A GUIDE TO THE HISTORY OF LOUISIANA

A GUIDE TO THE HISTORY OF LOUISIANA

Edited by Light Townsend Cummins
and Glen Jeansonne

REFERENCE GUIDES TO STATE HISTORY AND RESEARCH

GREENWOOD PRESS
Westport, Connecticut • London, England

Library of Congress Cataloging in Publication Data
Main entry under title:

A Guide to the history of Louisiana.

    (Reference guides to state history and research)
    Includes index.
    1. Louisiana--History--Bibliography--Handbooks,
manuals, etc. 2. Historical libraries--Louisiana--
Handbooks, manuals, etc. 3. Historical museums--
Louisiana--Handbooks, manuals, etc. 4. Archives--
Louisiana--Handbooks, manuals, etc. I. Cummins, Light
Townsend. II. Jeansonne, Glen, 1946-   . III. Series.
Z1289.G84 [F369]   016.9763   82-6108
ISBN 0-313-22959-7 (lib. bdg.)   AACR2

Copyright © 1982 by Light Townsend Cummins and Glen Jeansonne

All rights reserved. No portion of this book may be
reproduced, by any process or technique, without the
express written consent of the publisher.

Library of Congress Catalog Card Number: 82-6108
ISBN: 0-313-22959-7

First published in 1982

Greenwood Press
A division of Congressional Information Service, Inc.
88 Post Road West
Westport, Connecticut 06881

Printed in the United States of America

10 9 8 7 6 5 4 3 2 1

CONTENTS

Introduction ... ix

PART ONE: THE HISTORICAL LITERATURE

1. French Louisiana
   CARL A. BRASSEAUX ... 3

2. Spanish Louisiana
   LIGHT TOWNSEND CUMMINS ... 17

3. The Antebellum Period
   JOSEPH G. TREGLE, JR. ... 27

4. Civil War and Reconstruction
   JOE GRAY TAYLOR ... 41

5. The Gilded Age and Progressive Era
   WILLIAM IVY HAIR ... 51

6. The Long Era and Beyond
   GLEN JEANSONNE ... 59

7. Black Louisianians
   EDWARD F. HAAS ... 71

8. Urban New Orleans
   RAYMOND O. NUSSBAUM ... 85

9. Women in Louisiana History
   VAUGHAN BAKER SIMPSON ... 95

Contents

10. Oral History: An Overview
    HUBERT HUMPHREYS — 103

11. Quantification and Louisiana Historians
    THOMAS SCHOONOVER — 115

PART TWO: ARCHIVES AND SOURCES

12. Sources for Spanish Louisiana
    GILBERT C. DIN — 127

13. The Cartography of Colonial Louisiana
    JOSEPH D. CASTLE — 139

14. Louisiana State Archives
    ARTHUR W. BERGERON, JR. — 149

15. The Department of Archives and Manuscripts, Louisiana State University
    MARGARET FISHER DALRYMPLE — 153

16. Southwestern Archives and Manuscripts Collection, University of Southwestern Louisiana
    FREDERICK J. STIELOW — 167

17. Louisiana State Museum: Louisiana Historical Center
    JOHN R. KEMP AND EDWARD F. HAAS — 173

18. The Howard-Tilton Memorial Library, Tulane University
    WILBUR MENERAY — 183

19. The Historic New Orleans Collection: The Kemper and Leila Williams Foundation
    ROBERT D. BUSH — 199

20. The Amistad Research Center
    CLIFTON H. JOHNSON — 205

21. Louisiana Division: New Orleans Public Library
    COLLIN B. HAMER, JR. — 215

22. The Earl K. Long Library Archives and Manuscripts Department
    D. CLIVE HARDY — 223

23. Sources in Northwest Louisiana
    PATRICIA L. MEADOR — 229

24. Louisiana's Smaller Archives
    GLEN JEANSONNE — 247

Appendix I.
    Chronology of Louisiana History   257
Appendix II.
    Selected List of Organizations with Special Interests in
        Louisiana History   265
Index   269
About the Contributors   295

INTRODUCTION

THIS GUIDE GREW out of a series of informal discussions between two friends who were attending a meeting of the Louisiana Historical Association several years ago. As young historians who had both recently completed our graduate studies, we noted the lack of a guide to historical literature and major archives dealing with Louisiana. Such a volume would have facilitated our own research. Others as well, we surmised, might have found such a resource to be valuable. We concluded that the time had arrived to assemble such a guide.

This volume is primarily a tribute to the dynamics and diversity of the Louisiana historical community. The history of Louisiana is a subject of interest to numerous individuals from all walks of life. There are at present almost two dozen four-year colleges and universities in Louisiana, many offering courses on the history of the state. More than ten of these provide such courses for graduate credit. Hundreds of other institutions, including junior colleges, high schools, and other levels of our educational establishment, foster an active interest in the heritage of the Pelican State. There are, moreover, at least twenty-five associations and organizations that, in one form or another, provide forums for those interested in the state's history. A casual inspection of almost any full service bookstore in the state will reveal a shelf or two of volumes dealing with Louisiana's past.

Interest in the history of Louisiana, although not new, has grown more pronounced in recent decades. This growing interest reflects a national trend. The United States is fast becoming a society tied together by television, mass audience events, and a somewhat distressing uniformity in the retail sector. Restaurants, motels, airports, supermarkets, and shopping malls are much the same from Portland, Maine, to Portland, Oregon. A motorist driving into Baton Rouge on the interstate highway would have to observe carefully in order to distinguish passing roadside scenes from those in dozens of other cities. Regional distinctions have blurred. Although this process has positive benefits, there is a competing trend that resists a completely homogeneous nation. Family origin, ethnic background, sectional uniqueness, and community heritage have assumed greater value for many Americans. There is a burgeoning interest in "local history," a phrase once used to denote pedestrian interests. It has now become a fashionable term. Interest in local history has been manifested in Louisiana, as in other parts of the nation, by increased support for state, parish, and municipal activities that emphasize the past and one's personal relationship to it.

This guide is predicated on a view of local history as a more detailed and considered assessment of significant chapters in the national life. It is also based upon a conviction that the individuality of one's past is worth preserving. A sense of place, identity, and consciousness of heritage is a humanizing factor in our increasingly impersonal and technical world. Our appreciation of the past is accentuated.

Promising research techniques in recent decades, such as oral history, quantitative methods, and an increased appreciation of minority and ethnic consciousness, have worked a revolution on our views of the American past. Many new research methodologies have been employed first in state and local history because they are more easily applied on a community level.

Despite the growing importance of state and local history, we lack accessible, convenient guides to sources at this level. We hope this volume will address that need for Louisiana. It contains two general types of articles: first, historiographical essays treating major sources and interpretations for each chronological period and some topical considerations of the state's history; and, second, descriptions of major archival repositories written by archivists familiar with the collections. The former will define issues, problems, and opportunities while surveying the major historical literature. The latter will provide guidelines for finding topics and planning research in Louisiana. We assume that the user of this guide already has a general knowledge of significant events and personalities in Louisiana history, including familiarity with textbook survey literature.

This volume is designed as a general reference tool for all interested in the history of Louisiana, especially those contemplating new research projects. It makes no claim to comprehensiveness, especially since space limitations preclude anything but a general synopsis. This guide is not directed to specialized historians actively conducting detailed, original research on limited topics, although it may very well be useful to them in areas outside their own expertise. Instead, this guide represents an experiment in providing an overview of literature and archives relevent to a general student's interest. It will furnish a starting point rather than a definitive treatment of any particular historical period or archive. Its value should be that it collects in one reference a survey of the status of historical studies in Louisiana.

As editors, we have followed certain general guidelines. First, each essay was written exclusively for this volume. Each author was delegated great freedom to survey his or her topic. Uniformity seemed less important than providing each contributor the opportunity to be spontaneous and creative. Second, we found it difficult to select archives for inclusion, while rejecting others, because so many institutions and organizations have archival materials significant to the state's history. Many religious groups, governmental agencies, businesses and corporations, educational institutions, and various individuals have (to our specific knowledge) valuable historical documents and collections. Our criteria for inclusion considered the repository's holdings for a wide variety of topics and time periods; the more chronologically diverse and substantial, the more likely it was to be included. With the exception of the Spanish archives, there are no essays dealing with manuscript repositories outside Louisiana. Many such archives and their contents are noted in other guides and directories. An essay dealing with materials in Spain seemed appropriate because of the growing number of historians researching Spanish Louisiana coupled to microfilm projects bringing these documents to Louisiana repositories. Third, there was only limited effort to avoid duplication. In several cases, articles comment upon the same sources and deal with areas that overlap. We feel this desirable in providing timely comments on the status of particular works or concerns. As editors, we assume responsibility for the guide. Each author has permitted us to edit his or her respective contribution, in some cases without reading the final version prior to publication. Nevertheless, the opinions and comments expressed in each of the various essays remain those of its author. We hope that readers will bring errors and omissions to our attention.

PART ONE
THE HISTORICAL LITERATURE

1
FRENCH LOUISIANA
CARL A. BRASSEAUX

A HISTORIAN'S PERSPECTIVE of the world is colored by the cultural and intellectual milieu in which he develops and matures. This mental process is so deeply imbedded that he may unconsciously apply it in interpreting historical facts. Thus, the Romantic Age spawned romanticized historical narratives; the disillusionment of the "Lost" and Great Depression generations fostered Marxist writings; and the national revulsion against America's recent military involvement in Southeast Asia generated radically different historical interpretations by New Left historians. History is dynamic—ever changing.

The historiography of French Louisiana has not escaped this process. In fact, Louisiana's earliest French colonialists adhered closely to the tenets of the Romanticist—a broad panorama of historical events, occasionally only loosely based on fact, painted against a backdrop of an untamed, aborigine-infested wilderness. Romantic historians were also not averse to projecting their own personalities into that of their subjects. Finally, the Romanticists were preoccupied with politics and thus neglected other facets of colonial life.

The most significant Romanticists include Abbé Guillaume T. F. Raynal, *Découverte du Mississippi par les français* (Geneva, 1780); François-Xavier Martin, *The History of Louisiana from the Earliest Period* (New Orleans, 1827); François Barbé-Marbois, *Histoire de la Louisiane et la Cession de cette colonie par la France aux Etats-Unis* ... (Paris, 1829); Charles E. A. Gayarré, *History of Louisiana,* 4 vols. (New Orleans, 1854-1866); Grace King and John R. Ficklen, *A History of Louisiana,* 4 vols. (New York,

1904); Régine Hubert-Robert, *L'Histoire merveilleuse de la Louisiane française: Chronique des XVIIe et XVIIIe siècles et la Cession aux Etats-Unis* (New York, 1941).

Although general histories of Louisiana have not followed the classical Marxist-New Left pattern of much modern historical literature, modern general works treating French Louisiana have demonstrated a heightened interest in economics and other facets of colonial development. Moreover, modern historians, unlike their predecessors, have been critical of their archival resources. The result has been sounder scholarship. Most noteworthy of this new wave of historians is Marcel Giraud, whose four-volume *Histoire de la Louisiane française* (Paris, 1953-1974) is the definitive general work on the French experience.

A host of lesser writers have during the past two centuries contributed tomes chronicling the French colonization of the Mississippi Valley. This omnibus category includes Victor Debouchel, *Histoire de la Louisiane, depuis les premières découvertes jusqu'en 1840* (New Orleans, 1841); Rameau de Saint-Père, *La France aux colonies: Etudes sur le développement de la race française hors de l'Europe* (Paris, 1859); Francis Parkman, *A Half-Century of Conflict*, 2 vols. (Boston, 1892); Justin Winsor, *The Struggle in America Between England and France, 1697-1763* (Boston, 1895); V. Hout, *La Vallée du Mississippi au XVIIIe siècle* (Paris, 1904); Winston Arthur Goodspeed, *The Province and the States: A History of the Province of Louisiana Under France and Spain* (Madison, Wis., 1904); D.M.A. Magnan, *Histoire de la race française aux Etats-Unis* (Paris, 1913); Henry Edward Chambers, *Mississippi Valley Beginnings: An Outline of the Early History of the Earlier West* (New York, 1922); Georges Oudard, *Vieille Amérique: La Louisiane au temps des français* (Paris, 1931); and L. P. Kellogg, "France and the Mississippi Valley: A Resumé," *Mississippi Valley Historical Review*, 18 (June 1931). More recent works include James Burton Tharp, *La France en Louisiane* (New York, 1951); Joseph L. Ruteledge, *Century of Conflict: Struggle Between French and British in Colonial America* (Garden City, N.Y., 1956); Edwin Adams Davis, *Louisiana: The Pelican State* (Baton Rouge, 1959), *The Story of Louisiana* (New Orleans, 1960), and *Louisiana: A Narrative History* (Baton Rouge, 1961); and Howard Peckham, *The Colonial Wars, 1689-1762* (Chicago, 1964).

The exploration of the Mississippi Valley by intrepid French Canadians has long been a source of fascination for Louisiana historians. As a consequence, it is one of the few periods of French Louisiana history that has received considerable attention. Although the bulk of research regarding French expansion into the Mississippi Valley has been devoted to specific explorers, there are nevertheless a few excellent overviews. William J. Eccles clearly describes political and sociological causes of Canadian migrations into the Upper Mississippi Valley in *Canada Under Louis XIV, 1663-1701* (Toronto, 1964), and *The Canadian Frontier* (New York, 1969).

Frederick Austin Ogg's *The Opening of the Mississippi: A Struggle for Supremacy in the American Interior* (New York, 1904) offers a layman's introduction to this period, complemented by John Anthony Caruso's *The Mississippi Valley Frontier: The Age of French Explorations and Settlement* (Indianapolis, 1966). More succinct but romanticized accounts of the opening of the Mississippi Valley to settlement can be found in Isaac Joslin Cox, *The Early Exploration of Louisiana* (Cincinnati, 1905), Marshall Sprague, *So Vast, So Beautiful a Land: Louisiana and the Purchase* (Boston, 1974), and Henry E. Chambers, *Mississippi Valley Beginnings: An Outline of the Early History of the Earlier West* (New York, 1922).

Most material relating to the exploration of Louisiana is biographical. Raphael N. Hamilton's *Marquette's Explorations: The Narratives Reexamined* (Madison, Wis., 1970), and Jean Delanglez's *Life and Voyages of Louis Joliet, 1645-1700* (Chicago, 1948) are the recognized works on initial exploration of the Upper Mississippi Valley. Hamilton's work has replaced Agnes Replier's *Père Marquette: Priest, Pioneer and Adventurer* (Garden City, N.Y., 1929), a superficial biography, and Joseph P. Donnelly's uncritical *Jacques Marquette, S.J., 1637-1675* (Chicago, 1968).

René-Robert Cavelier de La Salle, who completed the exploration begun by Marquette and Joliet, has received more scholarly attention than any Louisiana personality except Huey Long, due largely to Francis Parkman's eulogy *La Salle and the Discovery of the Great West* (Boston, 1869). Parkman's *La Salle* is actually an extension of the author's own personality. Battling failing eyesight throughout his effort to record the French experience in North America, Parkman portrayed La Salle as a man attempting to realize his own dream—colonization of Louisiana—against overwhelming odds and constant opposition. On Parkman's projection see William R. Taylor, "A Journey into the Human Mind: Motivation in Francis Parkman's *La Salle*," *William and Mary Quarterly,* 3rd ser. 18 (April 1962). Parkman's reputation as a great historian, based largely upon his biography of La Salle, was destroyed by Jean Delanglez's *Some La Salle Journeys* (Chicago, 1938), which demonstrated Parkman's willingness to bend the facts. The best biography of the controversial French explorer is Edmund Boyd Osler's *La Salle* (Don Mills, Ont., 1967), a psychological study demonstrating that La Salle was paranoid. This biography may be supplemented by Gabriel Gravier's *Découvertes et établissements de Cavelier de La Salle de Rouen dans l'Amérique du Nord* (Paris, 1870), Pierre Leprohon's *Le Destin tragique de chev. La Salle* (Paris, 1969), and André Chevrillon et al., *Louisiane et Texas* (Paris, 1938). Less scholarly and error-filled are J. V. Jacks's *La Salle* (New York, 1931), William Dana Orcuitt's *Robert Cavelier: The Romance of the Sieur de La Salle and His Discovery of the Mississippi River* (Chicago, 1904), and John Stevens Abbot, *The Adventures of the Chevalier de La Salle and His Companions* (New York, 1875).

La Salle's voyage of discovery culminated with his claiming the Mississippi Valley for France. An excellent account of this act is Marc de Villiers du Terrage's "Cavelier de La Salle Takes Possession of Louisiana," trans. André Lafargue, *Louisiana Historical Quarterly*, 14 (July 1931).

After claiming Louisiana for France, La Salle returned there to organize a colonization expedition. Once in Paris, La Salle usurped the colonization scheme of Diego Peñalosa, a Spanish renegade, and persuaded Louis XIV to support the establishment of a French colony in the Lower Mississippi Valley. For detailed studies of Peñalosa's influence upon La Salle, see E. T. Miller, "The Connection of Peñalosa with the La Salle Expedition," *Texas State Historical Association Quarterly*, 5 (October 1901); and Cesareo Fernandez Duro, *Don Diego de Peñalosa y su descubrimiento del reino de Quivira* (Madrid, 1882). For an excellent account of the complex Versailles diplomacy preceding royal approval of La Salle's colonization scheme, see Marc de Villiers du Terrage's *L'Expédition de la Salle dans le Golfe du Mexique, 1684-1687* (Paris, 1931), the preeminent study of the ill-fated expedition.

La Salle's expedition was plagued by misfortune from the outset. Forced to share his authority with the naval commander of the Louisiana-bound flotilla, La Salle, now suffering from severe paranoia, quarreled constantly with his fellow officer. As a consequence, the expedition missed the fog-enshrouded mouth of the Mississippi River and landed on the South Texas coast, where, abandoned by the now irate French naval commander, the colony was quickly decimated by disease, hostile Indians, and dissension.

The exact location of La Salle's colony is disputed in Herbert E. Bolton's "The Location of La Salle's Colony in the Gulf of Mexico," *Mississippi Valley Historical Review*, 2 (September 1915), and Dickson H. Hoese's "On the Correct Landfall of La Salle in Texas, 1685," *Louisiana History*, 19 (Winter 1978). The colony's proximity to the incredibly rich New Mexico silver mines precipitated frantic efforts by the Mexican provincial government to locate and expel the French colonists. William Edward Dunn pioneered this topic with his *Spanish and French Rivalry in the Gulf Region of the United States, 1678-1702: The Beginnings of Texas and Pensacola* (Austin, Tex., 1917). This sound work has recently been complemented by Robert S. Weddle's *Wilderness Manhunt: The Spanish Search for La Salle* (Austin, Tex., 1973). Henry Folmer's *Franco-Spanish Rivalry in North America, 1524-1763* (Glendale, Cal., 1953) places the incident within the larger framework of imperial colonial rivalry. Capsulized accounts of the Spanish search for the French colonists can be found in William Edward Dunn's "The Spanish Search for La Salle's Colony on the Bay of Espiritu Santo, 1685-1689," *Southwest Historical Quarterly*, 19 (April 1916), and Irving A. Leonard's "The Spanish Reexploration of the Gulf Coast in 1686," *Mississippi Valley Historical Review*, 22 (March 1936).

The demise of La Salle's colony coincided with France's entrance into the War of the League of Augsburg, which forestalled further colonization until 1698. During the interim, however, French claims to the Mississippi Valley were kept alive by *voyageurs* and *coureurs de bois*, licensed and unlicensed fur trappers, respectively, who repeatedly plunged deeper into the Midwestern wilderness in search of more fertile trapping grounds. On this subject, Grace Lee Nute's superficial work, *The Voyageur* (New York, 1931), has happily been replaced by Marcel Giraud's masterful study of the French "mountain man," *Le Métis canadien: Son rôle dans l'histoire des provinces de l'Ouest*, 2 vols. (Paris, 1945), and Marc de Villiers du Terrage's *La Découverte du Missouri et l'histoire du fort d'Orléans, 1673-1728* (Paris, 1928). E.R.M. Murphy's *Henri de Tonti: Fur Trader of the Mississippi* (Baltimore, 1941) briefly discusses the efforts of La Salle's trusted lieutenant to exploit the Midwestern fur trade after the explorer's death. Much more substantial studies on the French Canadian exploration and subsequent settlement of the Upper Mississippi Valley are found in Natalia Maree Belting, *Kaskaskia Under the French Regime* (Urbana, Ill., 1948), and "The French Villages of the Illinois Country," *Canadian Historical Review*, 24 (March 1943); C. W. Alvord, *The Illinois Country, 1673-1818* (Springfield, Ill., 1920); Sydney Breese, *The Early History of Illinois from Its Discovery by the French Until Its Cession to Great Britain in 1763* (Chicago, 1884); and Joseph Wallace, *The History of Illinois and Louisiana Under the French Rule*... (Cincinnati, 1893).

France's interest in Louisiana, dormant for over a decade after La Salle, was revived in 1698. This renewed interest is analyzed in John C. Rule, "Jerome Phelypeaux, Comte de Pontchartrain, and the Establishment of Louisiana, 1696-1715," *Frenchmen and French Ways in the Mississippi Valley*, ed. John Francis McDermott (Urbana, Ill., 1969). In 1698, Pontchartrain selected Pierre Lemoyne d'Iberville to explore and colonize the Lower Mississippi Valley. Iberville's successful efforts are described in Guy Fregault's *Iberville le Conquérant* (Montreal, 1944); and Nellis M. Crouse's *Lemoyne d'Iberville: Soldier of New France* (Ithaca, N.Y., 1954). For Iberville's discovery of the Mississippi River's mouth, see Richebourg Gaillard McWilliams, "Iberville at the Birdfoot Subdelta: Final Discovery of the Mississippi River," *Frenchmen and French Ways*.

Having explored the lower Mississippi, Iberville established Fort Maurepas near present-day Biloxi, Mississippi, and returned to France. Jay Higginbotham's *Fort Maurepas: The Birth of Louisiana* (Mobile, 1968), and Dunbar Rowland's *Old Biloxi: The First Settlement in Mississippi* (Jackson, Miss., 1920) provide insight into the hardships encountered by the post's garrison during the long months of isolation following Iberville's departure. Higginbotham has also settled the scholarly debate over the identity of Ensign Sauvolle, the fort's first commandant, in "Who Was Sauvole?" *Louisiana Studies*, 7 (Summer 1968). Sauvole's successor, Jean-Baptiste Lemoyne de Bienville, the father of Louisiana, is less fortunate in his biographer. Grace King's *Jean-Baptiste Lemoyne, Sieur de Bienville* (New York, 1893), and "Notes on the Life and Services of Bienville,"

Louisiana Historical Quarterly, 1 (January 1918) are uncritical, error-filled eulogies. On the other hand, Charles E. O'Neill accurately and vividly portrays the father of Louisiana's twilight years and death in "The Death of Bienville," *Louisiana History*, 8 (Fall 1967).

In late 1701, Iberville ordered the colony transferred from Biloxi to Mobile, and the latter remained Louisiana's seat of government until the founding of New Orleans in 1718. Definitive on this critical period in Louisiana history are the first two volumes of Marcel Giraud's *Histoire de la Louisiane française*, entitled *La Règne de Louis XIV* (Paris, 1953), and *Années de transition, 1715-1720* (Paris, 1958). Dated but still useful is Peter J. Hamilton's *Colonial Mobile* (Boston, 1897). Jay Higginbotham's lengthy study of the colonial capital, *Old Mobile* (Mobile, 1977), is an enormous compilation of uninterpreted facts. The most controversial personality at Old Mobile, Antoine Laumet, better known as Lamothe Cadillac, has been the subject of two biographies. Agnes C. Laut's *Cadillac, Knight Errant of the Wilderness, Founder of Detroit, Governor of Louisiana from the Great Lakes to the Gulf* (Indianapolis, 1931) is highly romanticized. Four subsequent biographical essays by Jean Delanglez and appearing in *Mid-America* better reflect modern historical methodology: "Cadillac's Early Years in America," 26 (January 1944); "Antoine Laumet, Alias Cadillac, Commandant at Michilimackinac," 27 (April 1945); "Cadillac at Detroit," 30 (July 1948); and "Cadillac's Last Years," 33 (January 1951).

From 1717 to 1731, Louisiana enjoyed substantial demographic and economic expansion because of immigration policies adopted by proprietary companies founded by financier John Law. The two major biographies of Law—Georges Oudard, *John Law: A Fantastic Financier, 1671-1729*, trans. G.C.E. Massé (London, 1928), and H. Montgomery Hyde, *John Law: The History of an Honest Adventurer* (Denver, 1948)—lack documentation and are superficial and romanticized. Emile Levasseur's *Recherches historiques sur le système de Law* (Paris, 1854) is an excellent study of Law's meteoric rise to power in France. Pierre Heinrich's *La Louisiane sous la Compagnie des Indes, 1717-1731* (Paris, 1908), and Henri Gravier's *La Colonisation de la Louisiane à l'époque de Law* (Paris, 1904) are the standard works regarding the impact of Law's proprietary companies on Louisiana's development.

Law realized that the colonization of Louisiana would become a profitable venture only through enlargement of the province's population. Voluntary and forced French emigration to Louisiana under the proprietary regime have been the subject of numerous recent studies. On the subject of forced emigration, consult James D. Hardy, Jr., "The Transportation of Convicts to Colonial Louisiana," *Louisiana History*, 7 (Summer 1966); Walter Hart Blumenthal, *Brides from Bridewell: Female Felons Sent to Colonial America* (Rutland, Vt., 1962); Sheila T. Sturdivant, "Rich Man, Poor Man, Beggar Man, Thief: Frenchmen Exiled to Louisiana, 1717-1721" (M.A. thesis, University of Southwestern Louisiana, 1971); and

Glenn R. Conrad, "Immigration Forcé: A French Attempt to Populate Louisiana, 1717-1720," *Proceedings of the Fourth Annual Meeting of the French Colonial Historical Society* (Athens, Ga., 1979) (hereafter cited as *Fourth Meeting, FCHS*). For information regarding voluntary emigration, see Mathé Allain, "L'Immigration française en Louisiane, 1718-1721," *Revue d'histoire de l'Amérique française*, 28 (March 1976), Marie-Claude Guibert, Gabriel Debien and Claude Martin, *L'Emigration vers la Louisiane (La Rochelle, Nantes, Clairac), 1698-1754* (Paris, 1977), and Carl A. Brasseaux, "The Image of Louisiana and the Failure of Voluntary French Emigration, 1683-1731," *Fourth Meeting, FCHS*. For a perceptive study of French policy decisions regarding emigration to Louisiana, see Mathé Allain, "French Immigration Policies: Louisiana, 1699-1715," *Fourth Meeting, FCHS*.

The Germans were the most significant group of immigrants to reach Louisiana during Law's rule. Two groundbreaking but error-ridden studies of the German influx are J. Hanno Deiler's *Die ersten Deutschen am unteren Mississippi und due Creolen deutscher abstammung* (New Orleans, 1904); and *The Settlement of the German Coast of Louisiana and the Creoles of German Descent* (Philadelphia, 1909). Deiler's errors are corrected by René le Conte, "Les allemands à la Louisiane au XVIIIe siècle," *Journal de la Société des Américanistes de Paris* 16 (January 1924). For a synthesis of recent German research regarding Louisiana's Teutonic immigrants, consult Reinhart Kondert, "German Immigration to French Louisiana: A Reevaluation," *Fourth Meeting, FCHS*. Henry Yoes, III, *A History of St. Charles Parish to 1973* (Norco, La., 1973) describes German settlements above New Orleans, as does Lubin F. Laurent, "History of St. John the Baptist Parish," *Louisiana Historical Quarterly*, 7 (April 1924).

German immigration proved a stabilizing influence on the colony, which had been populated principally by Canadian and French adventurers, French orphan girls, and, during the Law regime, Parisian women of dubious virtue. Although the transportation of female colonists to French Louisiana has been the object of considerable interest among historians, the adaptation to the rigorous life of the frontier by these pioneer women has, until recently, been the subject of mere speculation. This historiographical void is considered in Vaughan Baker Simpson, "Les Louisianaises: A Reconnaissance," *Proceedings of the Fifth Annual Meeting of the French Colonial Historical Society*, ed. James J. Cooke (Athens, Ga., 1980) (hereafter cited as *Fifth Meeting, FCHS*). In addition, under the direction of Vaughan B. Baker Simpson, the Women in Louisiana Collection has launched an ambitious program to examine the role of women in French Louisiana, and a monograph on this subject is currently in progress. This work is being grounded upon the following preliminary studies: Mathé Allain, "Manon Lescaut et Ses Consoeurs: Women in the Early French Period, 1700-1731," *Fifth Meeting, FCHS*; and Amos E. Simpson, "Women and the Law in French Colonial Louisiana," *Fifth Meeting, FCHS*.

Once European immigrants reached Louisiana, they faced the backbreaking task of carving an existence from the densely wooded wilderness. A. Baillardel and A. Prioult paint a vivid portrait of colonial life in *Le Chevalier de Pradel: Vie d'un colon française en Louisiane au XVIIIe siècle* (Paris, 1928). Other excellent studies of French colonial pioneers include Gary Mills's "The Chauvin Brothers: Early Colonists of Louisiana," *Louisiana History*, 15 (Spring 1974); Norman W. Caldwell's "Charles Juchereau de St. Denys: A French Pioneer in the Mississippi Valley," *Mississippi Valley Historical Review*, 28 (March 1942); Henry P. Dart's, "Episodes of Life in Colonial Louisiana," *Louisiana Historical Quarterly*, 6 (January 1923); and E. Fabre-Surveyer's "The Rocheblaves in Colonial Louisiana," *Louisiana Historical Quarterly*, 28 (April 1935). For an idyllic view of pioneer life, see Grace King's *Creole Families of New Orleans* (New York, 1921).

Because of the difficulty faced by the French pioneers in clearing the land as well as in becoming acclimated to Louisiana's oppressively hot and humid climate, the colonists pressured the proprietary government to import slaves. Henry P. Dart discusses the origins of Negro slavery in Louisiana in "The First Cargo of African Slaves for Louisiana, 1717," *Louisiana Historical Quarterly*, 14 (April 1931). The best account of the French government's efforts to establish a legal framework in which slavery could exist in subtropical Louisiana is Mathé Allain, "Slave Policies in French Louisiana," *Louisiana History*, 21 (Spring 1980). The administration of these regulations is examined in Carl A. Brasseaux, "The Administration of Slave Regulations in French Louisiana, 1724-1766," *Louisiana History*, 21 (Spring 1980). For an uneven and error-riddled overview of slavery in French Louisiana, consult James Thomas McGowan, "Creation of Slave Society: Louisiana Plantations in the Eighteenth Century" (Ph.D. diss., University of Rochester, 1976). More accurate but uneven is Grady W. Kilman, "Slavery and Forced Labor in Colonial Louisiana" (M.A. thesis, University of Southwestern Louisiana, 1972). See also Kilman's "Slavery and Agriculture in Louisiana, 1699-1731," *Attakapas Gazette*, 6 (June 1971).

Not all blacks in French Louisiana were slaves, however. For an excellent study of the emergence and evolution of French Louisiana's small but significant free black population, see Laura Foner's "The Free People of Color in Louisiana and St. Domingue: A Comparative Portrait of Two Slave Societies," *Journal of Social History*, 3 (Summer 1970). For a brief discussion of the free person of color's role in French Louisiana society, see Donald E. Everett, "Free Persons of Color in Colonial Louisiana," *Louisiana History*, 7 (Winter 1966).

The introduction of blacks into the colony coincided with the transfer of Louisiana's capital from Mobile to New Orleans. Marc de Villiers du Terrage's *Histoire de la Nouvelle Orleans, 1717-1722* (Paris, 1917) is definitive. Heloise Hulse Cruzat's "New Orleans Under Bienville," *Louisiana Historical Quarterly*, 1 (January 1918) focuses on the events leading to New Orleans's founding.

Because of its strategic position, New Orleans controlled all commerce on the lower Mississippi. For an excellent account of the Crescent City's emergence as an entrepôt, see John G. Clark's *New Orleans, 1718-1812: An Economic History* (Baton Rouge, 1970). Dated but still useful are Nancy Miller Surrey's *The Commerce of Louisiana During the French Regime, 1699-1763* (New York, 1916), and "The Development of Industries in Louisiana During the French Regime, 1673-1763," *Mississippi Valley Historical Review*, 9 (December 1922). Glenn R. Conrad briefly discusses France's efforts to subject Louisiana to mercantilism in "An Historical Sketch of Various French Colonial Commercial Companies," *Attakapas Gazette*, 4 (September 1969).

Louisiana's exports consisted primarily of timber, furs, and agricultural products. For a masterful discussion of Louisiana's agricultural production, see Lauren C. Post's "The Domestic Animals and Plants of French Louisiana," *Louisiana Historical Quarterly*, 16 (October 1933). Jack D. L. Holmes sheds new light on the early development of a major, indigenous Louisiana crop in "Indigo in Colonial Louisiana and the Floridas," *Louisiana History*, 8 (Fall 1967). See also D. H. Thomas, "Pre-Whitney Cotton Gins in French Louisiana," *Journal of Southern History*, 21 (May 1965); and Edna F. Campbell, "Industries of Louisiana About 1750," *Geographical Review*, 10 (July 1920). Louisiana's crucial, Illinois-based fur trade is carefully examined in Norman W. Caldwell's *The French in the Mississippi Valley, 1740-1750* (Urbana, Ill., 1941). Many Louisiana products, especially timber, found their way to the French Antilles. For a discussion of this brisk commerce, see C. P. Gould, "Trade Between the Windward Islands and the Continental Colonies of the French Empire, 1683-1763," *Mississippi Valley Historical Review*, 25 (March 1939). Goods were also smuggled into Spanish Texas and Florida. For an excellent study of this illicit commerce, see Henry Folmer, "Contraband Trade Between Louisiana and New Mexico in the Eighteenth Century," *New Mexico Historical Review*, 16 (July 1941). See also Carl A. Brasseaux, "Private Enterprise vs. Mercantilism:The Cadillac-Duclos Affair," *A Franco-American Overview*, vol. 5: *Louisiana in the Eighteenth Century*, ed. Mathé Allain and Carl A. Brasseaux (Bedford, N.H., 1981). Ross Phares's *Cavalier in the Wilderness: The Story of the Explorer and Trader, Louis Juchereau de St. Denis* (Baton Rouge, 1953) is a romanticized biography of Louisiana's greatest smuggler.

Louisiana's nascent commercial relations with France and the French Antilles were irreparably damaged in 1729, when the Natchez Indians destroyed Fort Rosalie, the hub of the provincial tobacco industry. Jean Delanglez's "The Natchez Massacre and Governor Perier," *Louisiana Historical Quarterly*, 27 (October 1934), is a penetrating study of the

Natchez Massacre and French efforts to wreak vengeance upon the powerful Indian tribe. Clem G. Hearsey's "The Vengeance of the Natchez, 1729," *Louisiana Historical Quarterly*, 12 (April 1929) is romanticized. The long-term failure of Franco-Natchez diplomacy, culminating in the 1729 uprising, is considered in Patricia D. Woods, "The French and the Natchez Indians in Louisiana: 1700-1731," *Louisiana History*, 19 (Fall 1978).

The Natchez Massacre sounded the economic death knell for Louisiana's proprietor, the Company of the Indies, and, in 1731, the French crown resumed control over the colony. Little has been written about Louisiana's development during the three decades following the resumption of royal control, and, of the existing biographies, none offers anything more than an overview of their subjects' Louisiana careers. Guy Grégault's *Le Grand Marquis: Pierre de Rigaud de Vaudreuil et la Louisiane* (Montreal, 1952), while a superior biography of Canada's flamboyant governor, gives little more than passing mention to his Louisiana years. Marc de Villiers du Terrage's *Les Dernières Années de la Louisiane française* (Paris, 1904), on the other hand, contains a detailed, although biased biography of Vaudreuil's successor, Louis Billouart de Kerlerac, who governed Louisiana during the Seven Years' War. The best description of the war along the northern frontier is Guy Grégault's *La Guerre de la conquête, 1754-1760* (Montreal, 1955). Jean-Jacques-Blaise d'Abbadie chronicles his own Louisina career in Carl A. Brasseaux, ed., *A Comparative View of French Louisiana, 1699 and 1752: The Historical Journals of Pierre Le Moyne d'Iberville and Jean-Jacques-Blaise d'Abbadie* (Lafayette, La., 1979).

During the twilight stages of the war, France ceded Louisiana to Spain in the Treaty of Fontainebleau. E. W. Lyon's *Louisiana in French Diplomacy, 1759-1804* (Norman, Okla., 1934) is the best of several superficial works treating the change of domination. Also useful are Helen Wall, "Transfer of Louisiana from France to Spain" (M.A. thesis, Louisiana State University, 1960); Donald J. Lemieux, "The Mississippi Valley, New France, and French Colonial Policy," *Southern Studies*, 18 (Spring 1978); Mildred Stahl Fletcher, "Louisiana as a Factor in French Diplomacy from 1763-1800," *Mississippi Valley Historical Review*, 17 (December 1960); W. R. Shepherd, "The Cession of Louisiana to Spain," *Political Science Quarterly*, 19 (September 1904); and Arthur S. Aiton, "The Diplomacy of the Louisiana Cession," *American Historical Review*, 36 (July 1931).

Approximately fifteen months after the Cession, on February 10, 1763, the Treaty of Paris was concluded, ending the Seven Years' War and transferring Louisiana east of the Mississippi River to England. British representatives took possession of Mobile and shortly thereafter launched preparations for the occupation of Illinois. The best account of the change of domination in West Florida as well as the subsequent, futile English attempt to reach Fort Chartres, is Robert R. Rea's introduction to Philip Pittman's *The Present State of the European Settlements on the Mississippi*

(Gainesville, Fla., 1973). The British efforts to occupy Illinois from the north and east precipitated Pontiac's Uprising. For two blatantly pro-British studies of the Indian insurrection, see Francis Parkman, *The Conspiracy of Pontiac and the Indian War After the Conquest of Canada*, 2 vols. (Boston, 1891), and Howard H. Peckham, *Pontiac and the Indian Uprising* (Princeton, N.J., 1947). Miller Jacobs's "Was the Pontiac Uprising a Conspiracy?" *Ohio Archeological and Historical Society Quarterly*, 54 (January 1956) is a more dispassionate view of the upheaval.

Such Anglo-Indian disputes were inevitable. Since the founding of Louisiana, the French had utilized Indians as the mainstay of the colony's defenses against neighboring Spanish and English possessions. Elizabeth A. H. John's *Storms Brewed in Other Men's Worlds: The Confrontation of Indians, Spanish and French in the Southwest, 1540-1795* (College Station, Tex., 1975) is an award-winning study of the rival powers' efforts to maintain internal security through Indian alliances. Verner W. Crane's *The Southern Frontier, 1670-1732* (Durham, N.C., 1928) offers an English view of the Franco-English rivalry along Louisiana's eastern border. The French relied heavily upon traders to win and maintain the allegiance of strategic Indian tribes. Mathé Allain and Vincent H. Cassidy, "Blanpain, Trader Among the Attakapas," *Attakapas Gazette*, 3 (December 1968) is a sentient study of one such backwoodsman. Also of interest is William Beer's "The Visit of Illinois Indians to France in 1725," *Louisiana Historical Quarterly*, 6 (April 1923). The standard works on the Indian in French Louisiana are Frederick Webb Hodge, *Handbook of American Indians North of Mexico*, Smithsonian Institution Bureau of American Ethnology, Bulletin no. 30, 2 vols. (Washington, D.C., 1912), and John R. Swanton, *Indian Tribes of the Lower Mississippi Valley and the Adjacent Coast of the Gulf of Mexico* (Washington, D.C., 1911).

The French also influenced the Indians of the Mississippi Valley through missionaries. On this subject, see Jean Delanglez, *The French Jesuits in Lower Louisiana, 1700-1763* (New Orleans, 1935), and Claude L. Vogel's *The Capuchins in French Louisiana, 1722-1766* (Washington, D.C., 1928). Charles Edwards O'Neill, S.J., dispassionately depicts the priests' role in the field as well as in provincial politics in *Church and State in French Colonial Louisiana: Policy and Politics to 1732* (New Haven, Ct., 1966). Roger Baudier's *The Catholic Church in Louisiana*, 2 vols. (New Orleans, 1939) is an important religious reference work for French Louisiana. Henry C. Semple's *The Ursulines in New Orleans and Our Lady of Prompt Succor: A Record of Two Centuries, 1727-1925* (New York, 1925) is an overview of Louisiana's first women's order. The Ursuline convent served as a refuge for a few orphaned, exiled Acadians, who began arriving at New Orleans in 1764. On this subject, see James F. Geraghty, "Louisiana's First Acadian Religious," *Attakapas Gazette*, 12 (Winter 1977).

The best study of Acadian immigration during the 1760s is Jacqueline K. Voorhies's "The Acadians: The Search for the Promised Land," *The Cajuns: Essays on Their History and Culture*, ed. Glenn R. Conrad (Lafayette, La., 1977) (hereafter cited as *The Cajuns*). Also useful is Glenn R. Conrad's "The Acadians: Myths and Realities," *The Cajuns*. For a more general history of the exiles, Emile Lauvrière's pioneer work, *La Tragédie d'un peuple: Histoire du peuple acadien de ses origines à nos jours*, 2 vols. (Paris, 1924), has been supplanted by Oscar W. Winzerling's *Acadian Odyssey* (Baton Rouge, 1955).

Acadian immigration was profoundly influenced by Spanish Governor Antonio de Ulloa's arrival at New Orleans on March 5, 1766. On this subject, see Jacqueline K. Voorhies, "Les Problèmes d'installation des acadiens en Louisiane au XVIIIe siècle," *Proceedings of the First International Symposium on the Acadiens*, ed. Jean Daigle (Moncton, New Brunswick, 1979). The best account of Ulloa is John Preston Moore's "Antonio de Ulloa: A Profile of the First Spanish Governor of Louisiana," *Louisiana History*, 8 (Summer 1967), which is complemented by Arthur P. Whitaker's "Antonio de Ulloa," *Hispanic American Historical Review*, 15 (May 1935). Lacking necessary troops and short on funds, Ulloa refused to take possession of the colony at New Orleans and was thus compelled to rule the province jointly with the French military and administrative chiefs—Governor Charles Philippe Aubry and Commissaire-ordonnateur Denis-Nicolas Foucault. Carl A. Brasseaux's *"L'Officier du Plume*: Denis-Nicolas Foucault, *Commissaire-ordonnateur* of French Louisiana, 1762-1769" (M.A. thesis, University of Southwestern Louisiana, 1975) is the standard career biography of the controversial administrator.

The *commissaire-ordonnateur* also served as first judge of the Superior Council, Louisiana's quasi-legislative and judicial body. For an overview of the *ordonnateur*'s development as a judicial officer, see Donald J. Lemieux, "The Office of Commissaire-Ordonnateur in French Louisiana, 1731-1763" (Ph.D. diss., Louisiana State University, 1972), and "Some Legal and Practical Aspects of the Office of Commissaire-Ordonnateur of French Louisiana," *Louisiana Studies*, 14 (Winter 1975). Concise studies of the evolution of the colony's chief judiciary body include James D. Hardy, Jr., "The Superior Council in Colonial Louisiana," *Frenchmen and French Ways*, and Jerry Micele, "From Law Court to Local Government: Metamorphosis of the Superior Council of French Louisiana," *Louisiana History*, 9 (Spring 1968). Henry P. Dart, "Courts and Law in Colonial Louisiana," *Louisiana Historical Quarterly*, 4 (July 1921) is a seminal study of the laws enforced by the Superior Council.

Ulloa's inept rule and internal economic conditions precipitated the rebellion of October 29, 1768, which resulted in the Spaniard's expulsion. In August 1769 a Spanish army, commanded by Ulloa's successor, Alexander O'Reilly, occupied the colonial capital and tried and executed five rebel leaders. The insurrection's causes and the necessity of executing the rebel leaders have been hotly debated by scholars for 150 years. The sources of the controversy are conflicting French and Spanish accounts of the episode. Because few scholars are proficient in both eighteenth-century French and Spanish, research has necessarily reflected one or the other viewpoint. For example, the general histories of the French-born historians Barbé-Marbois and François-Xavier Martin are blatantly critical of the Ulloa regime and openly condemn O'Reilly's actions. But Charles Gayarré, whose grandfather was a Spanish colonial official held hostage by the insurrectionists, attempts to vindicate the Spanish governors. In the early twentieth century, John R. Ficklen, Grace King, and Alcée Fortier—self-proclaimed defenders of Louisiana's Creoles—portrayed the rebels as "patriot-martyrs" driven to rebellion by their love of liberty. Although more objective, Frenchman Marc de Villiers du Terrage also condemns the execution of the rebel leaders. Two of the three most recent works treating the rebellion—David K. Texada, *Alejandro O'Reilly and the New Orleans Rebels* (Lafayette, La., 1970), and John Preston Moore, *Revolt in Louisiana: The Spanish Occupation, 1766-1770* (Baton Rouge, 1976)—were produced by Spanish borderlands specialists who have relied most exclusively upon Hispanic sources. It is therefore hardly surprising that they stress economic problems in the Spanish empire as contributing to the rebellion and thereby exonerate Ulloa. On the other hand, Carl A. Brasseaux's biography of Foucault, based largely on French sources, cites confusion stemming from economic and governmental instability, especially Ulloa's administrative ineptitude, as the major cause of the rebellion. Thus the controversy persists.

By perusing this brief historiography of French Louisiana, one may justifiably conclude that events at the period's chronological extremities have captured the attention and imagination of most Louisiana historians. Although the period of exploration and development and the Rebellion of 1768 have been virtually saturated with historical writings, the three decades following the restoration of French royal control over Louisiana, a critical formative period for Louisiana's governmental and cultural development, have been virtually ignored. Moreover, there is no social history of French Louisiana, no comprehensive study of French trappers and traders in the Mississippi Valley, and no objective work on Franco-Indian relations. Only when such gaps are filled can one truly begin to understand the French experience in Louisiana.

2
SPANISH LOUISIANA

LIGHT TOWNSEND CUMMINS

THE HISTORY OF Spanish Louisiana has long attracted the interest and attention of those concerned with the state's past. The student who surveys the body of literature dealing with this era of the region's history is confronted with several rather immediate problems. First, the geographic limits of Spanish Louisiana differed at various times from the present boundaries of the state. Modern geographic perspective hence complicates the drawing of limits in one's bibliographic search. The eighteenth-century colonial history of the entire Mississippi Valley, along with that of the Gulf Coast from Florida to the coastal bend of Texas, has a direct bearing on Spanish Louisiana. Second, study of Spanish Louisiana has long been undertaken by historians whose primary interests were not related to a state-based perspective. Instead, historians of the Spanish experience in the Americas and scholars dealing with intercolonial rivalries have predominated as authors. The questions they ask and the methods they employ sometimes provide little continuity to studies of subsequent eras in the state's history. Third, many important studies of Spanish Louisiana are not available in English-language editions. Europe, especially Spain, is home to a significant and growing school of non-English-speaking historians who have produced an admirable literature dealing with Spanish Louisiana.

Keeping these factors in mind, what follows will provide the reader with an introduction to major titles in the expanding historical literature dealing with Spanish Louisiana. This literature is extensive, although the quality and comprehensiveness of some of the older studies might be lacking by modern standards. Two comprehensive bibliographies of Spanish colonial

Louisiana provide good coverage of the English- and foreign-language secondary literature. The first, Jack D. L. Holmes, *A Guide to Spanish Louisiana: 1762-1806* (New Orleans, 1970), lists most of the major monographs and articles dealing with the region's Hispanic period. In addition, it furnishes the reader with a chronology of significant events during the Spanish domination. The second, a special topical issue published in the *Latin American Research Review*, 7 (Summer 1972), is currently the most comprehensive assessment of secondary literature dealing with Spanish Louisiana and the southeastern Spanish borderlands. With an introduction by William S. Coker, this issue carries the following relevant articles: Jack D. L. Holmes, "Research in the Spanish Borderlands: Alabama"; Samuel Proctor, "Research Opportunities in the Spanish Borderlands: East Florida, 1763-1821"; J. Leitch Wright, Jr., "Research Opportunities in the Spanish Borderlands: East Florida, 1781-1821"; Jack D. L. Holmes, "Research in the Spanish Borderlands: Louisiana"; and William S. Coker, "Research in the Spanish Borderlands: Mississippi." There is also a forty-page bibliography, which is designed to note a "comprehensive and up-to-date listing of references without claiming by any means that it is definitive" (p. 5). Additional historiographical essays dealing with Spanish Louisiana are Jack D. L. Holmes "Research Opportunities in the Spanish Borderlands: Louisiana and the Old Southwest," *Louisiana Studies*, 1 (Winter 1962); James A. Servies, *Pensacola and West Florida: A Chronological Checklist of Printed Works, 1542-1969* (Pensacola, Fla., 1969); Jack D. L. Holmes, "Interpretations and Trends in the Study of the Spanish Borderlands: The Old Southwest," *Southwestern Historical Quarterly*, 74 (April 1971); Charles E. O'Neill, S.J., "The State of Studies on Spanish Colonial Louisiana," *The Spanish in the Mississippi Valley: 1762-1804*, ed. John Francis McDermott (Urbana, Ill., 1974); and Jack D. L. Holmes, "The Historiography of the American Revolution in Louisiana," *Louisiana History*, 19 (Summer 1978).

Nineteenth- and early twentieth-century historians laid the foundations for present-day studies of Spanish Louisiana. Although in some cases their work must be used with great caution, the modern student would be well advised to consult the following for general surveys of the era: C.E.A. Gayarré, *History of Louisiana*, 4th ed. (New Orleans, 1903); Alcée Fortier, *A History of Louisiana* (New York, 1904); and François-Xavier Martin, *The History of Louisiana from the Earliest Period* (New Orleans, 1882). An accounting of the earlier historians researching and writing on Spanish Louisiana may be seen in Herbert H. Lang, "Nineteenth Century Historians of the Gulf States" (Ph.D. diss., University of Texas, 1953).

The early years of this century witnessed the growing interest of academic, university-trained historians in the Spanish presence in the Americas. Woodbury Lowery's studies of Spanish settlements in the United States, although not dealing with Louisiana, influenced many scholars examining the Spanish heritage along the Gulf Coast. James A. Robertson provided a general survey in his *Louisiana Under the Rule of Spain, France, and the United States, 1785-1807*, 2 vols. (Cleveland, 1910-1911). In addition, Louis Houck, *The Spanish Regime in Missouri*, 2 vols. (Chicago, 1909), and Walter B. Douglas, *The Spanish Domination of Upper Louisiana* (Madison, Wis., 1914) gave readers fairly detailed, early overviews of political and economic events on the upper Mississippi during the Spanish era.

The studies undertaken by Herbert Eugene Bolton and his students subjected Spanish Louisiana to the first major, coordinated historical analysis by professionally trained historians. Bolton, working in the early decades of this century, almost singlehandedly defined and legitimized the Spanish borderlands as a field of historical study. His 1921 synthesis, *The Spanish Borderlands: A Chronicle of Old Florida and the Southwest*, was published by the Yale University Press as part of its Chronicles of America series. This slender volume surveyed the history of Spanish exploration and settlement in the United States from the era of exploration down to the time of annexation by the United States, covering a broad arc of territory running from Florida westward to California. Louisiana, as a major eighteenth-century Spanish province, received special attention in this landmark study. Bolton highlighted the defensive role that the colony played in the Spanish imperial system. The province, he pointed out, became Spanish primarily because policy makers at the court of King Charles III realized its defensive importance as a buffer between New Spain and English America. This view of Spanish Louisiana as a defensive borderland permeates as a fundamental assumption almost every subsequent study of the province published since the early 1920s.

Bolton followed this seminal study with a respectably sized bookshelf of volumes examining topics and individuals significant to the history of the borderlands. Of special interest to students of Spanish colonial Louisiana are his *Anthanase de Mézierès and the Louisiana-Texas Frontier, 1768-1780* (Cleveland, 1914), and *Texas in the Middle Eighteenth Century* (Berkeley, 1915). Perhaps more significant, however, in considering Bolton's contribution to the study of Spain's presence in the colonial southeast is the fact that he directed the research of over a generation of doctoral students in his seminar at the University of California at Berkeley. Many of these students, including David Bjork, John Caughey, Abraham Nasatir, and Lawrence Kinnard, helped to make the study of the Spanish borderlands a major area of academic endeavor. One Bolton student, John Francis Bannon, has updated his mentor's earlier synthesis with the publication of *The Spanish Borderlands Frontier: 1513-1821* (Albuquerque, 1974). Lawrence Kinnard provided a timely and useful compendium of translated Spanish Louisiana documents at the Bancroft Library in his three-volume *Spain in the Mississippi Valley, 1765-1794*, which appeared as the annual report of the

American Historical Association for 1945. Abraham Nasatir, one of Bolton's most productive students, has summed up over fifty years of his own scholarship on Spanish Louisiana with the interpretive analysis *Borderland in Retreat: From Spanish Louisiana to the Far Southwest* (Albuquerque, 1970). A complete assessment of Bolton and his students may be seen in John Francis Bannon, *Herbert Eugene Bolton: The Historian and the Man, 1870-1953* (Tucson, 1978).

In the years prior to World War II, while Bolton and his students were pioneering in the study of Spanish borderlands, another group of historians interested in the expansion of the United States into the Mississippi Valley also began to produce studies examining Spanish Louisiana. Their perspective rested on the historical factors that eventually influenced annexation of the region by the growing young American republic. For the most part, their studies were based on Anglo-American manuscript sources, although a few made use of Spanish and French archives as well. Clarence W. Alvord, *The Mississippi Valley in British Politics*, 2 vols. (Cleveland, 1917), and *The Illinois Country, 1673-1818* (Springfield, Ill., 1920) are significant for understanding Anglo expansion into the region. I. J. Cox, *The West Florida Controversy, 1798-1813* (Baltimore, 1918) is also important in this regard. One must also consider the work of Samuel Flagg Bemis, especially *Jay's Treaty* (New York, 1923), *Pinkney's Treaty* (Baltimore, 1926), and *The Diplomacy of the American Revolution* (Bloomington, Ind., 1935). The following studies made additional contributions to this perspective: T. P. Abernethy, *Western Lands and the American Revolution* (New York, 1937); Philip C. Brooks, *Diplomacy and the Borderlands* (Berkeley, 1939); James A. James's two studies *The Life of George Rogers Clark* (Chicago, 1928), and *Oliver Pollock: Forgotten Patriot of the American Revolution* (Indianapolis, 1938); and E. Wilson Lyon, *Louisiana in French Diplomacy, 1759-1804* (Norman, Okla., 1934). No survey of this literature would be complete without mention of the significant work accomplished by Arthur P. Whitaker. One should especially examine his *The Spanish American Frontier, 1783-1795* (Boston, 1927), and *The Mississippi Question, 1795-1803* (New York, 1934).

Spanish historians writing in the first half of this century also began analyzing colonial Louisiana and its historical role in the saga of Hispanic America. The work of Manuel Serrano y Sanz is most significant in this regard, especially three studies: *Documentos históricos de la Florida y la Luisiana, siglos XVI al XVIII* (Madrid, 1912); *El Brigadier Jaime Wilkinson y sus tratos con España para la independencia del Kentucky (años 1787 a 1807* (Madrid, 1915); and *España y los Indios Cherokis y Choctas en la segunda mitad del siglo XVIII* (Seville, 1916). For an analysis of Spanish Louisiana's role in the American Revolution, see Manuel Conrotte, *La intervención de España en la independencia de los Estados Unidos* (Madrid, 1920), and Juan J. F. Yela Utrilla, *España ante la independencia de los*

Estados Unidos, 2 vols. (Lérida, Spain, 1925). Antonio de Castillo analyzed the colony's ecclesiastical history in *La Luisiana y el Padre Sedilla* (San Juan, P.R., 1929). Vicente Rodríguez Casado produced a series of significant examinations of the colony, most notably *Primeros años de dominación española en la Luisiana* (Madrid, 1942). Also useful is the catalog of the papers in the Estado section of the Archivo Histórico Nacional of Spain compiled by Miguel Gómez del Campillo, which were published during 1945 at Madrid. This two-volume study, *Relaciones diplomáticos entre España y los Estados Unidos según los documentos del Archivo Histórico Nacional* (Madrid, 1944-1945), contains an historical introduction that pays valuable attention to the role the Mississippi Valley played in U.S.-Spanish relations in the late eighteenth century.

The post-World War II era has witnessed a dramatic expansion of scholarly interest in Spanish Louisiana from each of the perspectives: the borderlands, U.S. diplomatic, and Hispanic. The renewed accessibility of the Spanish archives after the violent upheavals of the 1930s and 1940s, the advent of relatively inexpensive air travel, the availability of microfilm, and increased grant support from both public and private sectors have worked a revolution on Spanish Louisiana scholarship. In addition, new methodologies borrowed from the social sciences have been increasingly used in analyzing the history of the province. Significant studies based on extensive research in American, British, and Spanish sources have been appearing on an annual basis for the last three decades. Although much remains to be done, the period since the 1950s has seen the appearance of dozens of volumes and hundreds of articles dealing with Louisiana's Hispanic heritage. Scholars including Jack D. L. Holmes, Gilbert Din, Eric Beerman, William S. Coker, Charles E. O'Neill, C. Richard Arena, and John Preston Moore have devoted great efforts to analyzing various aspects of Spanish Louisiana, while others, including Robert Rea, J. Leitch Wright, Jr., and Barton Starr, have added new dimensions to examining Anglo-Spanish rivalry in the region. Spanish scholars, most notably Francisco Morales Padrón, Luis García Navarro, Fernando Costa Solano, Bibiano Torres Ramirez, Vincenta Cortés Alonso, and Juan José Andreu Ocariz, have encouraged continued historical analysis of the Spanish province in the rich archives of Seville and Madrid. Since most of the historical literature written prior to the early 1970s has been noted in the bibliographies by Holmes and Coker mentioned above, what follows will highlight some of the more recent studies dealing with the political, economic, diplomatic, and social history of Louisiana during the Spanish period.

The political history of Spanish Louisiana has largely been told by examining the careers of various colonial administrators. For a general overview, see José Montero de Pedro (El Marqués de Casa Mena) *Españoles en Nueva Orleans y Luisiana* (Madrid, 1979). Additional general studies of Spanish colonial administration are found in Jack D. L. Holmes,

"*Dramatis Personae* in Spanish Louisiana," *Louisiana Studies*, 6 (Summer 1967); Jo Ann Carrigan, "Government in Spanish Louisiana," *Louisiana Studies*, 11 (Fall 1972); and Fernando de Armas Medina, "Luisiana y Florida en el reinado de Carlos III," *Estudios americanos*, 19 (1964). The best single overview of the Ulloa period is John Preston Moore, *Revolt in Louisiana: The Spanish Occupation, 1766-1770* (Baton Rouge, 1976). The career of Alejandro O'Reilly has been traced in David K. Texada, *O'Reilly and the New Orleans Rebels* (Lafayette, La., 1970). See also Bibiano Torres Ramirez, *Alejandro O'Reilly en las Indias* (Seville, 1969), and Eric Beerman, "Un bosquejo biográfico y genealógico del General Alejandro O'Reilly," *La Revista hidalguia* (March-April 1981).

The Gálvez period has long attracted the attention of scholars because of Louisiana's crucial role in the American Revolution. The best single study remains John W. Caughey *Bernardo de Gálvez in Louisiana, 1776-1783* (Berkeley, 1934). For additional perspectives on the Gálvez period, see José Rodulfo Boeta, *Bernardo de Gálvez* (Madrid, 1976); Gilbert Din, trans. and ed., *Louisiana in 1776: A "Memoria" of Francisco Bouligny* (New Orleans, 1977); Jack D. L. Holmes, *The 1779 "Marcha de Gálvez": Louisiana's Giant Step Forward in the American Revolution* (Baton Rouge, 1974); Light Townsend Cummins, "Spanish Agents in North America During the Revolution, 1775-1779" (Ph.D. diss., Tulane University, 1977); Ralph Lee Woodward, Jr., trans. and ed., *Tribute to Don Bernardo de Gálvez* (New Orleans, 1979). The role Spain played in the American Revolution has been analyzed in several recent studies in addition to the above, including N. Orwin Rush, *The Battle of Pensacola: Spain's Final Triumph over Great Britain in the Gulf of Mexico* (Tallahassee, Fla., 1966); Buchanan Parker Thomson, *La ayuda española en la guerra de la independencia norteamericana* (Madrid, 1966); James H. O'Donnell, III, *Southern Indians in the American Revolution* (Knoxville, Tenn., 1973); J. Leitch Wright, Jr., *Florida in the American Revolution* (Gainesville, Fla., 1975); J. Barton Starr, *Tories, Dons, and Rebels: The American Revolution in British West Florida* (Gainesville, Fla., 1976); Robert V. Haynes, *The Natchez District and the American Revolution* (Jackson, Miss., 1976); Mario Rodríguez, *La Revolución americana de 1776 y el mundo hispánico: Ensayos y documentos* (Madrid, 1976); Luis Angel García Melero, *La independencia de los Estados Unidos de Norteamérica a traves de la prensa española* (Madrid, 1977); and Maria Pilar Ruigomez de Hernandez, *El gobierno español del despotismo ilustrado ante la independencia de los Estados Unidos de América* (Madrid, 1978).

The best study of Esteban Miró remains Caroline M. Burson, *The Stewardship of Don Esteban Miró, 1782-1792* (New Orleans, 1940). Francisco de Borja Medina, *José de Espeleta* (Seville, 1981) provides significant comment on the province and Gulf Coast area for the 1780s through the perspective of a significant Spanish commander. Jack D. L. Holmes, *Gayoso: The Life of a Spanish Governor in the Mississippi Valley,*

1789-1799 (Baton Rouge, 1965) presents good background for the entire post-1783 period of the colony's history, with a detailed analysis of the 1790s. A curious study, Thomas M. Frehrer, "The Barron de Carondelet as Agent of Bourbon Reform: A Study of Spanish Colonial Administration in the Years of the French Revolution" (Ph.D. diss., Tulane University, 1977), places the career of one of Louisiana's last Spanish governors within the context of eighteenth-century imperial administration.

The military history of the colony has, along with its political history, also received attention from scholars currently writing on the colony's historical development. Jack D. L. Holmes, *Honor and Fidelity: The Louisiana Infantry Regiment and the Louisiana Militia Companies, 1766-1821* (Birmingham, Ala., 1965) is a convenient reference. J. Leitch Wright, Jr., *Anglo-Spanish Rivalry in North America* (Athens, Ga., 1971) places one of the basic sources of military pressure on Louisiana in larger perspective. W. James Miller, "The Militia System of Spanish Louisiana, 1769-1783," *The Military Presence on the Gulf Coast*, ed. William S. Coker (Pensacola, Fla., 1975) provides a valuable overview of military organization during the early Spanish period. Early Spanish attempts to provide for the military defense of the province are noted in Gilbert Din, "Protecting the Barrera: Spain's Defenses in Louisiana, 1763-1779," *Louisiana History*, 19 (Spring 1978). A valuable clue to sources for the colony's military history is found in Eric Beerman, "A Check-List of Louisiana Documents in the *Servicio Histórico Militar* in Madrid," *Louisiana History*, 20 (Spring 1979). The role of the British in West Florida as an influence on Spanish military policy may be appreciated by surveying the numerous articles by Robert C. Rea. Most notable are "Life, Death, and Little Glory: The British Soldier on the Gulf Coast, 1763-1781," *The Military Presence on the Gulf Coast*, ed. William S. Coker (Pensacola, Fla., 1978), "Brigadier Frederick Haldimand—The Florida Years," *Florida Historical Quarterly*, 54 (April 1976), and "Graveyard for Britains, West Florida, 1763-1781," *Florida Historical Quarterly*, 47 (April 1969).

The economic history of Spanish Louisiana is conveniently surveyed in John G. Clark, *New Orleans, 1718-1812: An Economic History* (Baton Rouge, 1970). Bruce Tyler, "The Mississippi River Trade, 1784-1788," *Louisiana History,* 12 (Summer 1971) gives the reader a valuable overview of commerce during the crucial period of growing Anglo-American interest. The research of several Spanish historians during the last decade has added substantially to the demographic and economic analysis of the region. Antonio Acosta Rodríguez, *La población de Luisiana española (1763-1803)* (Madrid, 1979) provides a full-scale analysis of population movements in the colony using census records from the Spanish archives. For comment on Acosta's methods and conclusions, see Jack D. L. Holmes, "A New Look at Spanish Louisiana Census Accounts: The Recent Historiography of Antonio Acosta," *Louisiana History*, 21 (Winter 1980). Pablo Tornero Tenajero has provided a close analysis of Florida trade with the United

States in his *Relaciones de dependencia entre Florida y los Estados Unidos (1783-1820)* (Madrid, 1979). Although the focus of this work is not on Louisiana, its conclusions about the economic dependency of the Gulf Coast region make it of signal importance. Tornero's "Canarian Immigration to America: The Civil-Military Expedition to Louisiana of 1777-1779," trans. and ed. Paul Hoffman, *Louisiana History*, 21 (Fall 1980) carries forward the earlier investigations of Francisco Morales Padrón.

A recent study, also the product of the Spanish school, neatly complements the investigations of Acosta and Turnero. Elena Sanchez-Fabres Mirat, *Situación histórica de las Floridas en la segunda mitad del siglo XVIII (1783-1819)* (Madrid, 1977) is essential to understanding the political economy of the entire region in the closing decades of the century. The Anglo-Spanish economic structure in Louisiana can be appreciated by reviewing the letter books of John Fitzpatrick, a merchant who lived upriver from New Orleans. See Margaret Fisher Dalrymple, ed., *The Merchant of Manchac: The Letterbooks of John Fitzpatrick, 1768-1790* (Baton Rouge, 1978). The extensive editing project directed by William S. Coker that will eventually make available the papers of Panton, Leslie, and Company will, when completed, provide a definitive view of trade relations with the Indians in the Gulf region. The full scope of Anglo merchant activity may be appreciated by a close reading of José A. Armas Vicente, *El Mississippi, frontera de España* (Zaragoza, Spain, 1977).

Studies dealing with the history of ethnic minorities, especially blacks and Indians, have been a welcome and timely addition to the recent literature. Those interested in the foundations of slavery are directed to Thomas M. McGowan, "Creation of a Slave Society: Louisiana Plantations in the Eighteenth Century" (Ph.D. diss., University of Rochester, 1976). For additional studies dealing with blacks and slavery, see also Juan José Andreu Ocariz, *Movimientos rebeldes de los esclavos negros durante el dominio español en Luisiana* (Zaragoza, Spain, 1977); Gilbert C. Din, "Cimarrones and the San Malo Band in Spanish Louisiana," *Louisiana History*, 21 (Summer 1980); Jack D. L. Holmes, "The Abortive Slave Revolt at Pointe Coupee, Louisiana, 1795," *Louisiana History*, 11 (Fall 1970), and "The Role of Blacks in Spanish Alabama: The Mobile District, 1780-1813," *Alabama Historical Quarterly*, 37 (Winter 1975). A general overview of Spain's policy regarding slavery prior to the founding of Spanish Louisiana is surveyed in John J. TePaske, "The Fugitive Slave: Intercolonial Rivalry and the Spanish Slave Policy, 1687-1764," *Eighteenth-Century Florida and Its Borderlands*, ed. Samuel Proctor (Gainesville, Fla., 1975).

Relations with the Southeastern Indians, especially within the context of Anglo-Spanish rivalry, is a significant topic of investigation, although much is still to be done. The most comprehensive study of Spanish Indian policy remains the three-volume treatment Vicenta Cortés Alonso, *Historia de los indios del sureste de los Estados Unidos durante la segunda mitad del siglo*

XVIII (Doctoral thesis, University of Madrid, 1956). An equally valuable comment on the foundations of European Indian policy in the region is *The "Memoire Justificatif" of the Chevalier Montault de Monberaut: Indian Diplomacy in British West Florida, 1763-1765*, trans. and ed. Milo B. Howard, Jr., and Robert Rea (University, Ala., 1965). Significant background is provided by John J. TePaske, "French, Spanish, and English Indian Policy on the Gulf Coast, 1513-1763," *Spain and Her Rivals on the Gulf Coast*, ed. Ernest F. Dibble and Earle W. Newton (Pensacola, Fla., 1971). Helen Hornbeck Tanner's essay "Pipesmoke and Muskets: Florida Indian Intrigues of the Revolutionary Era," *Eighteenth-Century Florida and Its Borderlands*, ed. Samuel Proctor (Gainesville, Fla., 1975) is an important addition to the extensive bibliography on Southeastern Indians in the English colonial revolt. Jack D. L. Holmes has, during the last decade, produced a significant series of articles dealing with Indian policy during the Spanish period. See especially his "Spanish Policy Toward the Southern Indians in the 1790s," *Four Centuries of Southern Indians*, ed. Charles M. Hudson (Athens, Ga., 1975), "Spanish Treaties with West Florida Indians, 1784-1802," *Florida Historical Quarterly*, 48 (October 1969), "Up the Tombigbee with the Spaniards: Juan de la Villebeuvre and the Treaty of Boucfouca (1793)," *Alabama Historical Quarterly*, 40 (Spring-Summer 1978), and "Juan de la Villebeuvre and Spanish Indian Policy in West Florida, 1784-1797," *Florida Historical Quarterly*, 58 (April 1980). The latest contribution to the extensive literature dealing with the Creeks is Thomas D. Watson, "Strivings for Sovereignty: Alexander McGillivary, Creek Warfare, and Diplomacy, 1783-1790," *Florida Historical Quarterly*, 58 (April 1980). At this writing Abraham Nasatir and Gilbert C. Din have forthcoming with the University of Oklahoma Press a major study dealing with the Osage Indians.

The foregoing citations show that Spanish Louisiana has attracted a talented and growing group of scholars during the period since World War II. The literature continues to expand. This short essay has only provided an introduction to basic reading. Students interested in fruitful areas for possible future research are directed to Chapter 12 in this volume by Gilbert Din.

3
THE ANTEBELLUM PERIOD

JOSEPH G. TREGLE, JR.

THE SUPREME IRONY of Louisiana historiography must surely be that the state's past lends itself so readily to the author's pen that very little of consequence or lasting significance has yet been written about it. Here is the classic case of an embarrassment of riches, in which a community's abundance of color, drama, exotic distinctiveness, and seductive Mediterranean earthiness have provided a glittering vein of material easily exploited by those satisfied to mine only the surface levels, so that hardly a year goes by without additional potboilers telling once again the story of "romantic" Louisiana. The easy accessibility of "pirates," "Cajuns," "Creoles," French and Spanish governors, and hosts of other familiar characters has provided ready-made themes and *personae* for these incestuous accounts. Thus, our history has been peopled largely by stereotypes of dubious reality or validity.

Adding immeasurably to this distortion is the unhappy fact that Louisiana enjoys the distinction of nourishing *two* "lost causes," that of the Old South, which she shares with her sister communities below the Mason-Dixon line, and that of the Creole, the supposed aristocratic master of a cultivated society too refined to withstand the onslaught of Anglo-Saxon numbers and crudity after 1803. As in most cases of mythology, these folk "memories," while possibly supportive of some deep psychological need in a distressed society, have none the less perverted and disfigured the historic past.

This has been especially true for the so-called antebellum period. Consequently, this survey of the historical literature of the era is best begun by a melancholy recitation of great needs still unfilled. To date, for example, despite the overwhelming importance of agriculture in the lives of antebellum Louisianians, there has been no satisfactory history of that industry in the state, no study even of the fundamental processes by which land was brought into private development and settlement throughout the various rural regions of the community. Nor is there any integrative examination of the commercial organism of New Orleans during an epoch when for a moment the Crescent City was the chief export center of the entire nation. Despite the preeminent rank of the state in reception of foreign immigrants during the antebellum years, no comprehensive treatment of this phenomenon has ever been written. In an even greater failure, the subtleties and shadings of the long and often disruptive process of amalgamation of Latin and Anglo-Saxon cultures that began in Louisiana after 1803 still awaits a proper telling.

Additionally, there is no survey of the growth of transportation in an area laced by waterways, no satisfactory account of the growth of technology, of the arts and letters, of education, religion, journalism, or the professions. There have been monographs on slavery and rural life, but even these rest on uncertain foundations because as yet there has been no careful delineation of the demographic patterns of antebellum Louisiana, no scientific analysis of class configuration, of distribution of wealth, of productivity of land, and only remarkably limited examination of the workings and profitability of the plantation economy and the state's two great staple crops, sugar and cotton. Most startling of all, there is not a single comprehensive history of the state's antebellum political experience, no rewarding account of her constitutional evolution, or even a single definitive biography of any major political figure active before 1860.

What follows, then, is a survey of a sadly exiguous literature, most valuable, it may be, in clarifying what remains to be done.

THE TERRITORIAL PERIOD: 1803-1812

The three indispensable guides to the history of the Territory of Orleans are Clarence E. Carter, ed., *The Territorial Papers of the United States*, 26 vols. (Washington, D.C., 1934-1962), 9 (New Orleans); Dunbar Rowland, ed., *Official Letterbooks of W.C.C. Claiborne*, 6 vols. (Jackson, Miss., 1917); and George Dargo, *Jeffersons's Louisiana: Politics and the Clash of Legal Traditons* (Cambridge, 1975). The Carter and Rowland volumes are lodes of undigested and frequently highly subjective and biased reports and observations on affairs and personalities active in the territory. They must therefore be used with caution. Dargo's work is the most analytical inquiry into the complicated task of bringing a non-Anglo-American region into partnership with the young republic, and although its particular focus is legal history, it uses that concentration to enlighten broad segments of social, political, and economic concerns. Unfortunately, it is largely limited to the five-year span from 1803 to 1808. Marietta LeBreton, "A History of the Territory of Orleans, 1803-1812" (Ph.D. diss., Louisiana State University, 1969), and Thomas P. Coffey, "The Territory of Orleans, 1804-1812" (Ph.D. diss., Saint Louis University, 1958) are detailed accounts of the entire period, but their usefulness is limited by their interpretative thinness.

Essential to a fleshing out of the coverage of the foregoing are the extensive manuscript collections of principals involved with the territory: Thomas Jefferson and James Madison (Manuscript Division, Library of Congress); and Albert Gallatin (New York Historical Society). Additional manuscript holdings of great value are the Daniel Clark-James Wilkinson Papers (Historical Society of Pennsylvania), Peters Family Letters (New York Public Library), Nicholas P. Trist Papers (Library of Congress and University of North Carolina at Chapel Hill), and Palfrey Family Papers (Houghton Library, Harvard University).

For a sense of the lay of the land and the profile of the territorial settlement, the best sources are [Jacob Wagner], *An Account of Louisiana* (Providence, 1803); William Darby, *Geographical Description of the State of Louisiana* (Philadelphia, 1816), and his *Emigrant's Guide to the Western and Southwestern States and Territories* (New York, 1818); Henry M. Brackenridge, *Views of Louisiana* (Baltimore, 1817); F. M. Perrin du Lac, *Voyage dans les deux Louisianes* (Paris, 1805); C. C. Robin, *Voyages dans l'intérieur de la Louisiane*, 2 vols. (Paris, 1807); Jedediah Morse, *The American Gazetteer... with a Particular Description of Louisiana* (Charlestown, S.C., 1804); and Amos Stoddard, *Sketches, Historical and Descriptive of Louisiana* (Philadelphia, 1812).

Biographical studies of leading figures in the territorial period are few and of limited value. Joseph T. Hatfield, *William Claiborne: Jeffersonian Centurion in the American West* (Lafayette, La., 1976) suffers from its one-dimensional portrayal of that complex man, and William B. Hatcher, *Edward Livingston* (Baton Rouge, 1949) is marred by uncritically laudatory treatment of its protagonist as well as the author's skimpy knowledge of the period in which he was working.

Perhaps the most useful of the many studies of the Aaron Burr story is that of Thomas P. Abernethy, *The Burr Conspiracy* (New York, 1954), which supports the familiar argument that Burr's purpose was to seize the western states and Mexico, a view that Francis S. Philbrick, in *The Rise of the New West, 1754-1830* (New York, 1965), sees as proceeding from insufficient historical evidence. The classic and still useful study of the tangled skeins of West Florida's relationship to Louisiana is Isaac J. Cox, *The West Florida Controversy* (Baltimore, 1918).

Economic aspects of the territorial period are best viewed in John G. Clark, *New Orleans, 1718-1812: An Economic History* (Baton Rouge, 1970), and Robert Earl Roeder, "New Orleans Merchants, 1790-1837" (Ph.D. diss., Harvard University, 1959). The monumental educational problems confronting the new community are discussed in Stuart Noble, "Governor Claiborne and the Public School System of the Territorial Government of Louisiana," *Louisiana Historical Quarterly*, 11 (October 1928), and Martin L. Riley, "The Development of Education in Louisiana Prior to Statehood," *Louisiana Historical Quarterly,* 19 (July 1936).

THE ANTEBELLUM STATE: PLACE AND PEOPLE

Louisiana's five decades of growth from 1812 to 1861 saw great changes in its physical and demographic characteristics. These may be at least partially glimpsed by judicious use of contemporary descriptions and travel accounts, among the most helpful of which are Timothy Flint, *History and Geography of the Mississippi Valley*, 2 vols. (Philadelphia, 1832), and *Recollections of the Past Ten Years* (Boston, 1826), the work of a literate and sharp-eyed migrant to the young community; Basil Hall, *Travels in North America*, 2 vols. (Philadelphia, 1829); Charles A. Murray, *Travels in North America During the Years 1834, 1835, and 1836*, 2 vols. (London, 1839); Joseph H. Ingraham, *The Southwest by a Yankee*, 2 vols. (New York, 1835); Tyrone Power, *Impressions of America*, 2 vols. (London, 1842); Louis F. Tasistro, *Random Shots and Southern Breezes*, 2 vols. (New York, 1842); Charles Lyell, *A Second Visit to the United States of North America*, 2 vols. (London, 1850); J. J. Ampère, *Promenade en Amérique*, 2 vols. (Paris, 1855). Unsurpassed for the 1850s is still Frederick Law Olmsted, *A Journey in the Seaboard Slave States* (New York, 1856).

The ethnically complex nature of Louisiana's polyglot antebellum population is treated in Joseph G. Tregle, Jr., "Early New Orleans Society: A Reappraisal," *Journal of Southern History*, 18 (February 1952), the findings of which are applicable to the entire state. Although George W. Cable's work was condemned by many of the area's Gallic citizenry, his *Creoles of Louisiana* (New York, 1884) is insightful and essentially reliable. The pro-French rejoinder is found in Charles E. A. Gayarré, *The Creoles of History and Romance* (New Orleans, 1885), a product of years that found Gayarré increasingly embittered by the Civil War and Reconstruction. Vaughn Baker's "The Acadians in Antebellum Louisiana: A Study in Acculturation," *The Cajuns*, ed. Glenn Conrad (Lafayette, La., 1978) is a compact and rewarding survey of that variously viewed segment of the community, whereas Lewis W. Newton, "The Americanization of French Louisiana: A Study of the Process of Adjustment Between the French and Anglo-American Population of Louisiana, 1803-1860" (Ph.D. diss., University of Chicago, 1929), although dated and limited in its appreciation of the subtleties of its topic, indicates at least the significance and importance of the subject. One of the less obvious components in the Louisiana melting pot is highlighted in Frank M. Lovrich, "The Dalmation Yugoslavs in Louisiana," *Louisiana History*, 8 (Spring 1967).

For the raw data on antebellum population one must, of course, go to the published U.S. Census Bureau returns for each decade, frequently supplemented by *Compendiums* as well as analytical and comparative tables. Even more detailed are the actual field returns to the Census Bureau, which have been microfilmed by the National Archives for each of the surveys from 1810 through 1860 and are available in most university libraries in the state.

Contemporary indigenous accounts of the people and places of antebellum Louisiana are relatively scarce. The most gripping and compelling is the memoir of the Reverend Theodore Clapp, *Autobiographical Sketches and Recollections During a Thirty-Five Years Residence in New Orleans* (Boston, 1857). Clapp's account of his spiritual reorientation from Presbyterian to Unitarian divine catches beautifully the emotional and intellectual dimensions of the blending of cultures in Louisiana, while his pages on the cholera and yellow fever epidemics of 1832-1833 and 1853 are deservedly famous. Also helpful in conveying a sense of the particular time and place are Vincent Nolte, *Fifty Years in Both Hemispheres* (New York, 1854), the reminiscences of an agent of the Barings in New Orleans from the territorial period to the beginnings of the Jacksonian era; W. H. Sparks, *The Memories of Fifty Years* (Philadelphia, 1870), especially good in its colorful and intimate character sketches of some of the outstanding prewar Louisianians; Henry S. Foote, *The Bench and Bar of South and Southwest* (Saint Louis, 1876), which is considerably more comprehensive than its title would suggest; Cyprien Dufour, "Local Sketches," a series of personality profiles reprinted in the *Louisiana Historical Quarterly*, 14 (April, July, October 1931); and John S. Whitaker, *Sketches of Life and Character in Louisiana* (New Orleans, 1847), descriptions of eminent citizens by a prominent jurist of the period.

Some regions of the state have stimulated local studies of considerable merit. Among them are J. Fair Hardin, *Northwestern Louisiana: A History of the Watershed of the Red River, 1714-1937* (Louisville, Ky., and Shreveport, La., n.d.); G. P. Whittington, *Rapides Parish, Louisiana: A History* ([Alexandria, La.], 1970); William H. Perrin, *Southwest Louisiana, Biographical and Historical* (1891; reprint ed., Baton Rouge, 1971); and Betsy Swanson, *Historic Jefferson Parish: From Shore to Shore* (Gretna, La., 1975).

No monograph or memoir, however good, is likely to match the immediate sense and feel of a community that can be gained by reading contemporary newspapers and manuscript collections. Antebellum Louisiana was particularly rich in the former, and files of many of her great journals are available in libraries and museums. Unfortunately, collections of personal correspondence from the period are not nearly so plentiful, although some may indeed be found in the various state depositories noted elsewhere in this volume. For the most comprehensive holdings, however, one must look outside Louisiana. Unmatched in richness, particularly in political matters, are the papers of Josiah Stoddard Johnston, centering on the years from 1820 to 1834 and located at the Historical Society of Pennsylvania in Philadelphia (microfilm copies are available in several Louisiana libraries). Also valuable are the Mansel White Papers, the J.F.H. Claiborne Papers, and the Grace King Papers (University of North Carolina at Chapel Hill), the Nicholas P. Trist Papers (Library of Congress and University of North Carolina at Chapel Hill), the James Colles Papers (New York Public Library) the E.G.W. Butler Papers and the J.D.B. De Bow Papers (Duke University).

THE BATTLE OF NEW ORLEANS

Robin Reilly's *The British at the Gates: The New Orleans Campaign in the War of 1812* (New York, 1974) is the most solid and reliable treatment of the subject, much superior to Charles P. Brooks, *The Siege of New Orleans* (Seattle, 1961), and Samuel Carter, *Blaze of Glory* (New York, 1971), both of which indulge in fanciful reconstruction of conversation and happenings unsupported by historical evidence. Reilly's work is especially good in placing the New Orleans campaign in proper relationship to the total war effort. Narrower in scope and more technical in approach is Wilbur S. Brown, *The Amphibious Campaign for New Orleans, 1814-1815* (University, Ala., 1969). For a suggestion as to the origins of the British attack plan against New Orleans, see Joseph G. Tregle, Jr., "British Spy Along the Mississippi: Thomas Hutchins and the Defenses of New Orleans, 1773," *Louisiana History*, 8 (Fall 1967). The role of Jean Lafitte and company in the engagement is told by Jane de Grummond, *The Baratarians and the Battle of New Orleans* (Baton Rouge, 1961).

The best contemporary accounts of the siege are George Robert Gleig, *The Campaigns of the British Army at Washington and New Orleans... in the Years 1814-15* (London, 1821), which has also appeared in altered form anonymously as *A Subaltern in America* (Philadelphia, 1826), and A. Lacarrière Latour, *Historical Memoir of the War in West Florida and Louisiana* (Philadelphia, 1816). Especially valuable as an "authorized" version of events by its great hero is John Henry Eaton, *The Life of Andrew Jackson* (Philadelphia, 1828), but for a closer examination of the Tennessean's part in all this one must turn to his correspondence, in manuscript at the Library of Congress and the Tennessee Historical Society (Nashville) and in the published collection edited by John S. Bassett, *Correspondence of Andrew Jackson*, 6 vols. (Washington, D.C., 1926-1933). For the tempest of controversy surrounding Jackson's leadership during the British attack, the most revealing sources are "Andrew Jackson and Judge D. A.

Hall (Report of the Committee of the Louisiana Senate, 1843)," *Louisiana Historical Quarterly*, 5 (October 1922), "Report of the Committee of Enquiry of the Military Measures Executed against the Legislature of Louisiana, Dec. 28, 1814," *Louisiana Historical Quarterly*, 9 (April 1926), and Bernard Marigny, "Reflections on the Campaign of General Andrew Jackson in Louisiana in 1814 and '15," *Louisiana Historical Quarterly*, 6 (January 1923).

THE ANTEBELLUM STATE: POLITICAL AND CONSTITUTIONAL DEVELOPMENT

The two greatest antebellum historians of Louisiana, François-Xavier Martin and Charles E. A. Gayarré, were each in a unique position to record recollections of affairs with which they were intimately connected for most of the period. Regrettably, both of their published works, Martin's *History of Louisiana from the Earliest Period* (New Orleans, 1827), and Gayarré's *History of Louisiana*, 4 vols. (New Orleans, 1885), give scant notice to the years after 1815 and, except for Martin's strictures against Andrew Jackson, reflect little of their authors' personal reaction to events.

In the absence of any comprehensive and integrated account of Louisiana politics from 1812 to 1861 (the volume by Perry Howard, *Political Tendencies in Louisiana* [Baton Rouge, 1971] is an essay in what its author calls "political ecology" and does not meet distinct historical need), one must pull the story together from bits and pieces. Joseph G. Tregle, Jr., "Louisiana in the Age of Jackson: A Study in Ego Politics" (Ph.D. diss., University of Pennsylvania, 1954) covers the 1820-1834 period; William H. Adams, *The Whig Party of Louisiana* (Lafayette, La., 1973) is a straightforward narrative whose value is weakened by careless and slipshod editing. D.L.A. Hackett, "The Social Structure of Jacksonian Louisiana"; "Slavery, Ethnicity, and Sugar: An Analysis of Voting Behavior in Louisiana, 1828-1844," "'Vote Early! Beware of Fraud!': A Note on Voter Turnout in Presidential and Gubernatorial Elections in Louisiana, 1828-1844," and "'The Days of this Republic Will Be Numbered': Abolition, Slavery, and the Presidential Election of 1836," a series of articles appearing in *Louisiana Studies*, 12 (Spring 1973), 13 (Summer 1974), and 14 (Summer 1975), is valuable for its employment of quantification methodology but demonstrative of the frequently unsatisfying shallowness that seems to beset that technique. James G. Greer, "Louisiana Politics, 1845-1861," *Louisiana Historical Quarterly*, 12 (July, October 1929), 13 (January, April, July, October 1930), an archaic survey of the period resting largely on newspapers, lacks any substantive theme. Marius M. Carriere, "The Know-Nothing Movement in Louisiana" (Ph.D. diss., Louisiana State University, 1977) sees the American party as essentially the product of the death of the Whigs, nativism, and persistent Unionism.

Carriere supplants the more general volume by W. Darrell Overdyke, *The Know-Nothing Party in the South* (Baton Rouge, 1959) and, by the same author, "History of the American Party in Louisiana," *Louisiana Historical Quarterly*, 15 (October 1932), 16 (January, April, July, October 1933).

Once thought to be a definitive study of society and politics from the 1840s through Reconstruction, Roger W. Shugg's *Origins of Class Struggle in Louisiana* (Baton Rouge, 1939) is so frequently unreliable and inaccurate as to be of questionable value, except for its still suggestive identification of a range of issues requiring attention. For a critique of Shugg's work, see Joseph G. Tregle, Jr., "Another Look at Shugg's Louisiana," *Louisiana History*, 17 (Summer 1976).

Biographical studies of leading Louisiana antebellum political figures are in scant supply. William B. Hatcher's *Edward Livingston* (Baton Rouge, 1940) is simplistically adulatory and insensitive to the real issues in the political life of the state, hardly more helpful than the worshipful *Life of Edward Livingston* by a family connection, Charles Havens Hunt, (New York, 1864). Louis M. Sears's *John Slidell* (Durham, N.C., 1925), and Robert D. Meade's *Judah P. Benjamin* (New York, 1943) are skimpy in their attention to the Louisiana careers of their protagonists, and Pierce Butler's *Judah P. Benjamin* (Philadelphia, 1907) is antiquated in outlook and sources. Some appreciation of Slidell's long and important public life may be gleaned from Joseph G. Tregle, Jr., "The Political Apprenticeship of John Slidell," *Journal of Southern History*, 26 (February 1960), Albert L. Diket, "John Slidell and the Community He Represented in the Senate, 1853-1861" (Ph.D. diss., Louisiana State University, 1958), and Charles R. Craig, "John Slidell, Louisiana Politico, 1793-1847" (M.A. thesis, Tulane University, 1949). For Benjamin, see Louis Gruss, "Judah Philip Benjamin," *Louisiana Historical Quarterly*, 19 (October 1939). Arthur Freeman, "The Early Career of Pierre Soulé," *Louisiana Historical Quarterly*, 25 (October 1942), and J. Preston Moore, "Pierre Soulé: Southern Expansionist and Promoter," *Journal of Southern History*, 21 (May 1955) touch tangents of the fiery Frenchman's career, but there is no satisfactory biography or fuller political study. Wendell Holmes Stephenson, *Alexander Porter, Whig Planter of Old Louisiana* (Baton Rouge, 1934) focuses on one of the most observant and irrepressible political figures of the 1820s-1840s, but it was unfortunately done without access to the richest file of Porter correspondence, his letters in the Josiah Stoddard Johnston Papers mentioned above.

Most of the antebellum governors of Louisiana have been subjects of master's theses at Louisiana State University, several of which have been published in the *Louisiana Historical Quarterly*: Diedrich Ramke, "Edward Douglas White, Sr., Governor of Louisiana, 1835-1839," 19 (April 1936); Sidney J. Aucoin, "The Political Career of Isaac Johnson, Governor of Louisiana, 1846-1850," 28 (July 1945); Albert L. Dupont, "The Career of

Paul Octave Hébert, Governor of Louisiana, 1853-1856," 31 (April 1948); and Thomas Landry, "The Political Career of Robert Charles Wickliffe, Governor of Louisiana, 1856-1860," 25 (July 1942).

In the more formal area of the structure and mechanics of the antebellum state government, an indispensable collection is the microfiche edition of Louisiana constitutional conventions, 1811-1954, published by Greenwood Press (Westport, Ct., 1973). This should be supplemented by the *Journals* and *Debates* of the Louisiana State Legislature, regrettably incomplete for the pre-1860 period but invaluable not only as an index to legislative proceedings but also as a repository of reports of agencies of the antebellum government not to be found elsewhere. (These early state archives are available in a microfilm publication, *Records of the States of the United States of America*, prepared for the Library of Congress by William Sumner Jenkins in 1949 and accessible from the Library of Congress through interlibrary loan). Most helpful as guides through the thicket of constantly changing statutory enactments are Louis Moreau Lislet, comp., *A General Digest of the Acts of the Legislature of Louisiana . . . 1804, to 1827, Inclusive*, 2 vols. (New Orleans, 1828), Henry A. Bullard and Thomas Curry, comps., *A New Digest of the Statute Laws of the State of Louisiana* (New Orleans, 1842), and U. B. Phillips, comp. *The Revised Statutes of Louisiana* (New Orleans, 1856).

Constitutional development may be followed in Cecil Morgan, *The First Constitution of Louisiana* (Baton Rouge, 1975); Philip D. Uzee, "The First Louisiana State Constitution" (M.A. thesis, Louisiana State University, 1938); Ted Ferguson, "The Louisiana Constitution of 1845" (M.A. thesis, Louisiana State University, 1948); and Wayne Everard, "Louisiana State Politics and the Constitution of 1852" (M.A. thesis, University of New Orleans, 1972). For an interpretation of the formative forces behind these constitutional structures, see Joseph G. Tregle, Jr., "Political Reinforcement of Ethnic Dominance in Louisiana, 1812-1845," *The Americanization of the Gulf Coast, 1803-1850*, ed. L. F. Ellsworth (Pensacola, Fla., 1971).

Robert Dabney Calhoun's "The Origin and Early Development of County-Parish Government in Louisiana," *Louisiana Historical Quarterly*, 18 (January 1935) is a detailed and sound examination of this unique Louisiana system. Roger W. Shugg's "Suffrage and Representation in Antebellum Louisiana," *Louisiana Historical Quarterly*, 19 (April 1936) suffers from the same weaknesses that plague his broader *Origins of Class Struggle in Louisiana*. Much more reliable but not as finely focused on the antebellum period is Emmett Aseff, *Apportionment in Louisiana* (Baton Rouge, 1950).

In the area of legal history the most helpful guides are Samuel B. Groner, "Louisiana Law: Its Development in the First Quarter Century of American Rule," *Louisiana Law Review*, 8 (January 1948); John T. Hood, Jr., "The History and Development of the Louisiana Civil Code," *Tulane Law Review*, 33 (December 1958); Henry P. Dart, "History of the Supreme

Court of Louisiana," *Louisiana Historical Quarterly*, 4 (January 1921); and Grant Lyons, "Louisiana and the Livingston Criminal Codes," *Louisiana History*, 15 (Summer 1974). A contemporary examination of the state's criminal procedures is found in Albert Voorhies, *A Treatise on the Criminal Jurisprudence of Louisiana...from the Year 1805 to the Year 1858* (New Orleans, 1860).

Louisiana antebellum politics were not played simply on a local level, of course. Indispensable to an understanding of its fuller dimensions are the many exchanges of correspondence between Louisianians and national leaders such as Andrew Jackson, Henry Clay, Martin Van Buren, William Henry Harrison, James K. Polk, Nicholas Biddle, John J. Crittenden, Andrew Jackson Donelson, William C. Rives, and Franklin Pierce, all of whose papers are preserved in the Manuscript Division of the Library of Congress. Other collections valuable in this fashion are the Josiah Stoddard Johnston Papers mentioned above; the Adams Family Papers (Massachusetts Historical Society); James Buchanan Papers (Historical Society of Pennsylvania); Daniel Webster Papers (Hanover, New Hampshire); and the Nicholas P. Trist Papers (Library of Congress and the University of North Carolina at Chapel Hill). In the antebellum years the U.S. secretary of state acted as a general federal patronage officer, and much intimate detail of Louisiana politics can be gleaned from the National Archives microfilm publications of "Letters of Application and Recommendation," arranged under presidential administrations.

As yet largely unexploited by historians, the records of the various state courts of antebellum Louisiana are now accessible at depositories described elsewhere in this volume. Archives of the U.S. Civil Courts in Louisiana are available at the National Archives branch in Fort Worth, Texas. A helpful study of political power in the lower South during the 1850s, which places Louisiana in the broader context of regional analysis, is Ralph A. Wooster's *The People in Power: Courthouse and Statehouse in the Lower South, 1850-1860* (Knoxville, Tenn., 1969).

THE ANTEBELLUM STATE: ECONOMY

There is no satisfactory history of Louisiana's primary antebellum industry, agriculture. The best general survey of the topic is found in the monumental study by Lewis C. Gray, *History of Agriculture in the Southern United States to 1860*, 2 vols. (Washington, D.C., 1933), which devotes considerable attention to the state's principal crops, varieties of soil and terrain, labor system, and profit returns. But even classics become dated, and Gray's methodology has been supplemented extensively by subsequent econometric scholarship. For the most extensive attention to these newer areas of inquiry, one should consult recent volumes of such serials as *Agricultural History*, *Journal of Economic History*, *Journal of Negro History*, and *Explorations in Economic History*.

First produced profitably in Louisiana in 1794, sugar had by 1828 become the leading money crop of the state, a position it would hold until the mid-1840s, when cotton, always the plant of the majority of farmers, would assert its primacy even in income return. Most satisfactory treatment of the Louisiana sugar industry is found in J. Carlyle Sitterson, *Sugar Country: The Cane Sugar Industry in the South, 1753-1950* (Lexington, Ky., 1953). This should be supplemented by David O. Whitten, "Antebellum Sugar and Rice Plantations, Louisiana and South Carolina: A Profitability Study" (Ph.D. diss., Tulane University, 1970), and Mark Schmitz, "Economic Analysis of Antebellum Sugar Plantations in Louisiana" (Ph.D. diss., University of North Carolina at Chapel Hill, 1974). For an examination of the state's shifting agrarian patterns and their expression in the political arena, see Joseph G. Tregle, Jr., "Louisiana and the Tariff, 1816-1846," *Louisiana Historical Quarterly*, 25 (January 1942). On the question of the "democratic" or "aristocratic" distribution of wealth in antebellum Louisiana, the two diametrically opposed interpretations are found in Harry L. Coles, Jr., "Some Notes on Slaveownership and Landownership in Louisiana, 1850-1860," *Journal of Southern History*, 9 (August 1943), and Fabian Linden, "Economic Democracy in the Slave South," *Journal of Negro History*, 31 (April 1946).

An informative review of antebellum agricultural affairs is found in Edmond J. Forstall, *Agricultural Productions of Louisiana* (New Orleans, 1845). Even more extensive coverage of agrarian topics may be found in the great quarterly published in prewar New Orleans, *De Bow's Review*, and in various regional periodicals such as *The Southern Cultivator* (Augusta, Ga.), *The Southern Agriculturist* (Charleston, S.C.), *The Southern Planter* (Richmond, Va.), and *Niles' Register* (Baltimore, Md.). A more recent examination of the economic hazards of agrarian life is found in Raleigh A. Suarez, "Louisiana's Struggling Majority: The Antebellum Farmer," *McNeese Review*, 14 (1963). For a more complete overview of rural life in general during the period, see Suarez's "Rural Life in Louisiana, 1850-1860" (Ph.D. diss., Louisiana State University, 1954), and Edwin A. Davis, ed., *Plantation Life in the Florida Parishes of Louisiana: The Diary of Bennett S. Barrow* (New York, 1943).

Astonishingly, there is practically no historical literature on the great mercantile economy of antebellum Louisiana centered in New Orleans. Robert Earl Roeder's "New Orleans Merchants, 1790-1837" (Ph.D. diss., Harvard University, 1959) is an excellent introduction, unhappily never expanded into the later decades as originally intended by the author. A more general survey of rural trade may be found in Raleigh A. Suarez, "Bargains, Bills, and Bankruptcies: Business Activity in Rural Antebellum Louisiana," *Louisiana History*, 5 (Summer 1966), and an interpretative examination of the area's commercial and financial estate in Merl E. Reed, "Boom or Bust: Louisiana's Economy During the 1830s," *Louisiana History*, 4 (Winter 1963).

The more specific topic of antebellum banking history has attracted wider and deeper scholarly attention. By far the most comprehensive and technical examination of the subject is that by George D. Green, *Finance and Economic Development in the Old South: Louisiana Banking, 1804-1861* (Stanford, Cal., 1972), which rejects older criticism that the state's banking development of the 1820s and 1830s was reckless and unsound. Adopting the techniques of the "new" economic history, Green argues that the importance of state banks in the growth of urban and regional economies has been largely underestimated and submerged in confusion centering on "wildcat" note issue and speculation. More traditional views are found in Stephen A. Caldwell, *A Banking History of Louisiana* (Baton Rouge, 1935), and Harold Heck, "A History of Banks and Bank Legislation in Louisiana" (D.C.S. diss., New York University, 1939). The pivotal place of the Louisiana banking experience in the nation's economic convulsions of the 1830s and 1840s has produced several studies of particular excellence, such as Ralph W. Hidy, "The Union Bank of Louisiana Loan, 1832: A Case Study in Marketing," *Journal of Political Economy*, 4 (April 1939); Irene D. Neu, "Edmond Jean Forstall and Louisiana Banking," *Explorations in Economic History*, 7 (Summer 1970), and "J. B. Moussier and the Property Banks of Louisiana," *Business History Review*, 35 (Winter 1961); Bray Hammond, "The Louisiana Banking Act of February 5, 1842," Federal Reserve Bank of Atlanta *Monthly Bulletin*, 27 (January 1942); and George D. Green, "The Louisiana Bank Act of 1842," *Explorations in Economic History*, 7 (Summer 1970). Also pertinent are Emile P. Grenier, "The Early Financing of the Consolidated Association of the Planters of Louisiana" (M.A. thesis, Louisiana State University, 1938), and "Property Banks in Louisiana" (Ph.D. diss., Louisiana State Univeristy, 1942).

An essential source for research into Louisiana antebellum banking and economy in general is the expansive Record Group 56 in the National Archives, including Treasury Department holdings such as "Letters to and from Banks" and "Letters to and from Collectors of Customs." Also helpful are the contemporary mercantile magazines such as *De Bow's Review*, *Hunt's Merchants' Magazine*, and *Niles' Register*.

In the field of transportation, most valuable are Merl E. Reed, *New Orleans and the Railroads: The Struggle for Commercial Empire, 1830-1860* (Baton Rouge, 1966), actually statewide in its coverage; Edwin Dale Odum, "Louisiana Railroads, 1830-1880: A Study in State and Local Aid" (Ph.D. diss., Tulane University, 1961); Marshall Scott Legan, "Railroad Sentiment in North Louisiana in the 1850s," *Louisiana History*, 17 (Spring 1976); John C. Andreassen, "Internal Improvements in Louisiana, 1824-1837," *Louisiana Historical Quarterly*, 30 (January 1947); Harry Howard Evans, "James Robb, Banker and Pioneer Railroad Builder of Antebellum Louisiana," *Louisiana Historical Quarterly*, 23 (January 1940); and Walter M. Lowrey, "Navigational Problems at the Mouth of the Mississippi River, 1618-1880" (Ph.D. diss., Vanderbilt University, 1956).

THE ANTEBELLUM STATE:
SOCIAL AND CULTURAL

There is no satisfactory social or cultural history of antebellum Louisiana. In the whole broad field, indeed, only one study stands out as a model of what is needed in a wide variety of special categories, John Duffy's *The Rudolph Matas History of Medicine in Louisiana*, 2 vols. (Baton Rouge, 1958-1962). Supplementary to Duffy is A. E. Fossier, "History of Medical Education in New Orleans from Its Birth to the Civil War," *Annals of Medical History*, 6 (1934), and Jo Ann Carrigan, "The Saffron Scourge: A History of Yellow Fever in Louisiana, 1796-1905" (Ph.D. diss., Louisiana State University, 1961).

Various religious sects have been the subjects of historical attention, most satisfactorily in such studies as Roger Baudier, *The Catholic Church in Louisiana* (New Orleans, 1939), badly in need of revision and updating; John T. Christian, *A History of the Baptists of Louisiana* (Shreveport, La., 1923); Robert C. Witcher, "The Episcopal Church in Louisiana, 1805-1861" (Ph.D. diss., Louisiana State University, 1969); and Hodding Carter and Betty W. Carter, *So Great a Good: A History of the Episcopal Church in Louisiana and of Christ Church Cathedral, 1805-1955* (Sewanee, Tenn., 1955).

Louisiana men of letters were not particularly numerous in the antebellum years. Among their biographies, most insightful and informative are Edward M. Socola, "Charles E. A. Gayarré: A Biography" (Ph.D. diss., University of Pennsylvania, 1954), Dagmar LeBreton, *Chahta-Ima: The Life of Adrien-Emmanuel Rouquette* (Baton Rouge, 1947), and Otis C. Skipper, *J.D.B. De Bow, Magazinist of the Old South* (Athens, Ga., 1958). Milton Rickels, "Thomas Bangs Thorpe in the Felicianas, 1836-1842," *Louisiana Historical Quarterly*, 39 (April 1956) explores the "Big Bear" school of fiction in the state. In a more general examination of the literary field, greater attention has been directed to French-language writers than to those in English: Ruby B. Caulfield, *The French Literature of Louisiana* (New York, 1929), and Edward L. Tinker, *Les Ecrits de langue française en Louisiane au XIXe siècle* (Paris, 1933). In the related field of journalism, there is Raymond R. McCurdy's *A History and Bibliography of Spanish-Language Newspapers and Magazines in Louisiana, 1808-1949* (Albuquerque, 1951).

Very little of substance has been written on the educational history of Louisiana. Edwin W. Fay, *The History of Education in Louisiana* (Washington, D.C., 1898), and Thomas H. Harris, *The Story of Public Education in Louisiana* (Baton Rouge, 1924) are superficial and obviously obsolete in any case. More helpful are Gary C. Mitchell, "Growth of State Control of Public Education in Louisiana" (Ph.D. diss., University of Michigan, 1942); Raleigh A. Suarez, "Chronicle of a Failure: Public Education in Antebellum Louisiana," *Louisiana History*, 12 (Spring 1971); James W.

Mobley, "The Academy Movement in Louisiana," *Louisiana Historical Quarterly*, 30 (July 1947), devoted to the development of private institutions; and Earl Niehaus, "Jefferson College: The Early Years," *Louisiana Historical Quarterly*, 38 (October 1955).

Little has been done in the history of the arts in Louisiana, except in the fields of music and architecture. The rich New Orleans tradition in these areas is noted elsewhere in this volume, but for the nonurban scene the following are helpful: Gladys Bumstead, *Louisiana Composers* (New Orleans, 1935); Louis Panzeri, *Louisiana Composers* (New Orleans, 1972); John Desmond, *Louisiana's Antebellum Architecture* (Baton Rouge, 1970); Philippe Oszucik, *Louisiana's Gothic Revival Architecture* (Baton Rouge, 1973); and Arthur Scully, *James Dakin* (Baton Rouge, 1973). Hard to classify but informative and enjoyable is Leonard V. Huber, *Louisiana: A Pictorial History* (New York, 1975).

4
CIVIL WAR AND RECONSTRUCTION

JOE GRAY TAYLOR

ABRAHAM LINCOLN WAS elected president of the United States in November of 1860, and in January of 1861 the Louisiana Secession Convention voted to take Louisiana out of the United States and into the Confederate States of America. In Louisiana the Civil War proper may be said to have begun with secession and to have continued until the surrender of the surviving fragments of Kirby Smith's Trans-Mississippi Army in June of 1865. In the meantime, however, in April of 1862, Commodore David Farragut's fleet had run past the batteries of Forts Saint Philip and Jackson on the Mississippi River below New Orleans; before the end of that April General Benjamin F. Butler had begun the Union occupation of the Crescent City, which would persist until April of 1877. Thus discussions of Civil War and Reconstruction as they apply to Louisiana are not naturally separate, physically, chronologically, or otherwise. For the purpose of clarity, this chapter will attempt to discuss the two separately, but the separation is largely artificial. The Civil War and Reconstruction went on side by side; a state government established by General Nathaniel P. Banks and recognized by President Lincoln existed during the Red River Campaign of 1864.

Because this particular chapter is strictly limited in length and because other parts of this book attempt to survey the contents of various depositories of published and unpublished source materials, this essay will not attempt to be a catalog except in the broadest sense of the word. Since the duration in time of the Civil War was much less than the duration of Reconstruction, it will not receive as much attention as Reconstruction; after all, once Vicksburg and Port Hudson had been surrendered, Louisiana became a military backwater. Richard Taylor's victory over Banks in the Red River Campaign of 1864 must have gratified nearly every Louisiana Confederate, except possibly General Kirby Smith, but it had no apparent effect on the outcome of the war. Nor, in the final analysis, were the advances and retreats along Bayou Teche between Morgan City and Alexandria any more significant.

The truth of the matter is that, except for the fall of New Orleans, events in Louisiana before or after 1863 had little bearing on the military outcome of the American Civil War. The military role of the state has been exhaustively studied in Jefferson Davis Bragg, *Louisiana in the Confederacy* (Baton Rouge, 1941) and in the accurate and more thoroughly researched work of John D. Winters, *The Civil War in Louisiana* (Baton Rouge, 1963). Memoirs well worth reading include Lieutenant Colonel Arthur J. L. Freemantle, *Three Months in the Southern States: April-June, 1863* (New York, 1864); F. Jay Taylor, ed., *Reluctant Rebel: The Secret Diary of Robert Patrick, 1861-1865* (Baton Rouge, 1959); and Richard Taylor's superbly written *Destruction and Reconstruction: Personal Experiences of the Late War* (New York, 1879). In a class by itself is John Q. Anderson, ed., *Brokenburn: The Journal of Kate Stone, 1861-1868* (Baton Rouge, 1955), which affords the reader a literate, charming, and accurate account of life on a Louisiana cotton plantation during the Civil War.

In order to understand how the civilian government of Confederate Louisiana managed to continue in operation despite isolation, defeat, and disaffection, every serious student of the Civil War in Louisiana needs to consult Vincent H. Cassidy and Amos E. Simpson, *Henry Watkins Allen of Louisiana* (Baton Rouge, 1964). Charles L. Dufour maintains, in his well-written *The Night the War Was Lost* (New York, 1960), that the fall of New Orleans made inevitable the eventual fall of the Confederacy. Joseph Howard Parks, *General Edmund Kirby Smith, C.S.A.* (Baton Rouge, 1954) gives much detail concerning the military administration of the huge area west of the Mississippi. Two other significant secondary works are Fred H. Harrington, *Fighting Politician: Major General N. P. Banks* (Philadelphia, 1948), and Robert S. Holzman, *Stormy Ben Butler* (New York, 1954).

Still other books that demand notice are E. Merton Coulter, *The Confederate States of America, 1861-1865* (Baton Rouge, 1950), volume 7 of Wendell Holmes Stephenson and E. Merton Coulter, eds., *A History of the South*; H. Allen Gosnell, *Guns on the Western Waters: The Story of River Gunboats in the Civil War* (Baton Rouge, 1949); Earl S. Miers, *The Web of Victory: Grant at Vicksburg* (New York, 1955); and Kenneth P. Williams, *Lincoln Finds a General*, 5 vols. (New York, 1949-1959). T. Harry William's biography of Louisiana's most famous soldier, *P.G.T. Beauregard: Napoleon in Gray* (Baton Rouge, 1954) has little to say about the war in Beauregard's home state. The books and articles published in scholarly journals, especially the now defunct *Louisiana Historical Quarterly* and the currently published *Louisiana History*, afford the student a rather complete and accurate account of the political and military events of the Civil War in Louisiana. There will be those, without doubt, who will wish to consult *The War of the Rebellion: A Compilation of the Official Records of the Union and Confederate Armies*, 128 vols. (Washington, D.C., 1880-1901) and manuscript collections at the Library of Congress, the National Archives, and such state universities as Louisiana State University at Baton Rouge and the Southern Historical Collection at the University of North Carolina at Chapel Hill. Only a few graduate students and other researchers working on a Civil War topic, however, will find themselves in need of more detail than is afforded by Winter's volume. Some matters are still in dispute concerning the Teche campaigns and the Red River Campaign, but, assuming that definite resolution of these disputes was possible, the effect upon the overall history of the Civil War would be negligible.

More intensive study of Louisiana's black people during the Civil War holds more promise for the aspiring historian. For years Bell I. Wiley's *Southern Negroes, 1861-1865* (New Haven, Ct., 1938) and Joe Gray Taylor's "Slavery in Louisiana During the Civil War," *Louisiana History*, 8 (Winter 1967) were the only published works available on the subject, but much new material has been added during the last two decades. Among items worthy of note are John W. Blassingame, *Black New Orleans, 1860-1880* (Chicago, 1973); Charles P. Roland, *Louisiana Sugar Plantations During the American Civil War* (Leiden, Netherlands, 1957); C. Peter Ripley, *Slaves and Freedmen in Civil War Louisiana* (Baton Rouge, 1976); Charles Vincent, *Black Legislators in Louisiana During Reconstruction* (Baton Rouge, 1976) (these last two volumes are really more concerned with Reconstruction issues than with the Civil War); and Herbert G. Gutman, *The Black Family in Slavery and Freedom, 1750-1925* (New York, 1976). Unfortunately, no significant literature at all is available concerning Louisiana women during the Civil War or the years that followed.

One additional area open to profitable scholarly study is the attitude of Louisiana's people before and during the Civil War and Reconstruction. It can at least be argued that the state's vote in the presidential election of 1860 and that the votes cast for delegates to the Secession Convention (see Charles B. Dew, "The Long-Lost Returns: The Candidates and Their Totals in the Louisiana Secession Election," *Louisiana History*, 10 [Fall 1969]) indicated a majority of voters opposed to secession in November of 1860. Yet, by the January meeting of the Secession Convention, only a small minority was willing to oppose the determination of the secessionist majority. However great this early enthusiasm for secession may have been, though, it soon wore away, and by the time Vicksburg and Port Hudson had fallen to the strength of Union arms, it seems probable that a majority of the people of Louisiana, almost certainly a majority of the poorer white farmers of the state, were opposed to continuing the war. Ethel Taylor, "Discontent in Confederate Louisiana," *Louisiana History*, 2 (Fall 1961) deals with this subject, but more research is needed, especially concerning the Jayhawkers who resisted both Northern and Southern armies and who were a danger to life and property wherever they appeared. In addition, very little is known about the several units of Louisiana soldiers, black and white, who were organized under the Union flag.

Whatever else may be said about the military Civil War, it can hardly be argued that Louisiana was not on the losing side. But Reconstruction is another matter entirely. Once the organized violence had ended, Louisiana whites succeeded, by cooperating with the whites of other ex-Confederate states, in establishing a system of social, economic, and political relations between the races that more nearly resembled slavery than it did whatever vague ideals may have been contemplated by former abolitionists, by other humanitarians of various stripes, and by the Radical Republicans who pushed the Military Reconstruction Acts through Congress to completion. The economy of the South did change, but this economic change resulted as much from alterations in the world cotton market as from the demise of chattel slavery. Furthermore, whether wage labor on sugar plantations and sharecropping on cotton plantations be termed a form of peasantry, peonage, or collective as opposed to individual slavery, black people in Louisiana certainly found themselves in a condition not greatly improved over antebellum slavery and a far cry from true freedom. This new economic system would persist for two generations, and it was almost as strong as slavery in maintaining its grip on Southern agriculture.

Because Reconstruction went on for so long and because Louisiana politics of any era becomes almost inextricably convoluted with personal and institutional complications, a large quantity of written material dealing with Reconstruction became available. The gathering of manuscript materials, especially at Louisiana State University and at the University of North Carolina, made it possible to study social and economic developments in much greater depth. The alert student quickly noted, however, that the people who lived through Reconstruction, except for a few who were actively engaged in politics, largely ignored the political quarrels that filled the columns of the newspapers. The ordinary Louisiana citizen was too concerned with living, dying, and earning his daily bread, with courting, marrying, and raising children, giving much of his concern to religious matters, to devote much thought to the complications of national, state, or parish politics. One outstanding exception to this rule must be noted. The manuscript collection accumulated by Radical Republican Governor Henry Clay Warmoth is an invaluable source on early Louisiana Republican politics and is highly useful in dealing with the politics of later years.

Louisiana newspapers of the Reconstruction years are an essential source that must not be ignored; nonetheless the researcher must always bear in mind that the truth is not in them. Unquestionably the most valuable single newspaper source is the New Orleans *Tribune*, published by two brothers, prewar free men of color Louis and Joseph Roudanez, and edited by Paul Trevigne. When the "Carpetbag Faction" won control of the Louisiana Republican Party in 1867, official printing went to the New Orleans *Republican*, and the *Tribune* was doomed. The *Republican* was far less interested in reporting the news than it was in making as many political points as possible against the rival "Conservatives." The Conservative papers of New Orleans had an abundance of real and manufactured atrocities and a plethora of corruption to report, but they would go to almost incredible length to depict some perfectly normal action by the Radical Republicans as a criminal conspiracy or to twist evidence so as to excuse some inexcusable Democratic offense against humanity. But as bad as the New Orleans papers were, sheets published outside the city were worse, and the Franklin *Planter's Banner*, the Baton Rouge *Weekly Advocate*, and the Shreveport *Times* probably were more filled with unmitigated lies than others, but all were permeated with falsehood. These Democratic newspapers, which echoed Democratic politicians and were echoed by them, succeeded in distorting the history of post-Civil War Louisiana into something much nearer to the imaginative and self-serving narratives created by Bourbon politicians than to the actual course of events. And it was their version of the history of the time that would predominate for almost exactly a century.

Before World War II, published sources, even including memoirs, had very little effect on Louisiana's Reconstruction history. Most Northern and foreign travelers who came South were at the least sympathetic with white control of government. Nearly all of them were unbending white supremacists, and many were unswerving Democrats. Early historians of Reconstruction never really used the dozens of volumes of testimony taken by congressional committees, which were discounted before they were read. If the committee or subcommittee that heard the testimony had a Republican majority, then it was taken for granted that witnesses had been chosen so as to support the Republican and weaken the Democratic point of view, and there was often more than a little truth in this assumption. Henry Clay Warmoth's well-written memoir, *War, Politics and Reconstruction: Stormy Days in Louisiana* (New York, 1930), might perhaps have been expected to be an ardent defense of Radical Republicanism and a well-informed assault upon the Bourbons. Unfortunately, it was no such thing. By 1930 Warmoth had been in Louisiana sixty-six years, two generations, and the pages of his book make it obvious that he had always shared the attitudes of white Louisianians toward black people and that he hoped by means of his memoir to make himself fully acceptable to the white Democrats of Louisiana with whom he already associated socially and economically.

The first formal histories of Reconstruction in Louisiana were written when the attitudes described above were not only dominant but, among whites, almost completely unchallenged. George Washington Cable was highly critical of the way black people were treated in Louisiana in the late nineteenth century, but he challenged few, if any, of the Bourbon myths of Reconstruction. John Rose Ficklen, a worthy pioneer, was unable to complete what he had hoped would be a history of the state through the entire Reconstruction period, and his *History of Reconstruction in Louisiana (Through 1868)* was published by the Johns Hopkins University Press in 1910. Ficklen had no thought of challenging the traditional attitudes toward Reconstruction, but he did report the facts as he saw them. His account of the New Orleans Riot of July 30, 1866, is surprisingly accurate.

Eight years after the appearance of Ficklen's work, Professor Ella Lonn published her *Reconstruction in Louisiana After 1868* (New York, 1918). This is a curious volume; Lonn was an unwearying researcher and sometimes had trouble distinguishing between a mountain and a molehill; she amassed a formidable array of facts, which she usually put together in the way that would be least interesting to her readers. Even though she herself was a Yankee lady, she took it for granted that Radical Republicans were rascals and that Louisiana Democrats, even newspaper editors, were gentlemen. Lonn was aware that an economic storm was raging over Louisiana after 1873, but she attributed this major depression entirely to Louisiana Reconstruction! Perhaps she realized that there was a national panic that damaged the nation's economy, but she took it for granted that Louisiana's economic troubles were brought about by a mountainous state debt, by relentless Radical taxation, by unfathomable corruption, and by the incredible extravagance of Radical Republican officeholders.

A more modern, albeit still backward-looking, version of early Louisiana Reconstruction came with the publication of Willie M. Caskey's *Secession and Restoration of Louisiana* (Baton Rouge, 1938). Three years later Garnie W. McGinty's *Louisiana Redeemed: The Overthrow of Carpetbag Rule, 1876-1880* (New Orleans, 1941) made its appearance. Probably the most influential Reconstruction book of all, although it did not deal directly with Louisiana, was Claude G. Bowers, *The Tragic Era: The Revolution After Lincoln* (Cambridge, 1929), which was widely read nationally and fixed popular attitudes toward Reconstruction so firmly that a generation of scholarship would be required to loosen them.

Despite the many obstacles, a revisionist attitude toward Reconstruction history did begin to manifest itself in Louisiana, especially among faculty and graduate students of the Department of History of Louisiana State University at Baton Rouge. T. Harry Williams had never specialized in Reconstruction history as such, but he had worked under William H. Hesseltine at the University of Wisconsin, and his studies of Abraham Lincoln inevitably made him aware of some of the standard misconceptions. His "An Analysis of Some Reconstruction Attitudes," *Journal of Southern History*, 12 (November 1946) was an early call for a new look at Reconstruction. More important, Francis Butler Simkins, coauthor with Robert

S. Woody of *South Carolina During Reconstruction* (Chapel Hill, N.C., 1932), spent three of his most productive years at Louisiana State University. His stay coincided with the "G.I. Bill rush" of graduate students that followed World War II, and he influenced men and women who would have a large voice in Southern history through the 1970s and beyond. No way of measuring a great teacher's influence has yet been invented, but Simkins must have had significant effect upon at least two dozen writing historians and upon at least as many more who influenced students only through the classroom. It should also be noted that after 1960 writers who had prepared manuscripts dealing with Southern history, including Louisiana history, received a much warmer welcome from university presses, including especially Louisiana State University Press, than had been the case in earlier years.

After 1950 one new Reconstruction book after another appeared in print, so many that only the most important ones, and those pertaining particularly to Louisiana, can be mentioned here. George R. Bentley's *A History of the Freedmen's Bureau* (Philadelphia, 1955) gave a far more objective view of that much maligned institution than had previously been available, and Howard Ashley White presented a well-researched and unbiased volume, *The Freedmen's Bureau in Louisiana* (Baton Rouge, 1970). Vernon Lane Wharton's *The Negro in Mississippi, 1865-1880* (New York, 1965) was a guide and an inspiration to historians interested in the history of black Southerners during those years. Blassingame's *Black New Orleans* and Vincent's *Black Legislators in Louisiana* have already been mentioned. Much work remains to be done in this area.

Gerald M. Capers combined his abilities as an urban historian with an interest in early Reconstruction in Louisiana to produce *Occupied City: New Orleans Under the Federals, 1862-1865* (Lexington, Ky., 1965). James E. Sefton's *The United States Army and Reconstruction* (Baton Rouge, 1967) is an essential study, as is Otis A. Singletary, *Negro Militia and Reconstruction* (Austin, Tex., 1957). E. Merton Coulter, *The South During Reconstruction 1865-1877* (Baton Rouge, 1947), volume 8 of Wendell Holmes Stephenson and E. Merton Coulter, eds., *A History of the South*, is an excellent social and cultural history of Reconstruction in the South, especially of white people; it also affords some good information on the economic developments of the period. Unfortunately, the author almost completely disregards new information and, perhaps more important, new attitudes, that have been brought to Reconstruction historiography since about 1940; he presents a political scene not at all incompatible with Bowers's *Tragic Era*.

In somewhat the same category as Coulter's *South During Reconstruction*, although not as broad in its conception, is Stuart Omar Landry, *The Battle of Liberty Place: The Overthrow of Carpetbag Rule in New Orleans —September 14, 1874* (New Orleans, 1955). The Battle of Liberty Place in New Orleans was one of the major events in Louisiana's Reconstruction history, but it was even more important because having borne arms against the legal government of the state in 1874 was a significant advantage to any man who sought political preferment in Louisiana for the rest of the century. In fact, it was an almost essential requirement for political prominence in New Orleans. Another book that must be mentioned, and one with a radically different point of view from Coulter or Landry, is Roger A. Fischer's *The Segregation Struggle in Louisiana, 1862-1876* (Urbana, Ill., 1974), which recounts the efforts to desegregate schools, streetcars, and places of public accommodation in Louisiana, especially in New Orleans, during Reconstruction.

This author's *Louisiana Reconstructed, 1863-1877* (Baton Rouge, 1975) is an attempt to combine the history of all the various aspects of Reconstruction in Louisiana into one volume. In general the political and social points of view are revisionist; the book makes a determined effort to survey social, cultural, and economic as well as political developments. The story of politics during almost any phase of Louisiana history can almost always be expanded almost indefinitely, but in general it would seem that adding further political detail to Louisiana's Reconstruction history brings on the risk of hiding the forest among the trees. Even so, attention must be given to the ideas set forth in C. Vann Woodward's *Reunion and Reaction: The Compromise of 1877 and the End of Reconstruction*, rev. ed. (Garden City, N.Y., 1956).

Some important and enlightening scholarly articles dealing directly or indirectly with Reconstruction in Louisiana must be mentioned. Howard K. Beale's "On Rewriting Reconstruction History," *American Historical Review*, 45 (July 1940), and Lawanda Cox's "The Promise of Land for the Freedmen," *Mississippi Valley Historical Review*, 45 (December 1958) stimulated additional research. Three especially important articles appeared in the *Louisiana Historical Quarterly*: Thomas Ewing Dabney, "The Butler Regime in Louisiana," 27 (April 1944), John Edmond Gonzales, "William Pitt Kellogg: Reconstruction Governor of Louisiana, 1873-1877," 29 (April 1946), and Walter M. Lowrey, "The Political Career of James Madison Wells," 31 (October 1948). Although short, H. Grady McWhiney and Francis B. Simkins, "The Ghostly Legend of the Ku Klux Klan," *Negro History Bulletin*, 14 (February 1951) is important. Also significant is Louis R. Harlan, "Desegregation in New Orleans During Reconstruction," *American Historical Review*, 68 (April 1962), and Roger Wallace Shugg, "Survival of the Plantation System in Louisiana," *Journal of Southern History*, 3 (May 1937). The latter made it clear that the census of 1870 had been misinterpreted. More recent noteworthy articles include Harold M. Hyman, "Johnson, Stanton, and Grant: A Reconsideration of the Army's Role in the Events Leading to Impeachment," *American Historical Review*, 46 (October 1960); Thomas J. May, "The Freedmen's Bureau at the Local Level: A Study of a Louisiana Agent," *Louisiana History*, 9 (Winter 1968);

T. B. Tunnell, Jr., "The Negro, the Republican Party, and the Election of 1876 in Louisiana," *Louisiana History*, 7 (Spring 1966); and Bernard Weisberger, "The Dark and Bloody Ground of Reconstruction Historiography," *Journal of Southern History*, 25 (November 1959).

Much work remains to be done on the social and cultural history of Louisiana, especially of black Louisianians, during and after Reconstruction. Taylor gives some attention to these topics and more to economic factors, but by no means does he exhaust the subjects. Almost surely it is in the area of social, cultural, and economic history that the most important Reconstruction studies in Louisiana, and probably the nation, may be anticipated from the next generation of Reconstruction scholars.

5
THE GILDED AGE AND PROGRESSIVE ERA

WILLIAM IVY HAIR

IN 1877 LOUISIANA became the last Southern state "redeemed" by conservative Democrats from the alleged horrors of Republican Reconstruction rule. Carpetbagger, Scalawag, and Negro Republicans at last lost possession of the Statehouse. For the next one hundred years (until the election of David Treen in 1980) every Louisiana governor would be a Democrat.

Redemption came to Louisiana in the person of Governor Francis T. Nicholls (1877-1879 and 1888-1892), a former Confederate general whose noblesse oblige approach reflected the best of the Old Regime. But his abbreviated first administration (cut short by a new state constitution in 1879) would be followed by governors and legislatures that usually acted repressively toward blacks and dissident whites and reduced state services—schools, institutions—to almost invisible levels. This leadership, particularly Governor Samuel D. McEnery (1881-1888), were the so-called Bourbons, who claimed to be restoring honesty and tranquility to Louisiana but in fact made the state a byword for corruption and political chicanery.

The only book-length effort to explain public affairs in Louisiana during the Gilded Age (the late nineteenth century) is William I. Hair's *Bourbonism and Agrarian Protest: Louisiana Politics, 1877-1900* (Baton Rouge, 1969). Because it emphasizes the clash between the Bourbon Democratic state machine and rural reformers, somewhat to the neglect of events in New Orleans, *Bourbonism* should be supplemented by Joy J. Jackson's *New Orleans in the Gilded Age: Politics and Urban Progress, 1880-1896* (Baton Rouge, 1969). An article by Wayne M. Everard, "Bourbon City: New Orleans, 1878-1900," *Louisiana Studies*, 11 (Fall 1972), shed some additional light on municipal politics, as does Raymond O. Nussbaum's "The Ring Is Smashed! The New Orleans Municipal Election of 1896," *Louisiana History*, 17 (Summer 1976). Events surrounding the end of Reconstruction are described in a dated but still useful book by Garnie W. McGinty, *Louisiana Redeemed: The Overthrow of Carpetbag Rule, 1876-1880* (New Orleans, 1941).

Aspects of state politics during the late nineteenth century have been illuminated by several doctoral dissertations and master's theses. The most significant of these, Philip D. Uzee, "Republican Politics in Louisiana, 1877-1900" (Ph.D. diss., Louisiana State University, 1950), describes GOP opposition to the Bourbon Democracy. The troubled effort of blacks to involve themselves in the political process is the subject of Clara Lopez Campbell's "The Political Life of Louisiana Negroes, 1865-1890" (Ph.D. diss., Tulane University, 1971). The infamous Louisiana Lottery Company's influence on state politics is emphasized in John T. White, "The History of the Louisiana Lottery" (M.A. thesis, Tulane University, 1939). Clarence Howard Nichols, "Francis T. Nicholls, Bourbon Democrat" (M.A. thesis, Louisiana State University, 1959) treats the career of the "redeemer" governor. Both Populism and early twentieth-century Progressivism are the subjects of Henry C. Dethloff's "Populism and Reform in Louisiana" (Ph.D. diss., University of Missouri, 1964).

Black Louisianians endured increasing repression as the nineteenth century approached its close. No comprehensive study of race relations in the state during the Gilded Age or Progressive Era has been made, but several books, articles, and graduate theses and dissertations touch upon racial themes in the state (especially New Orleans) for this crucial period. An outline of the problem is presented by Henry C. Dethloff and Robert R. Jones, "Race Relations in Louisiana, 1877-1898," *Louisiana History*, 9 (Fall 1968). A more detailed look at this subject in the state's metropolis is Dale A. Somers, "Black and White in New Orleans: A Study in Urban Race Relations, 1865-1900," *Journal of Southern History*, 40 (February 1974). Although it ends with 1880, John W. Blassingame's *Black New Orleans* (Chicago, 1973) offers much information on black life in the city during the generation of Civil War and Reconstruction. Efforts to control or minimize the black vote are described in Campbell's "The Political Life of Louisiana Negroes, 1865-1890," and in Allie Bayne Windham Webb, "A History of Negro Voting in Louisiana, 1876-1906" (Ph.D. diss., Louisiana State University, 1962). The first post-Reconstruction migration of blacks out of Louisiana is the subject of Earl Howard Aiken, "Kansas Fever" (M.A.

thesis, Louisiana State University, 1939), and Morgan Peoples, "Kansas Fever in North Louisiana," *Louisiana History*, 11 (Spring 1970). The standard account of this exodus movement across the South, Nell Irvin Painter's *Exodusters: Black Migration to Kansas After Reconstruction* (New York, 1977), puts Louisiana events into broader context. The long travail of black sugarcane workers is traced back to the 1880s by Thomas Becnel, *Labor, Church and the Sugar Establishment, 1887-1976* (Baton Rouge, 1980). That race relations in Louisiana, particularly in New Orleans, deteriorated during the closing years of the nineteenth century is exemplified in the life-and-times biography of a black nationalist who died violently in 1900: William I. Hair, *Carnival of Fury: Robert Charles and the New Orleans Race Riot of 1900* (Baton Rouge, 1976).

The Progressive Era (ca. 1900-1920) is enormously difficult to define for Louisiana or the nation, both from the standpoint of time and because of its amorphous nature. Supposedly Progressivism embraced—in the words of Willard Gatewood's article in the *Encyclopedia of Southern History* (Baton Rouge, 1979)—"a complex of reforms designed to promote corporate regulation, political democracy, public health and welfare, efficiency, and morality." According to Gatewood, Southern Progressivism strayed from the national mainstream only in that it took place in a one-party political environment and in that "Southern progressives were virtually unanimous in their adherence to the ideology of white supremacy."

Currently there is no book-length work dealing particularly with life and politics in Louisiana during the Progressive Era, which for this state may be defined as lasting approximately from the turn of the century to the election of Huey P. Long as governor in 1928. But certain books and articles have appeared that deal with aspects of public affairs in Louisiana during the 1900-1928 years.

Huey Long's Louisiana: State Politics, 1920-1952 (Baltimore, 1956), by Alan P. Sindler, devotes the opening chapter to Louisiana history prior to the 1920s and another chapter to the 1920s decade that brought Long to power. Sindler views Longism in the "broad framework of a continuing movement of class protest having its origins in nineteenth-century Louisiana." The gubernatorial election of 1928 was therefore a "class revolution" that "had its tap root in Louisiana history." In his analysis of state politics, specifically for the 1900-1920 period, Sindler declared it to have been "a civic vacuum," an uninterrupted continuation of the arch-conservative "government by gentlemen"—the term that Roger Shugg used to characterize antebellum Louisiana.

Sindler concedes that one pre-Long governor was to some degree progressive: John M. Parker, who served from 1920 to 1924, was according to Sindler a "gentlemanly reformer," a diffident spokesman for "enlightened conservatism" whose modest program for change failed because he "deliberately minimized his influence in the Legislature" and refused to intrude himself into local elections.

Perry H. Howard's *Political Tendencies in Louisiana* (Baton Rouge, 1971), in his expanded edition, devotes about fifty pages to the 1900-1928 years. Howard agrees with Sindler on most points. Howard declared that with a planter-merchant oligarchy in control of the state's ruling Democratic party, "the endemic pattern of elitism and ascription continued to prevail." Louisiana was thus a case of "seriously arrested socioeconomic development," and Huey Long eventually came to power by mobilizing the pent-up frustrations of the state's poor rural whites. Howard also concurs with Sindler's view of Governor Parker, except for pointing out that Parker did "fight fire with fire" in combatting the New Orleans political machine (the "Choctaws," or "Old Regulars"); as governor, Parker actively promoted a rival city machine, the Orleans Democratic Association.

T. Harry Williams's Pulitzer prize-winning biography *Huey Long* (New York, 1969) approvingly comments on the valuable information, especially election statistics, provided by Sindler and Howard, but Williams takes them to task for their "mechanistic view of history," their "assumption," in Williams's words, "that Huey Long was only a product and a reflection on his environment." Actually, neither Sindler nor Howard go quite that far, but they do have a mechanistic stance. Sindler stated it most emphatically: "Huey Long, *sui generis* or no . . . must be understood in the context of the origins of class struggle in Louisiana."

As to Williams's personal assessment of Louisiana's leadership during the generation prior to 1928, he is somewhat contradictory but does not differ substantially from Sindler or Howard. In one colorful passage, Williams describes the ruling hierarchy of the early twentieth century as "smug, satisfied with things as they were, devoted to the protection of privilege. Its leaders were gentlemen in frock coasts, string ties, and wide hats." They were "dignified," more or less honest, but "backward-looking." In a play upon Roger Shugg's often-quoted phrase, Williams summarized the pre-Long style of politics as "government by goatee."

Elsewhere in the Long biography, however, Williams states that Louisiana did experience "some of the impact of the progressive movement that was affecting the whole country." This mild Progressivism prior to Huey Long, Williams explains, was personified by Governor John M. Parker. In appearance and mannerisms Parker much resembled Williams's goateed gentry. Parker's great failing as a political leader, according to Williams, was in being a conciliatory idealist who believed in the essential goodness of humanity, including oil company executives. Huey Long was not hampered by any such gentlemanly conception.

Louisiana politicians seldom write memoirs, but one notable exception was Martin Behrman. New York-born, of German-Jewish parentage, Behrman was a five-term mayor of New Orleans (1904-1920 and 1925-1926) and headed the Old Regular (Choctaw) organization from 1904 until his death in 1926. During the early 1920s, temporarily out of the mayor's office, Behrman told his political life's story in installments written for the New Orleans

Item. Behrman was an urban boss of the Richard Daley type, seldom found in the South but familiar to Northern cities. In 1977 Behrman's memoirs, edited and annotated by John R. Kemp, were published by LSU Press under the title *Martin Behrman of New Orleans.* Behrman's story offers interesting details about events and personalities of his time but provides little information about the actual working of the city machine. These same Behrman memoirs in the *Item* were heavily mined by George M. Reynolds, author of an earlier book that is still the standard on the subject, *Machine Politics in New Orleans, 1897-1926* (New York, 1936).

Although dealing with a special topic spanning most of the state's history, Mark T. Carleton's *Politics and Punishment: A History of the Louisiana State Penal System* (Baton Rouge, 1971) contains perceptive observations about Louisiana's political leadership during the early twentieth century, the "second generation Bourbon Democrats," he calls them. They were not, writes Carleton, altogether "carbon copies of . . . elder statesmen," for they were at least slightly affected by the Progressive spirit. As to John M. Parker, Carleton describes him as "a Progressive of the genteel and conservative stripe . . . neither a liberal in the modern sense nor a charismatic leader, Parker was the transitional figure between his . . . relatively do-nothing predecessors and the aggressive neo-Populism which soon followed."

Two recent books dealing with the entire South during the progressive Era deserve comment because of their pertinence for Louisiana. J. Morgan Kousser's *The Shaping of Southern Politics: Suffrage Restriction and the Establishment of the One-Party South, 1880-1910* (New Haven, Ct., 1974) points out in detail that certain so-called Progressive reforms—the direct primary, new registration laws, the Australian ballot, and others—were not (at least in the South) democratic devices meant to bring government closer to the people but in fact were designed to limit political participation by the poor and ill-educated of both races, not just blacks. Jack Temple Kirby's *Darkness at the Dawning: Race and Reform in the Progressive South* (Philadelphia, 1972) grimly explores the paradox of "racist reformism" and concludes that whatever the positive benefits of Progressivism may have been, the obsession with color that permeated the South at that time widened an already formidable chasm between the races. "More than ever before," declares Kirby, "blacks became mere shadow people to whites—existing more as spectors or a part of the landscape than as real, human individuals."

Several articles, especially in *Louisiana History* and in *Southern Studies* (formerly known as *Louisiana Studies*), deserve mention for the light they shed on aspects of life in Louisiana during the early twentieth century. In *Louisiana Studies*, Riley E. Baker's "Negro Voter Registration in Louisiana, 1879-1964" #4 (Winter 1965) provides useful data and reveals that the all-time low for black registration came in 1922, when only 598—a third of one percent of the total registration—were listed in the state. Stephen Zink's

"Cultural Conflict and the 1928 Presidential Campaign in Louisiana," *Southern Studies,* 17 (Summer 1978) describes how the Al Smith-Herbert Hoover contest brought into the open a latent Catholic-Protestant conflict within the state.

Matthew J. Schott has provided *Louisiana History*'s readers with two analyses of political behavior in the state during the early twentieth century. "Class Conflict in Louisiana Voting Since 1877: Some New Perspectives," 12 (Spring 1971), and "Progressives Against Democracy: Electoral Reform in Louisiana, 1894-1921," 20 (Summer 1979). In the latter article, Schott finds Kousser's thesis valid for Louisiana, with some exceptions. Notably, Schott reports that the New Orleans Choctaw machine was able to protect the voting rights of its working-class white—including Italian immigrant—supporters, which the "good government" Progressives such as John M. Parker had hoped to disfranchise.

Did Louisiana have a Progressive movement? In this writer's opinion, not much of one. By 1928 large corporations were not yet subjected to meaningful state taxation or regulation. Because of the white primary, poll taxes, and (in some parishes) outright vote fraud, democracy was scarcely more of a reality than it had been in 1900. Public services were still below the level of most poorer Southern states. As to "efficiency and morality" (Progressive goals defined by Willard Gatewood), these never have been Louisiana's strong points.

Some gains were made, but progress was modest indeed; in some areas that was actual slippage in comparison with other Southern states. In 1900 Louisiana ranked forty-fifth out of forty-five states in illiteracy; by 1930 she was forty-seventh out of forty-eight, ahead only of South Carolina, a poorer state with a larger percentage of blacks. On the other hand, those in mental hospitals slept in beds instead of on the floor (as most black patients were forced to do as late as 1907), and by the 1920s the Louisiana penal system was not the Gehenna it had been a generation before. Race relations, however, had not improved. The number of lynchings declined, but segregation and disfranchisement became more entrenched. Only two white residents of any prominence seemed to concern themselves with black civil rights during the "Progressive" years: an Episcopal priest at Napoleonville, Reverend Quincy Ewing; and a professor at LSU, William O. Scruggs. (For Ewing, see Charles E. Wynes, "The Reverend Quincy Ewing: Southern Radical Heretic in the 'Cajun' Country," *Louisiana History*, 7 [Summer 1966.]) Professor Scruggs' racial liberalism is mentioned in Paul Ted McCulley, "Black Protest in Louisiana, 1898-1928" (M.A. thesis, Louisiana State University, 1970).

To the slim list of Louisiana Progressives should also be added the name of Jean Gordon, a woman of social position in New Orleans who became the city's factory inspector. An outspoken advocate of child labor reform and public health programs, she was also one of few Louisiana women to take a public stance for woman suffrage. Miss Gordon did not want *black* women to have voting rights, however, and in a 1911 letter to John M. Parker (quoted in Kirby's *Darkness at the Dawning*) she revealed prejudice toward Catholics and Jews.

Louisiana Progressives of the early twentieth century were not numerous, their Progressivism was qualified, and their influence was minimal. This is not to say that because of the lack of progress a political explosion of pent-up resentment from those deprived of public services and social justice was inevitable. But the ordinary people of Louisiana were ready for reform and also ready to listen to a master promiser, Huey P. Long, who swore that if he had power he would make their stunted lives "decent and respectable."

6
THE LONG ERA AND BEYOND

GLEN JEANSONNE

THE TOWERING FIGURE of Huey Pierce Long has cast his shadow over Louisiana since the 1920s. Every historian who has written of twentieth-century Louisiana has included an account of Long, and monographs proliferate. Long himself authored, or had ghosted, two books. His autobiography, *Every Man a King* (New Orleans, 1933), is an embellishment that excludes embarrassing episodes and grossly oversimplifies issues. *My First Days in the White House* (Harrisburg, Pa., 1935), published posthumously, is a whimsical account of what Long planned to do after becoming president—packed with wit, irony, and egotism.

Long's earliest biographers were either hostile journalists on one hand or apologists on the other. Webster Smith, *The Kingfish: A Biography of Huey P. Long* (New York, 1933), published before the peak of Long's national career, is harsh; five entire chapters are devoted to Long's impeachment. Smith's book, however, is moderate compared with John Kingston Fineran, *The Career of a Tinpot Napoleon: A Political Biography of Huey P. Long* (New Orleans, 1933). Fineran states in his opening sentence, "The story of Huey P. Long, like that of any other racketeer, is the story of a criminal who disregarded both law and justice in pursuit of his own purposes, and successfully evaded punishment for a time."

Forrest Davis, *Huey Long: A Candid Biography* (New York, 1935) is more evenhanded, although he too is critical. Based upon only a superficial survey of newspaper and periodical accounts, some observations are nonetheless perceptive. Davis predicts that Long will be viewed more favorably by posterity than by his contemporaries because of the tangible aspects of his accomplishments and the ephemeral nature of his dictatorship.

Carleton Beals, *The Story of Huey P. Long* (Philadelphia, 1935) is the best biography contemporaneous with the Long era. He details Huey's financial manipulations, ruthlessness, and unlimited ambition but does not consider Long an entirely evil influence. Although motivated by a fanatical quest for power, many of Long's programs were beneficial. As its title indicates, Thomas O. Harris, *The Kingfish: Huey P. Long, Dictator* (New Orleans, 1938) considers that "the political career of Huey Pierce Long is a danger signal" (284). Although critical, Harris tempers his judgment: "Neither saint nor devil, he was a complex and heterogeneous mixture of good and bad, genius and craft, hypocrisy and candor, buffoonery and seriousness" (p. 4).

Long's attempts to counter a hostile press during his lifetime culminated in founding his own newspaper, the *Louisiana Progress*. After his assassination, "The Memorial Services held in the House of Representatives" (1936) provided an opportunity to martyr the Kingfish. There followed a series of Longite eulogies. James A. Fortier, ed., *Huey Pierce Long: The Martyr of the Age* (New Orleans, 1937) includes an article by Governor Richard W. Leche, a chronology of Long's career, a list of his accomplishments, and his favorite poem, William Ernest Henley's "Invictus."

After a resounding victory in the gubernatorial election of 1936, the Long machine crumbled beneath an exposé that sent Governor Leche and other important state officials to prison. In the aftermath of these Louisiana scandals, New Orleans newsman Harnett T. Kane, in *Louisiana Hayride: The American Rehearsal for Dictatorship, 1928-1940* (1941; reprint ed., Gretna, La., 1971), concluded that Long was a power-starved individual who left a legacy of venality. Reviewing *Louisiana Hayride* for *New Republic* in 1941, Hamilton Basso stated: "It ought to stand as the definitive work on the subject" (p. 162). Major reviewers agreed that Kane's subtitle was appropriate, while none defended Long or his successors. Kane, a skilled writer with firsthand knowledge, was nonetheless not a systematic historian and in recent years has been criticized for factual errors and an anti-Long bias.

In the 1940s Long's partisans were overwhelmed politically and journalistically. When Long's law partner, Harvey G. Fields, published a laudatory, *True History of the Life, Works, Assassination and Death of Huey Pierce Long* (n.p., 1945), describing Long as "the most distinguished Louisiana citizen in the history of the state" (p. iii), he made little impression.

Allan P. Sindler, somewhat less critical than Kane, nevertheless provided academic sanction to Kane's conclusions in *Huey Long's Louisiana: State*

Politics, 1920-1952 (Baltimore, 1956), an exacting, analytical work. More than a study of Long or even of the Long machine, Sindler's book is rather an examination of Louisiana politics in the context of historical, geographic, economic, ethnic, and religious factors. Neither beginning nor ending with Long, he recognizes Long's contributions but does not conceal faults. He concludes that the Kingfish's legacy is harmful: "Widespread popular acceptance of the principle that the ends justify all means thus was Huey Long's morally enervating legacy" (p. 115).

Historians who studied Longism during the 1950s and 1960s could not ignore the rest of the Long family. Huey's brother Earl was governor, his son Russell a U.S. senator, and other relatives held or aspired to state and national offices. The first composite study of the Long family, Stan Opotowsky's *The Longs of Louisiana* (New York, 1960), devotes seven of twenty chapters to Huey. A New Orleans journalist, Opotowsky is repelled by the totalitarian Long machine but applauds its material improvements. Thomas Martin's *Dynasty: The Longs of Louisiana* (New York, 1960) resembles Opotowsky's work in length, interpretation, and scope. Critical but fair, devoting about half of the book to Huey, Martin unfortunately includes neither footnotes nor bibliography.

Two college-level collections of readings exist. Henry C. Dethloff, *Huey P. Long: Southern Demagogue or American Democrat?* (Lafayette, La., 1976), includes chapters from Long's autobiography and essays by a critical contemporary and a supporter as well as excerpts from writings by T. Harry Williams, V. O. Key, Jr., Arthur M. Schlesinger, Jr., Donald R. McCoy, and Allan P. Sindler. Hugh Davis Graham, *Huey Long* (Englewood Cliffs, N.J., 1970) is similar. He includes selections by Long himself, his contemporaries, and historians. In an "Afterward," Graham concludes that the search for both liberty and equality in America, sometimes incompatible, compelled Long by choosing equality to circumscribe liberty.

T. Harry Williams's Pulitzer Prize-winning *Huey Long* (New York, 1969) is a meticulously researched oral biography. More sympathetic than previous biographers, Williams condones Long's ruthlessness, arguing that it distinguished him from less successful predecessors. Long, forced to "fight fire with fire" by intractable, entrenched reactionaries, introduced realistic economic issues to Southern politics. But, in Williams, Long appears to operate in a vacuum, as Long himself said, *sui generis*. Williams discusses only vaguely the politicians who preceded Long, labeling their issues "false" without examining them. He employs labels such as "liberal" and "conservative" without defining them in the context of Louisiana politics. A facile cynicism detracts from this influential book, a cynicism that has tempted Louisiana voters to dismiss as "unrealistic" politicians who advocate government both humane and honest.

Williams's earlier article, "The Gentleman from Louisiana: Demagogue or Democrat?" *Journal of Southern History*, 26 (February 1960), succinctly expresses the thesis of his book and is widely reprinted, appearing in Dethloff's collection. Dethloff himself in "Huey Pierce Long: Interpretations," *Louisiana Studies*, 3 (Summer 1964) classifies Long's biographers as "great man" theorists, debunkers who merely label Long an "evil genius" or "demagogue," and those who consider Long the product of social conditions. Dethloff concludes that the complexity of the issue of Longism evokes differing interpretations at different times. Glen Jeansonne, "What Is the Legacy of the Longs?" *Louisiana Review/Revue de Louisiane*, 9 (Fall-Winter 1980) concludes that on the whole Long's influence was detrimental to his state. John Moreau Adam, "Huey Long and His Chroniclers," *Louisiana History*, 6 (Spring 1965) states that labels mean little unless precisely defined. Inveighing against vague categories, he calls for a new synthesis: "Such a book may convince us that the man was a democrat, a demagogue—or both, or something else" (p. 339).

Adam was one of many who awaited Williams's work. When published, the nearly 900-page biography was acclaimed as the long-awaited, definitive work. Articles published since then reflect Williams's influence. J. Paul Leslie, Jr., for example, in "Louisiana Hayride Revisited," *Louisiana Studies*, 11 (Winter 1972), attempts to rehabilitate the Leche administration Kane attacked so sharply in light of Williams's conclusions.

Scholars have advanced numerous theories about why Long gained power so quickly and wielded it so ingeniously. Joe L. Green, "The Educational Significance of Huey P. Long," *Louisiana Studies*, 3 (Fall 1974) constructs a "schematic model" of "the hero in history" and applies it to Long. He concludes that Long's appeal "was more psychological than logical," facilitated by personal charisma and the educational deficiencies of his constituents" (p. 274).

Robert E. Snyder, "Huey Long and the Presidential Election of 1936," *Louisiana History*, 16 (Spring 1975) furnishes a succinct analysis, if not a new interpretation, of Long's national ambitions. Snyder speculates that, although Long could not have won the presidency in 1936, "the evidence suggests that in 1936 Long might have denied FDR the presidency and would have kept a number of other politicians from winning office" (p. 143). Henry C. Dethloff, "The Longs: Revolution or Populist Retrenchment?" *Louisiana History*, 19 (Fall 1978) argues that Long differed from earlier Populists and Progressives less in program than in method and in choice of opponents. The Populists fought Bourbon planters; Long fought corporate capitalists. The Progressives believed that proper institutions would draw out man's goodness; Long sought to dictate utopia. Courtney Vaughn, "The Legacy of Huey Long," *Louisiana History*, 20 (Winter 1979) superficially surveys a very small portion of the literature on Long and states that demagogues are likely to emerge when those in power ignore the underprivileged. Glen Jeansonne, "Challenge to the New Deal: Huey P. Long and the Redistribution of National Wealth," *Louisiana History*, 21

(Fall 1980) concludes that Long was motivated by selfish ambition. Alan Brinkley, "Huey Long, the Share Our Wealth Movement, and the Limits of Depression Dissidence," *Louisiana History*, 22 (Spring 1981) argues that Long's support, although broad, was shallow, his Share Our Wealth organization fragmented and weak. Long was not a larcenous knave, but neither was he a serious threat to President Roosevelt.

Huey's multifarious facets have inspired numerous articles on minor aspects of his career. Robert E. Snyder, "The Concept of Demagoguery: Huey Long and His Literary Critics," *Louisiana Studies*, 15 (Spring 1976) examines four major novels based on Long, focusing on Hamilton Basso's *Sun in Capricorn*. He concludes that Basso, critical of other writers for romanticizing Long, is guilty of debunking distortion of his own. Snyder, "Huey Long and the Cotton-Holiday Plan of 1931," *Louisiana History*, 18 (Spring 1977), and Donald W. Whisenhunt, "Huey Long and the Texas Cotton Acreage Control Law of 1931," *Louisiana Studies*, 13 (Summer 1974) examine Long's aborted plan to raise cotton prices by prohibiting planting in 1932. Michael L. Gillette, "Huey Long and the Chaco War," *Louisiana History*, 11 (Fall 1970), and John R. Pleasant, Jr., "Ruffin G. Pleasant and Huey P. Long on the Prison-Stripe Controversy," *Louisiana History*, 15 (Fall 1974) reveal Long's attitudes toward Latin America and toward prisoners in the state penal institution. William F. Mugleston, "Cornpone and Potlikker: A Moment of Relief in the Great Depression," *Louisiana History*, 16 (Summer 1975) shows how Long utilized a comical controversy over the etiquette of crumbling or dunking cornpone to obtain national publicity.

The spectacle of Long's dictatorship, his charisma, and his death at the hands of an assassin have captured the attention of graduate students despite the absence of any substantial manuscript collection. The first unpublished studies of aspects of Long's career lack historical perspective and are therefore seldom consulted today. Emil Bertrand Ader, "An Analysis of the Campaign Techniques and Appeals of Huey P. Long" (M.A. thesis, Tulane University, 1942), and Leo Glenn Douthit, "The Governorship of Huey Long" (M.A. thesis, Tulane University, 1947) both fit this category, particularly because they rely excessively on newspaper sources. Elsie Boone Stallworth, "A Survey of the Louisiana Progresses of the 1930s" (M.A. thesis, Louisiana State University, 1948) is the sole study of an important aspect of Long's public relations, his political newspapers, published under five different titles from March 1930 to March 1940.

The best unpublished study of Long's early career is Betty Marie Field, "The Campaigns of Huey Long, 1918-1928" (M.A. thesis, Tulane University, 1969). "Huey Long in National Politics" (M.A. thesis, Johns Hopkins University, 1957), by Albert Edward Cowdrey, a New Orleanian who studied under C. Vann Woodward, is the most useful unpublished study of Long's national career. Cowdrey depicts Long as an ineffective senator primarily interested in promoting his own ambitions but concludes that he deserves to be remembered, "not because of his charlatanry in giving answers, but because of his insistence on asking questions of his society" (p. 153). Martha Mays Schroeder, "The Senate Career of Huey Long" (M.A. thesis, University of Texas, 1965) supplements and updates Cowdrey, and Edward Francis Renwick, "The Long's Legislative Lieutenants" (Ph.D. diss., University of Arizona, 1967) focuses on the role of subordinates in Long's machine. David A. Poe, "The Political Career of John Holmes Overton" (M.A. thesis, Northwestern State University, 1968) is a sympathetic account of a leading Longite. Edward F. Haas, "New Orleans on the Half-Shell: The Maestri Era, 1936-1946," *Louisiana History*, 13 (Summer 1972) is the account of a leading Longite who, as mayor of New Orleans, dominated the state's largest city for more than a decade after the Kingfish's death. The third-party movement inspired by Long and the attempt to carry on his Share Our Wealth Society after Long's assassination is the subject of David Louis Legendre, "Huey Long, Father Coughlin, Dr. Townsend and the Election of 1936" (M.A. thesis, Louisiana State University, 1975), overly dependent on secondary sources and a few newspapers. Glen Jeansonne, "Preacher, Populist, Propagandist: The Early Career of Gerald L. K. Smith," *Biography*, 2 (Fall 1979), and "Gerald L. K. Smith and the Share Our Wealth Movement," *Red River Valley Historical Review*, 3 (Summer 1978) describe the early career of Long's Share Our Wealth Society organizer.

Three books about Long's assassination each reach a different conclusion. By far the most reliable, although like the others undocumented, is Hermann Deutsch, *The Huey Long Murder Case* (Garden City, N.Y., 1963). Deutsch, an experienced New Orleans journalist, dismisses the possibility of a plot, concluding that Carl Austin Weiss, a successful, happily married physician, killed Long because the Kingfish questioned the racial origins of his wife's family. David H. Zinman, *The Day Huey Long Was Shot* (New York, 1963) relies on many of the same witnesses but reaches a different conclusion. Zinman believes that Weiss impulsively engaged Long in an altercation and Long was then struck by a wild shot fired by his bodyguards. Richard Briley III, in his deservedly obscure monograph, *Death of the Kingfish* (Dallas, 1960), advances the thesis that Huey was a puppet of the Capone mob.

The Great Depression in Louisiana produced political turmoil as well as privation. Betty Marie Field, "The Politics of the New Deal in Louisiana, 1933-1939" (Ph.D. diss., Tulane University, 1973) traces the complex patronage struggle between the Long machine and the Roosevelt administration, concluding that both selfishly placed politics ahead of alleviating human suffering. Such easily subdivided aspects of the New Deal as agriculture, relief, and public works are the subject of almost a dozen dissertations and theses. Rudolph Carrol Hammack, "The New Deal and Louisiana Agriculture" (Ph.D. diss., Tulane University, 1973) shows that farmers accepted planned agriculture only of necessity. The Roosevelt administration's policy, although temporarily beneficial, did little for tenant farmers and was no long-range solution. Donald Holley, "Activities of the Resettlement and Farm Security Administrations in Louisiana, 1935-1946" (M.A. thesis, Louisiana State University, 1964) points out that, although resettlement at the large Terrebonne cooperative failed, the federal government succeeded in reclaiming land for reforestation and waterfowl refuges and in underwriting farm loans. Robert E. Moran, "Public Relief in Louisiana from 1928 to 1960," *Louisiana History*, 15 (Fall 1973) argues that major improvements for the indigent, handicapped, and aged were not begun until after the Depression, and that even then it was the best-organized who received the best care. Hubert D. Humphreys, "In a Sense Experimental: The Civilian Conservation Corps in Louisiana" (M.A. thesis, Louisiana State University, 1964) discloses that the CCC taught thousands of illiterates to read and write (an accomplishment claimed by Huey Long), while developing parks and establishing a statewide system of drainage and erosion control. Humphreys's findings are summarized in his two articles in *Louisiana History* (Fall 1964, and Winter 1965). Kathryn Park, "The Federal Emergency Relief Administration in Louisiana, 1933-37" (M.A. thesis, University of Southwestern Louisiana, 1971) details the Long-Roosevelt patronage struggle, concluding that the FERA facilitated the creation of a permanent Department of Public Welfare. Virgil L. Mitchell, *The Civil Works Administration in Louisiana: A Study in New Deal Relief, 1933-34* (Lafayette, La., 1976) is a microscopic examination of the CWA rather than a study of the political struggle surrounding its administration. Ronnie W. Clayton, "A History of the Federal Writers' Project in Louisiana" (Ph.D. diss., Louisiana State University, 1974) emphasizes the work of Lyle Saxon, who as state director edited and wrote most of the published books himself but points out that some works of enduring value, such as the Dillard project, were not disseminated immediately. Clayton explores the latter facet in "The Federal Writers' Project for Blacks in Louisiana," *Louisiana History*, 19 (Summer 1978).

Huey's younger brother Earl, three-time governor and candidate for governor or lieutenant governor in all but one election between 1936 and 1960, has inspired countless popular vignettes but no definitive biography. The most useful accounts are in Allan P. Sindler, *Huey Long's Louisiana*, Thomas Martin, *Dynasty*, and Stan Opotowsky, *The Longs of Louisiana*, which treat him within the context of the Long family and state politics during his lifetime. Sindler, by far the most analytical, unfortunately ends prior to Earl's last term as governor. Sindler points out that Huey left monuments but it was Earl who created Louisiana's social welfare program. Popular with the masses, more compassionate and less vindictive than Huey, Earl nonetheless never moved out from the shadow of his more famous brother. Earl's folksy style and the melodrama of his last days are captured in A. J. Liebling, *The Earl of Louisiana*, 2nd ed. (Baton Rouge,

1970), and Morgan D. Peoples, "Earl Kemp Long: The Man from Pea Patch Farm," *Louisiana History*, 17 (Fall 1976). Liebling, a sympathetic journalist, is perceptive but uncritical, the book marred by factual error, and the conclusions chiefly intuitive. Peoples's article, episodic rather than systematic, is a treasury of anecdotes. Richard B. McCaughan, *Socks on a Rooster: Louisiana's Earl K. Long* (Baton Rouge, 1967) is more detailed but poorly written and inadequately researched. Glen Jeansonne, *Race, Religion and Politics: The Louisiana Gubernatorial Elections of 1959-60* (Lafayette, La., 1977) describes Earl's breakdown and his last statewide campaign. Jeansonne's findings are summarized in "Racism and Longism in Louisiana: The 1959-60 Gubernatorial Elections," *Louisiana History*, 11 (Summer 1970). Michael L. Kurtz, "Earl Long's Political Relations with the City of New Orleans: 1948-1960," *Louisiana History*, 10 (Summer 1969) deals with the relationship between Long and his nemesis, New Orleans Mayor deLesseps Morrison. Kurtz argues that, although both were relative liberals on social and economic issues, the actions of each were determined more by personal ambition than ideological commitment. John T. Baldwin, "Election Strategy and Tactics of Earl Kemp Long as Seen in His Gubernatorial Campaigns" (M.A. thesis, Louisiana Tech University, 1973) depicts Long as a consummate politician. Professor J. Paul Leslie of Nicholls State University is researching a biography of Earl.

Russell B. Long, Huey's son, who became U.S. senator, is not yet the subject of a monograph, but his career is sketched in Laurence Stern, "The Princefish Comes into His Own," *Reporter*, 33 (March 25, 1965) and also in several general accounts of Southern politics: Neal R. Pierce, *The Deep South States of America* (New York, 1974), Jack Bass and Walter DeVries, *The Transformation of Southern Politics* (New York, 1976), and William C. Havard, ed., *The Changing Politics of the South* (Baton Rouge, 1972). The latter is a state-by-state analysis of the states of the Old Confederacy modeled on V. O. Key's classic, *Southern Politics in State and Nation* (New York, 1949). Inferior to Key, it is nonetheless superior to any other recent study.

The color and longevity of the Long faction is such that accounts of Louisiana politics have devoted little attention to their opponents—the anti-Longs. The only study of John M. Parker, elected governor with Huey Long's assistance but soon a bitter enemy, is Matthew J. Schott, "John M. Parker of Louisiana and the Varieties of American Progressivism" (Ph.D. diss., Vanderbilt University, 1969). Schott argues that Parker's administration was the apogee of elitist Progressivism, but the dignified, conscientious Parker was no match for the charisma and bombast of the less-inhibited, less-principled Kingfish.

Hilda Phelps Hammond, *Let Freedom Ring* (New York, 1936) provides vignettes of anti-Long leaders. Adras Laborde, *A National Southerner: Ransdell of Louisiana* (New York, 1951), ploddingly narrates the fifty-year political career of the man whom Huey Long defeated in the senatorial election of 1930. A prominent anti-Long publisher driven from the state by the Kingfish is the subject of Lawrence F. Ingram's "Hodding Carter Rebels" (M.A. thesis, Southeastern Louisiana University, 1968). The campaigns of Sam Houston Jones, whose election as governor in 1940 temporarily vanquished the Long machine, are examined in Jerry P. Sanson, "The Louisiana Gubernatorial Election of 1940" (M.A. thesis, Louisiana State University, 1975), Otis P. Morgan, "A Rhetorical Study of the Radio Speaking of Sam Jones in the 1948 Gubernatorial Campaign" (M.A. thesis, Louisiana State University 1964), and Glen Jeansonne, "Sam Houston Jones and the Revolution of 1940," *Red River Valley Historical Review*, 4 (Summer 1979). An excellent broader study is found in Dennis Daugherty, "From Log Cabin to Governor's Mansion: The Story of Sam Houston Jones" (Senior thesis, Louisiana State University, 1970), based partly on interviews with Jones. The entire October-November 1971 issue of *Acadiana Profile*, a regional bimonthly published in Lafayette, Louisiana, is devoted to Jones, who is depicted as a clean-government liberal whose administration built upon the accomplishments of Huey Long while eliminating his abuses. Jones deserves more detailed and critical treatment, at least a Ph.D. dissertation, possibly a monograph. Gus Weill, *You Are My Sunshine: The Jimmie Davis Story* (Waco, Tex., 1977), superficial and uncritical, depicts Jones's successor as a man who lived out the American dream. Glen Jeansonne, "The Evolution of Politics in Louisiana," *Acadiana Profile* (October 1975) provides an overview of twentieth-century politics, and his "Political Corruption in Louisiana: Necessary Evil or Merely an Evil?" *Revue de Louisiane/Louisiana Review*, 3 (Summer 1974) examines a notorious aspect of the state's history, emphasizing the recent era.

Judge Leander Perez, political boss of Plaquemines Parish for nearly fifty years, is excoriated in James Conaway, *Judge: The Life and Times of Leander Perez* (New York, 1973), a popular but unreliable account. Glen Jeansonne, *Leander Perez: Boss of the Delta* (Baton Rouge, 1977) depicts Perez as a complex, ambivalent figure, paternalistic but authoritarian. A detailed analysis of Perez's local power base and financial empire is followed by chapters on his role in presidential politics and fanatical defense of racial segregation. See also Jeansonne's "Leander Perez: A Southern Demagogue and Reformer," *Louisiana Studies*, 14 (Fall 1975), and "Leander Perez and the Tidelands Fight," *Revue de Louisiane/Louisiana Review*, 5 (Winter 1976).

Although Perez was the most powerful rural boss, deLesseps S. Morrison, mayor of New Orleans (1946-1960), was the state's preeminent urban leader but three times failed to satisfy his gubernatorial aspirations. The most detailed account of Morrison's mayoral career is Edward F. Haas, *DeLesseps S. Morrison and the Image of Reform: New Orleans Politics,*

1946-1961 (Baton Rouge, 1974). Haas concludes that the image of reform was more apparent than real during Morrison's fifteen years as mayor. Michael L. Kurtz, "The Demagogue and the Liberal: A Study of the Political Rivalry between Earl Long and deLesseps Morrison" (Ph.D. diss., Tulane University, 1971) considers Morrison a "good-government" liberal, a theme he expands upon in "DeLesseps S. Morrison: Political Reformer," *Louisiana History*, 17 (Winter 1976). Joseph B. Parker, *The Morrison Era: Reform Politics in New Orleans* (Gretna, La., 1974) is a theoretical analysis of Morrison's Crescent City Democratic Association. Glen Jeansonne, "DeLesseps S. Morrison: Why He Couldn't Become Governor of Louisiana," *Louisiana History*, 14 (Summer 1973) concludes that Morrison was defeated in statewide elections because of his Catholicism, domicile in New Orleans, and moderate views on race—all handicaps among North Louisiana voters. Haas, "DeLesseps S. Morrison and the Governorship: A Reassessment," *Louisiana Studies*, 17 (Summer 1976) argues that Morrison could have won if he had chosen to run in 1952.

Some of Louisiana's lesser politicians have attracted biographers. Floyd Martin Clay, *Coozan Dudley LeBlanc: From Huey Long to Hadacol* (Gretna, La., 1974) is the story of an anti-Long politician who served as state representative, state senator, and member of the Public Service Commission, failing in campaigns for governor and Congress. LeBlanc became notorious as the impressario of Hadacol, a patent medicine that in the 1950s was a national fad and multi-million-dollar business. Jerry Brigham and Karlie K. Kenyon, "Hadacol: The Last Great Medicine Show," *Journal of Popular Culture*, 10 (Winter 1976) focuses on the sensational aspects of LeBlanc's business career. Mary Alice Fontenot and Vincent Riehl, *The Cat and St. Landry* (Baton Rouge, 1972), a biography of the colorful D. J. "Cat" Doucet, Saint Landry Parish sheriff (1936-1940; 1952-1968), is one of the better popular biographies. F. Edward Hebert, chairman of the House Armed Services Committee, is the subject of two flattering works, *Creed of a Congressman*, ed. Glenn R. Conrad and John McMillan (Lafayette, La., 1970), and *Last of the Titans* (Lafayette, La., 1976). Lawrence Franklin Ingram, "Edwin E. Willis, Louisiana Congressman, 1948-1968: A Career Biography" (Ph.D. diss., University of Southwestern Louisiana, 1973) relates the career of conservative Willis, who chaired the House Un-American Activities Committee.

Although popular works on Louisiana politics have outpaced serious academic studies, there are some important exceptions. Mark T. Carleton, *Politics and Punishment: A History of the Louisiana State Penal System* (Baton Rouge, 1971) is a model study of an unenlightened system plagued by public indifference, administration by political appointees, and demands that the system cost as little as possible.

The office of governor, unusually powerful in Louisiana, has been the subject of several limited studies. Miriam G. Reeves, *The Governors of*

Louisiana (Gretna, La., 1972), a series of biographical portraits, is useful as a reference but too superficial for serious scholars. Sidney J. Romero, "The Inaugural Addresses of the Governors of the State of Louisiana: Tweedledum-and-Tweedledee—or Contrariwise?" *Louisiana History*, 14 (Summer 1973) concludes that inaugural speeches are not consistent in length or ideology and not directly related to subsequent accomplishments. Edwin W. Edwards, "The Role of the Governor in Louisiana Politics: An Historical Analysis," *Louisiana History*, 15 (Spring 1974) examines executive power under each of Louisiana's nine constitutions. The events preceding the constitutional convention summoned by Governor Edwards are discussed in James L. Barnidge, "The Louisiana Constitutional Convention of 1973: The Road to Revision," *Louisiana History*, 15 (Winter 1974). The ratification is analyzed in Public Affairs Research Council, "Special Election on the Constitution, April 20, 1974," selection 31, *Readings in Louisiana Politics,* ed. Mark T. Carleton, Perry H. Howard and Joseph B. Parker (Baton Rouge, 1975). Selection 29 of the same book, Charles E. Grenier and Perry H. Howard, "The Edwards Victory," subjects to quantitative analysis the election of the "Cajun" governor. They conclude that successful state politicians in the future will be those relatively liberal on social and racial issues but conservative on economic issues. Joe Gray Taylor, *Louisiana: A Bicentennial History* (New York, 1976) concludes that the election of 1972 was a classic sectional confrontation but that "the change came in the fact that South Louisiana was more unified than ever before in support of one of its own and population shifts had turned the tables so that South Louisiana was far more powerful than North Louisiana at the polls" (p. 171).

For a long-range analysis of voting trends, Perry H. Howard, *Political Tendencies in Louisiana* (Baton Rouge, 1971) is indispensable. Howard subdivides the state into voter types based on topography, culture, and occupation and uses statistical analysis to explain the rise and fall of factional alignments. Matthew J. Schott, "Class Conflict in Louisiana Voting Since 1877: Some New Perspectives," *Louisiana History*, 12 (Spring 1971) postulates that factors such as region, religion, and race are indeed "real" issues that have been more important historically than class differences.

Scholars will find useful two collections of readings, the previously mentioned anthology by Carleton, Howard, and Parker, and Glenn R. Conrad, ed., *Readings in Louisiana History* (New Orleans, 1978). Both devote sections to modern Louisiana and include a selection of the articles mentioned above.

Recent Louisiana is ripe for additional research. Little has been done on national issues, nationally prominent Louisianians, or presidential contests, and scholarly biographies exist for only a handful of Louisiana's governors. Almost every archive in the state provides opportunities for research. Louisiana State University houses the papers of such recent figures as John B. Fournet and Charlton Lyons. Louisiana State University-Shreveport received the collection of William M. ("Willie") Rainach and has undertaken an ambitious oral history program emphasizing Shreveport history. The papers of Sam Jones have been donated to the Tulane University Library, which also maintains a large collection of political ephemera. Congressman Jimmy Morrison's papers are at Southeastern Louisiana University and the papers of Senator Allen J. Ellender are now at Nicholls State University. Such subjects as race, economics, education, music, art, journalism, and constitutional and institutional history all are expanding rapidly, outpacing the efforts of scholars to record Louisiana's recent past.

7

BLACK LOUISIANIANS

EDWARD F. HAAS

HISTORIANS HAVE BEEN slow to acknowledge the importance of blacks in the development of Louisiana. During the early twentieth century, scholarly interest in the topic was negligible. The standard work, Charles Barthelemy Roussève, *The Negro in Louisiana: Aspects of His History and His Literature* (New Orleans, 1937), was a regrettably superficial book. Roussève's pioneering volume, a published version of his master's thesis, attempted to survey the sweep of black contributions to Louisiana history and literature in only 191 pages. The author unfortunately compounded the problem of scope with inadequate research. For instance, he did not consult V. Alton Moody, "Slavery in Louisiana Sugar Plantations," *Louisiana Historical Quarterly*, 7 (April 1924), a vital supplement that was the basic study of the "peculiar institution" in Louisiana for its day. The result was a sketchy volume with gaps and limitations that Roussève, to his credit, readily perceived.

Despite its flaws, Roussève's book stood alone. Although a trickle of supporting essays appeared during the twenty-five years after its publication, no substantial monographs on black Louisianians were forthcoming. Historians generally ignored the subject. During the decade of the 1960s, however, a radical change occurred. The civil rights revolution and the rise of black power awakened scholars to the significance of blacks. Black history soon became a burgeoning field. Since its inception in 1960, *Louisiana History*, the state historical publication, has clearly reflected this growing trend in historical research. It is a rare volume of the journal that does not include an article on Louisiana blacks. A marked increase in the number of books on race relations and blacks in Louisiana has further signaled the end of scholarly neglect.

This recent interest in the state's black heritage, however, has not been uniform. Historians have focused disproportionate emphasis upon particular topics within one major historical period, the nineteenth century. For this reason, studies of slavery in antebellum Louisiana and black involvement in the Civil War and Reconstruction are plentiful, but other equally important times for black Louisianians have received scant attention.

The colonial period—for many scholars, the golden age of Louisiana history—is ironically one such era. Despite the presence of blacks in early Louisiana and their many contributions to the colony, literature on the subject is sparse. The best starting point is Thomas Fiehrer, "The African Presence in Colonial Louisiana: An Essay on the Continuity of Caribbean Culture," *Louisiana's Black Heritage*, ed. Robert R. Macdonald, John R. Kemp and Edward F. Haas (New Orleans, 1979). The introductory chapter of Joe Gray Taylor, *Negro Slavery in Louisiana* (Baton Rouge, 1963) is also good. A fine unpublished source is James T. McGowan, "Creation of a Slave Society: Louisiana Plantations in the Eighteenth Century" (Ph.D. diss., University of Rochester, 1976). Supportive material, however, is rather meager. Daniel H. Usner, Jr., "From African Captivity to American Slavery: The Introduction of Black Laborers to Colonial Louisiana," *Louisiana History*, 20 (Winter 1979), and James T. McGowan, "Planters Without Slaves: Origins of a New World Labor System," *Southern Studies*, 1 (Spring 1977) are good for the early French period. Mathé Allain, "Slave Policies in French Louisiana," *Louisiana History*, 21 (Spring 1980), and Carl A. Brasseaux, "The Administration of Slave Regulations in French Louisiana, 1724-1766," *Louisiana History*, 21 (Spring 1980) are also helpful. William Riddell, "Le Code Noir," *Journal of Negro History*, 10 (July 1925) is dated, however. John G. Clark, *New Orleans, 1718-1812: An Economic History* (Baton Rouge, 1970) contains some information on colonial slavery. Henry P. Dart, "A Louisiana Indigo Plantation on Bayou Teche, 1773," *Louisiana Historical Quarterly*, 9 (October 1926) is useful. Gilbert Din, "*Cimarrones* and the San Malo Band in Spanish Louisiana," *Louisiana History*, 21 (Summer 1980), Jack D. L. Holmes, "The Abortive Slave Revolt at Pointe Coupée, Louisiana, 1795," *Louisiana History*, 11 (Fall 1970), and E. R. Liljegren, "Jacobinism in Spanish Louisiana, 1792-1797," *Louisiana Historical Quarterly*, 22 (January 1939) examine black rebellion during the Spanish period. Laura L. Porteus, "The Gris-Gris Case: A Criminal Trial in Louisiana During the Spanish Regime, 1773," *Louisiana Historical Quarterly*, 17 (January 1934) discusses white reaction to one facet of black culture. Ronald R. Morazan, "'Quadroon' Balls in the Spanish Period," *Louisiana History*, 14 (Summer 1976) notes the colonial background of an important social event for blacks and whites in

New Orleans. Donald E. Everett, "Free People of Color in Colonial Louisiana," *Louisiana History*, 7 (Winter 1966) is quite good, but Alice Dunbar-Nelson, "People of Color in Louisiana," *Journal of Negro History*, 1 (January 1916) remains worthwhile. Emile Hayot, "Les Gens de couleur libres du Fort-Royal (1679-1823)," *Revue français d'histoire de'Outre-Mer* (1969) is also useful. Roland C. McConnell, *Negro Troops of Antebellum Louisiana: A History of the Battalion of Free Men of Color* (Baton Rouge, 1968) discusses black militiamen during the colonial period. McConnell, "Louisiana's Black Military History, 1729-1865," *Louisiana's Black Heritage*, offers a brief summary. Jack D. L. Holmes, *Honor and Fidelity: The Louisiana Infantry Regiment and the Louisiana Militia Companies, 1766-1821* (Birmingham, Ala., 1965) is also helpful on the same topic.

The relative wealth of sources on blacks in antebellum Louisiana rises in sharp contrast to the writings on the colonial period. The focal point of antebellum research is, of course, slavery, and the basic work is Joe Gray Taylor, *Negro Slavery in Louisiana*. It is the essential first study that all scholars must consult, but it should be supplemented with other treatments of Louisiana's "peculiar institution." A fine work is David C. Rankin, "The Tannenbaum Thesis: Slavery and Race Relations in Antebellum Louisiana," *Southern Studies*, 18 (Spring 1979). Two excellent slave narratives are Henry Bibb, *Narrative of the Life of Henry Bibb, an American Slave* (New York, 1849), and Solomon Northup, *Twelve Years a Slave*, ed. Sue Eakin and Joseph Logsdon (Baton Rouge, 1968). Tommy R. Young II, "The United States Army and the Institution of Slavery in Louisiana, 1803-1835," *Louisiana Studies*, 13 (Fall 1974); John Duffy, "Slavery and Slave Health in Louisiana, 1766-1825," *Bulletin of the Tulane University Medical Faculty*, 26 (February 1967); and David O. Whitten, "Medical Care of Slaves: Louisiana Sugar Region and South Carolina Rice District," *Southern Studies*, 16 (Summer 1977) are valuable specialized studies. John N. Cravens, "Felix 'Zero' Ervin: Louisiana Negro Slave and East Texas Freeman," *East Texas Historical Journal*, 10 (Fall 1972) is interesting. James H. Dorman, "The Persistent Spector: Slave Rebellion in Territorial Louisiana," *Louisiana History*, 18 (Fall 1977) examines a knotty antebellum problem. V. Alton Moody, "Slavery on a Louisiana Sugar Plantation," *Louisiana Historical Quarterly*, 7 (April 1924), is still useful. Avery O. Craven, *Rachel of Old Louisiana* (Baton Rouge, 1975) is a delightful tale of plantation life in the West Feliciana country. John Milton Price, "Slavery in Winn Parish," *Louisiana History*, 8 (Spring 1967) discusses plantation society in the hill country of northern Louisiana. Meloney C. Soniat, "The Tchoupitoulas Plantation," *Louisiana Historical Quarterly*, 7 (April 1924); Lane Carter Kendall, "John McDonogh, Slave Owner, Part I," *Louisiana Historical Quarterly*, 15 (October 1932); and "John McDonogh, Slave Owner, Part II," *Louisiana Historical Quarterly*, 16

(January 1933); Edwin Adams Davis, "Bennet H. Barrow, Antebellum Planter of the Felicianas," *Journal of Southern History*, 5 (November 1939); and Alice Pemble White, "The Plantation Experience of Joseph and Lavinia Erwin, 1807-1836," *Louisiana Historical Quarterly*, 27 (April 1944) are older accounts of the plantation community from the perspective of whites. Edwin Adams Davis, ed., *Plantation Life in the Florida Parishes of Louisiana, 1836-1846: As Reflected in the Diary of Bennet H. Barrow* (New York, 1943) is a primary source in a similar vein. Tom H. Wells, "Moving a Plantation to Louisiana," *Louisiana Studies*, 6 (Fall 1967), and Harry L. Coles, "Some Notes on Slaveownership and Landownership in Louisiana," *Journal of Southern History*, 9 (August 1943) are insightful. David O. Whitten, "Sugar Slavery: A Profitability Model for Slave Investments in the Antebellum Louisiana Sugar Industry," *Louisiana Studies*, 12 (Summer 1973) is an economic account. Joe Gray Taylor, "The Foreign Slave Trade in Louisiana After 1808," *Louisiana History*, 1 (Winter 1960), and James Paisley Hendrix, Jr., "The Efforts to Reopen the African Slave Trade in Louisiana," *Louisiana History*, 10 (Spring 1969) discuss the nineteenth-century African slave trade. General studies that rely heavily upon Louisiana sources are Kenneth M. Stampp, *The Peculiar Institution: Slavery in the Antebellum South* (New York, 1956); John W. Blassingame, *The Slave Community: Plantation Life in the Ante-Bellum South* (New York, 1972); Eugene D. Genovese, *Roll, Jordan, Roll: The World the Slaves Made* (New York, 1974); Herbert G. Gutman, *The Black Family in Slavery and Freedom, 1750-1925* (New York, 1976); and *Slavery and the Numbers Game* (Urbana, Ill., 1975). Joe Gray Taylor, "A New Look at Slavery in Louisiana," *Louisiana's Black Heritage*, summarizes these recent works.

William L. Richter, "Slaves in Baton Rouge, 1820-1860," *Louisiana History*, 10 (Spring 1969), and Terry L. Seip, "Slaves and Free Negroes in Alexandria, 1850-1860," *Louisiana History*, 10 (Spring 1969) are acceptable essays on slavery in secondary Louisiana cities, but there is unfortunately no adequate published work on black bondage in New Orleans. Joe Gray Taylor, *Negro Slavery in Louisiana*, largely overlooks the topic, and John S. Kendall, "New Orleans' 'Peculiar Institution,'" *Louisiana Historical Quarterly*, 23 (July 1940) is outmoded. The best published accounts of Crescent City slavery appear in Richard C. Wade, *Slavery in the Cities: The South, 1820-1860* (New York, 1964), Robert S. Starobin, *Industrial Slavery in the Old South* (New York, 1970), and John W. Blassingame, *Black New Orleans, 1860-1880* (Chicago, 1963). Loren Schweringer, "A Negro Sojourner in Antebellum New Orleans," *Louisiana History*, 20 (Summer 1979) is useful. Robert C. Reinders, "Slavery in New Orleans in the Decade Before the Civil War," *Mid-America*, 44 (October 1962) is also helpful. Laurence J. Kotlikoff and Anton J. Rupert, "The Manumission of Slaves in New Orleans, 1827-1846," *Southern Studies*, 19 (Summer 1980) is unique. The foremost scholarly treatment, however, is Charles Herman

Woessner, "New Orleans, 1840-1860: A Study of Urban Slavery" (M.A. thesis, Louisiana State University, 1967), a reassessment of Wade's work.

Historical fascination with Louisiana's free black population represents another manifestation of the strong interest in the antebellum era. There is, however, no suitable comprehensive work on free blacks before the Civil War. H. E. Sterkx, *The Free Negro in Antebellum Louisiana* (Rutherford, N.J., 1972) strives to fill this role, but its limitations are too many. Annie Lee West Stahl, "The Free Negro in Ante-Bellum Louisiana," *Louisiana Historical Quarterly*, 25 (April 1942) is also spotty. The most satisfactory general study is Ira Berlin, *Slaves Without Masters: The Free Negro in the Antebellum South* (New York, 1974), an excellent book that contains several sections on Louisiana. Equally important is Gary B. Mills, *The Forgotten People: Cane River's Creoles of Color* (Baton Rouge, 1977). Mills discusses a significant colony of *gens de couleur libre* who lived in the Cane River country of northwestern Louisiana, an area that historians have typically neglected. These unusual people adopted the French language and culture and acquired substantial wealth in property and slaves. Mills particularly notes the social differences that distinguished these Creoles of color from slaves and other free blacks in the region. Laura Foner, "The Free People of Color in Louisiana and St. Domingue: A Comparative Portrait of Two Three-Caste Slave Societies," *Journal of Social History*, 3 (Summer 1970) examines the same social development from a comparative viewpoint. David O. Whitten, "A Black Entrepreneur in Antebellum Louisiana," *Business History Review*, 45 (Summer 1971), a fine essay on Andrew Durnford, a free black sugar planter; J. M. Murphy, "Thomy Lafon," *Negro History Bulletin*, 7 (October 1943); and Robert C. Reinders, "The Free Negro in the New Orleans Economy, 1850-1860," *Louisiana History*, 6 (Summer 1965) focus on free blacks in the marketplace. Free black soldiers receive their due in Roland C. McConnell, *Negro Troops of Antebellum Louisiana*, "Louisiana's Black Military History, 1729-1865"; and Donald E. Everett, "Emigres and Militiamen: Free Persons of Color in New Orleans, 1803-1815," *Journal of Negro History*, 38 (October 1953), a broader work on Crescent City free blacks during the territorial period and the War of 1812. Terry L. Seip, "Slaves and Free Blacks in Alexandria, 1850-1869," Robert C. Reinders, "The Decline of the New Orleans Free Negro in the Decade Before the Civil War," *Journal of Mississippi History*, 24 (1962), and James E. Winston, "The Free Negro in New Orleans, 1803-1860," *Louisiana Historical Quarterly*, 21 (October 1938) are also useful. Frances Jerome Woods, *Marginality and Identity* (Baton Rouge, 1972) is a sociological study of a free black family that delves into the antebellum era. James Haskins, *The Creoles of Color of New Orleans* (New York, 1975) is less than scholarly.

The antebellum black community of New Orleans, slave and free, has attracted the special attention of several historians. Two introductions to black cultural achievements are Charles E. O'Neill, "Fine Arts and Literature of Nineteenth-Century Louisiana Blacks," *Louisiana's Black Heritage*, and the first chapter of Blassingame, *Black New Orleans, 1860-1880*. R. L. Desdunes, *Nos hommes et notre histoire* (Montreal, 1911); Rousséve, *The Negro in Louisiana*; and T. A. Daley, "Victor Sejour," *Phylon*, 4 (Winter 1943) are older works that cover the same ground. The foremost studies of antebellum black music and the quadroon balls are Henry A. Kmen, *Music in New Orleans: The Formative Years, 1791-1841* (Baton Rouge, 1966), and "The Music of New Orleans," *The Past as Prelude: New Orleans, 1718-1968*, ed. Hodding Carter (New Orleans, 1968). Emilie Le Jeune, "Creole Folk Songs," *Louisiana Historical Quarterly*, 2 (October 1919), Henry A. Kmen, "Old Corn Meal: A Forgotten Urban Negro Folksinger," *Journal of American Folklore*, 75 (January-March 1962), and John S. Kendall, "New Orleans Negro Minstrels," *Louisiana Historical Quarterly*, 30 (January 1947) are also available. Robert C. Reinders, "The Churches and the Negro in New Orleans, 1850-1860," *Phylon*, 22 (Fall 1961), and Blake Touchstone, "Voodoo in New Orleans," *Louisiana History*, 13 (Fall 1972) dwell upon different aspects of black religion. Marcus Christian, *Negro Ironworkers of Louisiana, 1718-1900* (Gretna, La., 1965) is a brief, well-done account of a largely forgotten black contribution to New Orleans architecture. Betty Porter, "The History of Negro Education," *Louisiana Historical Quarterly*, 25 (July 1942) is helpful for the antebellum period. Roger A. Fischer, "Racial Segregation in Ante-Bellum New Orleans," *American Historical Review*, 84 (February 1969) is an excellent discussion of race relations in the Crescent City before the Civil War. Fischer, like Richard C. Wade and Ira Berlin, contends that racial segregation was an antebellum phenomenon.

Several works chronicle Louisiana's "peculiar institution" during the Civil War. Joe Gray Taylor, "Slavery in Louisiana during the Civil War," *Louisiana History*, 8 (Winter 1967) is a good survey. C. Peter Ripley, *Slaves and Freedmen in Civil War Louisiana* (Baton Rouge, 1976), and Bell Irvin Wiley, *Southern Negroes, 1861-1865* (New Haven, Ct., 1938) are excellent. The transition from slavery to freedom receives detailed attention in J. Carlyle Sitterson, *Sugar Country: The Cane Sugar Industry in the South, 1753-1950* (Lexington, Ky., 1953). Sitterson, "Magnolia Plantation 1852-1862: A Decade of a Louisiana Sugar Estate," *Mississippi Valley Historical Review*, 25 (September 1938), "The Transition from Slavery to Free Economy on the William J. Minor Plantations," *Agricultural History*, 17 (Fall 1943), and "The McCollams: A Planter Family of the Old and New South," *Journal of Southern History*, 6 (August 1940) discuss this change on particular plantations. Charles P. Roland, *Louisiana Sugar Plantations During the American Civil War* (Leiden, Netherlands, 1957), and Clement Eaton, *The Mind of the Old South*, rev. ed. (Baton Rouge, 1967) are useful on the same topics.

For many black Louisianians, the Civil War involved a military experience. The best study of free black soldiers in Louisiana is Mary F. Berry, "Negro Troops in Blue and Gray: The Louisiana Native Guards, 1861-1863," *Louisiana History*, 8 (Spring 1967), but Donald E. Everett, "Ben Butler and the Louisiana Native Guards, 1861-1862," *Journal of Southern History*, 24 (May 1958), and Gary B. Mills, "Patriotism Frustrated: The Native Guards of Confederate Natchitoches," *Louisiana History*, 18 (Fall 1977) are also outstanding. Blassingame, *Black New Orleans, 1860-1880*; Ripley, *Slaves and Freedmen in Civil War Louisiana*; Dudley T. Cornish, *The Sable Arm: Negro Troops in the Union Army, 1861-1865* (New York, 1956); and Wiley, *Southern Negroes* contain worthwhile treatments of Louisiana blacks in the Union army. McConnell, "Louisiana's Black Military History 1729-1865," summarizes the topic but offers little that is new.

William F. Messner, "The Vicksburg Campaign of 1862: A Case Study in the Federal Utilization of Black Labor," *Louisiana History*, 16 (Fall 1975), Peyton McCrary, *Abraham Lincoln and Reconstruction: The Louisiana Experiment* (Princeton, N.J., 1978), and Ripley, *Slaves and Freedmen in Civil War Louisiana*, discuss the Union army's use of black workers. William F. Messner, *Freedmen and the Ideology of Free Labor: Louisiana, 1862-1866* (Lafayette, La., 1978) is also worthwhile. Louis G. Gerteis, *From Contraband to Freedmen: Federal Policy Toward Southern Blacks, 1861-1865* (Westport, Ct., 1973), and William F. Messner, "Black Violence and White Response: Louisiana, 1862," *Journal of Southern History*, 41 (February 1975) contend that federal military officials were conservatives who preferred social control over social change in Louisiana. Also helpful is Murray H. Horowitz, "Ben Butler and the Negro: 'Miracles Are Occurring,'" *Louisiana History*, 17 (Spring 1976).

The standard work on the new freedmen of Louisiana is Ripley, *Slaves and Freedmen in Civil War Louisiana*. Donald E. Everett, "Demands of the New Orleans Free Colored Population for Political Equality, 1862-1865," *Louisiana Historical Quarterly*, 38 (April 1955), however, is an important pioneering study of black participation in wartime politics. Ted Tunnell, "Free Negroes and the Freedman: Black Politics in New Orleans during the Civil War," *Southern Studies*, 19 (Spring 1980) is a more recent work. Blassingame, *Black New Orleans, 1860-1880*, and William F. Messner, "Black Education in Louisiana, 1863-1865," *Civil War History*, 22 (March 1976) are helpful sources on the education of freedmen during the Civil War.

Howard Ashley White, *The Freedmen's Bureau in Louisiana* (Baton Rouge, 1970) is an ably researched book that supersedes John Cornelius Englesman, "The Freedmen's Bureau in Louisiana," *Louisiana Historical Quarterly*, 32 (January 1949), but its value is mainly in administrative history. Thomas May, "The Freedmen's Bureau at the Local Level: A

Study of a Louisiana Agent," *Louisiana History*, 9 (Winter 1968), and "The Louisiana Negro in Transition: An Appraisal of the Medical Activities of the Freedmen's Bureau," *Bulletin of the Tulane University Medical Faculty*, 21 (February 1967) examine the daily operations of the federal agency. William McFeely, *Yankee Stepfather: General O. O. Howard and the Freedmen* (New York, 1970), and Thomas May, "Continuity and Change in the Labor Program of the Union Army and the Freedmen's Bureau," *Civil War History*, 17 (September 1971) also touch upon the problems of the Freedmen's Bureau in Louisiana. Claude F. Oubre, "'Forty Acres and a Mule': Louisiana and the Southern Homestead Act," *Louisiana History*, 17 (Spring 1976) discusses the quest for land.

Joe Gray Taylor, *Louisiana Reconstructed, 1863-1877* (Baton Rouge, 1977), the foremost synthesis, concentrates on politics and contains considerable information on the black man's role in Reconstruction. Agnes Smith Grosz, "The Political Career of Pinckney Benton Stewart Pinchback," *Louisiana Historical Quarterly*, 27 (April 1944) is a good study of the black politician that is far superior to James Haskins, *Pinckney Benton Stewart Pinchback* (New York, 1973), an unsuccessful popular biography. A. E. Perkins, "James Henri Burch and Oscar James Dunn in Louisiana," *Journal of Negro History*, 22 (July 1937), "Some Negro Officers and Legislators in Louisiana," *Journal of Negro History*, 14 (October 1929), and "Oscar James Dunn," *Phylon*, 4 (Summer 1943) are still helpful. An excellent collective biography of black leaders is David C. Rankin, "The Origins of Black Leadership in New Orleans During Reconstruction," *Journal of Southern History*, 40 (August 1974). Rankin, "The Politics of Caste: Free Colored Leadership in New Orleans During the Civil War," *Louisiana's Black Heritage*, is a revised and somewhat expanded version. Charles Vincent, *Black Legislators in Louisiana During Reconstruction* (Baton Rouge, 1976) contains a series of very useful biographical sketches that reflect intensive research, but the book fails to tie together loose ends. Other works that examine early black political activity include Howard J. Jones, "Biographical Sketches of Members of the 1868 Louisiana State Senate," *Louisiana History*, 19 (Winter 1978); Philip D. Uzee, "The Beginnings of the Louisiana Republican Party," *Louisiana History*, 12 (Summer 1971); William P. Connor, "Reconstruction Rebels: The *New Orleans Tribune* in Post-War Louisiana," *Louisiana History*, 21 (Spring 1980); T. Harry Williams, "The Louisiana Unification Movement of 1873," *Journal of Southern History*, 11 (August 1945); and T. B. Tunnell, Jr., "The Negro, the Republican Party, and the Election of 1876 in Louisiana," *Louisiana History*, 7 (Spring 1966). Roger A. Fischer, *The Segregation Struggle in Louisiana, 1862-1877* (Urbana, Ill., 1974) is a valuable study of black protest against racial discrimination.

An unfortunate result of this protest and black political participation was often violence. Three very good recent studies are Donald E. Reynolds,

"The New Orleans Riot of 1866, Reconsidered," *Louisiana History*, 5 (Winter 1964), and Melinda Meek Hennessey, "Race and Violence in Reconstruction New Orleans: The 1868 Riot," *Louisiana History*, 20 (Winter 1979). Older works that require careful reading are Manie White Johnson, "The Colfax Riot of April, 1873," *Louisiana Historical Quarterly*, 13 (July 1930), Frances P. Burns, "White Supremacy in the South: The Battle for Constitutional Government in New Orleans, July 30, 1866," *Louisiana Historical Quarterly*, 18 (July 1935), and Oscar H. Lestage, "The White League in Louisiana and Its Participation in Reconstruction Riots," *Louisiana Historical Quarterly*, 18 (July 1935). Otis A. Singletary, *Negro Militia and Reconstruction* (Austin, Tex., 1957) has a fine chapter on the involvement of black troops in the Battle of Liberty Place. Wayne R. Austerman, "Baton Rouge and the Black Regulars," *Louisiana History*, 21 (Summer 1980) is also worthwhile. Allen W. Trelease, *White Terror: The Ku Klux Klan Conspiracy and Southern Reconstruction* (New York, 1971) examines Klan activities in Louisiana. Allie B. Webb, "Organization and Activities of the Knights of the White Camelia in Louisiana, 1867-1869," *Proceedings of the Louisiana Academy of Science*, 17 (March 1954) is also useful.

Blassingame, *Black New Orleans, 1860-1880* is a sophisticated and admirably researched social history of Crescent City blacks during Reconstruction. David C. Rankin, "The Impact of the Civil War on the Free Colored Community of New Orleans," *Perspectives in American History*, 11 (1977-1978), is a parallel study of slightly more recent vintage. A useful work on black education is Joe M. Richardson "The American Missionary Association and Black Education in Louisiana, 1862-1878," *Louisiana's Black Heritage*. Louis R. Harlan, "Desegregation in New Orleans Public Schools During Reconstruction," *American Historical Review*, 67 (April 1962), the old standard, and Roger A. Fischer, "The Post-Civil War Segregation Struggle," *The Past as Prelude*, discuss school desegregation from different points of view. A good overview of black participation in Reconstruction is Charles Vincent, "Black Louisianians During the Civil War and Reconstruction: Aspects of their Struggles and Achievements," *Louisiana's Black Heritage*.

With the Compromise of 1877 and the return of Democratic rule, the status of the black man declined in Louisiana. Morgan Peoples, "'Kansas Fever' in North Louisiana," *Louisiana History*, 11 (Spring 1970), John Van Deusen, "The Exodus of 1879," *Journal of Negro History*, 21 (April 1936), and Nell Irvin Painter, *Exodusters: Black Migration to Kansas After Reconstruction* (New York, 1977) explore the deteriorating conditions of black Louisianians that motivated many to emigrate to Kansas. William Ivy Hair, *Bourbonism and Agrarian Protest: Louisiana Politics, 1877-1900* (Baton Rouge, 1969) is the premier study of white racism and social injustice that culminated in black disfranchisement during the late nineteenth century.

William Ivy Hair, "Henry J. Hearsey and the Politics of Race," *Louisiana History*, 17 (Fall 1976), and Arlin Turner, *George W. Cable* (Durham, N.C., 1956) are fine supplements. These works, however, focus upon white attitudes. There is no examination of Louisiana blacks in the late nineteenth century that is comparable to Vernon Lane Wharton, *The Negro in Mississippi, 1865-1890* (Chapel Hill, N.C., 1947), and George B. Tindall, *South Carolina Negroes, 1877-1900* (Columbia, S.C., 1952).

Two Louisiana studies support the Woodward thesis on the coming of segregation in the New South. Henry C. Dethloff and Robert R. Jones, "Race Relations in Louisiana, 1877-98," *Louisiana History*, 9 (Fall 1968), and Dale A. Somers, "Black and White in New Orleans: A Study in Urban Race Relations, 1865-1900," *Journal of Southern History*, 40 (February 1974) contend that race relations in Louisiana were fluid until the establishment of legal barriers in the 1890s. Paul A. Kunkel, "Modifications in Louisiana Negro Legal Status Under Louisiana Constitutions, 1812-1957," *Journal of Negro History*, 44 (January 1959), Riley E. Baker, "Negro Voter Registration in Louisiana, 1879-1964," *Louisiana Studies*, 4 (Winter 1965), and Germaine A. Reed, "Race Legislation in Louisiana, 1864-1920," *Louisiana History*, 6 (Fall 1965) review these legal restraints. J. Morgan Kousser, *The Shaping of Southern Politics: Suffrage Restriction and the Establishment of the One-Party South, 1880-1910* (New Haven, Ct., 1974) is a superb discussion of black disfranchisement in the South that examines Louisiana. George E. Cunningham, "The Italian, a Hindrance to White Solidarity in Louisiana," *Journal of Negro History*, 50 (January 1965), and Charles E. Wynes, "The Reverend Quincy Ewing: Southern Racial Heretic in the 'Cajun' Country," *Louisiana History*, 7 (Summer 1966) note two interesting sidelights to the race question. Geraldine McTigue, "Patterns of Residence: Housing Distribution by Color in Two Louisiana Towns, 1860-1880," *Louisiana Studies*, 15 (Winter 1976), and Zane L. Miller, "Urban Blacks in the South, 1865-1920: An Analysis of Some Quantitative Data on Richmond, Savannah, New Orleans, Louisville and Birmingham," *The New Urban History: Quantitative Explorations by American Historians*, ed. Leo Schnore (Princeton, N.J., 1975) are innovative essays that deserve close scrutiny.

C. Vann Woodward, "The Case of the Louisiana Traveler," *Quarrels That Have Shaped the Constitution*, ed. John A. Garraty (New York, 1962), and Otto H. Olsen, *Carpetbagger's Crusade: The Life of Albion Winegar Tourgee* (Baltimore, 1965) provide the best treatments of *Plessy* v. *Ferguson*, the Louisiana case that brought forth the legal doctrine of separate-but-equal. Barton J. Bernstein, "Case Law in *Plessy* v. *Ferguson*," *Journal of Negro History*, 47 (July 1962), and "*Plessy* v. *Ferguson*: Conservative Sociological Jurisprudence," *Journal of Negro History*, 48 (July 1963) are good technical supplements. Otto H. Olsen, ed., *The Thin Disguise: Turning Point in Negro History—Plessy v. Ferguson—a Documentary Presentation* (New York, 1967) is also helpful.

In a class by itself is William Ivy Hair, *Carnival of Fury: Robert Charles and the New Orleans Race Riot of 1900* (Baton Rouge, 1976). The book is both a biography of Charles and a narrative of the riot that he precipitated. Hair's use of scattered and incomplete records to reconstruct the black man's early life is exceptional, and his discussion of the violence is at once clear and exciting. The only flaw in this outstanding book is Hair's failure to show adequately the development of the black community in New Orleans during the late nineteenth century and to discuss the relationship between that community and Robert Charles.

Hair's book on the Charles riot also stands alone because supportive works have been extremely thin. Scholars have displayed surprisingly little interest in twentieth-century Louisiana blacks. The only significant exception to this rule is the contingent of music historians who have an almost fanatical attraction to black jazzmen and their music. Due to this fascination with jazz, studies of black musicians in Louisiana are numerous. Two of the best are Donald M. Marquis, *In Search of Buddy Bolden: First Man of Jazz* (Baton Rouge, 1978), and Tom Bethell, *George Lewis: A Jazzman from New Orleans* (Berkeley, 1977). Others include Alan Lomax, *Mister Jelly Roll* (New York, 1950); Stephen Longstreet, *The Real Jazz Old and New* (Baton Rouge, 1956); Al Rose and Edmond Souchon, *New Orleans Jazz: A Family Album* (Baton Rouge, 1967); Martin Williams, *Jelly Roll Morton* (New York, 1962), and *King Oliver* (New York, 1960); William J. Schafer with Richard B. Allen, *Brass Bands and New Orleans Jazz* (Baton Rouge, 1977); William J. Schafer and Johnnes Riedel with Michael Polad and Richard Thompson, *The Art of Ragtime: Form and Meaning of an Original Black American Art* (Baton Rouge, 1973); and Samuel B. Charters, *Jazz New Orleans, 1885-1963: An Index to the Negro Musicians of New Orleans* (New York, 1963). Al Rose, *Storyville, New Orleans* (University, Ala., 1974) contains important information on the black musicians who performed in the old red light district. Danny Barker and Jack V. Buerkle, *Bourbon Street Black* (New York, 1973) is a provocative sociological examination.

Other works on the early twentieth-century black community are at best fragmentary. Mark T. Carleton, *Politics and Punishment: A History of the Louisiana State Penal System* (Baton Rouge, 1971) explores the treatment of blacks in the state penitentiaries. Although his study begins in the antebellum period, the main thrust of the book is on twentieth-century conditions. Charles C. Alexander, *The Ku Klux Klan in the Southwest* (Lexington, Ky., 1965), David M. Chalmers, *Hooded Americanism: The History of the Ku Klux Klan*, rev. ed. (New York, 1981), and William Ivy Hair, "'Inquisition for Blood': An Outbreak of Ritual Murder in Louisiana, Georgia and Texas, 1911-1912," *Louisiana Studies*, 11 (Winter 1972) consider the question of violence. Thomas Bechel, *Labor, Church, and the Sugar Establishment: Louisiana, 1887-1976* (Baton Rouge, 1980) discusses black labor in the sugar industry. Doris Dorcas Carter, "Charles P. Adams and

Grambling State University: The Formative Years (1901-1928)," *Louisiana History*, 17 (Fall 1976), and Ernest J. Middleton, "The Louisiana Education Association, 1901-1970," *Journal of Negro Education* (Fall 1978) are valuable for an understanding of black education in Louisiana. Ronnie W. Clayton, "The Federal Writers' Project for Blacks in Louisiana," *Louisiana History*, 19 (Summer 1968) is unique and worthwhile. Doris Dorcas Carter, "Refusing to Relinquish the Struggle: The Social Role of the Black Woman in Louisiana History," *Louisiana's Black Heritage*, is a summary that concentrates on the twentieth century. Munro S. Edmundson and John H. Rohrer, eds., *The Eighth Generation Grows Up* (New York, 1960), and Woods, *Marginality and Identity*, are useful sociological studies.

Historical interest in race relations in Louisiana during the civil rights revolution of the mid-twentieth century is somewhat greater. Edward F. Haas, *DeLesseps S. Morrison and the Image of Reform: New Orleans Politics, 1946-1961* (Baton Rouge, 1974), and Glen Jeansonne, *Leander Perez: Boss of the Delta* (Baton Rouge, 1977) delve into the racial views of two intense political rivals who were both segregationists. James Conaway, *Judge: The Life and Times of Leander Perez* (New York, 1973) is a popular biography. Glen Jeansonne, "Racism and Longism in Louisiana: The 1959-60 Gubernatorial Elections," *Louisiana History*, 11 (Summer 1970) is a pivotal essay. Mary Lee Muller, "New Orleans Public School Desegregation," *Louisiana History*, 17 (Winter 1976) is the best treatment of the events that led to school desegregation in modern New Orleans. Morton Inger, *Politics and Reality in an American City: The New Orleans School Crisis of 1960* (New York, 1969), Robert L. Crain and others, *The Politics of School Desegregation: Comparative Case Studies of Community Structure and Policy-Making* (Garden City, N.Y., 1969), and Edward L. Penney and Robert S. Friedman, *Political Leadership and the School Desegregation Crisis in New Orleans* (New York, 1963) are also helpful. Haas, *DeLesseps S. Morrison and the Image of Reform* views the school crisis from the perspective of the politically expedient mayor of New Orleans. Peter Hernon, *A Terrible Thunder* (Garden City, N.Y., 1978) is a journalistic account of the Mark Essex case. Numan V. Bartley, *The Rise of Massive Resistance: Race and Politics in the South During the 1950s* (Baton Rouge, 1969), Neil R. McMillen, *The Citizens' Council: Organized Resistance to the Second Reconstruction, 1954-1964* (Urbana, Ill., 1971), Numan V. Bartley and Hugh Davis Graham, *Southern Politics and the Second Reconstruction* (Baltimore, 1975), and August Meier and Elliott Rudwick, *CORE: A Study in the Civil Rights Movement* (New York, 1973) are general studies that examine the Louisiana scene. All of these studies, with the exception of the book on CORE, it should be noted, discuss the civil rights movement in Louisiana from the perspective of the white Southerners.

This tendency to view the black experience from the standpoint of whites has been a common one among Louisiana historians. Concentration on nineteenth-century topics in black history has been another. Although old habits are hard to break, several scholars including John W. Blassingame, C. Peter Ripley, and David C. Rankin have recently attempted to move in new directions. Furthermore Clifton H. Johnson's essay, "Some Manuscript Sources in Louisiana Archival Repositories for Study of the History of Louisiana Blacks," *Louisiana's Black Heritage*, outlines numerous opportunities for fresh research. Historians who hope to develop a better understanding of the black experience in Louisiana would do well to broaden their horizons and become increasingly receptive to innovative approaches. The whole of Louisiana history would be richer for their efforts.

8

URBAN NEW ORLEANS

RAYMOND O. NUSSBAUM

THE PRESENT GENERATION of urban historians is not so much concerned about particular cities as it is about studying cities as cases in a wider pattern of urbanization. This chapter attempts to place New Orleans in that context. Little of the literature on the city, however, is written in that context. Indeed, it is the very uniqueness of the Crescent City that has attracted many historians to it—its romantic old buildings, quaint customs, and complex racial and ethnic structure. This essay attempts to be faithful to the city's special character while placing it in the broader framework of urban history.

Few works on the colonial period of New Orleans history are very satisfying academically. However, one study, John G. Clark's *New Orleans, 1718-1812: An Economic History* (Baton Rouge, 1970) is quite useful. In exploring economic problems, Clark also sheds much light on the political and social development of the city, concluding that the mercantilist French and Spanish regimes gave way to a laissez-faire economy following the Louisiana Purchase.

Three themes dominate the literature of New Orleans history from 1812 to 1860: the rise and later decline of the port; ethnic relations; and urban slavery. Almost all writers who have commented on the period stress the problem of the shifting fortune of the port as a central theme in antebellum New Orleans history. Clark, for example, in "The Antebellum Grain Trade of New Orleans," *Agricultural History*, 38 (July 1964), and "New Orleans and the River: A Study of Attitudes and Responses," *Louisiana History*, 8 (Spring 1967) considers in detail the process by which Eastern capitalists building a trans-Appalachian transportation network diverted much of the grain trade from New Orleans. Furthermore he shows that New Orleans businessmen contributed to their own decline by consciously choosing to rely almost exclusively on the river trade, when Eastern capital had already begun to show the clear advantages for many transportation needs of railroads over water. Lawrence H. Larsen in "New Orleans and the River Trade: Reinterpreting the Role of the Business Community," *Wisconsin Magazine of History*, 61 (Winter 1977) generally agrees with this but attributes the port's decline to the impersonal effects of a changing transportation network while minimizing the importance of the New Orleans business community's conservative investment stance. As Merl Reed shows in *New Orleans and the Railroads: The Struggle for Commercial Empire, 1830-1860* (Baton Rouge, 1966), some of the city's businessmen had been interested in railroads even in the earliest stages of their development in the East. In the 1850s some New Orleans investors had belatedly and rather unsuccessfully begun the construction of a railroad system to serve the city.

Despite the inadequacies of the city's transportation network, immigrants from a variety of ethnic groups did settle in New Orleans, and many historians have analyzed them. Among the best and most available of their works are Joseph Nau, *The German People of New Orleans, 1850-1900* (Leiden, Netherlands, 1938), and Earl F. Niehaus, *The Irish in New Orleans, 1800-1850* (Baton Rouge, 1965). The Creoles, many of them descendants of the French and Spanish settlers of colonial New Orleans, are discussed with penetrating insight in Joseph G. Tregle, Jr., "Early New Orleans Society: A Reappraisal," *Journal of Southern History*, 18 (February 1952). He finds them not the cultivated, urban people of legend and their own self-image but unsophisticated and mercurial while sensate and charming. Robert C. Reinders and William W. Chennault, "The Northern Born Community in New Orleans in the 1850s," *Journal of American History*, 51 (September 1964) stresses the role of that community in bringing new attitudes, values, and capital from a free labor society into New Orleans, where social ferment based on a slave labor system was so pervasive.

No ethnic group has attracted historians' attentions more than the blacks, and especially the slaves. Their main concern has been the adjustment of slavery, most characteristically a rural institution, to the demands of urban life. Richard C. Wade's *Slavery in the Cities: The South, 1820-1860* (New York, 1964) explores this problem by describing the tensions between the whites' need to discipline slaves and the freedom of action slaves experienced in the necessarily more open urban society and economy. Wade concludes that slavery adjusted to urban life but only tenuously and began to decline in the 1850s, when white masters felt threatened by pressure from Northern free soilers and abolitionists. While Wade is impressionistic, Claudie Goldin's *Urban Slavery in the American South, 1820-1860: A*

Quantitative History (Chicago, 1976), is, as the title implies, purely quantitative. She concludes that slavery had adjusted quite well to the urban environment and declined as a result of market forces rather than slaveowners's fears. Two case studies in New Orleans slavery, Jerry B. Martin, "New Orleans Slavery, 1840-1860: Testing the Wade Thesis" (M.A. thesis, Tulane University, 1972), and Herman C. Woessner, "New Orleans, 1840-1860: A Study of Urban Slavery" (M.A. thesis, Louisiana State University, 1967), while emphasizing different trends, find that although many of Wade's generalizations might hold for New Orleans the specific case of that city does not fit all of them.

New Orleans race relations were complicated further by the presence of a large population of free people of color (*gens de couleur*) who, unlike slaves, were often light-skinned, Roman Catholic, French-speaking, occasionally highly educated, and sometimes even quite wealthy. The historical literature on them, especially Donald Everett, "Free Persons of Color in New Orleans, 1803-1865" (Ph.D. diss., Tulane University, 1952), and David C. Rankin, "The Forgotten People: Free People of Color in New Orleans, 1850-1870" (Ph.D. diss., Johns Hopkins University, 1976) often portrays them as anomalous people occupying a place between whites and blacks in the city's class and racial structure.

A series of epidemics, especially yellow fever, made this antebellum period perilous for Orleanians, and those epidemics have found able historians in John Duffy and Jo Ann Carrigan. Duffy's *Sword of Pestilence: The New Orleans Yellow Fever Epidemic of 1853* (Baton Rouge, 1966), and "Nineteenth Century Public Health in New Orleans and New York: A Comparison," *Louisiana History*, 15 (Fall 1977) examine the 1853 epidemic and the city's generally poor public health system, which proved incapable of coping with the crisis. Carrigan's "Privilege, Prejudice and the Strangers' Disease in Nineteenth Century New Orleans," *Journal of Southern History*, 36 (November 1970), and "Yellow Fever in New Orleans 1853: Abstractions and Realities," *Journal of Southern History*, 25 (August 1959) analyze the effect of the epidemics on various socioeconomic classes of the city. In the midst of this terrible and recurring danger the city still preserved a lively cultural life. Henry A. Kmen's *Music in New Orleans: The Formative Years, 1791-1841* (Baton Rouge, 1966) traces the existence of elaborate balls and operas to a period quite early in the city's history.

The image of antebellum New Orleans that emerges here is that of a gumbo, but one that has only just begun to cook. The only attempt at synthesis is Robert C. Reinders, *End of an Era: New Orleans, 1850-1860* (New Orleans, 1964). Although useful as a narrative, this book fails to fully integrate the social, political, and racial aspects of this critical period.

Adherents of the new urban history will find little among these studies of antebellum New Orleans entirely satisfactory. They neither ask the same questions of the evidence nor use the same methodology to find answers.

Valuable insights into the city's past in this period might have come from investigations of social mobility, urban networks, and the transition from village to walking city and walking city to large city.

The Civil War and Reconstruction period in New Orleans history has been marred in earlier works by prejudice emphasizing the inefficiency and dishonesty of the Radicals. The best and most complete revisionist work on New Orleans is Gerald M. Capers, *Occupied City: New Orleans Under the Federals, 1862-1865* (Lexington, Ky., 1965). Although Capers recognizes that economic and social dislocation accompanied military occupation, he defends occupation commanders Benjamin Butler and Nathaniel Banks as able administrators forced by necessity to adopt repressive measures. David C. Rankin's study of Negro leadership during the occupation and the Reconstruction period, "The Origins of Black Leadership in New Orleans During Reconstruction," *Journal of Southern History*, 40 (August 1974), shows that most of the Negro leaders were from the *gens de couleur* and other black upper- and middle-class groups, not unprepared exslaves.

The most important change that Reconstruction brought was in race relations. The effects of abolition have been a matter of considerable debate for several years. The best general study is John Blassingame's *Black New Orleans, 1860-1880* (Chicago, 1973). Although incomplete and thinly researched, it is still valuable. Blassingame stresses the existence in the city, as early as antebellum times, of a black community with institutions that had developed independently of white repression. His blacks were largely the molders of their own destinies. David C. Rankin's "The Impact of the Civil War on the Free Colored Community of New Orleans," *Perspectives in American History*, 11 (1977-1978) has shown that, ironically, the *gens de couleur* lost status after abolition because many people placed them on the same social level with the freedmen.

C. Vann Woodward's thesis that segregation did not emerge fully until the late 1890s has spawned considerable historical literature, some of which concerns New Orleans. Roger A. Fischer, in "Racial Segregation in Antebellum New Orleans," *American Historical Review*, 74 (February 1969), believes that segregation was a way of life in antebellum New Orleans. Louis Harlan, "Desegregation in New Orleans Public Schools During Reconstruction," *American Historical Review*, 77 (April 1962) emphasizes the role of integrated schools in the city during Reconstruction, a rare phenomenon anywhere in the country at the time. Reinforcing Woodward's thesis, Dale A. Somers, "Black and White in New Orleans: A Study in Urban Race Relations," *Journal of Southern History*, 40 (February 1974) traces a fluid pattern of race relations that finally ended in 1900 with a riot discussed in great detail in William Ivy Hair's *Carnival of Fury: Robert Charles and the New Orleans Race Riot of 1900* (Baton Rouge, 1976).

The presence of an increasing number of Sicilians in postwar New Orleans added still another ingredient to the uncertain melting pot. In 1891 some Sicilians accused of assassinating police chief David C. Hennessy were lynched in a parish prison. There is abundant literature on the subject, but too much of it is marred by the authors' bias. John S. Kendall, "Who Killa de Chief," *Louisiana Historical Quarterly*, 22 (April 1939), John E. Coxe, "The New Orleans Mafia Incident," *Louisiana Historical Quarterly*, 20 (October 1937), and David L. Chandler, *Brothers in Blood: The Rise of the Criminal Brotherhoods* (New York, 1969) side with the lynch mob. Conversely, Richard Gambino's *Vendetta* (New York, 1977) is an even more grossly uncritical defense of the Italians. The account by Joy Jackson in *New Orleans in the Gilded Age: Politics and Urban Progress 1880-1896* (Baton Rouge, 1969) is fairly balanced but again tips toward the lynchers. The most balanced account is in Humbert S. Neilli's *The Business of Crime: Italians and Syndicate Crime in the United States* (New York, 1977).

Some of the better studies of Gilded Age New Orleans emphasize political history. Joy Jackson's *New Orleans in the Gilded Age* (Baton Rouge, 1969) stresses the conflict between a working- and middle-class-supported machine and an upper-class reform movement. Jackson's account sympathizes, sometimes uncritically, with the reformers, depicting them as idealists thwarted by the machine. She asserts that the machine's defeat in the municipal election of 1896 produced a fundamental reordering of New Orleans politics. However, as I have shown in "Progressive Politics in New Orleans" (Ph.D. diss., Tulane University, 1974), and "The Ring Is Smashed! The New Orleans Municipal Election of 1896," *Louisiana History*, 17 (Summer 1976), the election hardly changed political patterns. Instead of declining, the machine only regrouped. Fueled by an infusion of state patronage, between 1890 and 1900 the ring reorganized itself as the Choctaw Club, the dominant power in city politics until 1946. Wayne Everard's "Bourbon City: New Orleans, 1878-1900," *Louisiana Studies*, 11 (Fall 1972) discusses New Orleans Gilded Age politics in the context of C. Vann Woodward's analysis of Bourbonism.

The disfranchisement of blacks in 1898 produced a reordering of New Orleans politics that assured machine hegemony. The competition that had characterized Crescent City politics in the Gilded Age was facilitated by the black "swing vote," which forced opposing factions to compete for its support. As J. Morgan Kousser shows in *The Shaping of Southern Politics* (New Haven, Ct., 1974), the Choctaw Club, along with its rural allies, engineered black disfranchisement in order to achieve a monopoly of political power. The result of that maneuvering is well analyzed in George M. Reynolds's *Machine Politics in New Orleans, 1897-1926* (New York, 1936), still an excellent study of the Choctaws' heyday years.

The late nineteenth and early twentieth century was a critical era for New Orleans. Improved urban transportation developed simultaneously with an influx of destitute rural black migrants and Sicilian immigrants creating a city more deeply divided culturally, spatially, and socially. Such pervasive social ferment is grist for powerful historical writing, and some of the literature on the period is excellent. Roger Shugg's "The New Orleans General Strike of 1892," *Louisiana Historical Quarterly*, 21 (August 1938) is an incisive account. Gracefully written, it unfortunately lacks documentation. The origins of the most influential commercial organization in postwar New Orleans is analyzed in J. Tuffly Ellis, "The New Orleans Cotton Exchange: The Formative Years, 1871-1880," *Journal of Southern History*, 39 (November 1973).

The black underclass of New Orleans left little written evidence of its culture but had an enduring voice in jazz. The best studies of jazz and the social milieu of its origins are Alan Lomax, *Mister Jelly Roll* (Berkeley, 1973); Al Rose and Edmond Souchow, *New Orleans Jazz: A Family Album* (Baton Rouge, 1967); Don Marquis, *In Search of Buddy Bolden* (Baton Rouge, 1978); Nat Shapiro and Nat Hentoff, *Hear Me Talkin' to Ya* (New York, 1963); and Jack V. Buerkle and Danny Barker, *Bourbon Street Black* (New York, 1973). The most comprehensive sound recording of New Orleans jazz is "Jazz Odyssey: New Orleans, 1917-1947," three long-playing records from Columbia Products.

Some useful studies of other aspects of New Orleans culture in this period do exist. Dale A. Somers, *The Rise of Sports in New Orleans, 1850-1940* (Baton Rouge, 1972) provides insights into that avocation. Lyle Saxon's *Gumbo Ya-Ya* (New York, 1945), although not scholarly, contains much colorful and revealing material about ethnic, cultural, and neighborhood groups that shaped the city in the early twentieth century. Its primary sources include numerous WPA interviews.

Of all New Orleans institutions, Carnival is most revealing of the city's social underpinnings and values. Historically all of the city's socioeconomic classes, black and white, underclass, middle class, and elite, have participated but have celebrated in different ways. Carnival thus mirrors the New Orleans social hierarchy. Unfortunately there is little scholarly historical literature about it, but there are some worthwhile studies. Perry Young's *The Mistick Krewe* (New Orleans, 1969), first published in 1931, depicts and analyzes much of the social history of Carnival until that time. Robert Tallant's *Mardi Gras* (Garden City, N.Y., 1948) is a useful treatment. With much anthropological interest in ritual and festival, the New Orleans Carnival remains a fertile field for scholarly research into the social values of the city.

Some of the historical literature of twentieth-century New Orleans consists of biographies of the city's mayors. Most serious scholarship has concentrated on the administrations of Martin Behrman and deLesseps S. Morrison. The literature on Behrman, particularly Robert W. Williams, Jr., "Mayor Behrman and New Orleans Civic Development, 1904-1920," *Louisiana History*, 2 (Fall 1961), and "Martin Behrman, Mayor and Political Boss of New Orleans, 1904-1926" (M.A. thesis, Tulane University, 1952), praises his modernization but criticizes him for tolerating vice. He probably tolerated it because he knew Orleanians generally favored it. A good corrective to this thesis might come from a reading of Behrman's own memoirs, published serially in the New Orleans *Daily Item* in 1922 and 1923, and later edited and greatly condensed in John R. Kemp's, *Martin Behrman of New Orleans: Memoirs of a City Boss* (Baton Rouge, 1977).

Morrison's election in 1946 as a reform candiate finally ended the Choctaw hegemony Behrman had done so much to establish. The career of the last Choctaw mayor, Robert S. Maestri, is well studied in Edward F. Haas, "New Orleans on the Half Shell: The Maestri Era, 1936-1946," *Louisiana History*, 13 (Summer 1972). The fullest study of Morrison's fifteen-year administration is Haas's *DeLesseps S. Morrison and the Image of Reform* (Baton Rouge, 1974), which depicts Morrison primarily as an image builder who was not as committed to reform as he led people to think. Expecting such consistency is probably unreasonable; no politician completely lives up to his own propaganda. In any event, Morrison's reform measures and massive municipal building program were sufficient to prompt Michael Kurtz in "DeLesseps S. Morrison: Political Reformer," *Louisiana History*, 17 (Winter 1976) to comment somewhat uncritically that "deLesseps S. Morrison constantly tried to change things for the better." A different perspective is Joseph B. Parker's *The Morrison Era* (Gretna, La., 1974), which analyzes the mayor's political organization, the Crescent City Democratic Association, rather than his politics. Unfortunately, 65 of the book's 115 pages are a study not of the Morrison years but of twentieth-century New Orleans politics, material available in more useful form elsewhere.

During most of the period since 1900, blacks have been swept under the city's rug. Always a large part of the city's population, their participation in the city's civic and political life was minimal, except in the very latter part of the Morrison years. A 1960 federal court decision ordering the city to desegregate its public schools suddenly changed all this. School integration during the first year proved traumatic and not very successful. Inger Morton, *Politics and Reality in an American City: The New Orleans School Crisis of 1960* (New York, 1969), and Edward L. Pinney and Robert S. Freedman, *Political Leadership and the School Desegregation Crisis in Louisiana* (New York, 1963) trace this sad result to a failure of leadership on the part of the city government, state politicians, and the city elite. As an explanation of some of the specific events of 1960 that thesis is quite convincing, but as an elucidation of the ongoing failure to achieve school integration—the city's public schools are now mostly black—can probably be ascribed more to the deeply rooted patterns of white supremacy. The Louisiana State Advisory Committee to the United States Commission on Civil Rights, *The New Orleans School Crisis* (Washington, D.C., 1961) also analyzes and describes the 1960 events. A good narrative history of the integration crisis is Mary Lee Muller, "New Orleans School Desegregation," *Louisiana History*, 17 (Winter 1976).

Some of the best writing on the 1960 crisis can be described more precisely not as history or social science but as humanistic letters. John Steinbeck, during his journeys "in search of America," arrived in New Orleans at the height of violence near the affected schools, and he recorded his particularly vivid and perceptive impressions of the incidents in *Travels with Charley in Search of America* (New York, 1962). What impressed him most about the women who led the violence was the terrible way in which their fear of social change had reduced them to near animalism. Robert C. Coles's *Children of Crisis: A Study of Courage and Fear* (Boston, 1967) provides powerful understanding of the lives of blacks and whites involved in these events. His sympathies lie mostly with the small black children integrating the schools, but he also shows empathy for the whites who felt trapped and threatened by integration. The truth that emerges from reading Steinbeck and Coles is not the truth of behavioral science or empirical history but more like the truth of the best fiction, truth that affects the heart as much as the mind.

Race had always been the single most divisive factor in New Orleans society, and that became even more true after about 1900, when the drainage of swamp lands led to the development of all-white suburbs on the shores of Lake Pontchartrain. Until then almost all of the city's neighborhoods had been "mixed," with whites and blacks living within a few blocks of one another. Now it became possible for a black and a white New Orleans to emerge. The first study of this phenomenon was H. W. Gilmore's "The Old New Orleans and the New: A Case for Ecology," *American Sociological Review*, 9 (August 1944). Pierce J. Lewis, *New Orleans: The Making of an Urban Landscape* (Cambridge, 1976) asserts that residential segregation has become even more marked since Gilmore wrote, and he predicts that today's vigorous preservation movement might even accelerate this trend by moving whites into previously black neighborhoods, causing blacks to be displaced. Daphne Spain's "Race Relations and Residential Segregation in New Orleans," *Annals of the American Academy of Political and Social Sciences*, 441 (January 1979) reiterates many of these points in a broad historical context and arrives at a similarly gloomy conclusion. J. Lambert Molyneaux and Anthony V. Margavio, "Population Change in New Orleans from 1940-1960," *Louisiana Studies*, 9 (Winter 1970) uses sociological analysis to explore some of the same themes as Gilmore, Pierce, and Spain. A study by the New Orleans city planning firm of Curtis and Davis, *The New Orleans Housing and Neighborhood Preservation Study*, 3 vols. (New Orleans, 1974) is also useful. In this regard the City of New Orleans Office of Policy Planning is currently publishing a series of studies on each of the city's neighborhoods.

In addition to these works, preservationists have produced books that, although specifically designed to provide leadership for their movement, are of considerable value to historians. Several volumes in the series published by the Friends of the Cabildo are histories of former neighborhoods plus an additional volume on the city's distinctive aboveground cemeteries. The series edited by Mary Lou Christovich includes *New Orleans Architecture*, vol. 1: *The Lower Garden District* (Gretna, La., 1971), vol. 2: *The American Sector*, (1972), vol. 3: *The Cemeteries* (1974), vol. 4: *The Creole Faubourgs*, (1977), vol. 5: *The Esplanade Ridge* (1977); and Christovich and Roulhac Toledano, vol. 6: *Faubourg Treme and the Bayou Road* (1980). The New Orleans Chapter of the American Institute of Architects' *A Guide to New Orleans Architecture* (New Orleans, 1974) is arranged like a tour of the city designed to demonstrate the historic significance, quality, and variety of the city's architectural heritage.

Numerous untapped veins of potential historical understanding of New Orleans exist. Fuller use of the colonial manuscripts at the Louisiana State Museum will illuminate that only dimly seen period. The New Orleans Public Library's city archives collection has valuable materials on municipal development in New Orleans since colonial times. The little explored topic of labor unions, especially of teachers' unions, could be explored using materials in the University of New Orleans Archives. At Tulane University the papers of two of deLesseps Morrison's closest advisers, Scott Wilson and Dave McGuire, could offer more insights into the work of that pivotal mayor.

We need not only new answers to traditional research topics like labor, municipal development, and mayoral politics but new questions, questions that might emerge from a deeper study of the literature of the social sciences. The author's own research on New Orleans neighborhoods, for instance, uses tools derived from anthropology. Studies of race relations, labor, and the city elite, among many others could benefit from such analysis. Too little of the research on New Orleans places the city in a comparative perspective with other cities, a perspective that not only would help clarify the general problem of urbanization in America but would also help clarify the particular problems of urbanization in the Crescent City. The study of the history of education and of crime in various American cities has proven useful in the analysis of social stratification and assimilation; little such research has been done for New Orleans. Perhaps ten years hence some essay about the study of New Orleans history will be able to report many of these problems addressed and illuminated.

9
WOMEN IN LOUISIANA HISTORY

VAUGHAN BAKER SIMPSON

WHEN THE DISTINGUISHED Southern historian Avery O. Craven published *Rachel of Old Louisiana* (Baton Rouge, 1975), he insisted that it was merely a "little book"—not a scholarly exercise but simply a pleasant entertainment. It had, he said, no thesis; it was "just a love affair." Yet Craven's "little book" remains one of the few in print on the subject of the remarkable women who, like Rachel, managed plantations large and small in antebellum and Reconstruction Louisiana. After examining over three hundred of Rachel O'Conner's letters to her brother, David Weeks, and detailing the growth of her Feliciana Parish plantation to over a thousand acres worked by seventy-five slaves, he concluded that few men had done as well in the difficult business of successful cotton plantation administration between 1820 and 1846. Moreover, almost nonchalantly, Craven asserted that

> here in the South, Rachel and her kind had, perhaps unconsciously, launched an attack on the institution of Negro slavery. They had developed large plantations where the Negroes were largely born and reared and had taught the skills that forced a degree of equality and independence.... Slavery had disintegrated at a rapid rate in Rachel's hands. How widely her example had spread throughout the South we do not know. (p. 107)

For a book without deliberate thesis, Craven planted some of the most provocative seeds of thought in Louisiana historiography. That a historian of Craven's stature should so lightly dismiss the significance of Rachel's story loudly emphasizes the lack of status women's topics have merited in Louisiana—indeed, Southern—history.

Except for Craven's "little book," no account of women's role in antebellum Louisiana exists. Nor, for that matter, can substantive analyses be found in any period in Louisiana history. Serious studies of the role of women in Louisiana's past are woefully, abysmally lacking. Although more and more American and European historians are addressing research to topics focusing on—or at least including—women, few Louisiana writers have undertaken the task. With the plethora of unexploited primary source material that exists to support research on women's activities in Louisiana from colonial times to the present, the obvious question is, Why such neglect?

The answer is clearly a matter of methodology and historical theory. Louisiana history, until quite recently, has been written with a traditional narrative approach. Most of the standard works chronicle the drama of war or rebellion or detail the deeds of prominent leaders. In this orthodox methodology, women's topics ranked low on the list of the historian's priorities. Women did not play major roles in Louisiana's political development, nor did they serve in the front ranks of military affairs. The "drum-and-trumpet" focus therefore excluded them or relegated them to minor and insignificant roles. Women and their activities were merely footnotes to history.

History is now being redefined, however. With new historiographical emphases and new methodological approaches, the subject of women in history has gained a new significance. This new emphasis is not a matter of claiming for women a role they never played but of recognizing the role they did play, which means reexamining the dynamics of historical development. Although new bibliographies on women in American history abound, Louisiana historians have not yet addressed the task of delineating women's role in shaping the social, economic, and—if politics is defined in the broadest sense as the exercise of influence as well as power—political legacy of Louisiana's past. Avery Craven's casual "little" study of Rachel Weeks O'Connor clearly suggests a far more important role for women in Louisiana history than has yet been recognized.

In the colonial period, any mention of women in the standard literature is difficult to find. Marcel Giraud's description, in his four-volume *Histoire de la Louisiane française* (Paris, 1958), of the early experiences of female immigrants to the fledgling Gulf Coast settlement remains an exceptional treatment; Giraud, in volume 3, also discusses in colorful detail the later women deportees. As a model approach, however, Giraud's is disappointing. Although characterized by his usual meticulous research, his treatment nevertheless avoids any interpretive analysis of female participation in shaping the settlement in the wilderness. The French Colonial Documents (Archives des Colonies: La Correspondence Générale de la Louisiane, 67 reels; Archives de la Marine, 10 reels; Archives Nationales, series B, 386 reels) on deposit at the University of Southwestern Louisiana's Center for Louisiana Studies are, however, abundant in their evidence of the importance of women to the hopes of the colonial administration both for populating and civilizing the wilderness. The Superior Council Records housed at the Louisiana State Museum and the early civil records also attest to the active and vital role women played in the developing colony, particularly economically.

Published studies of women in the period are scanty. Heloise Hulse Cruzat's "The Ursulines of Louisiana," *Louisiana Historical Quarterly*, 2 (January 1919) reveals a pathbreaking interest in the religious order that pioneered education in Louisiana; the subject richly deserves further examination. The Archives of the Ursuline Convent in New Orleans hold valuable materials for a yet-to-be-written exploration of the contribution the Ursulines made to the religious, social, and educational development of the colony. These sources can be supplemented with Gabriel Gravier's *Relation du voyage des dames religieuses ursulines de Rouen a la Nouvelle Orleans* (Paris, 1872), and Marion Ware's translation of "An Adventuresome Voyage to French Colonial Louisiana: the Narrative of Mother Tranchepain, 1727," *Louisiana History*, 1 (Summer 1960) to provide a new picture of early conditions in a French settlement at New Orleans.

Walter H. Blumenthal's *Brides from Bridewell: Female Felons Sent to Colonial Louisiana* (Rutland, Vt., 1962) serves as a dismally shallow, single published study of the women deported to Louisiana in the early French period. More substantive exploratory work can be found in Mathé Allain's "Manon Lescaut et ses consoeurs: Women in the Early French Period, 1700-1731," and Vaughan Baker's "Les Louisianaises: A Reconnaissance," both in *Proceedings of the Fifth Meeting of the French Colonial Historical Society, March 29-April 1, 1979* (Washington, D.C., 1980). These authors plow untilled ground and promise further contributions.

Primary source materials in the Spanish period are even richer in unexploited treasure on women in early Louisiana. The only widely recognized woman of the period, the colorful and dynamic Baroness Michaela de Almonester y Pontalba, lacks a full-scale biography. Leonard Huber's small pamphlet, *Baroness Pontalba's Buildings* (New Orleans, 1964) merely tantalizes. The Records of the Spanish Cabildo of Louisiana (1769-1803) at the Louisiana State Museum in New Orleans contain judicial records, marriage contracts, estate inventories, and successions replete with data on women in Spanish Louisiana that has been barely skimmed. Rich information yet unused exists in the Spanish commandants' reports, which relate family disputes and internal relationships supportive of demographic and historical anthropological analyses as well as details of the lives of individual women appropriate to more traditional methodological approaches. The Archives General de Nice y Sevilla; Papeles procendentes de Cuba (*legajos* 187a-220b), on deposit at the Center for Louisiana Studies at the

University of Southwestern Louisiana, contain these reports and significant supplementary materials on women's economic activities under the Spanish administration. Beginning with the territorial period, civil and parish records increase abundantly, becoming even more numerous after statehood. A cursory examination of wills, suits, claims, and conveyances shows active participation of women in Louisiana's rapid growth.

The subject of women and slavery in Louisiana remains virtually untouched. Several manuscript collections promise important new insights into the impact of the institution on women and of women on the institution. Beyond the church and civil records, which have much of quantitative value to reveal, and the letters of Rachel Weeks O'Connor, now housed in the LSU Department of Archives and Manuscripts, the Amistad Research Center in New Orleans holds several important collections pertaining to women and slavery. The records of the American Home Missionary Society, over one million items dating between 1816 and 1836, includes information on slavery throughout the South as well as in Louisiana. The Slavery in Louisiana Collection dating between 1785 and 1869 housed at the Historic New Orleans Collection and the exslave narratives and manuscripts collected in the WPA Papers (Louisiana State Library, Louisiana Section) and WPA Ex-Slave Narrative Project (Louisiana State Library, Archives and Manuscripts Division) can all reveal new insights on the subject of slavery viewed from the women's perspective.

The activities of women in the field of education have been well documented if not very well interpreted in Louisiana. The vital presence of women's religious groups and the leadership exhibited by individual secular women in the field of Louisiana education has meant the preservation of numerous documentary collections that could support interpretive studies. Supplementing the records of the Ursulines are the Carmel Archives from 1824 to the present, housed at the Mount Carmel Generalate in Lacombe; the archives from 1638 of the Saint Vincent Sisters of the Daughters of the Cross Convent in Shreveport; and the records of the Religious of the Sacred Heart, an order that established three schools in Louisiana after 1821. The Sacred Heart Papers are presently available at the academies in New Orleans and at Grand Coteau, Louisiana, and through the Southwestern Archives at the University of Southwestern Louisiana. The records of the American Missionary Association at the Amistad Research Center in New Orleans contain interesting information on women schoolteachers who came to Louisiana and other areas of the South in the Reconstruction period.

Papers of individual women educators richly deserve scrutiny. Helen C. Wilkerson's correspondence, speeches, programs, and family papers (1905-1959) illuminate her career as assistant dean of women at Louisiana State University (LSU Department of Archives and Manuscripts). The Anna Estelle Many Papers concern her long career at Newcomb College (Tulane

University Archives). Sophie Bell Wright's scrapbooks from 1866 to 1912 (LSU Department of Archives and Manuscripts) relate to her career as principal of the Home Institute, a day and boarding school for girls, and as organizer of the Free Night School for Working Men and Boys. Edith Garland Dupré's Papers in the Southwestern Archives at the University of Southwestern Louisiana detail her career on the Southwestern faculty from 1901 to 1944, as well as her activities serving in Red Cross centers in Europe during and after World War I. The Anna Marie Hansen Jamison Papers at the Amistad Research Center are particularly interesting in illumating her teaching career from 1917 to 1937 in Southern black schools. The Rosa Freeman Keller Papers, also at the Amistad Research Center, although a small collection of only thirty-five items, contain documents concerning Keller's participation in the suit leading to the integration of Tulane University. The Hotel Dieu Hospital Library in New Orleans holds the archives from 1904 to 1974 of the Hotel Dieu School of Nursing. The scrapbooks and papers of the University of Southwestern Louisiana Nursing School are on deposit in the Women in Louisiana Collection at USL's Center for Louisiana Studies. The Dodd College Records at Centenary College in Shreveport contain information on a private Junior College for Women from 1927 to 1943.

Manuscript collections concerning women artists, writers, and musicians are also sufficient to support probing analyses. The Grace King Papers (LSU Department of Archives and Manuscripts) contain nearly 5,000 items. Leona Queyrouse's Papers (LSU Department of Archives and Manuscripts), over 2,000 items from 1800 to 1950, amply document the career of this French writer, poet, and musician. The papers of Ada Jack Carver, a short story writer and playwright, are deposited in the archives at Northwestern State University. The Women in Louisiana Collection at the University of Southwestern Louisiana contains an extensive collection of documents on Mary Alice Fontenot, presswoman and author of children's books. Regrettably, the papers of Lillian Hellman, one of the most noted of Louisiana women writers are on deposit at the University of Texas. Tulane University's William Ransom Hogan's Jazz Archive contains both documents and recordings of a number of Louisiana women musicians, including Lillian Armstrong, Billie Holiday, Billie Pierce, Bessie Smith, and Mary Lou Williams. The role of women in developing and perpetuating Louisiana music has not yet been even cursorily examined, nor has an assessment of women's contribution to Louisiana's artistic and literary legacy been made.

Although women's clubs and organizations have contributed richly to Louisiana's cultural and even political development, no scholar to date has undertaken an assessment of that contribution. Several collections of organizational records contain useful data: the records of the Jennings,

Louisiana Women's Auxiliary to the Grand Army of the Republic from 1917 to 1960 (USL Women in Louisiana Collection); the American Association of University Women's records (Women in Louisiana Collection and Archives Department, Northwestern State University); the Baton Rouge Business and Professional Women's Club Records (LSU Department of Archives and Manuscripts); the Local Council of Women of New Orleans (New Orleans Public Library, Louisiana Division); and the Records of the Christian Women's Exchange (Tulane University Library, Special Collections) are but a few. Two of the most significant women's organizational collections are the records of the ERA Club, a suffrage organization with extensive reform interests and activities, and the records of the Women's Anti-Lottery League, both deposited in the Louisiana Division of the New Orleans Public Library.

Papers of individual women active in Louisiana politics are unfortunately few, and published works virtually nonexistent. The central question of women's suffrage in Louisiana awaits interpretation. One single master's thesis, Patricia Loraine Spiers, "The Woman Suffrage Movement in New Orleans" (Southeastern Louisiana University, 1962), has surveyed the topic.

Since the issue of enfranchisement for women in Louisiana was often bitterly tied to such issues as federalism versus states' rights and to the question of enfranchisement of blacks as well as women, it deserves in-depth examination and promises to elucidate the present as well as the past. The aforementioned ERA Club Papers at LSU; the Merrick Family Papers (Historic New Orleans Collection), which contain items pertaining to women's rights leader Caroline Merrick; the McConnell Family Papers (Tulane University Library, Special Collections), with items concerning Elizabeth Logan McConnell; the Judith Hyames Douglas Papers (LSU Department of Archives and Manuscripts); and the papers of United States Senators Edward J. Gay and Joseph E. Ransdell (LSU Department of Archives and Manuscripts) richly supplement the unexploited newspaper and legislative records of the period to provide unequaled research sources on the subject.

Since active participation on the political scene is but a twentieth-century phenomenon, it can be hoped that materials on women in politics will grow. The Women in Louisiana Collection, established in 1977 at the University of Southwestern Louisiana's Center for Louisiana Studies has been charged with building source materials on women's activities in the state from colonial times to the present. Increased awareness of the significance of women's materials and increased research activity on subjects concerning women has already resulted from the activities of the staff of the Women in Louisiana Collection and promises a brighter future for the subject in Louisiana literature than has been true in the past.

Writings at present are scant, bibliographies are presently nonexistent. One recent shining aid to researchers has been Andrea Hinding's *Women's*

History Sources: A Guide to Archives and Manuscripts Collections in the United States (New York, 1979). Although the Louisiana section is, happily, already out of date and incomplete, it does serve as a useful beginning guide to documentary collections concerning women in Louisiana. The presence of women in Louisiana history has, until very recently, been spectral. With the new attention being given to the significance of women in history, it can be hoped that the ghostly shapes of Louisiana's women will soon take on solid form.

10
ORAL HISTORY: AN OVERVIEW

HUBERT HUMPHREYS

ORAL HISTORY AS it is used today grew out of post-World War II technology. Allen Nevins at Columbia University gave it recognition and developed its possibilities. Although there are several basic variations of contemporary definition and use, it is essentially a sound recording of eyewitness accounts of historical events. But it is an obvious historical fact that, stripped of its technology, this method of conveying historical information from eyewitnesses to others predates recorded history. The collecting of the oral narrative was modified when historians began to talk to and prepare a written record of stories told by such witnesses. For example, historians are aware of such research by Herodotus, Michelet, and Bancroft. Modern electronics provides an added dimension, a verbatim sound recording, which opens new possibilities. It also raises new theoretical and philosophical questions in historiography.

The first extensive attempt to investigate the use of oral history in Louisiana came as a result of this author's research project for the National Endowment for the Humanities, and that research is the basis of this essay. The original version was published in *Louisiana History*, 11 (Winter 1980), and the footnotes of this more detailed account reflect the research sources used, including the "Oral Historians of Louisiana" tapes located in the

An earlier version of this essay was given as the presidential address, Louisiana Historical Association, March 1979, and was based on research under grants from the Shreveport-Bossier Foundation and the National Endowment for the Humanities.

Archives at Louisiana State University in Shreveport. The twenty-one transcribed tapes form a unique body of original material on the individual experiences of oral history researchers in the state. The National Endowment for the Humanities project culminated in *Oral History in Louisiana: A Catalog* (Shreveport, La., LSU-Shreveport Bookstore, 1980), the first attempt to catalog and report on the diverse interview projects and collections in the state. The researcher also may consult Joel Gardner, *Oral History for Louisiana* (Baton Rouge, 1980).

In the absence of a statewide oral history project in Louisiana, the individual historian, conducting his own interview for a specific research goal, is responsible for much of the early self-conscious collecting of oral history material. It is difficult to establish the exact time the oral history movement began in the state. There are some very early activities that could be called oral history. For example, Collin L. Hamer, Jr., of the New Orleans Public Library, reports finding in the library basement typescripts of interviews conducted by employees of the WPA Writers' Project, specifically, from the Negro Writers' Project. The New Orleans Art Museum reports a small packet of typescripts of verbatim interviews of New Orleans artists from the 1930s, another WPA project. There are, of course, the slave narratives located in several depositories. For example, there is a fine collection at Northwestern State University in Natchitoches, which is currently being reevaluated and used. These projects predate any sound recorded eyewitness accounts by historians, although recently Joel Gardner in *Oral History for Louisiana* suggested that oral history as now defined, that is, a sound recorded interview for historical purposes, may have started in Louisiana. This took place in the 1930s when Huddie Leadbetter (Leadbelly) was interviewed in Shreveport by folklorist John Allan Lomax.

No evidence of any oral history-type projects was found from the 1940s. The exception might be the phono-disc collections from radio stations in the state, in which skilled radio interviewers conducted specialized interviews of persons who had witnessed or participated in some historic event of interest. Recorded interviews from radio stations often end up in oral history collections. In the early 1950s both the phono-disc and the early erratic wire recorder were being used to record various events; for example, the minutes and citizens' debates at the New Orleans City Council meetings. Although collectively this material is in the category of sound recorded events and does not narrowly fit into our definition of oral history, it is often catalogued in an oral history collection and is certainly important in its own right. But it was not until the mid-1950s that a Louisiana historian began self-consciously to record interviews electronically for research.

Evidence gathered in this study reveals that between 1956 and 1959 three research projects, two by established historians and a third that was more archival in nature but was guided by the hand of a professional historian, were begun or planned: the late T. Harry Williams's preparation for research for his book on Huey Long; John Loos's research for *Oil on Stream*; and an archival-type project at the New Orleans Jazz Archives at Tulane.

Williams, after careful study of the Columbia Project, characteristically and, in the case of the Williams research, of necessity, made a forthright commitment to use the oral history method to collect materials and write a biography of Huey Long. With his usual confidence, Williams set out in 1956 to adapt the Columbia experience selectively and pragmatically to the creation of his own private oral history collection on Long. This collection, since deposited in the Louisiana State University Archives, in turn would serve his research. Approximately twelve years later, when the Pulitzer Prize-winning book came off the press, Williams gained national recognition as a creative oral historian. The research experience made him an enthusiastic supporter for both the immediate research use of oral history as well as a later archival use. In a taped telephone interview shortly before his death, Williams reported that he and his wife were hard and enthusiastically at work on a biography of Lyndon B. Johnson.

Within a year of Williams's first interview, John Loos at Louisiana State University entered into an agreement with the Interstate Oil Pipeline Company to write a history of the company and decided it was necessary to gather information by interviewing. After extensive research into the company's records he began interviewing in June of 1957. In two years he traveled all over the United States and conducted taped interviews with over one hundred former and present employees. The research was of a national corporation with deep roots in Louisiana, particularly in Shreveport. *Oil on Stream* was published by the Louisiana State University Press in 1959. The tapes and transcripts are still part of the company's records in Houston but will soon be transferred to the LSU archives. These interviews contain not only extensive information on the company's history but considerable information on the political and social history of Louisiana.

Almost simultaneously a third and somewhat different oral history project was taking shape in New Orleans. In the mid-1950s Richard Allen, the former curator of the Hogan Jazz Archives at Tulane, was for his own enjoyment occasionally conducting interviews with New Orleans jazz personalities in his French Quarter record shop. Recognizing the historical importance of such material, Allen went to the late William R. Hogan, chairman of the Tulane History Department, with the idea of doing a master's thesis on the history of jazz that would be partially based on this type of material. The idea for a thesis became, under the creative imagination of Allen and Hogan, a proposal to the Ford Foundation to establish a jazz archive based largely on taped interviews. Running interference for them at the foundation was the Tulane dean of liberal arts, historian Fred Cole. The result is the internationally known William R. Hogan Jazz Archives. Obscure as well as famous jazz musicians gave information on their music and their lives that create unique and vivid pictures of the jazz era. It is appropriate that jazz music had a seminal influence on the oral history movement in Louisiana. The scope of these interviews and the use of the collection have long since spread beyond New Orleans, and more recently the transcripts of many of these interviews have been made available to research libraries around the world by the Microfilm Corporation of America.

The works of Williams, Hogan, Loos, and Allen were rarely publicized in the early days of their research, but their experience was influential in their graduate history classes at Louisiana State University and Tulane. No doubt many graduate students in the next decade first learned this method of research as a result of these three projects. Consideration of subsequent oral research by Louisiana historians presented here is neither narrowly chronological nor in order of importance.

Joy Jackson of Southeastern Louisiana University and Sue Eakin of LSU-Alexandria are two consistent exponents of oral history who have utilized tapes in their own research. Both had extensive newspaper experience before committing themselves fully to professional history and were influenced by the interview techniques of journalism in gathering and using historical material. Both have also published books and articles and presented papers that are partially based on extensive interviewing. Each has directed students in oral history research projects. They have a special interest in the cultural and ethnic history of their respective communities and regions of the state. Eakin has used such material as the basis of a well-received newspaper column, "Back-tracking," from the Alexandria *Daily Town Talk*, and has a large private collection of tapes on such topics as Louisiana socialists and black academies. Part of Joy Jackson's Louisiana Historical Association presidential address, 1978, was based on oral research.

For the past few years Bennett H. Wall, formerly of Tulane University, has been using the oral history method to research a book on the Exxon Corporation, which has a long-time and significant Louisiana connection. He confirms John Loos's experience that many large companies, certainly in the oil industry, have a practice of periodically discarding or destroying a major part of their archives. Although Wall, like Loos, began to use the tape recorder in corporate history, he was no novice and recalls lugging an old Montgomery Ward recorder around Kentucky over twenty-five years ago collecting material in a research project. He is thoroughly convinced that such material, if judiciously gathered, not only provides facts otherwise unavailable but also is "unsurpassed in providing the tone and color that makes historical reconstruction reflect some of the excitement and vitality of the original participants." On the other hand, though, he correctly raises some questions, as did John Loos, about its proper use.

The pioneering research of Loos and Wall in corporate history suggests many possibilities for collecting, preserving, and researching Louisiana economic history, such as the offshore oil and gas industry, post-World War II use of the state's rivers and canals, and many other twentieth-century developments. Trained historians are available, but well-planned projects and the necessary funding for them are not yet a working reality.

Several younger Louisiana historians who have published well-received books or articles have, in tapes prepared for this particular study, commented on their first use of oral history for research. They often report that their first experience came in preparing a thesis or dissertation in the late 1960s or early 1970s. Frequently this material was collected for a political biography. For example, Edward F. Haas and Glen Jeansonne have used oral history very successfully in writing their respective biographies of New Orleans Mayor deLesseps Morrison and Plaquemines Parish boss and segregationist Leander Perez. Although both did their first research in oral history in graduate schools outside the state, each is a native of Louisiana, and each wrote on Louisiana subjects. Both have been influenced by the pioneering work of Williams as well as the successful Columbia-type projects. Jeansonne's masters' thesis on the 1959-1960 gubernatorial campaign, later published in the University of Southwestern Louisiana monograph series, utilized interviews with all of the principal candidates. Both Haas and Jeansonne believe interviews crucial for supplying important material not otherwise available. Both basically confirmed the Williams experience as to the value of the taped interview in writing political biography as well as some of the limitations, although their approach to interviewing is as different from Williams' as are their personalities and ideological preferences. Jeansonne is currently interviewing in preparation for a biography of Share Our Wealth organizer Gerald L. K. Smith.

Thomas Becnel of Nicholls State University, lacking printed information needed for his thesis on the Louisiana shrimp industry, began to interview older Gulf Coast fishermen. Since this was before the tape recorder was widely used, he did not record these interviews electronically. Convinced by this research experience that a significant part of the material was essentially verifiable, he later moved into various other research projects, many of them dealing with local history, using a tape recorder. One such project, partially funded by the National Endowment for the Arts, was to conduct a cultural inventory of the Lafourche Parish area. Although aware of the innate problems in oral history research, he became thoroughly convinced that judiciously used it has great potential. But Becnel also considers the proper processing and cataloguing of interviews for future research use a presently critical problem. Michael Kurtz of Southeastern Louisiana University raised many of the same questions discussed by Becnel, particularly questions on transcribing and processing the interview in a format that would make the information easily retrievable by the researcher. Kurtz's areas of research include local history, state politics, and some specialized interviewing on the Kennedy assassination, particularly the New Orleans connection. Other historians contributing to this study have posed additional questions in their critical evaluations of oral history, both in its present use as well as in its potential for researching twentieth-century Louisiana topics. All were confident, even excited, about such research.

One of the youngest oral history experiments in the state is at Louisiana State University in Shreveport. A joint project of the Social Sciences Department and the University Archives, its specific purpose is to document selected aspects of Northwest Louisiana history. A brief synopsis of its origins reflects the diversity of Louisiana oral history projects. The pilot project came about when attempts to acquire Shreveport-area archival materials revealed acute gaps on some of the most important twentieth-century events in the area's history. A chance remark to the effect that what was needed in lieu of the missing material was an oral history project brought a meeting with a prominent Shreveporter who suggested the possibility of obtaining funds for such a project from the local Shreveport-Bossier Foundation. He had read Williams's book on Long and was intrigued by the oral history research method. Subsequent events led to the writing of a proposal and the funding of a pilot project by the foundation. The purposes of the project were defined, the equipment purchased, preliminary research conducted, and the challenges of making the plan work realistically faced.

Most of the interviews in the LSU-Shreveport project are transcribed, a preface written placing the interview in the proper context, and a signed release obtained. The memoir is then processed for the university archives. Since the amount of time and money to complete this undertaking was underestimated, there were the usual problems of implementing a new program. The first interview conducted was what might be called a "seed interview." A former mayor with deep roots in the community and a sense of history, who knew practically everyone and their relationships to each other, was interviewed about whom should be interviewed and why and how that person fit into area history. These types of interviews provide a valuable source in the first year or two of any planned local history project. The oldest persons were interviewed first; several have since died. Three of these significantly reflect important aspects of Northwest Louisiana history: Carl Jones, eighty-one, a pioneer in the early oil development of the area; Don Ewing, a longtime influential editor of the Shreveport *Times*; and State Senator William Rainach, a candidate for governor in the 1959-1960 election. Each placed on the record significant material that would not have otherwise been preserved. Carl Jones vividly recalled Howard Hughes, Sr., and Hughes's peddling of his famous oil drill bit in the Pine Island Oil Field in North Caddo Parish around 1908-1909. Senator Rainach outlined his deliberate plan, in the wake of the 1954 Brown decision, to maneuver the Louisiana Legislature into massive resistance of racial desegregation and gave a post-mortem on that crusade. Don Ewing explained his rationale for deciding which candidates would get the support of the Shreveport *Times*.

Others interviewed for the LSU-Shreveport program include former mayors, state representatives, judges, parish officials, and state political leaders such as Arthur Watson, chairman of the Democratic State Central Committee. One of the most exciting interviews was with Cecil Morgan, former Caddo legislator who later became a judge and eventually dean of the Tulane Law School. He was a leader in the fight to impeach Huey Long and has written a critical book review of Williams's biography of Long. Morgan persuaded Harney Bogan, a colleague from the Caddo delegation in those years, to join the discussion of the impeachment. These interviews were videotaped, and they capture the drama and excitement of the impeachment days as the participants, seemingly with direct recall, vividly relive those events. Because both Morgan and Bogan had read Williams's book, these interviews, plus one other such interview, raises serious questions for historians. What happens to the memoirs of a participant in a historic event if in the intervening years he reads influential articles and books about that event? How damaging is this to a historical reconstruction of the event and its meaning at the time? How different is the memoir elicited by the questions of a trained historian and the traditional memoir under the distortions of time and widely disseminated books and articles on the subject?

The LSU-Shreveport program also includes some interview projects related to the cultural history of the area. There is presently underway or in the planning stage a series on the Shreveport Little Theater, dating back to the 1920s, and on the Shreveport Symphony. The interviewers for the projects are knowledgeable about the subject as well as the persons to be interviewed. An unexpected bonus has been the occasional acquisition of important traditional archival materials as a direct result of having conducted an interview. The archive that has both the written records and an oral interview strengthens the potential quality of research.

Although the genesis and scope of oral history projects by Louisiana sociologists, political scientists, anthropologists and other related social scientists will not be extensively examined here, it can be said that a number of researchers are engaged in projects that are of value to the historian as well as being significant in their own right. For example, a most unique and fascinating scholarly self-tape was graciously prepared for this study by Dr. Hiram "Pete" Gregory, distinguished anthropologist at Northwestern Louisiana University. This tape reviews over fifteen years of experience in using the recorder to collect and study material on Louisiana Indians and related ethnic groups. He also has generously identified and recognized the work of a variety of students and scholars in Louisiana and around the country who have worked with him. Gregory and his colleagues have collected an impressive amount of original material. Much of Gregory's own field work has been done with illiterate or semiliterate people. The work is primarily on the history and ethnology of Louisiana Indian communities, dozens of them, such as the Louisiana Choctaw and Jena Choctaw, Creole, and mixed ethnic groups including the Spanish-American Indian community in Sabine Parish. Material gathered is deposited at appropriate anthropological centers in the United States, with individual Indian tribes, and more recently at the Northwestern Folk Life Center. As an anthropologist, Gregory is using the term "oral history" in its original sense: preliterate peoples passing the tribal or folk history from father to son, from tribal leader to those preparing for tribal leadership, by word of mouth. He has found the material gathered quite verifiable.

An Ethnic Heritage Oral History Project, financed by a sizable federal grant to the New Orleans Saint Marks Community Center, is another unique state project. Under the direction of Margery Freeman, a paid staff of adults and students have, since 1977, engaged in a community history project of the New Orleans Treme-Seventh Ward with emphasis on blacks and other ethnics. Preliminary reports indicate the collection, preservation, and community use of a remarkable amount of such source material. Approximately a hundred people have been interviewed. Fifteen of these were taped for a videotape that is being used at the center and in several area schools.

Some of the most exciting history interviews in the state are conducted by local history enthusiasts. Two of the most interesting in this category are the work of nonprofessionals knowledgeable about the cultural heritage of their own communities and the state. Mrs. Dorothy Schlesinger started collecting oral history as a result of membership on the Board of the Friends of the Cabildo in New Orleans, while Mr. Goodloe Stuck was the first president of Shreveport Historical Preservation. Both were born and educated outside Louisiana, and both have given enthusiastic leadership to the preservation of the colorful local history of their adopted state.

For her own pleasure Mrs. Schlesinger began to record and transcribe the experiences and stories of a native New Orleanian friend. Other friends, including Connie Griffith, Tulane archivist, encouraged her. The Board of Friends of the Cabildo agreed to support the project and provide volunteer interviews. Six years later, undaunted by inevitable problems, she had interviewed 163 people from all walks of life, and the tapes had been transcribed. Mrs. Schlesinger obtained the cooperation of professional historians, archivists, graduate students, and many average citizens. Copies of this body of material are now deposited at the Louisiana State Museum Archives as well as at the Tulane Archives.

After reading Professor Williams's book on Long, Goodloe Stuck decided that the tape recorder would be of real value to him in trying to document his own private research. Stuck's interviews about a large old house in the Shreveport "Bottoms" area turned up fascinating information. This structure had been a house in the old red light district and home of Annie McCune, one of Shreveport's more famous madames. With his tape recorder he pursued Annie's ghost through memories of former delivery boys, bankers, and policemen. The search, which has carried him into nursing homes, bars, and quiet, tree-shaded, older homes, will result in a book. Edited transcripts of these interviews will be deposited in the Louisiana State University-Shreveport Archives.

Strictly archival oral history projects in the state are often difficult to identify because many such projects have been ad hoc cooperative ventures between an archives staff and an independent researcher. Moreover, traditional archives in Louisiana have suffered from a lack of funds and planning. Archival oral history projects have ranked at the bottom of priority lists. Nevertheless, there are some commendable efforts and permanent achievements. Many of the tapes and/or transcripts located in the state's libraries or archives were made by historians or other researchers for a specific purpose and have been donated to the archives after the researcher's project was complete. But many other items or collections are the result of the activity of an archivst or librarian taking scarce time and money to preserve an unusual eyewitness account or memoir. Such interviews, often by a historian-archivist, are to be found at a number of the state's colleges. Often the interview is not transcribed and may even be uncatalogued, making it difficult for a potential researcher to use. Other limited projects were funded by small grants for some local history project. Although there is great diversity in the nature, scope, and quality of the material, evidence suggests a commendable pervasive sense of history that will not let valuable source material disappear. So an interview is deliberately made with a last Indian chief, a first woman legislator, Huey Long's personal aide, an ex-governor, a steamboat captain, an old socialist, or the community patriarch. All end up in an archives with the hope that they will some day be transcribed, catalogued, and made available to future researchers. Maybe it will take a future WPA-type project for unemployed historians or archivists to fund, rediscover, and more properly evaluate these materials.

Without comment on their merit or quality, a brief sampling of these college archival projects reflects persistent efforts to record disappearing historical evidence. Over one hundred interviews at Northwestern Louisiana University conducted by faculty and others in the last fifteen years include a substantial number of nationally known people who have a Louisiana connection, and many are prominent Louisianians.

At the University of Southwestern Louisiana there is a significant collection on the rice industry, on prominent southwestern Louisiana families, and on area history. At LSU a variety of small projects include a family history project and an American in Viet Nam Project. Nicholls State University has preserved a rather large Bicentennial project on many facets of area history. Most state colleges have done some interviewing on the history of their own institution.

Although only the most cursory analysis has been made of these preliminary inventories, several tentative observations can be made. First, there is documentation on important Louisiana topics or people that would never have been available in traditional archival material and that supplements with color and insight more formal records. It also includes a great deal of trivia, but then that is true also of regular archival collections. As previously noted, there is a great gap in proper cataloguing and final processing, a problem that must eventually be addressed. There are oral history projects on the same subject and even on the same people within a university, but due to the lack of communication or central archival coordination there may be little or no contact between the two research efforts.

At least a dozen parish or city libraries have attempted oral history projects on local history. Most have been in the last five years and are Bicentennial projects, with an occasional historic preservationist or genealogist responsible for collecting. Most of these have had only limited success. There is only meager information available on a variety of private or specialized items from churches, clubs, unions, and businesses, which, for their own narrowly defined historical or educational purposes, have proceeded to document on tape some aspect of the organization's history. There is an occasional project in the elementary and secondary schools of the state. In 1980 two events of note took place in Louisiana that should encourage and strengthen these groups. The Southwest Library Association, under a national grant, sponsored two pilot institutes on oral history for public libraries, at the Saint Charles Parish Library and the Richland Parish Library. The second event was a one-day workshop on oral history in Baton Rouge sponsored by the Louisiana Committee for the Humanities and the Louisiana State Archives.

Research on the nature, scope, and status of oral history in Louisiana revealed some unexpected information. A surprising number of researchers have at one time or another used the method either as a research tool or simply to preserve memoirs of significant persons. All are convinced that their own research has been strengthened and some of the flavor of the times recaptured. Others reflected on the personal satisfaction that came to both the interviewer and the memorist as they recorded a wealth of opinions and suggestions. They also raised critical questions about such topics as funding, standards, and potential areas of reseach. Others were concerned with the role of the archivist and of the Louisiana Historical Association in providing a forum for these and related topics. Also implicit in many comments is the need for a clearer understanding of the oral history tape or transcript as a historical document.

The experiences of the WPA Writers' Project, as well as the pioneering work of Williams, Loos, Hogan, and Allen in the 1950s, have contributed to our understanding of twentieth-century Louisiana. Other Louisiana historians since have significantly added to that work. Archivists and librarians are attempting to define their role in generating or preserving oral history archival material. Although nationally there is an increasing number of professional articles calling for a more critical reappraisal of oral history, in Louisiana history it is not so much a reappraisal as a first appraisal. This essay leaves to others a more definitive assessment of the collective experience. Finally, Louisiana's historians owe a note of thanks to all those interviewees who have been willing to participate in the various research projects. They have not only provided significant new information, and on occasion a challenge to historical and ideological misconceptions about their lives, but they have also become our friends. Out of their rich experiences they have reminded us of the virtues of the human condition.

11
QUANTIFICATION AND LOUISIANA HISTORIANS

THOMAS SCHOONOVER

LOCAL AND STATE historians should neither overlook nor neglect the increasingly common use of computers and statistical techniques. Moreover, not only college instructors, but social science teachers in the upper elementary and high schools as well as laymen should familiarize themselves with this new methodology in order to read critically the research studies it produces. Up to the present, with the lone exception of political history, Louisiana historians have been negligent in applying this new methodology. Even in political history much of the valuable quantitative analysis has been accomplished by political scientists and sociologists. After a brief review of existing scholarship and suggestions for quantifiable sources, this essay will discuss generally some books and articles that can serve as models and methodological aids and finally will review the three main study guides that can introduce scholars and researchers to quantitative methodology from "a" to "z."

In the area of political sociology and political analysis Louisiana has benefited considerably from computer-assisted research and statistical analysis done by political scientists and sociologists. William C. Havard, *The Changing Politics of the South* (Baton Rouge, 1972) contains a chapter on Louisiana. Perry H. Howard, *Political Tendencies in Louisiana*, rev. ed. (Baton Rouge, 1971) offers an excellent study of social politics from the early nineteenth century through the late 1967 elections. The nativist Know-Nothing movement of the mid-nineteenth century attracted articles by Richard Tansey, "Prostitution and Politics in Antebellum New Orleans," *Southern Studies*, 18 (Winter 1979), and Marius Carriere, "Political Leadership of the Louisiana Know-Nothing Party," *Louisiana History*, 21 (Spring 1980), which analyze social and economic aspects of the nativists' movement in Louisiana. In addition, Terry L. Seip's essay, "Municipal Politics and the Negro: Baton Rouge, 1865-1880," *Readings in Louisiana Politics*, ed. Mark T. Carleton, Perry H. Howard, and Joseph B. Parker (Baton Rouge, 1975), uses statistical data on occupation, interracial living groups, city finances, and voting to seek sociopolitical understanding of Reconstruction Baton Rouge. Scholars have analyzed the political and social impact of the 1928 election upon Louisiana politics in essays by Barbara C. Wingo, "The 1928 Presidential Election in Louisiana," *Louisiana History*, 18 (Fall 1977), and Steven D. Fink, "Cultural Conflict and the 1928 Presidential Campaign in Louisiana," *Southern Studies*, 17 (Summer 1978). The Long era has undergone extensive voting analysis in Allan P. Sindler's *Huey Long's Louisiana* (Baltimore, 1956). Two other essays in *Readings in Louisiana Politics* provide models for sociopolitical analysis of recent elections: Charles E. Grenier and Perry H. Howard, "The Edwards Victory," uses factor matrices and multivariable correlations to create and then to examine three sociopolitical groups that he calls "urban Republicanism," "Catholic moderates," and "black power"; and James Chubbuck, Edwin Renwick and Joe E. Walker, "The Emergence of Coalition Politics in New Orleans," uses a multifactor, socioeconomic model to analyze New Orleans politics in the 1960s and early 1970s. Finally, the 1960 gubernatorial and presidential elections have been exhaustively studied in William C. Havard, Rudolph Heberle, and Perry H. Howard, *The Louisiana Elections of 1960* (Baton Rouge, 1963).

Unfortunately, neither the economic, agricultural, social, nor urban history of Louisiana has been the object of extensive quantitative study. Not only Louisiana economic history, including agricultural history, has been neglected, but there has been general neglect of Southern economic history (except the economics of slavery) by scholars employing quantification techniques. For the work completed in Southern economic history and suggestions and bibliography for areas or problems for future study, however, two essays can be consulted with great benefit: Gerald D. Nash, "Research Opportunities in the Economic History of the South After 1860," *Journal of Southern History*, 32 (August 1966), and Harold D. Woodman, "Sequel to Slavery: The New History Views Postbellum South," *Journal of Southern History*, 43 (November 1977).

Although interesting quantitative studies of Louisiana history are uncommon, articles by Laurence J. Kotlikoff, Anton J. Rupert, David G. Rankin, Geraldine McTigue, David O. Whitten, and Gary B. Mills should be noted. Kotlikoff and Rupert, "The Manumission of Slaves in New Orleans, 1827-1846," *Southern Studies*, 19 (Summer 1980) uses data on age, sex, and price to reveal a significant role for free blacks in the emancipation process during the early nineteenth century in New Orleans. Rankin's study, "The Origins of Black Leadership in New Orleans During Reconstruction," *Journal of Southern History*, 40 (August 1974) demonstrates one imaginative application of prosopography (collective biography) to an era and elite, blacks during Reconstruction, for whom it is normally difficult to obtain personal data. McTigue's study, "Patterns of Residence: Housing Distribution by Color in Two Louisiana Towns, 1860-1880," *Louisiana Studies*, 15 (Winter 1976) uses manuscript census data to reveal the scattered residential patterns of the late nineteenth century but also to suggest that the clustered settlements were not necessary at the time because the blacks' place in Southern society was so well defined that it permitted physical proximity. Later, as socially and politically defined boundaries became blurred, physical distance became necessary as the means for defining black places in society. This essay is suggestive, but such studies must be carried out for other Southern towns and neighborhoods and for longer time periods in order to develop a clearer picture of settlement patterns over generations rather than just decades.

Many studies of Negro slavery based upon quantitative methods could serve as models for studying slavery in Louisiana. Perhaps the best introduction to the historiography of computer-assisted scholarship on slavery is Paul A. David et al., *Reckoning with Slavery: A Critical Study in the Quantitative History of American Negro Slavery* (New York, 1976). An intriguing study that examines mortality among blacks for the last fifteen years of slavery and the first two generations of freedom is Edward Meeker, "Mortality Trends of Southern Blacks, 1850-1910: Some Preliminary Findings," *Explorations in Economic History*, 13 (January 1976). Meeker relates mortality to the broader questions of health and life expectancy. His study could also provide a useful model for investigating mortality, life expectancy, and health conditions in Louisiana, not only for blacks but for the whole population.

Several preliminary or related studies have tentatively examined slavery in Louisiana. David O. Whitten's essay about the profitability of slavery in the sugar industry, "Sugar Slavery: A Profitability Model for Slave Investments in the Antebellum Louisiana Sugar Industry," *Louisiana Studies*, 12 (Summer 1973), is an econometric study that attempts to find a formula for evaluating the various factors in the sugar industry in order to arrive at a model-formula for determining profitability. Whitten's essay requires considerable expertise in mathematics, economics, or statistical methods to follow closely. On a more general but supplementary level, one can profitably examine several articles by Randolph Campbell and Richard Lowe on slavery, slave profitability, and slave wealth in Texas and east Texas for perspectives and ideas that might be applicable to northern and western Louisiana: Lowe and Campbell, "Slave Property and the Distribution of Wealth in Texas, 1860," *Journal of American History*, 63 (September 1976), Lowe and Campbell, "The Slave-Breeding Hypothesis: A Demographic Comment on the 'Buying' and 'Selling' States," *Journal of Southern History*, 62 (August 1976), and Campbell, "The Productivity of Slave Labor in East Texas: A Research Note," *Louisiana Studies*, 13 (Summer 1974).

Still other recent studies of local resources in Louisiana reveal significant bodies of data for computer-assisted social and economic studies. Such essays include Collin Bradfield Hamer, Jr., "Records of the City of Jefferson (1850-1870) in the City Archives Department of the New Orleans Public Library," *Louisiana History*, 17 (Winter 1974). Hamer's essay lists and describes holdings that include tax receipts, cash books, financial reports, ledgers, voucher books, journals of receipts, budgets, tax lists, tax rolls, death records, marriage certificates, property transfers, and other miscellaneous records that would permit computer-assisted investigation of many social and economic trends of the city of New Orleans and its inhabitants in the mid-nineteenth century. Blaise C. D'Antoni, "The Church Records of North Louisiana," *Louisiana History*, 15 (Winter 1971) reports on the early records for Avoyelles and Natchitoches parishes indicating the wealth of baptismal, funeral, and marriage records, many dating from the early or mid-eighteenth century, that are available to researchers. The Avoyelles and Natchitoches records offer excellent data for quantitative research projects in social, particularly family and demographic, history. Certainly every Louisiana parish and city possesses records for the nineteenth and in some cases for the eighteenth century that are similar in kind to those described in these essays. Taken together with manuscript census returns, the local records offer an excellent opportunity for authoritative social and demographic histories of Louisiana's cities and parishes. One study proposed along these lines and recently funded by the National Endowment for the Humanities will be described below.

Other recent studies collect, compile, and broadly analyze series of data. Such works, while not new, may be partly inspired by modern quantification research. These compilations of data, particularly if new series of data are being brought together, represent useful and desirable labor. Unfortunately, many of the recent studies have been based merely upon arranging statewide or parish data that are easily available from federal census returns. Normally these studies do not add additional statistical tests to the data they have gathered. Examples of the genre of studies that essentially only arrange available data are three studies by Derek L. A. Hackett, in *Louisiana Studies*: "Vote Early! Beware of Fraud! A Note on Voter Turnout in Presidential and Gubernatorial Elections in Louisiana, 1829-1844," 14 (Summer 1975), "Slavery, Ethnicity, and Sugar: An Analysis of Voting

Behaviour in Louisiana, 1828-1844," 13 (Summer 1974), and "The Social Structure of Jacksonian Louisiana," 12 (Spring 1973). Of a similar nature is Charles Shanalruch, "The Louisiana Immigration Movement, 1841-1907: An Analysis of Efforts and Attitudes and Opportunities," *Louisiana History*, 18 (Spring 1977). Basing his work upon parish census data for 1880 to 1910, Shanalruch does little to analyze or manipulate the data. These studies are valuable, but they suffer from one of the common pitfalls of present quantitative research, namely, too much data and too little verbal analysis and interpretation. Joseph G. Tregle, Jr., "Another Look at Shugg's Louisiana," *Louisiana History*, 17 (Summer 1976) likewise uses global census data for parishes to suggest that certain assumptions by Shugg of the sociocultural characteristics of antebellum Louisiana should be questioned. Tregle does not claim to refute Shugg definitively but rather to point out weaknesses and suggest alternative directions. One of the directions he points to for a model of technique and methodology for studying nineteenth-century Louisiana is Gavin Wright's essay, "Economic Democracy and the Concentration of Agricultural Wealth in the Cotton South, 1850-1860," *Agricultural History*, 14 (January 1970).

Under grants from the National Endowment for the Humanities, Professors John Cameron and Judith Gentry have been involved in an ambitious five-year, computer-assisted research project. Using parish and church records and federal manuscript census reports, they have investigated a host of questions, including but not restricted to elites, kinship patterns, rural-urban tensions, prices, fecundity, morbidity, wealth, family, and slavery. This study promises great value and utility both in terms of the depth of study and because of its potential as a model for other researchers and other regions of Louisiana. Cameron and Gentry have presented one paper, which was on eighteenth-century slavery in Acadiana. Ultimately, Professors Cameron and Gentry propose to write a social, economic, and demographic history of the French Acadiana region in Louisiana from 1765 until 1865.

In seeking current models for explanations, techniques, or stimulation with regard to one's own research, various other essays or collections of essays can serve as starting points. Several that treat ethnocultural and political history as well as the relationship between ethnocultural and political history deserve mention. This field of quantitative research is particularly suited to Louisiana, with its demographic divisions between an urbanized, Catholic, French-influenced south and an agricultural, rural, Protestant, Anglo-Saxon north. Suggestions for possible research topics and models in ethnocultural political history can be found in Robert P. Swierenga, "Ethnocultural Political Analysis: A New Approach to American Ethnic Studies," *Journal of American Studies*, 5 (April 1971); Paul Kleppner, "Beyond the 'New Political History': A Review Essay," *Historical Methods Newsletter*, 6 (December 1972); Samuel T. McSeveney,

"Ethnic Groups, Ethnic Conflicts, and Recent Quantitative Research in American Political History," *International Migration Review*, 17 (Spring 1973); and Matthew J. Schott, "Class Conflict in Louisiana Voting Since 1877: Some New Perspectives," *Louisiana History*, 12 (Spring 1971).

Very early, the interested investigator or layman should examine Robert P. Swierenga's excellent review article, "Computers and American History: The Impact of the 'New' Generation," *Journal of American History*, 60 (March 1974), which surveys recent writings on the methodology and summarizes the major research writings and main trends in quantitative investigations. Swierenga's essay describes various possible models to guide the prospective researcher's own projects and bibliographical citations of recent quantification studies to guide the lay historian. Swierenga's earlier work, *Quantification in American History: Theory and Research* (New York, 1971), introduces investigators to samples of quantitative research as practiced in the 1960s as well as an excellent bibliography of prior quantitative research. Swierenga wrote a brief but informative introductory essay and then divided his selected essays and bibliography into six categories— "General: Method and Theory," "Content Analysis," "Legislative and Judicial Behavior," "Popular Voting Behavior," "Economic History," and "Social and Demographic History"—which should prove useful to both novice and experienced historian interested in computer-assisted research. Excellent models of research from other states may guide Louisiana historians. For example, Stephen Thernstrom's *The Other Bostonians: Poverty and Progress in the American Metropolis, 1880-1970* (Cambridge, 1973), and Allan G. Bogue's *From Prairie to Corn Belt: Farming on the Illinois and Iowa Prairies in the Nineteenth Century* (Chicago, 1963) could serve as guides for urban-social history or rural-agricultural history.

Another volume that reflects the variety of approaches to state and local history currently being used in computer-assisted research is David C. Klingamen and Richard E. Veddes, eds., *Essays in Nineteenth Century Economic History: The Old Northwest* (Athens, Ohio, 1975). In addition to the research review essays by Swierenga, Kleppner, and McSeveney, Louisiana historians interested in considering the application of quantification techniques should consult one of the three standard introductory volumes described below. These guides can serve as an initiation into quantification theory, methodology, and historiography.

The sources available to Louisiana historians are numerous and varied. Moreover, some Northern data archives offer useful segments of Louisiana data on tape, available to any researcher merely for the price of a tape and postage. By far the most significant data archive is the Inter-University Consortium for Political Research (ICPR), University of Michigan, Ann Arbor, which not only serves as a repository for raw data deposited by researchers after they have completed their investigation but has also undertaken large-scale programs to reduce blocks of data to machine-readable form on tapes available to researchers.

For example, the ICPR contains census data by county-parish and/or state from 1790 to 1970, election statistics by candidate's name since 1824, and governmental data by county/parish since 1824, referenda and primary election data since the mid-nineteenth century, and the partisan division of state governments since 1834. The ICPR also possesses farm real estate values by parish since 1850 and other socioeconomic public policy and political data by state since 1890. A letter to either the ICPR or the Social Science Data Archive (SSDA), University of Iowa, a smaller but nevertheless significant archive for national machine-readable data, will elicit a response indicating the full scope of their holdings relative to Louisiana. As an additional valuable service, the ICPR and the SSDA often can supply copies of programs used by researchers in analyzing data donated and stored in their archives. In sum, the data archives present the potential researcher with large bodies of readily usable, valuable data at low cost, vastly easing the beginning quantifier's introduction to computerized research.

Another archival center for quantitative data is the Machine-Readable Archives Division of the National Archives. This center's holdings can be examined in the recently published second edition of the *Catalog of Machine-Readable Records in the National Archives of the United States* (Washington, D.C., 1977). Of course, most of the material in this archival center relates to the post-World War II period, and often to the last twenty years. Thus, at present this archive does not offer major data holdings for the study of Louisiana, but it may well become a major research source center within the next several decades.

Very often the established historian, his professional training behind him, feels reluctant to undertake a time-consuming, tedious learning process in an area for which he feels neither equipped—since it is too mathematical and scientific—nor inclined—because of his humanities proclivity. Yet, many historians probably have considered the possibility of undertaking some quantitative research. Some would experiment with the methodology if they were convinced that with relative ease they could acquire the necessary fundamental knowledge, the terminology, the tests, and their potential applications. They need no longer feel helpless or hesitant. Recently three very instructive books have been published, certainly soon to be followed by others, that inform and direct the neophyte quantifier. Two of these new guides will also be useful to secondary school teachers and lay historians who desire only to obtain the ability to read critically quantification scholarship.

Edward Shorter's *The Historian and the Computer: A Practical Guide* (Englewood Cliffs, N.J., 1971) is the simplest, most readable of the three. Since Shorter's personal research interest lies in social history, his book emphasizes statistical tests and examples from this field, particularly useful for potential quantifiers of social history. Structured as a step-by-step guide for undertaking a research project—from conceiving the problem in statistical terms and designing the codebook to selecting and analyzing the appropriate test statistics—Shorter's work is "a practical guide" to statistical historical research. Although more readily suited to social historians, it should be easily understandable to even the most nonmathematically inclined investigator. Given its brevity and uncomplicated presentation, this book offers an excellent introduction to critical comprehension of computer research.

Roderick Floud, *An Introduction to Quantitative Methods for Historians* (Princeton, N.J., 1973) is more systematically organized in presentation of the basic statistical terms and assumptions and applications of test statistics. Whereas Shorter emphasizes the "how-to-do-it" aspects of the statistical technique, Floud clearly elaborates the theoretical structure of statistics. Selecting his examples from various fields of historical research, Floud never loses sight of his goal: to teach the rule or principle, not the specific application. Nevertheless, Floud strives to offer the neophyte all the essential practical guidance necessary to undertake his own research project. In sum, Floud's book is a bit more theoretically and less practically oriented than Shorter's. Still it is well written, easily understood, and an excellent brief introduction to statistics for historians. Although the text is more sophisticated than Shorter's, Floud's *Introduction* should serve well both schoolteachers and lay historians.

Charles Dollar and Richard Jensen have written an excellent advanced study, *Historian's Guide to Statistics: Quantitative Analysis and Historical Research* (New York, 1971). Perhaps too advanced for the majority of beginners, it is more suited for use as the interested historian's second book on computer research. Dollar and Jensen present the same basic statistical concepts as Shorter and Floud, but more summarily. Then they proceed to statistical tests and applications that are more complex than those proposed and explained by either Shorter or Floud. Hence, this book will not function as a convenient primer for most lay historians.

Nevertheless, the Dollar-Jensen book has several strengths. In fact, the assets of these three books are complementary, and collectively they provide the prospective investigator with commentary on any aspect of quantitative research procedure. Most historical quantitative projects involve a historiographical reference to what has and is being done in the area under study, the location and identification of data sources, a research design (including construction of a code book), the collection and processing of data, the application of statistical tests, and the interpretation of the test results. The three guides under review treat all these aspects of quantitative research, but each is especially strong in one or more aspects. Dollar and Jensen offer a sixty-three-page bibliographical guide to source materials for numerical data, statistical manuals, and data archives as well as articles and books reflecting quantitative research results. Shorter discusses constructing a code book and coding practices, that is, gathering the data, in great detail. Dollar and Jensen best describe the machinery and technology of data processing. Floud is easily the most thorough guide to the fundamental terms, assumptions, and statistical tests—simple descriptive statistics, analysis of time series, correlation and regression—whereas Dollar and Jensen effectively present the more complex statistical applications such as Gutman scaling, content analysis, and cluster analysis. Floud's presentation emphasizes the limits of its applicability to the kinds of data with which historians normally work. He carefully prepares his reader to recognize the limits to which chosen test statistics can be used in analysis, a necessary skill for the person concerned with acquiring a critical reading ability.

One final reason that might induce most Louisiana high school or college teachers to add one or more of these titles to their urgent reading list is that research work increasingly relies, at least in part, upon application of statistical methods. Passing these findings on to high school and undergraduate students will be an integral part of every teacher's task when fulfilling the professional duty to update. More importantly, Louisiana historians involved in undergraduate and graduate education have an additional obligation to offer their students not just the best introduction, guidance, and training of which they are capable but to prepare their students to teach in Louisiana's schools and colleges in the 1980s and 1990s. Increasingly future teachers will require at least the ability to read critically and comprehend statistical research, if not the ability to utilize the methodology. Edward Shorter, Roderick Floud, and Charles Dollar and Richard Jensen have made it possible for any interested historian to acquire a comprehension of quantitative methodology. It is hoped that their efforts will enable the next generation to acquire a higher level of expertise.

PART TWO
ARCHIVES AND SOURCES

12
SOURCES FOR SPANISH LOUISIANA

GILBERT C. DIN

THE BEST HISTORY is based on primary documents, and the Spanish archives are rich in original documents on Spain's presence in Louisiana. These documents have been exploited in part, and, consequently, much remains to be learned about the Spaniards in the Mississippi Valley from 1766 to 1803. The first Louisiana historian to write a history based on Spanish documentation was Charles Gayarré in his monumental, four-volume *History of Louisiana* (New Orleans, vols. 1-3, 1854; vol. 4, 1866). He obtained copies of documents from Spain, which he used in his second and third volumes. After Gayarré, however, several decades passed before writers of Louisiana history again employed Spanish documents. Then a torrent of historical works appeared. This was due in large part to Professor Herbert E. Bolton, the "Moses of the Spanish borderlands," who encouraged research on the Spanish period of American history at the University of California. From his seminars emerged such historians as John W. Caughey, Abraham P. Nasatir, Lawrence Kinnaird, and several more who first used the Spanish documents in the Bancroft Library at Berkeley before journeying to Spain to explore the archives. From the 1920s greater numbers of graduate students and professors mined the Spanish archives for Ph.D. dissertations, articles, and monographic studies about Spain's stay in the Mississippi Valley. Their research has greatly increased our knowledge of this area two hundred years ago, but enormous quantities of unused documents remain.

A Spaniard once told me that his people were *papeleros*—great users of paper, bureaucrats buried in their own paperwork. The fact that, in governing Louisiana and their other New World colonies, Spaniards required that virtually everything be committed to writing has been a blessing to the historian, who depends on the written word. Not only did the Spaniards write down almost everything of an official nature (and some things not official), but often they sent several copies across the hazardous Atlantic. Governors in New Orleans also retained a copy of any document dispatched to the captain general in Havana or to Spain. The captain general made yet another copy before remitting his dispatches to Spain. Today the original document, as well as most, if not all, of the copies, can be found in the Spanish archives. Important, too, for historians of a later day is that Spanish authorities generally used high-quality paper for their dispatches. Today the documents often appear remarkably fresh even after two hundred years. A number of the documents, however, have not withstood the test of time. The ink has eaten through the paper, and the documents are difficult or impossible to read. Handling them is also risky as they tear easily. Fortunately, these manuscripts are in the minority, and the important reports from top officials are not among them. Also, for those knowing modern Spanish, eighteenth-century Spanish vocabulary and handwriting are easily mastered. Vocabulary has not changed radically in two centuries, and scribes of that era wrote in a fairly uniform style that makes reading these documents easy—for the most part.

As for research topics, there remains a vast assortment, despite the fact that many studies have been published or have appeared as dissertations in recent decades. General topics awaiting the researcher today are still some of the old topics because better and fuller studies are needed based on Spanish archival holdings. These are biographies of governors or studies of their administration (Ulloa, Unzaga, Gálvez, Miró, Carondelet, Casa Calvo, Salcedo) as well as biographies of other government officials such as Juan Ventura Morales, Gilberto Guillemart, Bishop Luis Peñalver, Colonel Pedro Piernas, and numerous other army officers, post commandants, bureaucrats, and distinguished citizens. Other topics include many aspects of Spain's relations with Indian nations in friendship, alliance, and trade. The military in Louisiana has only been lightly touched on, although documentation of this nature is voluminous. Certain aspects of trade and commerce have been worked, but no thorough studies have yet emerged on trade with Havana, France, Spain, and the United States or its western settlements. Agriculture is another fertile topic for research for such crops as tobacco, sugar cane, cotton, hemp and flax, and rice. Land ownership has also received little attention. The study of slavery and blacks has been all but ignored in Spanish Louisiana but offers great possibilities. Other local topics include customs, classes, and religious affairs.

In a nutshell, numerous topics remain that can be seen immediately from consulting the archival catalogs. Once the topic has been selected, the investigator must search out the documents, blow away the dust, and breathe life into them again. Without doubt, many pleasant surprises await the patient investigator who diligently wades through scores of *legajos* (the bundles in which the documents are stored) and sniffs out the manuscripts needed to restore the past. Because documents were often stored haphazardly in the *legajos*, with little relationship as to time and subject, research often resembles putting together a gigantic jigsaw puzzle. Patience is a prime virtue for the archival worker.

A word of caution for the researcher who goes to Spain. Summer is usually not the best time to be there because archives are either on a half-day schedule or closed altogether. At other times of the year, Christmas or Holy Week, they tend to close for several days or longer. Also the siesta prevents one from working all day since the archives are closed for about three hours in the early afternoon. However, the main archives permit the microfilming of documents and generally do a good job. In addition to the guides and catalogs to the archives listed below, each archive has manuscript guides that are also useful and should be consulted.

Several general guides should be noted: Dirección General de Archivos y Bibliotecas, *Guía de fuentes para la historia de Iberoamérica conservadas en España*, 2 vols. (Madrid, 1966-1968); *Guía histórica y descriptiva de los archivos, bibliotecas y museos de España* (Madrid, 1921); Jack D. L. Holmes, *A Guide to Spanish Louisiana, 1762-1806* (New Orleans, 1970), and "Maps, Plans and Charts in Spanish and Cuban Archives: A Checklist," *Louisiana Studies*, 2 (Winter 1963); Ministerio de Educación Nacional, *Guía de los archivos de Madrid* (Madrid, 1952); and William R. Shepherd, *Guide to the Materials for the History of the United States in Spanish Archives* (1907; reprint ed., New York, 1965).

Spain's Office of Cultural Relations of the Ministry of Foreign Affairs is publishing a twelve-volume series, *Documentos relativos a la independencia de Norteamérica en los archivos españoles*. Several of these volumes are now available. These volumes catalog the holdings of the principal Spanish archives in Seville, Madrid, and Simancas that relate to the American Revolution. Several monographic studies by Spanish scholars will also be a part of the series.

There are three principal locations in Spain for documents bearing on the history of Louisiana: the Archivo General de Simancas (AGS) near Valladolid in north-central Spain; the city of Madrid, which has a number of research centers, the Archivo Histórico Nacional (AHN) being the most important; and Seville with the Archivo General de Indias (AGI). They shall be dealt with in order from north to south. By far the most important archive is the AGI at Seville, and it is possible, in some instances, to bypass the other archives and consult only it. But for many topics it is best to visit the other archives, particularly the Archivo Histórico Nacional in Madrid.

Permission is required in order to use the archives, but it is not difficult to obtain. Once permission has been granted to use one national archive, a *tarjeta de investigador* is issued that is also good at the other national archives. However, this card does not open the door to all repositories. In some cases a letter of introduction from the U.S. embassy's cultural attaché is required. This is a mere formality and regularly done. Also small photographs are usually required in obtaining entrance to the archives. Therefore it is useful to have a dozen or so made up in advance if several archives are to be consulted.

Of the major archives, the Archivo General de Simancas is the most difficult to reach and the one often omitted by researches. The archive is a medieval castle in the village of Simancas, about seven miles west of Valladolid. Most researchers today stay in Valladolid and ride out to Simancas on the bus that takes the Spanish staff to work at the archive in the morning. The AGS is primarily important for Spanish history and has about 80,000 *legajos*, totaling some 33 million documents. In the eighteenth century most of the colonial documents were sent to Seville, but a number of documents dealing with Louisiana are still there. They are mostly of a military nature.

In the section of Guerra Moderna, *legajos* 6,799 to 7,327, are found documents pertaining to the Spanish colonies, including Louisiana. The materials deal with the regular army, the militia, service records of military personnel, fortifications, the military operations of Bernardo de Gálvez from 1779 to 1784, and sundry other military activities. There are also documents on American schemes in the Mississippi Valley in the 1780s, a proposal to make Louisiana and the Floridas into a captaincy-general, the American Revolution, Southern Indians, trade relations with the Americans, Kentucky, diplomatic affairs between Spain and the United States, and invasion scares extending from 1790 to 1802. Of these documents, probably the most original—those not having copies elsewhere—are those of military importance. But no study should be carried out based solely on AGS documentation.

The important guides to Simancas are Angel de la Plaza, *Archivo General de Simancas, guía del investigador* (Valladolid, 1962); and Patronato Nacional de Archivos Históricos, *Hojas de servicios de América*, vol. 22: *Catálogo del Archivo de Simancas, Secretaría de Guerra (siglo XVIII)* (Valladolid, 1958). Two reels of microfilm of service records from Louisiana and Florida, 1787 to 1797, for both the regular army and militia units, from *legajos* 7,291 and 7,292, are available for purchase from the Servicio Nacional de Microfilm (Publication no. 12) at the Centro Nacional de Microfilm, Calle Serrano 115, Madrid.

The Archivo Histórico Nacional of Madrid was started in the mid-nineteenth century to house the documents from suppressed monasteries. It was located in the Real Academia de la Historia until 1896, when it was moved to the Biblioteca Nacional. Over the years it has received state papers of various councils of government, the Inquisition, military and religious orders, extinct universities, Jesuit missions abroad, and nineteenth-century colonies. Also present is the "Cedulario Indico," forty-one volumes of copies of royal decrees from the sixteenth to the nineteenth centuries.

For the last twenty years the AHN has been housed at a modern facility at Calle Serrano 115, Madrid. For the study of Louisiana history, the most important section is Estado, which in 1921 contained 8,602 *legajos*. A number of these *legajos*, 3,882 to 3,902, deal with Spain's relations with the United States over the Mississippi Valley and West Florida. The documents were catalogued by Miguel Gómez del Campillo in his *Relaciones diplomaticas* (see below). These documents are available for purchase on microfilm in thirty-three reels from the Centro Nacional de Microfilm. These nearly 10,000 documents contain a wealth of information on governors' reports, royal orders, court instructions, immigration, Indians, military defenses, conspiracies, adventurers (Clark, Wilkinson, Bowles, O'Fallon, Gênet), the fur trade, diplomatic relations with the United States, Spain's reaction to the American Revolution, and much more. The collection is skimpy until 1777 and increases significantly after 1790. Although there is little on Louisiana after 1808, the documentation on East and West Florida continues in other *legajos* in Estado.

Other items of interest for the Louisiana researcher are the *residencias* of the Louisiana governors and the trial records of the French Creole leaders of the 1768 revolt; they are in Consejos de Indias. Also of interest are the minutes of the Suprema Junta de Estado and Supremo Consejo de Estado, the highest decision-making bodies in Spain. Those documents dealing with Louisiana are in Estado, *legajos* 917 to 927. No researcher should overlook the AHN for a topic after 1783.

There are several important guides for the AHN: Miguel Gómez del Campillo, *Relaciones diplomaticas entre España y los Estados Unidos*, 2 vols. (Madrid, 1944-1946); Angel Gonzalez Palencia, *Extracto del catálogo de los documentos del Consejo de Indias conservados en la sección de Consejos del Archivo Histórico Nacional* (Madrid, 1920); and Abraham P. Nasatir and Ernest R. Liljegren, "Materials Relating to the History of the Mississippi Valley, from the Minutes of the Supreme Councils of State, 1787-1797," *Louisiana Historical Quarterly*, 21 (January 1938).

Although the Biblioteca Nacional in Madrid does not contain a significant number of documents on Louisiana in its Sección de Manuscritos, it is worth consulting nevertheless. Of primary interest are three volumes called "Documentos de la Luisiana" (ms. 19,246-19,248). These documents are originals or authentic copies, and some of these several hundred manuscripts do not have copies elsewhere. Of peripheral interest are two volumes of manuscript documents on Spanish Florida (ms. 19,508-19,509) for the period 1709 to 1817. The repository also has a copy of Francisco Bouligny's "Memoir," dated August 16, 1776 (ms. 19,265), which is missing a number of pages, however. A few additional documents relating to Louisiana are also present scattered throughout the manuscript collection. The reader is directed to two guides for this repository: Julian Paz, *Catálogo de manuscritos de América existentes en la Biblioteca Nacional* (Madrid, 1933), and Pedro Roca, *Catálogo de los documentos que pertenecieron a D. Pascual Gayangos, existentes hoy en la Biblioteca Nacional* (Madrid, 1904).

The library of the Palacio de Oriente in Madrid is located near the center of the city and contains a few manuscripts of interest to Louisiana in Manuscritos de América, Miscelenea de Ayala. For its holdings consult Jesús Domínguez Bordona, *Catálogo de la Biblioteca de Palacio: Manuscritos de América*, vol. 9 (Madrid, 1935).

The Royal Academy of History is located in an older part of Madrid, Calle Leon, in an eighteenth-century building. Dark, overcrowded, and musty, it is open only from 3:30 to 7:30 P.M. and closed in summer. It contains very little pertinent to Spanish Louisiana. It does, however, have an abundance of royal decrees on the Spanish colonies of America. Of peripheral interest, too, is the Colección Muñoz for documents on colonial Spanish America. The guide for these manuscripts is the *Catálogo de la colección de Don Juan Bautista Muñoz*, 3 vols. (Madrid, 1954-1956). For the rest of the manuscripts, consult the manuscript catalog prepared by Antonio Rodríguez Villa at the Real Academia.

Several military centers in Madrid and one in nearby Segovia also conserve documents on Spain's presence in the Mississippi Valley. The Servicio Histórico Militar, at Mártires de Alcalá 9, has a few of them among its holdings of over 12,000 manuscripts and over 10,000 maps and plans. Consult the *Catálogo de la Biblioteca Central Militar*, pt. 1: *Documentos*, and pt. 2: *Mapas y planos* (Madrid, 1945), issued by the Archivo del Servicio Histórico Militar. A more convenient guide is Eric Beerman, "A Check-List of Louisiana Documents in the 'Servicio Histórico Militar' in Madrid," *Louisiana History,* 19 (Spring 1978). He lists twenty-three entries, each containing a number of documents. These manuscripts deal mainly with military plans, Louisiana's boundary in 1804, and the retrocession of Louisiana to France. Most of the documents date in the 1804-1805 period.

The Museo Naval of Madrid is located at the Ministerio de la Marina, Montalban 2, which also has a museum of Spanish ships. Although the manuscript section of the Museo Naval does not have many documents on Spanish Louisiana, it does have some on naval matters. It was here, for example, that Jack D. L. Holmes found the papers of José de Evia's coastal reconnaissance of the Mexican Gulf Coast (Florida to Texas) from 1783 to 1796, which he published in Spain in 1968. One may consult guides available in the research room at the Museo Naval.

The Archivo General Militar is located in Segovia, about a two-hour train ride from Madrid, in the castle that dominates the town. In this old fortress Isabel I had herself proclaimed queen of Castile in 1474. Today it is used by the Corps of Army Engineers, but it also stores military service records of the eighteenth and nineteenth centuries. Of particular interest for Spanish Louisiana are the files of the officers who served in the army and navy in Louisiana, which provide biographical information. These files are found in the Personal section. A guide to the files was published by Enrique de Ocerín, *Indice de los expedientes matrimoniales de militares y marinos que se conservan en el Archivo General Militar*, vol. 2 (Madrid, 1959). Permission to consult the AGM must be obtained in advance in Madrid from the subsecretary of the army, at the Ministry of the Army.

Archivo del Ministerio de Asuntos Exteriores at Madrid, which contains Spain's diplomatic papers with other nations largely from the mid-nineteenth century, is not very valuable for Spanish Louisiana. The few documents on this subject treat Louisiana before it became a Spanish possession and the problems Spain had establishing a boundary between Texas and Louisiana after 1804. The only guide available for the AMAE is the *Guía de los Archivos de Madrid* (Madrid, 1952), pp. 94-108.

By far the most important collection of documents for the history of Spanish Louisiana is stored at the world-famous Archivo General de Indias in Seville, which is vital for the entire history of colonial Spanish America. It began largely through the efforts of Juan Bautista Muñoz, an annalist, and José de Gálvez, minister of the Indies (1776-1787) and uncle of Louisiana's Governor Bernardo de Gálvez, who saw the need for having a single repository for papers relating to the Indies. The first documents came from the AGS in 1785, when 253 boxes packed into 24 carts left Simancas for Seville. From the start the manuscripts were housed in the Casa Lonja, a sixteenth-century edifice. Other papers came later from the House of Trade, the AMAE, and other government agencies. In the period 1888-1889, the Papeles Procedentes de Cuba (Papers from Cuba) were added. These last documents consisted of 2,350 *legajos* on Louisiana, the Floridas, and a few other places. Eight *legajos* were left behind in Cuba, where they are today. (They are described in Luis Marino Perez, *Guide to the Materials for American History in Cuban Archives* [Washington, D.C., 1907]. The Cuban archives also have other documents on Louisiana.)

The Papeles de Cuba (PC) on Louisiana comprise over 500 *legajos* and constitute the most important single collection of documents on Spanish Louisiana with the most varied assortment of topics. Within these *legajos* can be found reports of governors, intendants, post commandants, and sundry other officials and agencies in Louisiana: accounting offices, hospital records, warehouse ledgers, military reports and statements, diaries, petitions, criminal and civil court records, documents on religious affairs, relations with the United States, censuses, information on various individuals and officials, agriculture, fur trade, adventurers, to name only some. The topics are too numerous to mention here. Unfortunately, the PC documents are not conveniently catalogued, nor are they arranged in order within the *legajos*. The *legajos* range in size from one to several books or ledgers to as many as 2,000 letters. The larger *legajos* require considerable time to sort through carefully. The documentation was too extensive to be fully detailed by Roscoe Hill in his *Descriptive Catalogue* (listed below); nevertheless, Hill's remains the best guide to the massive Louisiana documentation in PC.

Also in the AGI, in section 5, Audiencia de Santo Domingo, are some 148 *legajos*, numbering from 2,528 to 2,689, consisting of 140,000 pages of additional documentation on Louisiana. In the 1960s these documents were arranged in a coherent order within the *legajos* and catalogued by Peña and others (see below). Although smaller in size than PC, the documentation in Santo Domingo (SD) is still quite important and should be consulted along with the PC manuscripts. Topics, among others, in the SD papers are commerce and smuggling, military affairs and service records, the Louisiana militia, religious affairs, immigration, accounting and treasury records, relations with the United States, correspondence of the governors, captains general of Cuba, and other officials, slavery and blacks, and agriculture. Although some of the same letters can be found elsewhere (PC, AHN, and AGS), the SD papers relating to Spanish Louisiana should not be overlooked.

Besides PC and SD, additional documents on Louisiana can be found in other places of the AGI. In section 9, *legajos* 1-19 deal with the Audiencia of Santo Domingo (Cuba, Puerto Rico, Louisiana, and Florida) in the period from 1729 to 1860. Moreover, in the same section, the Audiencias of Mexico and Guadalajara have items dealing with Texas and the Louisiana frontier. Also section 5: Audiencias e indiferente (Courts and Miscellaneous) and section 10: Papeles del Ministerio de Ultramar (Papers of the Overseas Ministry) have more manuscripts. No doubt scattered through some of the other sections of the AGI one can find additional items relating to Spanish Louisiana.

There are, relative to other Spanish archives, more useful guides to the AGI, among them, Cristobal Bermudez Plata, *Catálogo de documentos de la sección novena del Archivo General de Indias*, vol. 1, series 1a and 2a: *Santo Domingo, Cuba, Puerto Rico, Luisiana, Florida y Mexico* (Seville, 1949); José María de la Peña y Cámera et al., *Catálogo de documentos del Archivo General de Indias, Sección V. Gobierno. Audiencia de Santo Domingo sobre la época española de Luisiana*, 2 vols. (Seville, 1968); José de la Peña y Cámera, *Archivo General de Indias de Sevilla. Guía del visitante* (Seville, 1958); and Roscoe R. Hill, *Descriptive Catalogue of the Documents Relating to the History of the United States in the Papeles Procedentes de Cuba Deposited in the Archivo General de Indias at Seville* (1916; reprint ed., New York, 1965).

Complete collections of documents from the Spanish archives in the United States are rare, although efforts to increase holdings through microfilm have been increasing in the last few years. The Spanish government has helped considerably by allowing the microfilming of the entire section 5, SD, of the AGI for Loyola University of New Orleans and offering for sale the documents from the AHN, Estado, *legajos* 3,882-3,902, described by Paz (see above). In addition, a number of libraries in Louisiana and elsewhere have scattered collections of documents, but they are incomplete or cover principally one area or individual. Although these latter collections are useful, in most instances they do not replace the need to refer to the Spanish archives. Inasmuch as American libraries are buying or engaging in microfilm projects, the following information is offered as a guide that is by no means complete.

Loyola University of New Orleans has the complete set of documents on microfilm from the AGI, SD (Sección V. Gobierno). Although copies of the documents cannot be made in New Orleans, they can be ordered from Seville. For this the catalog by Peña and others is very useful. Loyola University also intends to continue its cooperation with Spanish archivists for the cataloguing of documents relating to Spanish Louisiana.

The University of Southwestern Louisiana has a project to microfilm all the materials on the Acadians in the AGI, PC, and to obtain a complete set of commandant reports. USL would like to extend its project to microfilm all the documentation in the AGI on Spanish Louisiana.

The Howard-Tilton Library of Tulane University and Louisiana State University (Baton Rouge) both have extensive collections of documents from the Spanish period that are not from the Spanish archives; however, LSU has obtained a number of assorted documents from Spain on microfilm or as photostats or photocopies. Located at both institutions are the Dispatches of the Spanish Governors of Louisiana 1766-1792, which were translated by a WPA project. For fuller treatment of the holdings of both institutions, see Connie G. Griffith, "Collections in the Manuscript Section of the Howard-Tilton Memorial Library, Tulane University," *Louisiana History*, 1 (Fall 1960), 320-27; and Brian E. Coutts, "An Inventory of Sources in the Department of Archives and Manuscripts, Louisiana State University, for the History of Spanish Louisiana and Spanish West Florida," *Louisiana History*, 19 (Spring 1978): 213-50. Although not very satisfactory, see also Stanley Clisby Arthur, *Index to the Dispatches of the Spanish Governors of Louisiana 1766-1792* (New Orleans, 1975).

The Bancroft Library at the University of California, Berkeley, has a Louisiana Collection of documents that never made it from Cuba to Spain. They are Spanish originals or authentic copies acquired in Havana in the late nineteenth century. Many of these documents were published as volumes 2-4 of the *Annual Report* of the American Historical Association for 1945: Lawrence Kinnaird, ed., *Spain in the Mississippi Valley, 1765-1794*, 3 pts. (Washington, D.C., 1949). The documents after 1794, however, were not published. The Bancroft also has other transcripts of documents from the Spanish archives and is heir to Professor A. P. Nasatir's personal collection of about 200,000 pages of documents, which come mainly from the AGI, PC, and which deal extensively with upper Louisiana but also include Natchitoches.

The McClung Collection, Lawson McGhee Library, Knoxville, Tennessee, has eighteen boxes of photostats and typescripts of materials on the Old Southwest, which were assembled by A. P. Whitaker in the 1920s from the AGI and AHN. Beginning in 1937, Duvon C. Corbitt has been translating and publishing them in "Papers from Spanish Archives Relating to Tennessee and the Old Southwest," in *Publications* of the East Tennessee Historical Society.

The Mississippi Valley Collection at the John Brister Library, Memphis State University, contains 277 reels of microfilm of documents from the AGI, PC; 4 reels from the AHN, Consejo de Indias on the Louisiana governors; 16 reels from the AGS, Guerra Moderna, on the military; and many more reels from the New Mexico State Archives, Bexar Archives, and the Archivo General de la Nación (Mexico City), which contain valuable information on Louisiana.

The Missouri Historical Society, Saint Louis, is rich in Spanish documents, particularly about the people of Saint Louis, the fur trade, and Indians. Louis Houck deposited many of his transcripts from the AGI, PC, *legajos* 2,357-13,375, here, although many of the documents were published in his *Spanish Regime in Missouri*, 2 vols. (Saint Louis, 1909).

The Library of Congress has an extensive collection of transcripts and microfilm on Spanish Louisiana. Many of these documents were collected by Roscoe R. Hill at the time he was cataloguing the AGI, PC, sixty years ago. Since then other collections of documents, copies, and microfilm have been deposited there. For more information on the Library of Congress, consult *Information Bulletin*, 26 (February 1967) and the issues of (Library of Congress) *News from the Center*, from its inception in 1967, which list major microfilming projects in foreign manuscript collections and other important information on manuscript holdings in the United States.

The Department of Archives and History, Jackson, Mississippi, has many documents from the AGI, PC, *legajos* 2,351-2,356, which are available on microfilm. Although largely of Natchez and the Mississippi region of West Florida, the documents also contain much for Louisiana history. They are listed in the now outdated James Alexander Robertson, *List of Documents in Spanish Archives Relating to the History of the United States, Which Have Been Printed or of which Transcripts Are Preserved in American Libraries* (Washington, D.C., 1910; reprinted).

In addition to those mentioned, other libraries, particularly in the Southeast, have documents from the Spanish archives. Consult the following articles and books for suggestions and hints for research on the Spanish period of Louisiana history: V. L. Bedsole, "Collections in the Department of Archives and Manuscripts, Louisiana State University," *Louisiana*

History, 1 (Fall 1960); Ernest J. Burrus, S.J., "An Introduction to Bibliographical Tools in Spanish Archives and Manuscript Collections Relating to Hispanic America," *Hispanic American Historical Review*, 35 (November 1955); William S. Coker and Jack D. L. Holmes, "Sources for the History of the Spanish Borderlands," *Florida Historical Quarterly*, 49 (April 1971); Philip M. Hamer, ed., *A Guide to Archives and Manuscripts in the United States* (New Haven, Ct., 1961); A. Otis Hébert, Jr., "Resources in Louisiana Depositories for the Study of Spanish Activities in Louisiana," *The Spanish in the Mississippi Valley, 1762-1804* ed. John Francis McDermott (Urbana, Ill., 1974); Jack D. L. Holmes, "Interpretations and Trends in the Study of the Spanish Borderlands: The Old Southwest," *Southwestern Historical Quarterly*, 74 (April 1971); "Research Opportunities in the Spanish Borderlands: Louisiana and the Old Southwest," *Louisiana Studies*, 1 (Winter 1962); "Research in the Spanish Borderlands in Louisiana," *Latin American Research Review*, 17 (Summer 1972); and William Stetson Merrill, "Transcripts from the Spanish Archives at the Newberry Library, Chicago," *Illinois Catholic Historical Review*, 2 (1919).

Almost all of the Spanish repositories noted above vary their reading room hours according to the season of the year. In addition, civil and religious holidays determine days which the archives are open to the public. It is best for the researcher to inquire locally about such matters. Spanish archives do not normally handle mail or telephone requests from researchers. A personal visit to the archive is recommended.

13
THE CARTOGRAPHY OF COLONIAL LOUISIANA

JOSEPH D. CASTLE

THE HISTORICAL CARTOGRAPHY of Louisiana may be divided into three periods: primary, descriptive, and modern. Within each of these periods, various maps clearly illustrate a progressive improvement in cartographical methods and accuracy of detail. The earliest stage of development, the "foundation maps," incorporated knowledge derived from the new discoveries and explorations. A foundation map was so superior to other maps that its representation of a region was copied for a long time. The appearance of such maps was commonly followed by derivative maps produced by imitative and inferior mapmakers. These cartographical copies often exhibited degeneration in accuracy and detail. The influence of a foundation map, however, might linger for a hundred years after new and better maps had corrected its errors. Maps based upon findings of an earlier period frequently persisted long after subsequent discoveries and settlements of a later generation were widely known.

The first period of Louisiana cartography lasted from the time of the earliest maps until the final decade of the sixteenth century. The maps of

I wish to acknowledge the assistance of Robert E. Macdonald, Edward F. Haas, Stephen Webre, and Susan Gibbs Lemann.

this period were based on the reports of early official expeditions, supplemented by information received from individual pilots and adventurers. Usually the product of geographers and mapmakers in Europe who never ventured into the unknown wilderness of the new continent, these early maps attempted to synthesize incomplete, vague, erroneous, and contradictory information. The information supplied the mapmakers was based on crude observations of latitude, dead-reckoning longitude, hand sketches from personal observation, and lists of rivers, bays, and headlands sighted. The resultant maps, artistically filled with pictures of curious animals and geographical extravaganza, were confused, contradictory, and inaccurate. Nonetheless, they are today valuable for their evidence of increasing geographical knowledge. To attempt any modern interpretation of these maps is a fundamentally fallacious procedure. They must be interpreted in the light of the intellectual limitations that dictated their scope. Even then, their value usually lies more in their contribution to our understanding of the expansion of geographical knowledge than in the identification of specific locations.

One map of this early period merits special comment because of its importance in the evolution of the cartography of the Louisiana region. Abraham Ortel, better known by the Latinized form of his name, "Ortelius," published a map of Florida in 1584. It was based on information derived from the Spanish royal cartographer Hieronymo Chiaves and other European sources. Although this map was not as accurate as others, it was the first printed map of the region. It remained the basis for the charts of many continental mapmakers for over a century.

The second cartographical period, the descriptive, extended from the end of the sixteenth to the middle of the eighteenth century. Maps of this period were based upon actual, albeit crude, surveys. Specific details were more plentiful and can usually be identified on modern maps. The place-name nomenclature was that of the Indians, early explorers, and settlers. The delineation, however, was informative rather than accurate. It became more distorted as the area shown extended away from the settlements and depended on the impressions of explorers and Indian traders. The two most important foundation maps in this period were those of Nicolas Sanson d'Abbeville and Guillaume de l'Isle. In 1656, Sanson, who has been called the founder of the French school of geography, published his "Le Nouveau Mexique, et La Floride," which extended from Port Royal on the South Carolina coast westward to California and from northern Mexico through the interior of the continent to Canada and the Great Lakes. The boundary lines separating the colonial possessions were of special interest because of Sanson's official position with the French government as royal geographer. "Floride française" on the map was probably depicted for the first time to designate the Georgia-South Carolina area as part of the French possessions in the New World. This map was a good example of liberal boundary enlargement, a method both French and English official geographers employed to augment the claims of their sovereigns to territory in the New World. First published in Paris as a loose map, it was included in several Sanson atlases. it became a foundation map for the southern region of the United States until the publication of the de l'Isle map in 1718.

Guillaume de l'Isle's "Carte de la Louisiane," published in 1718, was of greater importance and had more impact than Sanson's map. De l'Isle (1675-1726) was one of the foremost European cartographers of his time and became royal geographer to Louis XIV. His chief merit was his application of scientific methods and his careful examination of original sources. Unlike the Amsterdam mapmakers who made their maps for profit and copied errors so often that they became accepted as truth, de l'Isle was continually revising and eliminating errors in light of new scientific information. The de l'Isle map of 1718 was the first modern attempt to trace the route of Fernando de Soto. The path of the de Soto expedition noted by de l'Isle was close to the identifications made by recent investigators. The routes of Alonso de Leon (1689), Saint-Denis (1713-1716), and other western explorers were also traced. The cartography of this map was notable for its employment of new information, its wealth of detail, and the relative accuracy of its depiction of the Mississippi Valley, particularly in the improved detail concerning the lower reaches of the Mississippi River and the other rivers flowing into the Gulf of Mexico. Numerous editions of this map had appeared by the beginning of the nineteenth century. Among the imitations of this map were those by Johann Homann in 1720, Isaak Tirion in 1740, and Antonio Zatta in 1788.

The third, or modern, period of cartography began in the middle of the eighteenth century. Maps of this period were the work of professional surveyors using refined instruments and methods. They were in striking contrast to the detail of the maps that preceded them. One of the best examples of this period was an untitled manuscript map of southern Louisiana done by Juan Pedro Walke (John Peter Walker?) between 1799 and 1803.

Much care was taken in the preparation of this map, and its detail included a number of categories. Settlements were carefully indicated by small squares, Indian villages placed on the map, and the bayou system extensively noted. A large portion of the land to the west of the Mississippi River was carefully shaded to indicate swampland or marsh, and the pine forests and plains were clearly delineated.

Walke's work is a good example of how modern students of cartography use detail to date a map. Because of the abundance of specific detail, the map can be conclusively dated between 1799 and 1803. By 1799, the 31st parallel had been surveyed and recognized by both Spain and the United States as their common boundary, the U.S. territory of Mississippi organized, and Fort Adams established on the east bank of the Mississippi just above the 31st parallel. The cartographer recognized the 31st parallel as "limites de la Floride occidentale," while to the north lay the "Territorio del Misisipi," and "Fuerte americano" was located on the site of Fort Adams. An indication that the map was completed before 1803 is seen by the location of the "Avoyeles" Indians along the Red River. Shortly after the Louisiana Purchase, the Avoyelles Indians were forced from their historic home.

Walke's map lies at the end of a long evolutionary process beginning with the cartography of the years immediately following the discoveries of Columbus and his successors. The first explorations of the Louisiana area came from the southeast under the auspices of the Spanish crown. Ponce de León landed on the coast of Florida in March 1513 and died still believing that Florida was an island. His explorations produced no known maps. The so-called de Soto map, which is the only extant contemporary map to illustrate the extensive explorations of the expedition that Fernando de Soto and his followers made in the years 1539-1543, is an unsigned, undated sketch in the Archivo General de Indias. The entire area covered by de Soto's expedition was given on the manuscript map, which showed the interior as far north as contemporary North Carolina and Tennessee and the coast from the vicinity of South Carolina to Mexico. The rivers along the southern Atlantic coast flowed correctly in a southeasterly direction, and the Appalachian Mountains appear for the first time. This map is interesting because it was probably the first map to show the interior of any part of the present United States. The Ortelius-Chiaves printed map of 1584 was based upon this map and other Spanish sources. The Spanish, however, failed to follow through with these early explorations, and it was left to the French to continue the exploration of the Mississippi Valley. They approached the region from an entirely different direction, north out of Canada.

In 1534, Jacques Cartier sailed for the New World, and the next year he entered the Saint Lawrence estuary, venturing as far as the site of Montreal. Among his protégés was Jean Nicolet, who went west in 1634. Nicolet was the first white man known to have passed through the straits of Mackinac and to have voyaged to Green Bay. Some time between 1654 and 1663, two of the boldest and most successful fur traders, Médard Chovart, sieur des Grosseilliers, and his brother-in-law, Pierre d'Esprit, sieur de Radisson, made two journeys to the west and possibly reached the Mississippi River.

It was not until 1673, however, that Louis Jolliet and Père Jacques Marquette explored the upper Mississippi. Having traveled as far as the confluence of the Mississippi and Arkansas rivers, the explorers calculated from their position that the Mississippi emptied into the Gulf of Mexico rather than the Gulf of California or the Pacific Ocean, as others had believed. Jolliet's journal and his reports on the exploration were lost when his canoe capsized while he was returning to Quebec. However, his recollections and Marquette's journal served as records of their experiences, and news of their discoveries was published in Paris in 1681 in Thevenot's *Recueil des voyages*, which included a map of the area.

Almost a decade later, in 1682, Robert Cavelier, sieur de La Salle, along with Henry de Tonti and a small expedition, retraced the path of Jolliet and Marquette and proceeded to the mouth of the Mississippi. La Salle's geographical misconceptions regarding the country he traveled are reflected in the map produced by Jean Baptiste Louis Franquelin. The map was ill proportioned north to south, with the Great Lakes too far south and incorrectly located. Contemporary knowledge of the North American continent and the position of the course of the Mississippi River was reflected on the map to the confluence of the Missouri and Mississippi rivers. At this point Franquelin showed the Mississippi taking a ninety-degree westward turn, terminating the river in the Gulf of Mexico near Matagorda Bay.

While La Salle was exploring the lower reaches of the Mississippi, Louis Hennepin, a Belgian Recollect priest, was traveling through the upper Mississippi and Illinois River territory. In 1683 he obtained permission from the crown to publish his *Description de la Louisiane nouvellement découverte au sud-ouest de la Nouvelle France,* in which he included a map of his explorations. This map was one of the first made by a Frenchman from on-the-spot observations, and it therefore represented an important cartographic stepping stone. Hennepin pointed his "River Colbert" straight south and, with a dotted line, continued it to the Gulf of Mexico at almost the exact geographic spot where it presently flows into the Gulf.

Hennepin, however, played a much more important role in the exploration and settlement of Louisiana than the simple publication of a book and a map. Ordered by his superiors to return to America, he refused and fled to Antwerp. There he took service with Prince William of Orange, who was also King William III of England. From 1697 to 1699, three editions of Hennepin's travels were issued in English. Dedicated to King William, they called upon him to take possession of the territory and extolled the vast economic, political, and military potential of Louisiana. The successful French settlements in the Lower Mississippi Valley had an important impact on mapmaking. D'Iberville began the exploration of the country. He committed numerous people to this task, including Louis Juchereau de Saint-Denis, Pierre Charles Le Sueur, the Jesuit missionary Paul du Ru, and his brother, Jean-Baptiste Le Moyne, sieur de Bienville. Bienville and Saint-Denis were entrusted with the exploration of the Red River in hopes of establishing a western base to exploit the mines of the Spanish or to discover mines of their own. Le Sueur was sent to the land of the Sioux up the Missouri to begin the exploitation of copper mines discovered during earlier exploration.

The information received from these explorers enabled d'Iberville to funnel journals and manuscript maps continually to Guillaume de l'Isle in Paris. The result of this flood of information can be seen in the number of maps that de l'Isle issued between 1700 and 1718: a printed map of North America in 1700 attempted to show the boundaries of various possessions in the New World; a manuscript map in 1701 showed the trading path of the English from Charlestown to the Mobile River ten years before it appeared on English maps; a manuscript map in 1702 with five large sheets was based on information from the third voyage of d'Iberville; a printed map in 1702 used many details from his 1701 and 1702 maps but added much more detail; and, finally, his most important map, the "Carte de la Louisiane et du cours du Mississippi," published in 1718, incorporated the founding of New Orleans that same year by Bienville.

De l'Isle was not the only cartographer to make use of the information that d'Iberville provided. In 1701, Nicolas de Fer produced a map of the Gulf Coast and part of the Mississippi River from the earlier voyages of La Salle and d'Iberville. Although de Fer may have relied upon the explorations of La Salle and d'Iberville to prepare this map, he did not make adequate use of the information. The Mississippi was shown entering the Gulf of Mexico near its present-day location, but the course of the river was located too far to the west. The territory around Lake Pontchartrain and the Mississippi coast settlement established by d'Iberville was vague and did not incorporate much of the material forwarded to France by d'Iberville. Although this information had been forwarded to de l'Isle, it should have been available as well to de Fer as geographer to the French court.

De l'Isle's 1718 map has importance other than its historical locations. His expansion of French claims on the continent touched off a "war of maps" between France and England that paralleled the struggle for empire waged by traders and colonial representatives. Toward the south, de l'Isle contained the British from Bay Saint Mathieu (now Saint John's Bay) to a line on the Savannah River. Even in the region to the north he asserted the Carolinas had been named for Charles IX of France. According to de l'Isle, "Caroline," was first discovered, named, settled, and possessed by the French. Charles Town, he claimed, was the French "Charlefort."

In 1720, de l'Isle was answered by Herman Moll with his "A New Map of Ye North Parts of America Claimed by France." Moll was a propagandist for English territorial claims in North America. A Dutchman who lived in England, Moll had a distinctive cartographical style. Moll combined blunt clarity of lettering and considerable detail without flourishes or extraneous design. He frequently scattered short explanatory legends over his maps. In his 1720 map, he extended the English Carolina borders westward and even indicated some claim to the territory drained by the Mississippi River.

Moll was not alone in defending the English territorial claims to the interior of the North American continent. In 1733, Henry Popple published his twenty-sheet map of British North America. One of the most important of all maps of America, it was to that date the best English map of North America. It was especially remarkable for its grand scale. The 1734 edition published by Covens and Mortier and, in particular, the "Nouvelle carte particulière de l'Amérique" reflected the English view of the Gulf Coast. While some of Popple's information was derived from de l'Isle's "Carte de la Louisiane," he also relied upon the English cartographer Colonel John Barnwell's 1722 manuscript map of the area as well as other English explorations. Popple asserted the English claim to Carolina and included a great many subtle differences from the version of de l'Isle. Popple showed quite a different river system flowing into Mobile Bay. His map was extremely rich in Indian place names and gave a great number of the French settlements in Louisiana.

The next entry in the "war of maps" was by Jacques Nicolas Bellin. In 1750 he published his "Carte de la Louisiane et des pays voisins." Bellin attempted to locate the Spanish, French, and English settlements along the coast, keeping the English colonies all closely contained east of the Appalachians. Bellin was one of the better imitators of de l'Isle's 1718 map, but he omitted De Soto's route and several outdated references and introduced new information.

Other maps were used for other purposes. In 1721 John Senex published "A Map of Louisiana and of the River Mississippi" and dedicated it to William Law, father of John Law. While the spectacular collapse of the "Mississippi Bubble" in 1720 ruined many European investors, it made Louisiana famous. This map has been nicknamed "The Mississippi Bubble Map." Senex can be accused of plagiarism of de l'Isle, for the map was closely based on the 1718 de l'Isle map showing De Soto's route, the route of Saint-Denis in 1713-1716, and other features without giving de l'Isle the appropriate credit. The Carolina part of Senex's map was vacant and did not have de l'Isle's reference to the French priority of settlement, although Senex indicated that Charles Town was "called by the French Charlefort."

The "war of maps" ended with the French and Indian War. Having little or no information concerning their new possessions, the Spanish had to rely largely on French sources and maps to understand the extent of the territory they controlled. One of the first maps available to the Spanish was Thomás López's 1762 "La Luisiana," which not only showed lower Louisiana but also included an insert of New Orleans done in 1744 by Bellin and an insert of the upper Mississippi, "where the course of the river is known." López located the various forts that the French had constructed on the Mississippi, Ohio, and Wabash rivers as well as Fort Conde on Mobile Bay. He included extensive information on the Indian tribes and the river system but very little regarding British positions in the East Coast colonies.

The British also desired up-to-date information on their newly acquired territories east of the Mississippi River. In 1765, a military expedition was sent to make an official survey of the Mississippi Valley territory. The result was the first map of the British occupation of the Illinois country, "Course of the River Mississippi." First published by Robert Sayer in London in

1772, it was one of the finest maps of the Mississippi River. It showed the French settlements found by the English upon occupation of the east bank, from Fort Chartres in the north to the mouth of the Mississippi in the south. Subsequent editions of this map differed from the first by the inclusion of several features in the neighborhood of New Orleans, such as Forts Saint Leon and Saint Mary. The map also indicated the depth of the river at Balise, at the bar, and for ten, twenty, and thirty leagues out from the pass. British concern over the proximity of the Spanish to Baton Rouge led them to establish Manchac at the juncture of the Iberville River (now Bayou Manchac) with the Mississippi.

The Ross map of the river and Bernard Roman's "A General Map of the Southern British Colonies, in America" were available to both the British and the colonists during the Revolutionary War. Thomas Jefferys published the Ross map in his *American Atlas* in 1775, and Roman's map was included in *The American Military Pocket Atlas... of the British Colonies, Especially Those Which Now Are, or Probably May Be the Theatre of War*. Roman's man was invaluable to both sides. It contained great detail concerning the river, creek, and bayou systems of the area in the south controlled by the British as well as the trading paths used to travel from the eastern seaboard to the Indian nations to the west and on the Mississippi and Mobile rivers. It showed navigable rivers such as "Yazoo River navigable above forty-five leagues from its mouth" and located Fort Bute on the Iberville River, while Forts Saint Leon and Saint Mary were placed on the Mississippi below New Orleans.

Interest in the navigability of the Mississippi River also extended to the navigability of the Gulf Coast and the harbors, bays, and rivers feeding into it. This information was of vital importance to the competing European governments. Up-to-date charts were necessary if naval operations were to be carried out quickly and efficiently. The governments concerned themselves, therefore, with keeping a continuing flow of current charts coming from their cartographers.

The French were among the first to produce such a chart in 1720, with "Carte de la côte de la Louisiane depuis l'embouchure de Mississippi jusqu'à la baye de Pensacola par M. de Serigny en 1719 et 1720." Not only does this map show the Mississippi River from the entrances to above New Orleans, but it also provided soundings of the gulf from the mouth of the river to Pensacola Bay. A note in the upper right-hand corner stated that it was difficult to find one's way safely across the gulf unless constant soundings were taken. Thomas Kitchen provided the British with an excellent map of the Gulf Coast in 1761, "A New Map of the River Mississippi from the Sea to Bayagoulas." As in the previous map, Kitchen gave information showing the river from the entrances to the Bayagoulas, but he also stated that the area from East Pass to Bay Saint Louis was very shallow water with many small islands. He indicated that he had relied upon Spanish charts for some of his information.

One of the most prolific French cartographers in the middle of the eighteenth century, Jacques Nicolas Bellin, produced many excellent maps of Louisiana and Florida. He also made many accurate charts of the Gulf Coast. His *Le Petit Atlas maritime* (1764), included two maps of the Gulf Coast. "Carte de la coste de la Floride depuis la baye de la Mobile jusquaux cayes de St. Martin," showed the soundings of Mobile Bay, Pensacola Bay, Santa Rosa Bay, and Bay Saint Joseph, while the locations of the major rivers emptying into the gulf were also given. The second plate of the Gulf Coast, "Cours du fleuve Saint Louis depuis ses embouchures jusqu'à la rivière d'Iberville et costes voisines" provided similar information from the entrance of Mobile Bay west to the entrances of the Mississippi River. Detailed soundings were given around the barrier islands off the present day Mississippi and Alabama coasts, the Chandeleur Islands, and the pass of the Mississippi River. This map also showed the course of the Mississippi from the passes to the Iberville, with the locations of New Orleans, the Colapissas, the Bayagoulas, and the Houmas.

One of the best coastal charts was produced by the most prolific and important English map publishers of his time, Thomas Jefferys (ca. 1710-1771). An engraver, geographer, and publisher, Jefferys was appointed geographer to Frederick, prince of Wales, and later to George III. Published posthumously, "The Coast of West Florida and Louisiana ... the Peninsula and Gulf of Florida or Channel of Bahama with the Bahama Islands" gave extensive information in feet and fathoms for the area from the passes of the Mississippi River east to Mobile Bay. He also provided information on the soundings for the entire coast around Florida to the mouth of Saint John's River.

The American Revolution revived French hopes of regaining the Louisiana territory. Inspired by this hope, the Department of the Marine ordered a new coastal chart. Completed in 1778, this "Carte d'une partie des côtes de la Floride et de la Louisiane" gave extensive soundings for the mouth of the Mississippi River and the bays of Mobile, Pensacola, Saint Rose, and Saint Joseph.

Interest in maps did not decrease when the American government purchased the Louisiana territory. In 1803 President Thomas Jefferson requested the Spanish governor of Louisiana to forward maps of the Louisiana territory. The governor replied that he wished he could do so, but the French had removed all maps of the area when they left in the 1760s. While in possession of the colony, both the French and Spanish regularly sent manuscript maps of the territory to their respective governments. Most of the maps remaining in the colony, along with a majority of the governmental records, were removed to the mother country when the colony changed hands. This was done because the French and Spanish governments did not wish knowledge of their fortifications and settlements to be made available to other powers.

We now turn our attention to those map collections in New Orleans that will aid the researcher interested in the colonial era. The largest map collection in the area is that of the Louisiana Historical Center of the Louisiana State Museum. This collection totals over 2,000 maps; approximately 850 are of colonial Louisiana. At this writing, these maps are housed in the Historical Center Archives, the Presbytère, 751 Chartres Street, opposite Jackson Square in the French Quarter. Current plans call for this facility to relocate in the near future to the newly renovated U.S. Branch Mint, 400 Esplanade Avenue, on the edge of the French Quarter.

The manuscript maps in this collection are primarily of the New Orleans area and were done by surveyors who were residents of the colony, such as Ignace Broutin and Gonichon during the French period and Carlos Trudeau during the Spanish regime. Most of the printed maps in the collection are of French provenance. English maps are also well represented. However, there are fewer Spanish items as the Spanish did not produce many printed maps. These maps provide extensive information concerning locations of forts, settlements, Indian villages, and resources. Information on rivers and other waterways was continually updated as the period progressed.

The cartographic holdings of the Historic New Orleans Collection, 533 Royal Street, contain approximately 400 items, of which the majority are nineteenth-century maps with some twentieth-century materials. The colonial period is fairly well represented by printed editions. This collection contains three important manuscript maps: a 1732 map of New Orleans done from Gonichon, a 1732 map of New Orleans, and the 1799-1803 Juan Pedro Walke map already discussed.

The third significant map collection in New Orleans is located in the Louisiana Collection of the Howard-Tilton Memorial Library, Tulane University. This collection contains approximately 171 printed maps of colonial Louisiana. Although there are no manuscript maps in the collection, all time periods in the colonial era are represented.

14
LOUISIANA STATE ARCHIVES

ARTHUR W. BERGERON, JR.

Street address:	1515 Choctaw Drive
Mailing address:	P.O. Box 44125
	Baton Rouge, Louisiana 70804
Telephone:	(504) 342-5440
Days and hours:	Monday-Friday, 8 A.M. to 4:30 P.M.

UNFORTUNATELY LOUISIANA HAS lagged behind most states in the preservation of her public records. Because of neglect, carelessness, and apathy, thousands of priceless documents have been destroyed. The majority of surviving records from the colonial period are now located in parish courthouses and in the Louisiana State Museum. Even these records have been subjected to theft and damage by fire, insects, and water, due to improper storage. Practically all state records from the antebellum period (1812-1860) were destroyed during the Civil War and Reconstruction. Fortunately most local records from this period have survived in the parish courthouses, although the same destructive elements have taken their toll.

It was not until the 1930s that something was done to preserve Louisiana's public records. The Louisiana Historical Records Survey under Dr. Edwin A. Davis located and inventoried public records throughout the state. Many of the state records that now survive were placed temporarily at LSU. From 1954 to 1956, Dr. Davis was chief consultant to the Louisiana Archives Survey, which he planned and originated. One of the recommendations of the survey was that a state archives be established as a central depository for noncurrent state, parish, and local records.

In 1956 Dr. Davis coauthored the bill that created the State Archives and Records Service and influenced its passage in the legislature. The State Archives created by this legislation acted as an independent agency under the direction of the Louisiana State Archives and Records Commission, then composed of the secretary of state as chairman, the attorney general, and the state comptroller. This arrangement continued until 1972, when the commission was abolished and State Archives was transferred to the secretary of state's office. Under the commission and under the secretary of state, State Archives until quite recently was primarily a records management and microphotographic agency. It was empowered to accept for preservation historical records but had no full-time archival program. Finally, in March 1977, an archivist was hired to head the manuscript section.

State Archives was originally located in the subbasement of the State Capitol. In 1959 it moved to the ground floor of Old Peabody Hall, a building near the capitol that had been constructed prior to 1900 and had been condemned by the State Fire Marshall. Two years later the archives were transferred from the ground floor to the second floor of Old Peabody Hall, where more space was available. The need for still more room resulted in an appropriation from the Board of Liquidation in 1967 permitting the archives to move to its present location. The archives are now housed in a former hardware store and warehouse. This building does not have the needed environmental controls, but much renovation has been done to provide temperature consistency and a pleasant research area. The legislature has approved construction of a new archives building.

The first major accessions to the archives section came in 1961, when records from two parish courthouses were transferred to Baton Rouge for preservation. The clerk of court of Saint Landry Parish transferred all unneeded records prior to 1860. Most of these documents are from the colonial period, 1764-1803. Colonial records from Avoyelles Parish were also moved to State Archives. These latter documents were calendared and microfilmed, and State Archives published *Calendar of Louisiana Colonial Documents,* vol. 1: *Avoyelles,* in 1962. In 1963 the archives published a second volume of its colonial calendars covering the Saint Landry records up to 1785. Additional Saint Landry colonial records came into the archives in subsequent years, and the process of sorting and calendaring the remaining documents was completed in 1979.

A major acquisition was made in late 1961. The National Archives returned to the state its collection of records of the Louisiana Confederate government, which had been confiscated by the Union army during the Civil War. In all, some nine cubic feet of loose material and eighty bound volumes were given to State Archives. The loose documents consist of letters received by Governor Thomas O. Moore and Governor Henry W. Allen, ordinances and resolutions of the secession convention, acts of the legislature, election returns, military correspondence, and records of several state departments. Among the bound volumes are orders and correspondence of the adjutant general, lists of militia officers, and records of the executive and other departments. All of these Confederate records contain much information as yet little used by researchers.

Unlike many state archives, the Louisiana State Archives has few parish records in original form or on microfilm. A recently initiated program will begin to remedy this situation, however. State Archives has begun microfilming the records of several parish clerks of court as an ongoing program. In addition to the Avoyelles and Saint Landry parish records previously mentioned, State Archives has microfilmed or obtained film copies of colonial documents from the following parishes for the specified time periods: Saint Charles (1740-1803; 13 reels); Natchitoches (1732-1819; 25 reels); Saint James (1782-1787; 1 reel); and East Baton Rouge (Spanish West Florida records) (1782-1810; 13 reels). Most of these records are written in French and Spanish, but a few are in English.

All of these colonial period records contain a wealth of information for researchers. The types of documents included are land sales, slave sales, marriage contracts, successions, petitions for land grants, labor contracts, apprenticeship agreements, powers of attorney, suits, mortgages, manumissions, and some official decrees and correspondence. Most of the slave sales include the name, description, and place of origin (usually an African tribe) of the slave being sold. Several labor contracts for the construction of houses provide descriptions of the structures to be built. Some of the petitions and correspondence deal with depredations committed by runaway slaves living in "maroon" (fugitive slave) colonies.

In addition to the records of the Louisiana government transferred from the National Archives, State Archives has several other types of records pertaining to Confederate Louisiana, including microfilm copies of service records of the state's Confederate soldiers. Supplementing these are applications for pensions by Confederate veterans and their widows. These files sometimes contain original documents from the war years or letters from veterans to the Board of Pension commissioners, furnishing historical data on the units in which they served. Several volumes from the state treasurer's and state auditor's offices that were not captured by the Union army or were retained by the War Department for only a short period of time are also a part of the archives collection. These include Appropriation and Expenditure Record (1860-1861); Endorsed Journal of Receipts and Expenditures (1861-1863); Journal of Receipts and Expenditures (1863-1865); Journal of Receipts and Expenditures for the Louisiana Militia (1862); Swamp Land Ledger (1861-1864); and Auditor's Order Book (1862).

Because State Archives has been associated closely with the secretary of state's office since its creation, many of the records in the archives collection come from that office. Included here are original signed copies of acts of the legislature (1804-1865; 280 volumes); records of commissions of state and parish officials (1846-1928; 25 volumes); lists of municipal officials (1892-1928; 10 volumes); official acts of the governor (1868-1877; 3 volumes); voter registration books (1898; 64 volumes for 56 parishes); special executive orders (1862-1863; 1 volume for U.S. military governor); motor vehicle division correspondence and financial records (1921-1932; 6 cu. ft.); and letterpress copybook of letters sent (1902; 1 volume).

Correspondence of state departments, agencies, and boards comprises a sizable portion of the archives collection. Practically all of this correspondence is for the years between 1870 and 1930, although there are a few items before and after these years. The available records are as follows: Department of Agriculture and Immigration (1916-1929; 22 cu. ft.); Board of Appraisers (1898-1917; 1 volume and 1 cu. ft.); State Auditor (1864-1952); 10 volumes and 2 cu. ft.); Attorney General (1916-1919; 2 cu. ft.); Board of Audit and Exchange (1892-1910; 1 volume); Department of Education (1863-1925; 16 volumes and 27 cu. ft.); Board of Health (1877-1879; 1 volume); Department of Highways (1911-1922; 39 volumes); State Land Office (1865-1927; 322 volumes and 29 cu. ft.); Railroad Commission (1899-1918; 24 volumes and 9 cu. ft.); State Treasurer (1870-1932; 41 volumes); Louisiana Relief Committee (1922; 3 cu. ft.); and Department of Commerce and Industry (1971-1975; 2 cu. ft.).

Another category of important records for researchers is the minutes of meetings of public agencies. State Archives has the following in its collection: Board of Pension Commissioners (1898-1932; 2 volumes); Board of Commissioners for the Port of New Orleans (1896-1960; 15 reels); State Board of Health (1866-1868, 1908-1972; 22 volumes); Board of Audit and Exchange (1892-1916; 1 volume); Funding Board (1880-1886; 1 volume); State Board of Appraisers (1899-1916; 4 volumes); State Advisory (1934-1944; 2 cu. in.); and State Board of Equalization (1907-1916; 1 volume).

Many documents at State Archives remain to be properly identified and catalogued. For example, more than 1,000 volumes of ledgers, journals, and records from the state treasurer's and state auditor's offices are currently being processed. All volumes dating prior to 1865 have been identified, as well as some after that date. This entire group constitutes a valuable portrait of the state's financial transactions. The following may serve as an example of what is available: journals of receipts and expenditures (1847-1860; 9 volumes); and records of appropriations and expenditures (1847-1859; 6 volumes). Remaining volumes will probably be organized by decades. Notices of newly catalogued items appear in the State Archives *Newsletter*, published quarterly. State Archives is also publishing a complete listing of its archival holdings in installments in the *Newsletter*. Available issues will be mailed to interested persons upon request.

15
THE DEPARTMENT OF ARCHIVES AND MANUSCRIPTS, LOUISIANA STATE UNIVERSITY

MARGARET FISHER DALRYMPLE

Street address:	202 Middleton Library, Louisiana State University Baton Rouge, Louisiana 70803
Mailing address:	Same
Telephone:	(504) 388-2240
Days and hours:	Monday-Friday, 7:30 A.M. to 4:00 P.M.; Saturday, 8:00 A.M. to noon; closed Sunday and most university holidays

THE LOUISIANA STATE University Department of Archives and Manuscripts was established in 1935 by Edwin Adams Davis, a member of the university's history department. Davis recognized the need to preserve the historical manuscripts that make up part of the state's cultural heritage and wished to assemble a body of original research materials that could be

---

The author wishes to thank M. Stone Miller, Jr., head of the Department of Archives, and his staff for their assistance in the preparation of this essay.

utilized by local scholars. He persuaded the university administration to create an autonomous department for the purpose of collecting and preserving manuscripts relating to the history and culture of Louisiana and the Lower Mississippi Valley, and he was appointed its first director. A year later, in 1936, Davis was instrumental in bringing about the passage of Louisiana Act 258, which empowered the university, through its Department of Archives, to "receive and collect public records or documents and materials bearing upon the history of the state, edit and publish official records and other historical materials, and make a survey of the official records of the state, its parishes and other subdivisions." The act also provided that all public officials could turn over their noncurrent records to the department "for permanent preservation therein."

In 1937, Louisiana State University was named sponsor of the Louisiana Historical Records Survey (HRS), a statewide project of the Works Progress Administration (WPA), and John C. L. Andreassen was named its chief administrator. The project, which employed over 500 people, inventoried and described many of the state's historical documents, both public and private, for the survey's publications; other documents were transcribed, translated, indexed, and otherwise made more accessible to researchers. When the HRS was disbanded in 1943, many of its records and products, both published and unpublished, were deposited in the Department of Archives.

In 1946 Davis resigned the directorship of the Department of Archives to return to full-time teaching. His archival work was carried on by his successors, William R. Hogan, Vergil L. Bedsole, John M. Price, and the present head, M. Stone Miller, Jr. In 1958, the department moved into quarters in the newly constructed Middleton Library and surrendered its autonomous status to become a division of the university library system. Its role as a repository of public records ended in 1956, when the state legislature created the Louisiana State Archives and Records Commission to house, adminster, and preserve all noncurrent records generated by state and local agencies. Most of the materials of this nature housed at LSU were transferred to the State Archives in 1970.

The Department of Archives, which presently holds over 4,000 collections and nearly 4 million separate items dating from the seventeenth century to the present, has become a major repository for scholarly source materials pertaining to the Lower South. Its collections are acquired through gifts, purchases, and loans and include, in addition to original manuscripts, microfilms, photographs and other visual items, rare imprints, maps, tape recordings, motion picture films, and memorabilia.

The oldest major group of manuscripts in the department pertain to colonial Louisiana. The papers (1719-1954; 407 items) of the Chevalier Jean-Charles Pradel (1692-1764), a French nobleman who was among the first settlers of Louisiana, reflect the military and economic history of the colony and include valuable information about the development of Pradel's plantation, the colony's economic ties with France, and the family life of upper-class colonists. Letters written by Pradel's wife, Alexandrine de la Chaise, are among the earliest personal expressions of the activities and thoughts of a Louisiana woman. Smaller collections of papers of planters, farmers, and merchants, as well as civil and military records, further document the history of French colonial Louisiana. The department also owns microfilms of Louisiana documents in the Archives Nationales de France (Archives des Colonies, series 13a, 1694-1807; 69 reels).

Large resources also exist for research in the history of Spanish Louisiana.[1] The New Orleans Municipal Records (1765-1877; 3,409 items) include civil and legal documents from the New Orleans Cabildo, such as commercial regulations, petitions, bills for repairs to public structures, revenue reports, land sale documents, and surveys. The Natchitoches Parish Records (1732-1932; 3,998 items) and the Opelousas District Papers (1777-1800; 119 items) contain documents pertaining to Spanish civil and military administration in these areas.[2] There are also scattered papers of such Spanish officials as Governors Gálvez, Miró, Gayoso de Lemos, Casa Calvo, Carondelet, and Salcedo; José Vidal, commandant of Concordia Post; Baton Rouge militia officer Philip Hicky; and Juan Filhiol, commandant of Fort Miró. Many of the plantation collections contain documents from this period dealing with land purchases, commerce, slavery, and local administration; and there are also several small collections of papers of merchants, traders, and farmers active during the period of Spanish rule.

Recently acquired microfilms of Spanish archival documents have greatly enhanced research possibilities in the history of colonial Louisiana. These include copies of the service records of Louisiana militia units (Hojas de Servicios Militares de América, 1787-1799; Sección de Guerra Moderna, Archivo General de Simancas; 2 reels); the Jack D. L. Holmes collection of documents dealing with the history of colonial Louisiana, primarily from the Papeles Procendentes de Cuba (12 reels); and the sections of the Stetson Collection at the University of Florida that pertain to Spanish Louisiana and Spanish West Florida (5 reels). The Middleton Library, through the Department of Archives, has joined Loyola University of New Orleans in a project to microfilm all documents in the Archivo General de Indias (Papeles Procedentes de Cuba) that pertain to Louisiana and the Gulf Coast. To date, 110 reels have been received, *legajos* 488-560, which pertain largely to commerce and economic matters. Additional reels will be added as the filming continues. Documentation of British activities on the Gulf Coast during this period is provided by microfilms of the Frederick Haldimand Papers (1769-1772; 1 reel) in the British Library and of the West Florida Records in the Public Record Office (Colonial Office, series 5, volumes 574-622; 15 reels), which are held by the Middleton Library.

The Department of Archives also has transcriptions of colonial records prepared by the Historical Records Survey and the Survey of Federal Archives. These include the Spanish West Florida Records (1782-1816; 19

volumes and index; originals in the office of the Clerk of Court of East Baton Rouge Parish); Dispatches of the Spanish Governors of Louisiana (1766-1796; 17 volumes; originals in the Archivo General de Indias, Seville); and the Vicente Pintado Survey Papers (1792-1818; 11 volumes).

Several exceptionally large and hitherto little-exploited collections offer opportunities for the study of long-term trends in plantation history. These include the Edward J. Gay and Family Papers (1805-1925; 70 lin. ft.), which cover five generations of a planter family of Iberville Parish, Louisiana, and document the development and administration of a still-operating sugar plantation and the history of the family (including the careers of two members who served as a U.S. congressman and a U.S. senator). The Uncle Sam Plantation Records (1815-1934; 23 lin. ft. and 406 volumes), the Pharr Family Papers (1848-1934; 85,762 items and 220 volumes), and the Smithfield Plantation Records (1900-1970; 35 lin. ft. and 191 volumes to date) richly document the nineteenth- and twentieth-century Louisiana sugar plantation as an aspect of agribusiness development in the South.

Because a majority of the plantation collections come from fairly limited geographical areas (Natchez and vicinity, the Feliciana parishes, the Lower Mississippi Valley, and South Louisiana), concentrated regional studies of various aspects of plantation economy are possible. Another line of research is suggested by the fact that many of the collections were generated by families related through ties of blood, marriage, and business. Socioeconomic studies of the planter class could reveal much about the nature of traditional Southern politics, economic practices, and social values.

Other aspects of the rural history and economy of the Lower South are illustrated by the papers of small farmers, both white and black, from several regions of Louisiana and Mississippi. This body of archival materials suggests investigation of such topics as settlement patterns and population movements, the impact of the Civil War and of various national and regional economic crises on the middle- and lower-class rural population, religious and social values, and education. The Family History Project Papers (1972-; 4 lin. ft. to date), produced by students in university history classes, contain much otherwise unavailable information about recent Southern rural life and folk traditions.

The urban institutions that resulted from or sustained the rural economy of the Lower South are well represented in the department's collections. There are records of several defunct banks, including the Commercial Bank of Natchez (1836-1864; 151 volumes), the Bank of the United States-Natchez Office (1830-1846; 63 volumes), the Consolidated Association of Planters of Louisiana (1791-1912; 10,000 items and 85 volumes), the city Bank of New Orleans (1832-1852; 6 lin. ft.), the Louisiana State Bank (1817-1888; 14 lin. ft.), the Merchants' Bank of New Orleans (1857-1860; 1 letter-file book), and the Planter's Bank of Natchez (1835-1844; 2 volumes, and ca. 100 items). Personal papers of a number of bankers and their families provide further information about nineteenth-century banking practices. The papers of the State Agricultural Credit Corporation (ca. 1927-1971; 16 lin. ft.) illustrate more recent trends in agricultural financing.

Papers of merchants and factors who dealt with rural producers further illustrate economic aspects of Southern agriculture. They include the records of several firms of factors, commission merchants, and general merchants who were located in New Orleans, New York, and in some of the smaller towns of the Lower South. A number of these collections are quite voluminous and span several decades; consequently, they offer potential for cliometric studies of economic trends on both the local and regional levels. One example of these collections is the Meyer Brothers Store Records (1853-1909; 10 lin. ft. and 245 volumes), which document the business activities of a firm of general merchants in Clinton, Louisiana, and reflect in detail the various economic activities and fluctuations of that largely agrarian community.

Changing trends in agricultural experimentation and science are also reflected in the department's collections. The papers of Thomas Affleck, Texas horticulturalist and agricultural writer, and of John Carmichael Jenkins, Mississippi planter and experimental agriculturist, reflect nineteenth-century agricultural science. The LSU Agricultural Extension Service Papers (1909-ca. 1975; 140 lin. ft. to date) include annual narrative and statistical reports submitted by parish (county) agents, correspondence, publications, speeches, circulars, photographs, and scrapbooks. Of particular interest within this collection are reports of several New Deal agricultural relief agencies and the records (1924-1955) of a separate black extension service, which document living conditions among Louisiana's rural black population. The Louisiana Sugar Planters' Association Records (1897-1911; 850 items) and the Louisiana Sugar and Rice Exchange Records (1884-1936; 175 items and 6 volumes) reflect attitudes of growers toward changing market conditions and technological developments. The papers of several twentieth-century agronomists and agricultural scientists working on rice, sugar, yams, cotton, and other crops further illustrate the recent history of Southern agriculture.

Materials pertaining to other aspects of the economic history of the Lower South are also abundant. The Department of Archives has been designated as official repository of the Forest History Society and as such has been the recipient of donations of records from many regional lumber companies, as well as from several lumber producers and dealers. The largest collection, that of the Southern Forest Products Association (formerly the Southern Pine Association) to date consists of approximately 500 linear feet of records dating from ca. 1900 to ca. 1975; additional accessions are made periodically. Other collections include the records of the Crosset Lumber Company (1900-1962; 132 volumes), the Fordyce Lumber Company (1920-1963; 64 volumes and 70 reels of microfilm), the Jackson

Lumber Company (1902-1953; 20 volumes), the Johns-Manville Timberlands (1939-1972; 26 lin. ft.), the Kellogg Lumber Company (1918-1961; 7 lin. ft.); and the Springfield Lumber Company Corporation (1899-1934; 134 volumes). These collections contain information about the history and economics of the Southern lumber industry, the impact of World Wars I and II on lumber production and use, conservation and environmental aspects of the industry, labor relations, research in wood sciences, effects of mechanization, and the political activities of lumber producers.

The history of steamboating in the Lower South is represented by several large and useful collections. The E. B. and N. Philip Norman Collection (1833-1960; 1,140 items and 116 volumes) contain several hundred photographs of steamboats and river scenes, as well as manuscripts, research notes, published materials, and steamboat models and memorabilia. The Sophie Cooley Pearson Papers (1843-1966; 567 items and 14 volumes) include an unpublished memoir of life in a steamboating family (the late Mrs. Pearson was a daughter of steamboat owner-master Captain L. V. Cooley), as well as numerous photographs, two steamboat logbooks, and other materials. Papers of Captain Thomas P. Leathers and his family and of Captains Orramel Hinckley, Jesse K. Bell Rea, and John Reynaud illustrate other aspects of steamboating, as does the Robert H. Barrow Photograph Collection.

There are also collections of economic interest that pertain to such industries as railroads, tobacco growing, moss production, wagon building, blacksmithing, and livestock raising. The Jennings-Heywood Oil Syndicate Records (1901-1970; 13 lin. ft.) contain information about the early oil industry in Texas and Louisiana, and the papers of Charlton H. Lyons (1942-1973; 2 lin. ft. and 10 volumes) include materials relative to Louisiana oil production and the activities of the Independent Petroleum Association of America from the 1940s until the early 1970s. The papers (1916-1979; 519 items and 10 volumes) of Collett Everman Woolman, founder of Delta Airlines, and the C. Dreaux Boudreaux Papers (1972-1974; 1 volume) contain information about the development of aviation in the South.

The department's collections offer numerous opportunities for research in black history. Plantation records contain a wide variety of materials that deal with aspects of slavery in the Lower South, including its development during the colonial period; relations between slave and planter families; work assignments; slave discipline; health and mortality; emancipation; slave family life; slaves as wage earners, craftsmen, and small tradesmen; religion; and slave culture. The role of free blacks in the antebellum South is illustrated by several collections of papers from members of this group, including small farmers, planters, a barber, and several storekeepers.

Abundant materials pertaining to black history during the Civil War and Reconstruction include information on such topics as the activities and performance of black federal military units and the treatment of Confederate slaves, contrabands, and freedmen. An unpublished transcript of the 1861 trial of a group of Natchez slaves involved in an insurrection conspiracy reflects aspects of rural slave life and the slaves' understanding of the issues of the Civil War. Abundant records of postbellum planters employing free black labor and records of storekeepers who dealt with freedmen suggest the possibility of statistical studies of rural economic conditions after emancipation and of the evolution of the tenant and sharecropping systems of the Lower South.

More recent manuscripts dealing with black history are less numerous. The LSU Agricultural Extension Service Records, mentioned above, document many aspects of rural black life. The Screwmen's Benevolent Association Records (1851-1917; 1,854 items and 11 volumes) reflect urban working conditions involving a New Orleans longshore workers' union. There are also small collections of papers of black businessmen and craftsmen, including a New Orleans woman undertaker and a Baton Rouge plasterer. Although there is an abundance of material pertaining to civil rights problems from the mid-nineteenth century until the 1960s, most of it reflects mainly white responses and attitudes.

The department also contains considerable information for the study of other ethnic groups in the Lower South. Louisiana's Francophone population is well represented by manuscripts dating from the early eighteenth century up to the present. These include papers of French colonial officials and settlers, planters, farmers, businessmen, writers, scholars, educators, public officials, and other people of French origin. Of particular interest to students of Acadian culture are the poems, sermons, and other papers (1840-1860; 359 items and 27 volumes) of Father Adrien Rouquette; the papers (1882-1950; 17 items and 22 volumes) of Sidonie de la Houssaye (1821-1894), which include manuscript drafts of her short stories; the manuscript writings and other papers (1870-1965; 70 items and 11 volumes) of Judge Felix Voorhies (1839-1919), Saint Martinville lawyer and author; the records (1939-1962; 8,772 items and 152 volumes) of the Acadian Handicraft Project, a WPA effort to preserve and encourage various traditional crafts; and the papers of André Olivier, Saint Martinville historian and writer. There are also a number of collections that pertain to Francophone culture in New Orleans and elsewhere in Louisiana. The papers (1862-1909; 385 items) of New Orleans journalist and diplomat Henry Vignaud (1830-1922), of interest in themselves for the information they contain about the career of this famous Louisianian, include substantial bodies of letters from newspaper editor Eugene Dumez and journalist-poet L. Placide Canonge. There are also numerous bodies of personal letters, diaries, and business and legal papers written in French by South Louisianians, as well as imprints, photographs, and other materials that document the culture of the region.

Collections pertaining to Jewish life in the Lower South also offer potential for study. Extensive records of several business firms in New Orleans, Natchez, Baton Rouge, and elsewhere reflect Jewish participation in the

Southern economy since the middle of the nineteenth century. Other collections contain personal and family correspondence in English, German, and Yiddish; records of a burial society in late nineteenth-century Clinton; cashbooks from a Jewish congregation in Natchez (1902-1934); and the records of Jewish charitable organizations in New Orleans (1917-1944). A diary (1861-1862) kept by Clara Solomon includes information about the social and cultural life of a young Jewish girl in Confederate New Orleans.

Louisiana's German population is represented by several collections of interest. The Max Nuebling Letter Book (1822-1826; 2 volumes) consist of copies of letters written by a German immigrant residing in Saint Francisville to his family in Germany and includes information about work and living conditions in West Feliciana Parish. The diary (1864-1868, 1871, 2 volumes) of Eduard Hansen, a native of Luxembourg and a naturalized Louisianian, concerns his military service with the Union Army during the Civil War. The George Speeg Papers (1895-1918; 562 items and 58 volumes) consist of German-language accounts, periodicals, and other items kept by a German immigrant blacksmith in Lobdell, West Baton Rouge Parish. Papers of several members of the Kleinpeter family extend from 1813 to 1918 and include business papers, Confederate soldiers' letters, and plantation records. The diary (1908-1923; 47 items and 5 volumes) of Louis Leonpacher, a German immigrant who became a Baton Rouge veterinarian, includes copies of letters received as well as photographs and colored sketches. An unexploited collection of interest to students of the Civil War is the Luise Weydemeyer Family Correspondence, which includes six letters (1822-1866) from Elise Sigel, wife of Union army general Franz Sigel, in which she discusses federal military campaigns and relations within the high command of the Union army.

The department's collections also contain information about several other ethnic groups. There are collections pertaining to Irish immigrants throughout the nineteenth century, to Italians in New Orleans and elsewhere, and to Chinese laborers who arrived in Louisiana after the Civil War. A number of collections include information about Indians and Indian relations in the late eighteenth and early nineteenth centuries. There are also many collections with information about Louisiana's Spanish settlers and their descendants.

Since its founding in 1935, the Department of Archives has been actively collecting manuscripts pertaining to women and their history, and the present collection offers unusually rich opportunities for the study of Southern women from colonial times until the present. Colonial legal and civil documents from New Orleans, Natchitoches, Opelousas, and elsewhere, as well as some personal letters, reflect the role of women in the early history of Louisiana. The collections from the nineteenth and twentieth centuries contain extensive bodies of papers generated by women and girls of both rural and urban families from all economic levels and ethnic backgrounds. These papers, consisting of letters, diaries, notebooks, scrapbooks, literary efforts, and other writings, touch on every aspect of feminine experience, including education, social life and values, marriage, childbearing and rearing, health practices, fashions, homemaking, recreation, religion, wage earning, and participation in politics, philanthropic organizations, business, and the arts. Several collections contain papers of women planters, and others reflect the important role played by women in plantation management during and after the Civil War. Other collections pertaining to women's history include such diverse materials as the letters of a Louisiana housewife describing civilian life in a small town during World War II; letters from an unusually articulate farm wife discussing the economic disintegration of the plantation system after the end of the Civil War; the letters and diaries of schoolgirls; patterns for sewing and needlework; the diary of a governess living with a plantation family; letters and notebooks expressing religious convictions and experiences; the papers of professional and business women in several fields; and recipes.

The roles played by Southern women in the arts and professions are also documented in the department's collections. The vast corpus of papers (1833-1954; 14,094 items and 245 volumes) of New Orleans author Grace King and her family illustrate not only the career of this nationally known writer but also the cultural and intellectual life of New Orleans in the late nineteenth and early twentieth century. Other Southern woman writers whose papers are found in the department are Kate Lee Ferguson, Cora E. Carey, Emma Wilson Emery, Eleanor Percy Ware, Leona Queyrouse, Frances Parkinson Keyes, Sidonie de la Houssaye, and Helen Gilkison. There are also a number of unpublished literary works by women, including a novel about the Colfax Riot of 1873 written by an eyewitness to that event. The papers (1897-1955; 578 items and 2 volumes) of New Orleans lawyer and suffrage leader Judith Hyams Douglas (1879-1955) reflect the legal and civic influence of a feminist activist during the first half of this century, and the recently acquired papers of Baton Rouge lawyer Sylvia Roberts, chief legal counsel for the National Organization for Women (NOW) show more recent trends in the women's rights movement. The department also holds records of a number of associations of professional women, including the Louisiana divisions of the American Association of University Women, the Baton Rouge Business and Professional Women's Club, the Louisiana State Nurses' Association and several other professional nursing organizations, and several LSU campus organizations involving women.

The complex political history of Louisiana and the Lower South is amply documented in the department's collections. An unpublished letter book of William C. C. Claiborne and letters of Thomas Bolling Robertson provide new materials for the study of the early national period. Letters and diaries in collections of personal papers dating from the nineteenth and twentieth centuries reflect many aspects of local, state, and national political affairs in Louisiana and Mississippi, as do the papers of political leaders such as Louisiana Governors Thomas Overton Moore, Benjamin F. Flanders, William Pitt Kellogg, Jared Y. Sanders, and Henry L. Fuqua, U.S. Representative Edward J. Gay, and a number of state and local officials.

More recent political history is also well documented and includes a number of significant new and/or unexploited collections. The papers of Huey P. Long (1914-1936; 49 lin. ft.) contain materials that were inaccessible to T. Harry Williams when he wrote his biography of Long. The papers and scrapbooks of Governor Richard W. Leche (1935-1956; 100 lin. ft. and 172 volumes) offer untapped information about his career and about economic and political conditions in Louisiana during the later 1930s. The papers of John B. Fournet (1927-1970; 70 lin. ft.), a close associate of Huey Long and longtime chief justice of the Louisiana Supreme Court, offer further information on this period. Regional and national politics during the 1930s are reflected in the papers (1912-1940; 495 items) of Mississippi politician Archibald S. Coody, which include letters from Senator Theodore G. Bilbo. The papers (1904-1972; 5,828 items and 10 volumes) of Louisiana Governor Robert F. Kennon have been recently accessioned, as have papers, scrapbooks, and other items (1937-1977; 513 items and 12 volumes) relating to the administrations of Governor Earl K. Long. The department also has extensive bodies of papers of two recent leaders of the state's Republican party, Harrison G. Bagwell (1947-1969; 4 lin. ft.) and Charlton H. Lyons (1942-1973; 2 lin. ft. and 10 volumes). Other materials of interest to students of recent politics include a small body of Ku Klux Klan imprints and papers of members of the White Citizens' Council. The papers (1836-1974; 336 items and 3 volumes) of Leon Jastremski, Polish-born mayor of Baton Rouge and U.S. consul in Peru, include information about state and local politics and international diplomacy.

Several Louisianians active in national politics are also represented in the department's collections. These include Senators Edward J. Gay, Jr., Joseph E. Ransdell, Donelson Caffrey, and John Holmes Overton, and U.S. Representatives James G. Aswell and Ladislas Lazaro. The papers (1905-1970; ca. 6,000 items) of U.S. Representative Overton Brooks include information about his influential role in national defense policies and in the early U.S. space program. The papers (1852-1960; 1,528 items and 31 volumes) of New Orleanian Ernest Lee Jahncke, Sr., who served as assistant secretary of the navy from 1929 to 1933, include information about his broad civic and cultural interests.

Considerable potential exists for research in Louisiana legal history. The recorded proceedings of the Constitutional Convention of 1973 (215 reels) have been recently accessioned. There is also a constantly growing collection of papers of Louisiana judges and lawyers. These include papers of state supreme court justices John B. Fournet, E. Howard McCaleb, Joe W.

Sanders, Albert Tate, Jr., Joseph B. Hamiter, James Govan Taliaferro, and Walter B. Hamlin and of district judges Sam A. LeBlanc, Minos D. Miller, Jr., J. Cleveland Fruge, and C. Ellis Ott. There are also papers of a large number of practicing lawyers of the nineteenth and twentieth centuries, from both Louisiana and Mississippi, as well as of several local judges.

The Department of Archives holds a large body of materials pertaining to the Civil War and to Reconstruction in the Lower South, and new accessions in this area are constantly being added. Collecting policy concentrates on the history of this epoch in Louisiana and Mississippi and along the lower Mississippi River, and as a result the department has unusually strong resources for the study of Port Hudson, Vicksburg, and Red River campaigns; the federal occupation of New Orleans, Baton Rouge, and South Louisiana; and military activities in Mississippi and Tennessee. These resources include letters, diaries, and other papers of officers and enlisted men from both sides; official reports and orders; muster rolls; letters and diaries of Confederate civilians commenting on aspects of the war; imprints; and photographs. There are also considerable bodies of manuscripts dealing with such topics as military medicine, music, Confederate refugees, prisoners of war, and Confederate politics and diplomacy. A recently acquired collection of unusual interest are the papers (1862-1865; over 1,000 items), of Captain John W. McClure, assistant quartermaster, USA, for the Department of the Gulf in New Orleans. McClure was responsible for quartermaster stores in the New Orleans area and also for the confiscation and sale of rebel property, and his papers contain detailed information about federal economic activity in occupied New Orleans as well as itemized lists of the property of such prominent Confederates as John Slidell and Judah P. Benjamin and of nearly 200 others. The records of the United Confederate Veterans' Association (1889-1936; 144 lin. ft.) include minutes, correspondence, rosters, scrapbooks, and other materials relating to this organization.

The intellectual and cultural history of the Lower South is also well documented by the department's collections. There is information pertaining to education in private academies and other schools in the antebellum era; to religion; to musical training, performance, and composition; to theatre and drama; to newspaper publication; to literature; to medicine; and to the fine arts and architecture.

Considerable bodies of materials exist for the study of religious history, and there are manuscripts that pertain to most of the major denominations of this region. A current project of interest is the microfilming of the records of Baptist churches in the Florida Parishes. Two recently acquired collections of research potential are the William H. Head and Family Papers, which include over one hundred sermons and addresses dating from 1844 to the 1880s, as well as correspondence and a diary of a Mississippi Baptist minister; and the papers of J. Norris Palmer, late minister of the

Baton Rouge First Baptist Church, which cover the years 1917 to 1974 and include correspondence, diaries, scrapbooks, and materials pertaining to various administrative committees of the Southern Baptist Convention and to foreign missions.

The department holds several collections of interest for the study of literature in the South. The Grace King and Family Papers, mentioned above, include voluminous correspondence, diaries, manuscripts, and other materials that document King's career in great detail. The several groups of papers (1720-1940; 948 items and 15 volumes) of New Orleans historian Charles Gayarré include correspondence, research materials, and a number of unpublished manuscripts on various historical subjects. The papers (1899-1960; 15 lin. ft.) of James Aswell, Jr., a Louisiana-born novelist and newspaper columnist, include manuscripts, letters, and a diary kept by his wife that records Aswell's early efforts at fiction writing. The department also contains letters and other papers of George Washington Cable, H. L. Mencken, Lyle Saxon, Edward Clifton Wharton, Charles Dudley Warner, Harnett T. Kane, Samuel Clemens and his family, and other literary figures.

Music is another art represented in the department's collections. There are papers of several musicians, composers, and music teachers; published sheet music; a number of pieces of unpublished music; an unpublished two-volume manuscript by Charles Cior, a New Orleans music teacher, discussing a music-training technique that he developed; programs, broadsides, and announcements relating to musical performances; descriptions of performances in letters and diaries, including references to such notable artists as Louis Moreau Gottschalk and Jenny Lind; correspondence with Metropolitan Opera baritone Pasquale Amato, a scrapbook containing clippings and other materials relative to his career, and an unpublished biography of his life; and a group of letters from soprano Adelina Patti. The collection also includes papers of several members of the LSU School of Music; programs and scrapbooks pertaining to opera productions presented by that department; and papers of the Louisiana Music Teachers Association.

The history of medicine is documented in a number of collections of physicians' papers. New Orleans doctor and scientific writer Joseph Jones (1833-1896) is represented by a large collection (1832-1919; 3,360 items and 74 volumes) that includes correspondence, medical writings, a diary, and research notes. The papers (1826-1864; 67 items and 2 volumes) of Samuel A. Cartwright, New Orleans physician and professor of "Negro medicine," include materials on medical theory and antebellum political and racial ideas. Other collections include resource materials on homeopathic medicine, pharmacy, rural medical practice, military medicine, medical care of slaves, epidemics, treatment of various diseases, medical watering places, and medical training. The New Orleans Charity Hospital Record Books

(1882-1884; 4 volumes) contain detailed information about the background, condition, and treatment of individual patients. The various nursing association records mentioned above and the papers of Julie C. Tebo (1904-1966; 1 lin. ft.) reflect the development of the nursing profession in Louisiana. The largely unexploited Leper Home Records (1890-1921; 13 lin. ft. and 16 volumes) contain information about the operation of the Carville hospital before it was taken over by the U.S. Public Health Service.

The University Archives, which constitute yet another section of the manuscript collection, pertain to the history and administration of Louisiana State University from its founding in 1860 until the present. The early history of the university is reflected in the personal and official papers of the institution's first presidents, William T. Sherman (1860-1861), David French Boyd (1865-1880, 1884-1886), and Thomas Duckett Boyd (1896-1927); and in the Walter L. Fleming Collection, which includes letters and other papers of early administrators and faculty members. Official records held in the department include noncurrent files of the Board of Supervisors, the president's office, and the chancellor's office. The collection also includes records, reports, scrapbooks, and other materials generated by various academic departments; records of student and faculty organizations; professional and personal papers of past and present faculty members; printed items and ephemera; bachelor's theses (1898-1936); and a large collection of photographs.

Many of the collections of the University Archives contain materials that could be used for research in areas other than the history of LSU and of Southern education. The papers of Presidents Sherman and David Boyd contain valuable comments on the secession movement and on Reconstruction politics and economic problems. Official university records contain references to state politics, to the administration and influence of Huey P. Long, to race relations, and to the effects of World War II on the university. Other groups of papers contain information for research in such diverse fields as history, music, folklore, linguistics, biological sciences, sociology, geology, and geography.

A collection of visual materials, consisting of photographs, engravings, lithographs, motion picture films, and other materials, reflect most of the major subject areas of the document collection. Photographic materials, including early daguerrotypes, tintypes, and other nineteenth-century media, illustrate Southern plantation and urban life, the Civil War, industries, politics, and other topics. The photographs of Andrew Lytle (b. 1834), an early Baton Rouge photographer, depict Civil War scenes in Baton Rouge and the surrounding area, local buildings and landscapes, social and civic activities, and people. Photographs of George Francois Mugnier (1855-1936) depict buildings and scenery in the New Orleans area. The newly acquired Marshall Durham Photograph Album contains nearly two hundred carte-de-visite photographs of Louisiana during the Civil War, including unpublished photographs of New Orleans, Donaldsonville, and Port Hudson. The photograph files of Jasper E. Ewing and Sons concentrate on Baton Rouge subjects in the 1930s and 1940s. Other photographic collections include substantial bodies of materials pertaining to southwestern Louisiana, the lumber industry, steamboats, the Mississippi River flood of 1927, the geography and culture of the Acadian parishes, and state and national political figures and their activities.

The Department of Archives is also developing a small but steadily growing oral history collection.[3] Transcribed interviews with former LSU personnel give information on the history of the university as well as on many other topics. Of particular interest is a growing body of interviews (thirty to date) with veterans of the Vietnam War that provide rare firsthand descriptions of the American military experience in Southeast Asia. There are also interviews with Louisiana artist Caroline Durieux; two former residents of the New Llano socialist colony; former Louisiana Governor Sam H. Jones; and people involved in the early history of the Southern petroleum industry.

The department has facilities for limited copying, and research assistance can be provided for persons unable to visit the department in person. Finding aids include an extensive subject-index catalog and detailed inventories of most large collections.

NOTES

1. For a descriptive list of most of the holdings on this subject, see Brian E. Coutts and Merna W. Whitley, "An Inventory of Sources in the Department of Archives and Manuscripts, Louisiana State University, for the history of Spanish Louisiana and Spanish West Florida," *Louisiana History*, 19 (Spring 1978): 213-50.

2. The civil records listed above were acquired by the department from private collectors or manuscript dealers and are therefore not among the materials received by the department in its former role as state repository of public records.

3. For a detailed list of oral history holdings, see Merna W. Whitley, "Oral History Materials in the Department of Archives and Manuscripts, February, 1979," an unpublished inventory available in the department.

16
SOUTHWESTERN ARCHIVES AND MANUSCRIPTS COLLECTION, UNIVERSITY OF SOUTHWESTERN LOUISIANA

FREDERICK J. STIELOW

Street address: 3rd floor, Dupré Library
University of Southwestern Louisiana
Lafayette, Louisiana 70504
Mailing address: Same
Telephone: (318) 264-6031
Days and hours: Monday-Friday, 8:00 A.M. to 4:00 P.M.

THE SOUTHWESTERN ARCHIVES and Manuscripts Collection is a division of the University of Southwestern Louisiana Library and serves two primary missions. Its first role is specifically as the archives, the

This essay was written with the assistance of Glenn R. Conrad, James Geraghty, and Donald Saporito.

depository and place of organization, for the noncurrent records of the university. More importantly for the researcher, the archives also act as a research facility and repository for historical materials relating to the Mississippi Valley and, in particular, for those areas of southern Louisiana known as Acadiana.

The Southwestern Archives were the offspring of the History Department and its program. The archives were officially begun in January 1965 to complement a recently established graduate program, with Henry C. Dethloff, an agricultural historian, as their first archivist. Under Dr. Dethloff's guidance, the archives were able to gain intellectual control over the records of the university and established strong area collections in his field of expertise. In addition, Dr. Dethloff's efforts led the archives to be designated as the official depository for the rice industry.

In 1968, management of the archives passed into the hands of colonial historian Glenn R. Conrad. Mr. Conrad was especially successful in bringing to USL the most extensive collection of colonial material on Louisiana within the United States. During his tenure, Conrad's efforts also led to the formation of the Center for Louisiana Studies, which is now a separate department of the university under his direction with offices in the Dupré Library. Research materials generated by the staff of the Center for Louisiana Studies are ultimately deposited in the Southwestern Archives and Manuscripts Collection. Two significant and ongoing efforts in this vein are the Women in Louisiana Collection, directed by Vaughan Baker Simpson, and the Acadian and Creole Folklore Project, under the direction of Barry Ancelet.

In the summer of 1980, the archives were moved from quarters at the center to more spacious accommodations within the library. As part of expanded goals for the archives, the author, a professional archivist trained as a social historian with interests in southern Louisiana French culture, was brought in to head the department.

The archives are located on the third floor of USL's Dupré Library, and access is gained through the staff of the Jefferson Caffery Louisiana Room. The archives entertain a symbiotic relation with the Louisiana Room, its extensive vertical file, and some 15,000 monograph and microfilm editions on Louisiana subjects. The archives consist of some 90 manuscript and 30 folklore and oral history collections that encompass a million discrete items.

The University Archives (1899-present), with more than 1,300 feet, form the most extensive collection. Included in the holdings are twenty-five series, such as the records of USL's presidents (1900-1965), the early Board of Trustees (1900-1922), the registrar's office, and the faculty senate. The collections also contain a wealth of material on student life and athletics, as well as a large volume of photographs.

Beginning with a 1967 feasibility study, the archives were able to initiate an extensive Louisiana Colonial Records Program (1605-1803). Currently operated under the auspices of the Center for Louisiana Studies, this program is designed to microfilm manuscripts in foreign depositories relating to the French, Spanish, and British experiences in Louisiana. To date, this project has produced the largest collection of French materials dealing with Louisiana located outside of France. Processed materials from the Archive de Colonies include selections from series A and B on royal decrees, series C on general correspondence, series D on military affairs, and a variety of religious, financial, and transportation records from series F. The collection also holds microfilmed documents from the Archives du Ministère des Affaires Etrangères, Archives de la Guerre, Archive de la Marine, Archive du Ministère de la France d'Outre-Mer, Depôt des Cartes et Plans de la Marine, Bibliothèque Nationale, and elsewhere.

Through the cooperation of various Canadian depositories, the archives and the Center for Louisiana Studies were also able to microfilm manuscripts pertaining to the French experience in Canada, the Great Lakes region, and the Upper Mississippi Valley. In addition, British materials dealing with West Florida have been secured. At the present time, efforts are concentrated upon filming in Spain. Copies have been produced of documents within the Archivo Histórico Nacional and Archivo General de Simancas. It will require another ten years before all the pertinent holdings in the Archivo de Indias in Seville are filmed.

The Manuscripts Collection includes several collections dealing with the period from the end of the colonial era into the Civil War years. The Governor Alexander Mouton Papers (1813-1885; 350 items) contain correspondence from Louisiana's first Democratic governor, 1843-1846, and previously U.S. senator, 1837-1842. The John Mills Papers (1772-1812; 500 items) includes land titles, slave sales, and inventories from the Opelousas *Post*, and the Attakapas Day Book consists of the daily account of a trading post between 1813 and 1815. The Dalton Watson Papers (1793-1930; 2,000 items) provide a potpourri of correspondence and the plantation records of families in the Port Gibson, Mississippi-Waterproof, Louisiana, areas, as well as material on the Spanish Civil War and Indians in the West.

The Civil War era receives treatment in a number of collections. The Louis Stagg Papers (1855-1863; 25 items), for example, contain letters in French depicting conditions in the western theatre at Camp Moore, Tupelo, and Chattanooga. In addition to considerable information on the early history of Lafayette, Louisiana, the Givens-Hopkins Papers (1840-1860; 5,000 items) hold Civil War correspondence and Confederate pay vouchers. Similarly, the Debaillon Family Papers (1852-1944; 3 lin. ft.) contain information on such topics as the Know-Nothing party, the White League, and the Attakapas Vigilantes. The Declouet Family Papers (1811-1930; 400 items) concentrate upon the correspondence of Confederate Congressman Alexandre Declouet, 1861-1865, with his family.

Political history after the Civil War is treated in the papers of former Louisiana Senator Walter J. Burke (1866-1941; 1 lin. ft.) and a variety of other collections including those relating to U.S. Senator Donelson Caffery,

Congressman Garland Dupré (1873-1924; 1 lin. ft.), Congressman Edwin E. Willis (1948-1968; 200 lin. ft.), Lieutenant Governor J. Emile Verret, and Lieutenant Governor Albert Voorhies (1853-1948; 3 lin. ft.). Also of particular interest are the papers of Governor John M. Parker (1900-1936; 16 lin. ft.); they contain information on the Ku Klux Klan, the Dallas Calmes Affair, Huey P. Long, and other assorted topics.

Although they range beyond American borders, the papers of USL graduate and benefactor Jefferson Caffery (1902-1955; 60 lin. ft.) form one of the most prized collections. Mr. Caffery led a long and brilliant career as a Foreign Service officer, including twenty-nine years on an ambassadorial level. He served under every president from Taft to Eisenhower. His duties included acting as Woodrow Wilson's chief of protocol at the Versailles Peace Conference, as assistant secretary of state under Franklin Roosevelt, and, during the crucial years at the end of World War II, as the first career diplomat to head the Paris embassy. His postings covered the globe: Sweden, Greece, Spain, Japan, Germany, Belgium, El Salvador, Colombia, Cuba, Brazil, France, Egypt, Iran, and Pakistan.

On more localized topics, the Minutes of the Louisiana Conference of the South Methodist Episcopal Church (1889-1964; 64 volumes) and records of Lutheran churches in Crowley and Iota, Louisiana, help balance our scattered holdings on the Catholic church in southern Louisiana. In addition, a cooperative arrangement with the Lafayette Catholic Diocese and the new Lake Charles Diocese establishes a firm working relation and bridge to those other institutions.

The Manuscripts Collection contains material on a variety of other topics. For example, the David Reichard Williams Papers (1890-1962; 15 lin. ft.) and Owen Southwell Papers (n.d.; 30 lin. ft.) illustrate two strong collections in architecture, which are augmented by the recent donation of a collection of pre-nineteenth-century monographs. The Espy Williams Papers (1874-1910; 3,000 items), Ernest J. Whisler Papers (1964; 50 items), Marc Connelly Papers (1914-1966; 50 items), and Deep South Writers' Conference Papers (1961-present; 1.5 lin. ft.) serve as examples of the archive's holdings on literary figures. Of agricultural and horticultural interest are the Louisiana Camellia Society Papers, the Louisiana Iris Society Papers, the Jennings Nursery Collection, and the New Orleans Botanical Gardens Papers. Genealogical holdings are particularly well represented in the Mouton Papers (1872-1967), Jean Labranche Papers, Hébert Papers, and elsewhere.

Among the most actively pursued areas of collection are those dealing with the study of women in the state. Currently the archives house the records of a local branch of the American Association of University Women from its organization in 1927 together with selections from the Louisiana Division, Southeast Central Region, and National Office. Other collections include the Edith Dupré Papers, the Lucile Mouton Griffin Papers, and the

Marie Campbell Papers, as well as those from the Women in Louisiana Collection.

Business interests in southwestern Louisiana from the end of the colonial era to the present are particularly well documented within the collections. There are collections relating to the practice of law and medicine, lumbering, banking, and a variety of mercantile interests. On a more specialized level and as the official depository of the rice industry, there is a specific Rice Archives. The Rice Archives consist of sixteen individual collections on the rice industry in Louisiana and Mississippi, as well as information on cultivation in California, Texas, Cuba, India, and Puerto Rico. Among the more significant of these holdings are some forty feet of Pritchard Rice Milling Co. Papers and the Rice Millers' Association Archive (1906-1965; 10 lin. ft.). A rather unique feature of these collections is the presence of sixteen taped interviews with leading experts and figures in the industry.

The Sugar Archives provide further examples of USL's extensive holdings on agricultural topics. In addition to Louisiana, these sixteen printed and manuscript collections contain data on Cuba, Florida, the former French Empire, and elsewhere.

The Petroleum Archives reflect USL's strong interest in this region's major enterprise, concerns that are strengthened by the university's efforts in petroleum-related subjects and Lafayette's position as the oil center for the state. The Heywood Papers, for example, relate to the discovery and development of the Jennings Field. This collection and the recently acquired Fred Gerwick Collection also contain a number of valuable early photographs on the industry in the state. The more than 700 feet of the Zimmer Papers, which are currently in process, will provide a wealth of information on petroleum development and other geological topics. In addition to drilling logs and reports, these papers include Louisiana Department of Conservation hearings and orders for the area's oil fields.

The archives are actively expanding their photographic and pictorial collections. At this writing, a project is underway in the preparation and computer-oriented indexing of the 55,000 negatives of the Freeland Collection (1902-1960). Adjudged by experts from the Smithsonian Institute as a unique reflection of the social history of a small Southern city, this collection is being developed under the first National Historical Publications and Records Commission (NHPRC) grant awarded to a Louisiana institution. The importance of the collection has been underscored by the national success of the "Becoming Women: A Sequence of Louisiana Portraits" exhibit. Among other significant photographic holdings are the Froitzheim Pictorial Collection and the early oil field photos already mentioned.

A grant from the National Endowment for the Humanities for Francophone studies has helped underwrite the newest and potentially most valuable special collection—a tape archive of Acadian and Creole oral literature, history, and music. Working with experts from the Library of

Congress, Laval Université in Canada, and the faculty of several university departments, the archives are currently processing more than 500 taped interviews on Acadian and Creole music and culture for computer indexing. These tapes, which were secured through the Acadian and Creole Folklore Project of the Center for Louisiana Studies, are located in the recently completed Folklore/Oral History Room of the Dupré Library. They illustrate the desire of the University of Southwestern Louisiana to preserve and record the unique social character of the region.

In addition to folklore, these special collections are expanding to house the oral history collections. As previously indicated, the archives have interviews from the Rice Archives oral history program, but they also include recorded speeches from the Acadian Bicentennial Celebration and from several of the political figures within the collections as well as recordings from the Women in Louisiana Project. There are several other tapes of interest, such as the A. C. Bernard interviews with four hours of conversation about the formation of New Iberia, Louisiana, and the Spanish American War of 1898.

In conclusion, the Southwestern Archives and Manuscripts Collection is interested in materials relating to the university and its graduates as well as to the agricultural, industrial, and cultural facets of life in Acadiana. They are particularly interested in acquiring historical manuscripts and early photographs pertaining to the settlement and development of Louisiana, Acadiana, and the Lower Mississippi Valley region from the days of Cajun and Creole settlement to the oil industry of today. The archives invites inquiries from potential donors and researchers into such topics or other areas of interest within its holdings. A more detailed account of the archives will be found in the new edition of the *Guide to the Southwestern Archives and Manuscripts Collection* (Lafayette: University of Southwestern Louisiana, 1981).

17

LOUISIANA STATE MUSEUM: LOUISIANA HISTORICAL CENTER

JOHN R. KEMP AND EDWARD F. HAAS

Street address:	400 Esplanade Avenue
	New Orleans, Louisiana 70116
Mailing address:	751 Chartres Street
	New Orleans, Louisiana 70116
Telephone:	(504) 568-6968
Days and hours:	Monday-Friday, 8:30 A.M. to 4:45 P.M.

THE LOUISIANA STATE Museum, known to several generations as the Cabildo and Presbytère, is progressively becoming one of the most important resources in the state for the study of Louisiana's history and heritage. Its combined collections of architecture, decorative arts, industrial artifacts, folk art, costumes and textiles, paintings, prints, photographs, and archival holdings spanning the eighteenth through twentieth centuries are unequaled. The Louisiana Historical Center, a research facility that includes a library and archives, is one of the museum's newest departments.

The authors acknowledge their appreciation to the following members of the Louisiana State Museum's staff for their assistance in compiling this guide: Robert R. Macdonald, Director; Stanley Hordes, former Curator of Colonial Archives, Louisiana Historical Center; Joseph D. Castle, Associate Curator of Colonial Archives, Louisiana Historical Center; Ghislaine Pleasonton, former Associate Curator of Colonial Archives, Louisiana Historical Center; Vaughn L. Glasgow, Chief Curator, Curatorial Department; and, Donald Marquis, Curator of Jazz Collections.

The Louisiana State Museum has always held an important place in the state's cultural community since its creation by the General Assembly in 1906. Actually, the museum had its beginning in 1904 at the Louisiana Purchase Exposition in Saint Louis, Missouri. The Louisiana Board of Commissioners to the exposition collected a wide variety of artifacts that it deemed representative of the state's "archaeology, history, education, commerce, flora and fauna, minerals, and agriculture." With an appropriation of $2,500, the exhibition was returned to Louisiana in 1904 at the close of the exposition. The question of where to locate the new museum soon arose. After a brief squabble between the Board of Commissioners and officials from Louisiana State University, who wanted the collections in Baton Rouge, the museum opened its doors in the first floor of the Washington Artillery Hall as the "Louisiana State Exhibit and Museum." Two years later, on January 30, 1908, the New Orleans City Council and Mayor Martin Behrman transferred the Cabildo-Presbytère-Arsenal complex to the Board of Curators of the Louisiana State Museum. The buildings, however, were not occupied until January 1, 1911.

During those early years, annual attendance at the museum was 150,000 visitors, and the state legislature appropriated $12,500 for the institution. By 1950 the annual budget had increased to $87,150. In 1980 the museum complex received over a quarter of a million visitors and operated with a budget of $2.6 million.

In compiling a guide to the Louisiana State Museum's Historical Center, a repository of books, manuscripts, and maps, it would be remiss if additional museum collections were not mentioned. The museum, unlike libraries, has a special advantage in studying the history of the people of Louisiana because it also collects dimensional and visual artifacts. To study the culture of a people, in the anthropological sense, researchers must examine and evaluate the various objects that a culture produces. At the Louisiana State Museum, these materials are available. Museum collections can be divided into seven categories: buildings, paintings and graphic arts, furniture and decorative arts, costumes and textiles, science and technology, photographs, and jazz.

The museum properties, consisting of eight historically and architecturally significant structures in the New Orleans French Quarter, are themselves important historical documents. Five of these buildings have been declared National Historic Landmarks: the Cabildo, Presbytère, Lower Pontalba Building, Madame John's Legacy, and the New Orleans Branch of the U.S. Mint. Three additional structures—the Arsenal, Jackson House, and Creole House—are important to state and local history.

The museum's paintings and graphic arts collections consist of more than 1,000 paintings and 3,000 prints and drawings, including a large collection of eighteenth- and nineteenth-century portraits. Regional landscapes and townscapes form a significant portion of this collection. Within the section is a complete elephant folio of *Audubon's Birds of America*. The collection also includes the work of such noted artists as Richard Clegg, Jr., Francisco Bernard, George Coulon, Jean Joseph Vaudechamp, Julien Hudson, Jules Lion, and William A. Walker.

The furniture and decorative arts collections contain many important examples of materials made and used in Louisiana during the eighteenth and nineteenth centuries. They range from early country pieces to Eastlake and other nineteenth-century models, including furniture by the noted cabinet makers Mallard and Seignouret. The decorative arts collection includes glass, ceramics, and decorative accessories dating from the early nineteenth century to the early decades of the twentieth century. The museum houses important collections of silverware by the New Orleans firm of Hyde and Goodrich and an excellent collection of Newcomb-style crafts. There are approximately 6,000 items in this section.

The museum's holdings in costumes and textiles document fabrics, dress, and accessories from the end of the eighteenth century to the middle of the twentieth century. Of special note is the Mardi Gras collection of costumes, invitations, favors, and other materials related to this important Louisiana tradition. Ethnic materials include costumes and accessories and an especially fine group of Louisiana Indian baskets. There are approximately 8,000 items in this section.

The nucleus of the science and technology section includes architectural fragments, models, medical equipment, hardware, and implements that reflect the industrial, commercial, and scientific history of the state. One of the most important and popular objects in this section is the submarine *Pioneer*, which was developed during the Civil War and believed to be the oldest surviving submarine. The science and technology collections are estimated at over 5,000 objects.

The museum holds photographic collections numbering approximately 75,000 images, including several hundred negatives by such noted photographers as George Francois Mugnier, Robert Tebbs, and John Teunesson. In addition, several hundred examples of the earliest forms of photography, such as daguerreotypes, ambrotypes, ferrotypes, albumen prints, and "wet" and "dry" plate negatives, are located in these collections.

The New Orleans Jazz Museum has been turned over to the Louisiana State Museum for exhibition and archival use. An exhibition of jazz materials will be located in the Old Mint Building on Esplanade Avenue. The jazz collection is one of the largest and most comprehensive of its kind in the world. The main visual attractions are numerous musical instruments, including those once used by such greats as Louis Armstrong, Sidney Bechet, Bix Beiderbecke, Gene Krupa, and King Oliver. For the researcher there are also hundreds of rare photographs and thousands of phonograph records. Nearly 1,000 reels of taped music and interviews and boxes of original sheet music are included in the Jazz Museum. A very rare collection of New Orleans jazz on film will be available to the public.

The Louisiana Historical Center constitutes an eighth and distinct segment of the museum's collections. Created in 1977, the Historical Center consists of the museum's research library and archives. The library contains approximately 35,000 books and 10,000 pamphlets on Louisiana topics. Moreover, it has an excellent collection of New Orleans newspapers dating from 1802 to 1940. Both historians and genealogists have made extensive use of the library's collections, particularly the indexes to New Orleans cemeteries, scrapbooks, pamphlets, vertical files, rare books, and transcriptions from French and Spanish archives. In addition to published works, the library houses many important transcriptions and translations, such as Dispatches of the Spanish Governors of Louisiana (1766-1796; 27 volumes), prepared by the Works Progress Administration (WPA), which include material on Ulloa, Unzaga, O'Reilly, Gálvez, Miró, and Carondelet. Among the additional transcriptions (one volume unless indicated otherwise) are: Louisiane Recensements (1706-1741); Louisiane Correspondance Générale (1678-1706; 2 volumes); Louisiane Générale (1719-1724); Louisiane Correspondance Générale (1768-1769; 2 volumes); Louisiane Passages (1718-1724); Louisiane Concessions (1719-1724); Louisiane Etat Civil (1720-1734); and Archives of the Spanish Government of West Florida (June 3, 1782, to September 12, 1810; 18 volumes). The Records of the City Council of New Orleans, accessioned by the WPA, include Book 4083, 1770-1792; Book 4089, 1815-1822; Book 4087, 1794-1803, 2 volumes; Book 4084, 1823-1835; and Book 4088, 1800-1803.

The archival and manuscript collections are divided into two basic groups: general collections; and colonial archives, including the judicial records of the French Superior Council of Louisiana (1714-1769) and the Spanish judicial records (1769-1803). The general collections, which vary in type and subject matter, comprise the most diverse segment of the Louisiana Historical Center's holdings. They range from carnival invitations to Civil War correspondence and date from the territorial period to the twentieth century. Because the documents in this section have never been thoroughly catalogued or indexed, they are now undergoing reorganization.

Several collections pertain to the territorial period in Louisiana. The James Wilkinson Papers (early nineteenth century; 11 items) relate to the Aaron Burr conspiracy and the Spanish in West Florida. The Nathaniel Cox Papers (1802-1809; 17 items) contain information relative to social, political, and economic conditions in New Orleans as well as the cotton and sugar industries, Aaron Burr, and the Embargo Act. The Charity Hospital Papers (1811-1812; 1 lin. ft.) are also useful for medical history.

Holdings on antebellum economic history are particularly rich. The John Smith Collection (1799-1869; 1.5 lin. ft.) pertains to trade, commerce, and politics in New Orleans, the Gulf Coast region, and various American,

European, and West Indian ports. The James Colles Letterbooks (1801-1870; 5 volumes, mimeographed) and the Lewis Henry Webb Diaries (January 12, 1853 to July 5, 1853; 5 volumes) relate to social and business matters in New Orleans. Colles, a grocer, was affiliated with the firm of Dudley and Nelson; Webb was a young merchant from North Carolina who lived in New Orleans for one year. The Freret Collection (1880-1839; 25 items) contains information relative to Hunt and Smith Company, a mercantile firm in Huntston near Natchez, Mississippi. The P. A. Giraud, D. A. Chaffraix, Champomier and Giraud, and Lelong Papers (ca. 1837-1910; ca. 16 lin. ft.) include the business records of these New Orleans merchants.

Other collections relate to the agricultural sector of the economy. The John Flathers Papers (nineteenth century; 0.5 lin. ft.), a collection of receipts, bills of sale, and claims of title, pertain to the Orleans and Valentine plantations. The Bonaventure Plantation Ledger (1850-1851; 1 volume); and Mavis Grove Plantation Journal (1856-1859; 1 volume) are also available.

Additional antebellum collections are quite varied. The Battle of New Orleans Papers (1814-1815; ca. 71 items) include reports, orders, and correspondence concerning W.C.C. Claiborne, Andrew Jackson, and David B. Morgan. The Louisiana Civil Records (1812-1858; ca. 36 lin. ft.) constitute an uncatalogued collection that includes such records as state treasurers' annual reports, secretaries of state papers, district court records, and correspondence concerning executive clemency and patronage to several governors, including Edward Douglas White, Isaac Johnson, and Robert C. Wickliffe. The John McDonogh Papers (1813-1846; 2 lin. ft.) contain correspondence to and from business associates, members of the American Colonization Society, and former slaves in Liberia as well as extensive correspondence (104 items) to McDonogh from Andrew Durnford, a free black planter in Plaquemines Parish, Louisiana. The Beebe Papers (ca. 1840-1865; 1 lin. ft.) contain information relative to social, political, and economic conditions in New Orleans during the late antebellum period, including the yellow fever epidemic of 1853, the Vigilence Committee uprising of 1858, and the U.S. occupation of the city during the Civil War. The John Slidell Papers (ca. 1840-1870; 3 lin. ft.) include legal papers, correspondence, and land claims in Louisiana. The Henry Wilcox Papers (1825-1878; 0.5 lin. ft.) relate to military activities and Indian warfare in Louisiana, Alabama, Florida, and western Tennessee. The Historical Center also houses the Louisiana Militia Book (January 28, 1815-February 27, 1827; 1 volume). The W. P. Riddell Diary (1853-1858; 1 volume) is the diary of a chemistry professor at the University of Louisiana. The Valcour Aime Diaries (1821-1858; 4 volumes) relate to Saint James Parish. The H. M. Hyams Letterbook (October 1855-December 1857; 1 volume) pertains to matters in New Orleans and Saint Francisville.

Several collections pertain to the Civil War era. One is the Official Journal of the Convention of the State of Louisiana (January 23, 1861; 1 volume), the journal of the secession convention. The Brent Collection (ca. 1864-1865; 3 lin. ft.) consists of correspondence and dispatches to and from Lieutenant General Richard Taylor, commander of the Confederate Department of Alabama, Mississippi, and East Louisiana, October 1864 to May 1865, and muster rolls of the paroled members of Taylor's command that were surrendered at Mobile and Citronelle, Alabama, in May 1865. Principal correspondents include Jefferson Davis, Robert E. Lee, Joseph E. Johnston, P.G.T. Beauregard, Edward Farrand, W. J. Hardee, Dabney H. Maury, Nathan Bedford Forrest, Joseph Wheeler, E.R.S. Canby, P. G. Osterhaus, G. Granger, Frank Gardner, and G. W. Smith. The collection also contains material relative to the Department of the Trans-Mississippi and Duncan Kenner.

The George Moss Papers (1854-1868; 1 lin. ft.), a collection of Civil War correspondence from Louisianians fighting in Virginia and Mississippi, pertain to economic, military, and social conditions during and after the Civil War, journals, correspondence from Alabama, Louisiana, and Mississippi, land sales, legal documents, a genealogical chart, and death notices and contain information relative to the Briant family of Saint Martinville and New Orleans. The William S. Mitchell Papers (1859-1892; 40 items) are the personal papers of a Louisiana surgeon in the First Louisiana Infantry who served in northern Virginia during the Civil War. The P.G.T. Beauregard Papers (ca. 1855-1878; 30 items) relate to the construction of the Customs House in New Orleans, the Civil War, activities in New Orleans after the Civil War, and the genealogy of the Toutant family. The James Currell Papers (1864-1865; 14 items) relate to the exchange of Confederate and Union prisoners of war in the Mobile area.

The Jefferson Davis Papers (ca. 1861-1880s; 17 items) relate to the Civil War and events in the 1880s. The Bernard Janin Sage Papers (1851-1899; 135 items) contain legal notes in defense of Jefferson Davis and secession as well as correspondence with the Lewis family of South Louisiana. Sage had been chosen as counsel for the defense in the projected trial of Jefferson Davis. The Duncan Kenner Papers (1863-1877; 23 items) pertain to negotiations for a Confederate loan, the 1867-1868 Louisiana Constitutional Convention, and the 1876 gubernatorial elections. Principal correspondents include B. Baruc; G. A. Trenholm, secretary of the treasury of the Confederate States of America; Judah P. Benjamin; and James Madison Wells.

The Louisiana Historical Center also houses manuscript collections that relate to various Louisiana governors. Most of these collections consist of a few miscellaneous documents. The James Madison Wells Papers (1816-1878; 23 items), however, are more substantial and contain correspondence to and from the Wells family, John Sherman, Joseph Casey, and James S.

Hallowell, as well as the Scott family of Louisiana, Alabama, and Mississippi.

Several collections pertain to Louisiana in the nineteenth century. The John B. Fleitas Diary (1876; 1 volume) contains information on the Corine Plantation (formerly the Villere Plantation) in Saint Bernard, Louisiana. The Cenas Family Papers (1786-1916), a collection of letters, papers, and memorabilia of the Cenas family, relate to the social, political, economic, and military history of Louisiana. The Charles Patton Dimitry Papers (72 items) contain manuscript lectures and addresses that pertain to New Orleans and Louisiana in the nineteenth century. The Justin F. Denechaud Collection (1882-1903; 66 items) includes correspondence, pamphlets, broadsides, and memorabilia that relate to Louisiana politics.

Twentieth-century holdings are extensive. The Grace Chamberlain Papers (early twentieth century; 1 lin. ft.) relate to women's suffrage in Louisiana; the National American Woman's Suffrage Association and the ERA (Equal Rights for All) Club. The World's Panama-Pacific Exposition Commission Papers (ca. 1910; 8 lin. ft.) contain the records of the Louisiana Committee of the Panama Canal Exposition. The Louisiana State Board of Agriculture and Immigration Papers (ca. 1912-1915; 6.5 lin. ft.) contain records and correspondence. The Louisiana Engineering Society Papers (early twentieth century; 1 lin. ft.) constitute a collection of reports, receipts, accounts, and minutes of meetings. The George Hebard Maxwell Papers (1897-1938; 6.5 lin. ft.) relate to Maxwell's work in the national irrigation program with the National Irrigation Association (later renamed the National Reclamation Association). The James Parkerson Kemper Papers (ca. 1912-1915; 43 items) include published and manuscript articles, reports, and papers that contain information relative to Kemper's work in flood control in Louisiana as well as biographical sketches of the first families of the Bayou Teche region of Louisiana. The Walter Hamlin Papers (ca. 1950s-1970s; 3 lin. ft.) contain copies of the speeches and lectures of Walter Hamlin, associate justice and chief justice of the Louisiana Supreme Court. Scrapbook 100, by George Coulon, is a collection of notes, clippings, and biographies of Louisiana artists.

The Louisiana Historical Center has in its collections approximately 3,000 maps, atlases, and architectural plans pertaining to the colony and the state of Louisiana dating from the seventeenth to the twentieth century. Notable in the cartography collection are the Confederate manuscript maps of Louisiana, 1864; and Dudley's 1661 chart of the Gulf of Mexico. Among the architectural materials are the Historical Architectural Buildings Survey, a collection of field notes and drawings for Louisiana buildings, and the research notes for the first three volumes of the Friends of the Cabildo series on New Orleans architecture.

The judicial records of colonial Louisiana, however, constitute the Historical Center's largest and most significant collection. Covering the years from the earliest settlement in 1714 to the Louisiana Purchase in 1803, these records of the French Superior council and Spanish Louisiana contain a wide variety of civil and criminal proceedings that illuminate the economic, social, political, and cultural life of colonial Louisiana. While most of the documents (approximately a half-million pages) deal with attempts by creditors to recover commercial obligations, the collection includes a large number of successions. These proceedings contain a wealth of social, economic, biographical, and architectural data concerning the inhabitants of Louisiana. Among the inventories of plantations and estates are surveys of plantations, architectural descriptions of houses, accounts of administration of estates, commercial transactions, correspondence and copies of wills, marriage contracts, and parish baptismal, marriage and burial records. Also included in the colonial archives are petitions to governing officials by slaves for emancipation, by merchants for licenses to conduct public sales of their goods, by ship captains for absolution from responsibility for losses at sea, and by traders for permission to engage in commerce with Europe, the West Indies, and the English colonies in North America (later the United States).

In addition to the judicial records, the Louisiana Historical Center also holds other collections that relate to eighteenth-century Louisiana. One, "Mississippi Valley, French Manuscripts," is a compilation of original documents relating to French colonial administration, especially in Louisiana. Among these documents are such important items as the Code Noir of 1724 and letters of patent to Antoine Crozat in 1712 and the Company of the West in 1717. Another is a four-volume set of transcriptions of documents from the archives of Spain made in the mid-nineteenth century under the direction of Charles Gayarré. Most of the transcriptions consist of official correspondence among governors, intendants, ecclesiastical officials, and ministers in Spain and cover a wide variety of topics, ranging from trade and treaties with the Indians, to commercial restrictions and duties, to jurisdictional disputes with the Church. Although the bulk of the material was copied from the Archivo General de Indias in Seville, some of the documents originated in the Archivo de la Contaduria del Consejo de Indias de Madrid, and the Archivo General de Simancas. Two additional collections are the Julien Poydras Letterbook (1794-1800; 1 volume), a manuscript entitled "Private and Commercial Correspondence of an Indigo and Cotton Planter, 1794-1800," and the Mossmeier Papers (ca. 1750-1854; 1 lin. ft.), a collection of legal documents, inventories, official records, and family papers that relate to Haiti in the eighteenth century and New Orleans in the early nineteenth century.

The Louisiana Historical Center also houses several microfilm collections that pertain to colonial Louisiana. Among these materials are the Pontalba-Almonester-Miró Papers (1792-1796; 7 reels) and the colonial records of the following parishes: Saint Charles (1740-1792; 9 reels), Saint Landry (1764-

1793; 8 reels), and Avoyelles (1793-1796; 3 reels). Available also are the Dispatches from U.S. Consuls in New Orleans, 1798-1807 (March 17, 1798-February 6, 1807; 1 reel), the Records of the Diocese of Louisiana and the Floridas (1576-1803; 12 reels), and the Notarial Records of the Notaries of Spanish Louisiana and Court Proceedings of the Spanish Cabildo of Louisiana (1769-1803; 201 reels). These materials, manuscripts, and microfilm altogether constitute the largest collection of colonial Louisiana materials in the world.

The documents contained in the colonial holdings of the Louisiana Historical Center, furthermore, offer the researcher a rare glimpse into the everyday life of colonial Louisiana. While most other repositories contain official pronouncements, laws, and correspondence, the colonial collections of the Historical Center reflect a cross section of Louisiana residents, wealthy and indigent, black and white, free and slave. They relate public and private feuds, business ventures, political controversies, and revolts. They document the social, political, and economic evolution of the colony and are indispensable to the understanding of life in French and Spanish Louisiana.

Through funds from the National Endowment for the Humanities initially, and later with support from the state of Louisiana, members of the museum staff are preparing the colonial records for microfilming as well as writing detailed calendars for each document. Because the WPA used cellophane adhesive tape to mend the documents during the 1930s, long-range plans include restoration and stabilization. If these documents are left unattended, the chemicals in the adhesive will eventually destroy the papers.

Researchers wishing to use the colonial documents will find a partial index and incomplete calendars in the museum library. These finding aids were prepared by the Louisiana Historical Society and the WPA. Although existing guides will be obsolete with the completion of the current project, the previous numbering system will be noted and retained in the new calendars.

The completion of this work will undoubtedly lead to a thorough reexamination of early Louisiana history. Topics for historical research abound. Documentary sources on slavery and race relations alone are overwhelming. The succession records of white and black slaveowners, for instance, contain vital information on bondsmen as well as detailed lists of agricultural tools, supplies, and housing facilities. Other documents relate to emancipations, runaways, and health care for slaves. Additional materials pertain to the free black community. Among the judicial records are inventories of clothing, furniture, and books that will be valuable to cultural historians. Suits for payment of debts and for absolution of damages offer important possibilities to economic historians. With the present availability of these judicial records, students of Louisiana history will be forced to reevaluate old historical interpretations and to consider new ideas on the people and institutions of early Louisiana.

18
THE HOWARD-TILTON MEMORIAL LIBRARY, TULANE UNIVERSITY

WILBUR MENERAY

Street address:	Freret Street and Newcomb Place
	Tulane University
	New Orleans, Louisiana 70118
Mailing address:	Howard-Tilton Memorial Library
	Tulane University
	New Orleans, Louisiana 70118
Telephone:	(504) 865-5685
Days and hours:	Monday-Friday, 8:00 A.M. to 5:00 P.M.;
	Saturday, 10:00 A.M. to noon

THE HOWARD-TILTON Memorial Library of Tulane University contains several divisions with sources for the study of Louisiana, most associated with the Special Collections Division. Special Collections is composed of the Rare Books Section, the William Ransom Hogan Jazz Archive, the Tulane University Archives, the Manuscripts Section, and the Southeastern Architectural Archive. The Louisiana Collection, the largest section of printed material about Louisiana, is housed elsewhere in the library.

The nucleus of the Louisiana material came from the Charles T. Howard Memorial Library, founded in 1889 as a privately endowed and administered research library open to the public. One of the main goals of the Howard

Library was to provide material relating to the region, pioneered by Director William Beer (1891-1922). In 1941 the holdings of the Howard Library were merged with those of the Frederick W. Tilton Memorial Library of Tulane University and the library of Newcomb College, creating the present Howard-Tilton Memorial Library.

Of the areas of Special Collections, the Rare Book Section contains the fewest sources on Louisiana, since many of the "rare" Louisiana books are housed within the Louisiana Collection. The Rare Books Section does have, however, several discrete collections and individual items that are important in the study of Louisiana. Among the individual items are the "Thwaites's" *Jesuits Relations*, *American Archives* and numerous travel accounts mentioning Louisiana.

Among the special collections of books is the Favrot Library with 866 titles, many related to Louisiana, Baton Rouge, and New Orleans. Over one-half of the titles in the Favrot Library are not found elsewhere in the library. The Favrot Library contains histories of the state, novels, and poetry (mainly nineteenth-century by Louisiana authors), state and local publications dating from 1805, early law works, political pamphlets, printed speeches, and business charters. The earliest work dealing with Louisiana is John Frédéric Bernard, *Relations de la Louisiane et du fleuve Mississippi* (Amsterdam, 1720). Among rare works are the *West Florida Ordinance Adopted by the Convention of West Florida* (Natchez, La., 1810) and Alejandro O'Reilly, *Le Procès qui a été fait à cause du soulèvement qu'il y a eu dans cette colonie* (New Orleans, 1769).

The William B. Wisdom Collection contains prominent histories and novels along with a number of first editions of early travel accounts. The book section of the Rosemond E. and Emile Kuntz Memorial Collection contains 301 volumes that comprise a good working collection on Louisiana history. Some of the works belonged to Charles Gayarré and have his notes in the margins. The Lafcadio Hearn Collection contains 427 volumes of works either by or about Hearn.

The University Archives of Tulane University document the major higher educational movement in New Orleans from 1836. The archives contain records of the College of Orleans, the University of Louisiana, and Tulane University. The archives's holdings include the minutes of the Board of Administrators of the University of Louisiana (1847-1884) and of its successor, the Board of Administrators of the Tulane Educational Fund (1884-present); reports of presidents of Tulane University to the Board of Administrators; presidential correspondence (see also the Manuscripts Section); lists of graduates (1836 to present); student and university publications such as catalogs, newsletters, student journals, and newspapers; a clipping file dating from 1882; matriculation records (1903-1937); papers of Newcomb College; and photographs, memorabilia, and information files on selected alumni, faculty, and administrators.

The Manuscripts Section of the Special Collections Division contains over 2,000 individual manuscript collections, which range in size from 1 item to over 100,000 items. Nearly three-quarters of these collections relate in some fashion to Louisiana, and many of them to the New Orleans metropolitan area. Although the material concerning Louisiana dates from the late seventeenth century, the bulk is from the second half of the nineteenth century, increasing in size as one approaches the middle of the twentieth century.

In describing the holdings of the Manuscripts Section an effort has been made to organize material into three general time frames: the colonial period, which goes up to 1803; the antebellum era, including the Civil War; and the postbellum, or modern period, starting in 1865. Since the lives, careers, or papers of an individual or institution do not break neatly at these arbitrary chronological divisions, most collections are discussed in the time span of the bulk of the papers, or when the individual or institution flourished. For the antebellum and postbellum periods several topics, such as plantations, business, politics, charities, medicine, and religion, are repeated in each era. Many of the entire collections are fully described in the Special Collections Division of the Howard-Tilton Memorial Library.

The colonial era created the uniqueness of Louisiana. Over one hundred collections in the Manuscripts Section contain material on the colonial period in the state. A number of these collections, however, contain only scattered personal or business documents, such as baptismal, marriage, and death records, land grants, sales and surveys, business receipts, and military or government commissions. Among collections with more extensive documentation are family papers, governmental documents, business records, and reproductions from French and Spanish Archives.

The Favrot Family Papers (1669-1803; 825 items), are mainly the official and family correspondence of Claude Joseph Favrot, who served with the French army in Louisiana from 1731 to 1767, and those of his son, Pierre Joseph Favrot, who served with the French and Spanish armies in the region and who held several local administrative posts. The Barrow Family Archive contains the family correspondence of Spanish Governor Manuel Gayoso de Lemos (1797-1800; 21 items) and some of the Wickoff family of Opelousas (1781-1809; 18 items). The Urquhart Collection of the Bringier, Charest-DeGournay-Duborg, and Tureaud Papers holds a number of original and copied personal and sales documents.

The Grima Family Papers (1792-1806; 25 items), Nicolas Low Papers (1791-1811; 30 items), and Julien Poydras Recordbook (1792-1803; 1 volume) all deal with business activity in the late colonial period. There is a collection of French land grants (1733-1769; 55 items) and of Spanish land transactions in the Florida parishes and upriver from New Orleans (1786-1807; 52 items).

The New Orleans Municipal Papers (1770-1803; 70 items) contain information on the daily local governmental operations, as do many of the papers in the colonial sections of the John Minor Wisdom Collection (1717-1803; 83 items).

The Rosemonde E. and Emile Kuntz Collection holds a wealth of colonial material. For the French period (1665-1768; 179 items) there are family letters, correspondence of representatives of the Company of the Indies, land transfers, official documents, and material relating to the opposition to the cession to Spain. For the Spanish period (1769-1803; 279 items) there is additional material on the revolt of 1768, reports of Francisco Bouligny, numerous land transfers, and local governmental documents.

The Manuscripts Section also holds some of the proclamations of Pierre Clement Laussat regarding the retrocession of Louisiana to France (1803; 9 items).

There are fifty-one reels of microfilm from the Archives Coloniales, mainly series 13C, and twenty-five volumes of photographs of the Papeles de Cuba from the Archivo de Indias. The Spanish documents have been translated.

As in other Southern states, the antebellum era in Louisiana left an "oppressive legacy," the plantation agricultural system, with its institution of slavery. Plantation papers from the period include those of the Ackel Family (1825-1853; 165 items) in West Feliciana Parish; Robert Ruffin Barrow (1800-1865; 241 items) in Terrebonne Parish; the Brou Plantation (1808-1869; 250 items) in Saint John the Baptist Parish; Walthall Burton (1806-1860; 42 items) in Saint Landry Parish; Colomb Plantation (1850-1863; 1 volume in the Kuntz Collection) in Saint James Parish; Andrew Durnford (1829-1868; 63 items), a black planter in Plaquemines Parish; Jean Baptiste Ferchaud (1858; 1 volume); Alexis Ferry (1842-1883; 5 volumes), and Eugene Forstall (1851-1855; 2 letter books); all three in Saint James Parish; Prosper Foy (1790-1878; 2 volumes) in Saint Charles Parish; Willis P. Griffith (1840-1855; 72 items) in Saint Martin Parish; the Grima Family (1808-1865; 320 items) in several parishes; John Hoey (1840-1854; 9 volumes) in Jefferson Parish; Lestan Prudhomme (1826-1854; 978 items) in Natchitoches Parish; David Rees (1806-1835; 110 items) in Saint Martin Parish; the Roman family (1828-1865; 116 items) in Saint James Parish; Samuel Walker (1806-1807; 1 volume), location not identified; and Archibald P. Williams (1824-1866; 114 items) in Rapides Parish. In addition, there are seven small collections from the period in the Plantation Series and twenty-six similar collections in the Slavery Series. Material on plantations is also located in the Personal Documents Series, the Land Transactions Series and estate inventories, and slave and land sales in numerous other collections.

Louisiana's agricultural economy was an export economy in which merchants played an important role. Merchant records can be found in the papers of John McDonogh (1800-1852; 6,600 items), containing a large amount of commercial correspondence, bills of lading, and other financial papers. Other merchant's papers are those of Charles Alter (1840-1898; 490 items); André Brousseau (1852-1854); Carroll, Hoy and Company (1861-1869; 640 items); Collins Family (1844-1859; 100 items); John Dunlop (1827-1869; 170 items); New Orleans Cotton Broker Correspondence (1831-1850; 48 items); New Orleans Commission Merchant Ledger (1852-1853; 1 volume); New Orleans Wholesale Merchant Ledger (1817-1818; 1 volune); New Orleans Wine Merchant's Daybook (1828-1835; 1 volume); Roberts and Company (1854-1867; 12 volumes); Smith, Hubbard and Company (1834-1851; 116 items); and Paul Tulane (1834-1888; 435 items). Correspondence of several New Orleans commission agents and Mississippi planters can be found in the Albert Lieutaud Collection. The Frank M. Besthoff Collection contains commercial correspondence of the firms of Glendy Burke, John Watt, Louis de Saulls, and Gabriel Lavie (1808-1856; 215 items). The Cotton Trade Series contains eleven small collections on antebellum cotton trade. The collection has recently received the papers of the Mississippi Valley Association, an organization now known as the Water Resources Congress.

For financial records of the era, consult the Citizens Bank and Trust Company Papers (1833-1865; 32 volumes), the New Orleans Canal Bank and Trust Company Papers (1831-1865; 5 volumes) and the papers of Jules de la Vergne (1838-1843; 125 items), concerning the operations of the Louisiana Bank. Insurance company records include the *La Compagnie d'Assurance de la Nouvelle Orléans* Dividend Ledger (1808-1849; 1 volume). The Jackson, Riddle and Company Papers (1834-1839; 69 items) concern the discounting of bank notes. The Brizzard Collection contains a number of issues of state, local, bank, and private company currency.

The Pontchartrain Railroad Company Minute Book (1829-1839; 1 volume) and the Steamship *Louisiana*'s Records (1824-1825; 100 items) both deal with transportation. The library has recently received the papers of the Standard Fruit and Steamship Company for the period from 1919 to 1956.

James Damaré Recordbook (1857-1870), Saint James Parish, Meyer and Hymel Daybook (1856-1857), Thibodaux, and the Dufossard Landry Accountbook (1847-1848), Assumption Parish, all record the business operations of general stores.

Papers dealing with state politics located in collections relating to Louisiana congressmen include those of Whig Representative Henry Hosford Curley (1815-1831; 41 items), Democratic Representative Isaac Edward Morse (1833-1850; 150 items), Democratic Representative Louis St. Martin (1842-1889; 150 items), Democratic Representative and Senator John Slidell (1829-1860; 169 items), and scattered papers of other political leaders, such as Pierre Soulé and Judah P. Benjamin. The Albert Lieutaud Collection has material on elections in Saint John Parish (1818-1862; 41 items).

The most extensive governmental papers are those relating to the municipal government of New Orleans and its suburbs. Most of these can be found in the New Orleans Municipal Papers (1,021 items), the Kuntz Collection (692 items), and the John Minor Wisdom Collection (779 items). All of these collections were constructed from varying sources over a period of years. As a result, the three collections are comprised of similar, and often complementary, material. In general, these contain pay bills, receipts, license bonds, petitions to the City Council, correspondence of the mayor's office and financial records. Common themes in these documents are police matters, contracts, markets, levee and street repair, and slaves hired by the city. Items deserving of special mention are an 1805 Census of New Orleans; Bonds of Free Persons of Color in the First Municipality, 1843-1844; Tavern Bonds, 1830-1837; and clipped ordinances of the town of Carrollton, 1857-1870 (all in the Wisdom Collection). The letter book of the mayor's office, December 1803-May 1804, is a major item from the New Orleans Municipal Papers.

In the general Manuscripts Section can be found the Census of Carrollton (1857, 1859, 1860; 1 volume), receipts and reports on Carrollton (1840-1868; 194 items), and material on the town of Lafayette (1838-1844; 340 items).

For papers of antebellum charitable and assistance organizations, see the papers of John Page (1836-1849; 15 volumes), superintendent of the Waldo Burton Home; and the Poydras Home [Female Orphan Society] (1818-1865; 4,600 items). Several other organizations had their roots in the antebellum period but developed during the postwar years. For those collections consult the postbellum section.

The papers relating to medicine in Louisiana during the antebellum era include those of George Colmer (1847-1880; 2 volumes), Springfield, Louisiana, physician; John H. Harrison Papers (1840-1847; 94 items), professor of pathology at the University of Louisiana; Pierre Antoine and Pierre Alexander Lambert (1798-1862; 298 items), physicians and pharmacists in France and New Orleans; Joseph Montegut (1756-1805; 24 items); and John Leonard Ridell (1831-1879; 317 items), medical professor and inventor of the binocular microscope. There are also five small items concerning medicine in Louisiana, as well as numerous mentions of disease in the various family papers.

The bulk of the antebellum religious papers is found in the Episcopal Diocese of Louisiana Archive. These include records of Christ Church (1805-1862; 600 items), Saint Luke's (later Trinity) (1856-1859; 1 volume), and Saint Paul's Vestry Minutes (1839-1859; 1 volume), as well as the journal of the Annual Conventions (1838-1850; 1 volume) and the papers of individual ministers, such as William T. Leacock (1822-1862) and Greer B. Duncan (1843-1844; 1 volume). See also a record of Charles L. Howard as senior warden of Christ Church concerning the conflicts with General Benjamin F. Butler (1862-1865; 1 volume).

Other church-related collections include the records of Lafayette, Andrew, and Steele Chapels (later Rayne Memorial Methodist Church) (1848-1857; 1 volume); First Presbyterian Church Recordbook (1858; 1 volume); Presbyterian minister Thomas R. Markham (1842-1892; 50 items in the Louisiana Historical Association Collection); and papers of the Dispersed of Judah (1829-1865; 4 volumes) and the Gates of Mercy (1839-1865; 12 volumes) for Jewish records.

Papers dealing with the War of 1812, especially the Battle of New Orleans, include those of the Louisiana Historical Association (1813-1815; 241 items), being mainly morning reports and rosters but also containing the diary of Benjamin Story (1814-1815) during his capture by the British. Other papers relating to the conflict include those of Captain John Ballinger (1812-1813; 4 items) and subscription lists in the Kuntz Collection. The John Minor Wisdom Collection contains a fragment of a narrative of General William Carroll concerning the Battle of New Orleans (1815; 1 item). The papers of Hugues de la Vergne (1814-1815; 16 items), then an aide to Jacques Villere; Philogène Favrot (1814-1815; 53 items), serving in the U.S. army; the David Morgan Papers (1814-1815; 14 items); the William Priestly Narrative of the Expedition of General Carroll (1828; 1 volume); and the David Rees Papers (1813-1815; 7 items, mainly subscription lists) all recount various phases of the impact of the war on Louisiana. In addition, there are thirteen miscellaneous collections concerning the War of 1812 in Louisiana.

Probably no single period in Louisiana history is better documented in the Manuscripts Section than the Civil War. The Manuscripts Section holds over one hundred collections relating directly to the Civil War, plus the extensive holdings in the Louisiana Historical Association Collection. The majority of papers are letters and diaries of Louisiana soldiers and officers, describing camp conditions and combat situations in the state and in all theatres of conflict during the war. There are others, however, which describe home conditions and also Union descriptions of their side of the lines. There are even several journals of Louisianians who avoided the conflict by escaping to Europe. It would consume too much space to list each individual collection; rather, it is thought better to point out more important and typical collections.

Among the more important collections are a letter book of the correspondence between Albert Sidney Johnston and Pierre Gustave Toutant Beauregard during the Shiloh Campaign (1862); General Richard Taylor's letter and telegraph books (1864-1865; 5 volumes); the New Orleans Committee of Subsistance Papers (1862; 111 items); Henry D. Ogden Papers (1862-1865; 96 items); and U.S. General George G. Shepley Letterbook (1864). Typical of the soldiers' papers are those in the Pierson Family Letters (1860-1865; 148 items in the Kuntz Collection). The Pierson letters are from three brothers who served in different theatres of the Civil War and are highlighted by those of David Pierson, who had been a Unionist delegate from Winn Parish to the Secession Convention but who later joined the Third Louisiana and rose to the rank of captain.

The Louisiana Historical Association Collection, formerly housed in the Confederate Memorial Hall in New Orleans, contains a wealth of material relating directly to the participation of Louisiana in the Confederacy and to the efforts of various Confederate memorial organizations to keep the memory of the Confederacy alive well past the cessation of fighting.

Of particular interest for this essay are the correspondence, reports, and order books from the Trans-Mississippi Department (1862-1865; 438 items); Washington Artillery (1861-1865; 422 items); Orleans Guard Artillery (1861-1865; 82 items); and the Confederate departments west of the Mississippi (1861-1865; 544 items). The collection also contains 298 diaries and reminiscences of Louisiana soldiers, as well as a file on nearly 2,000 Louisiana Confederates. The papers of individuals involved in the war include those of James B. Walton of the Washington Artillery (1861-1878; 232 items); John L. Brent from the Trans-Mississippi Ordinance Department (1862-1865; 420 items); George W. Brent order books and letter books from the Military Department of the West (1863-1865; 31 items); letter books and orders of John T. Purvis as inspector of field transportation of the District of the Gulf (1862-1865; 54 items); and William H. Thomas, chief commissary, Trans-Mississippi Department (1862-1865; 721 items).

The papers of postwar memorial groups include the Louisiana section of the United Confederate Veterans (1875-1956; 3,239 items); the United Daughters of the Confederacy (1861-1958; 3,204 items); the United Sons of Confederate Veterans (1861-1951; 5,355 items); the Association of the Army of Northern Virginia (1870-1954; 9,607 items, including the record rolls of the 1st, 2nd, 5th, 6th, 7th, 8th, 9th, 10th, 14th, and 15th Louisiana Regiments, the Donaldsonville Artillery, the Crescent Rifles, the Louisiana Guards, the Louisiana Zouaves and the Orleans Cadets). The Washington Artillery Papers (1858-1956; 2,579 items) contain correspondence, orders, reports, membership photographs, and a record roll of that organization.

The Louisiana Historical Association Collection also holds over 8,000 items on more than eighteen other organizations whose goal was to construct individualized or general Confederate monuments. The papers of the Louisiana Historical Association (1890-1960; 12,598 items) likewise reflect a desire to perpetuate the memory of the Confederacy. The papers of Joseph A. Chalaron (1842-1881; 1,846 items) illustrate his wartime career and active leadership of veterans.

Distinct from the papers of the Louisiana Historical Association Collection, the Manuscripts Section contains the papers of the Henry Watkins Allen Monument Association (1870; 1 volume); and the papers of United Daughters of the Confederacy leader Daisy L. Hodgson (1870-1940; 98 items) contain Civil War letters and note the postwar memorial efforts of Mrs. William J. Behan. The George Moorman Scrapbooks (1863-1890; 7 volumes) mention his activity with the Confederate Calvary Veterans

Association. On the Union side are the papers of the Joseph A. Mower Post of the Grand Army of the Republic (1883-1890; 430 items). The bulk of the material in the Manuscripts Section, however, is from the late nineteenth and twentieth centuries.

For plantation records the Barrow Family Papers continue the records of the postbellum period and also contain the journals of David Barrow (1881-1887; 3 volumes), Pointe Coupee Parish; papers from the Adeline Sugar Refining Company (1892-1923; 2,148 items), Saint Mary Parish; the Lemann Family Papers (1840-1965; 14,865 items) contain records on several plantations in Ascension Parish as well as business records of a general store in Donaldsonville. The Polmer Brothers Papers (1892-1960; 14 cu. ft.) contain records of rural general stores, as well as papers of the Lafourche-Terrebonne Levee District. There is also a volume of a country store in Bunkie (1877-1880).

The most extensive postbellum business records are those relating to the New Orleans Canal and Banking Trust Company and its successor and allied banks. These include records of the Canal Bank (1865-1932; 507 volumes); the Citizens Bank and Trust (1865-1924; 83 volumes); Commercial-Germania Trust and Savings (1902-1919; 18 volumes); Commercial National Bank (1901-1919; 74 volumes); Commercial Trust and Savings (1902-1919; 29 volumes); German American National Bank (1865-1905; 39 volumes); Germania National Bank (1868-1910; 6 volumes); Germania Savings Bank and Trust (1883-1912; 5 volumes); Louisiana National Bank (1865-1905; 39 volumes); Marine Bank and Trust (1918-1928; 65 volumes); Provident Bank and Trust (1894-1905; 8 volumes); and United States Trust and Savings (1893-1919; 19 volumes).

The second most extensive group of business records are those of the New Orleans Cotton Exchange (1871-1965; ca. 1,000 volumes, being minute books and financial records). Among those papers of individuals having dealings with the Cotton Exchange are those of Edward H. Keep (1891-1895; 1 letter book) and of Norman Mayer (1902-1941; 667 items); M. A. Rogers (1880-1930; ca. 21 cu. ft.) and Edgar B. Stern (1880-1920; 2,734 items, including the records of Lehman-Stern Company).

Other business collections include those of lumber companies such as the Otis Lumber Company (1899-1961; ca. 6,500 items); the Openweyer Cypress Lumber Company (1900-1932; 8 volumes); and the Poitevent-Favre Lumber Company (1872-1936; 2,036 items); manufacturers such as the drug firm of E. J. Hart (1920-1941; 24 cu. ft.); Jackson Brewing Company (1890-1970; 16 cu. ft.); and the Marine Paint and Varnish Company (1917-1959; ca. 60,000 items); insurance concerns, including those of Lafayette Insurance Company (1869-1977; 18 cu. ft.); financial papers of the New Orleans Board of Underwriters (1874-1924; 2 volumes); and the papers of insurance rater Stephen H. Allison (1902-1910; 4,063 items). For realty companies there are the Jules Andrieu Letterbook (1894); Lafayette Realty

Company (1911-1920; 6 cu. ft.); Frank McGloin (1889-1904; 1 volume); and the Verret Canal and Land Company (1905-1909; 1 volume).

Transportation records include the New Orleans Railway and Light Company Papers (1905-1922; 28 items); New Orleans and Carrollton Railroad (1834-1896; 243 items); the Teche Lines (Bus) (1924-1935; 93 items); the Bayou Teche Railroad and Light Company Minutebook (1906-1908); and sixteen small collections in the Railroad Series. The Joseph Merrick Jones Collection of the papers of Donald T. Wright concentrates heavily upon river travel and contains over 35,000 photographs of river vessels, nearly 4,000 bills of lading, over 800 books and periodicals, and riverboat ephemera. The Cooley Family Papers (1890-1966; 1,177 items) and the Thomas P. Leathers Papers (1805-1959; 66 items) record the experience of river captains. The New Orleans Wharfinger's General Cargo and Vessel Book (1890-1892, 1 volume) documents shipping in New Orleans during a brief period.

Other business records include those of New Orleans merchant Charles A. Crawford (1867-1892; 210 items); representative of the Sugar Exchange Daniel de Saussure (1890-1917; 150 items); merchants Franck and Danneel (1865-1885; 2 volumes); the St. Charles Hotel Papers (1789-1930; 1,913 items); and those of Samuel A. Trufant (1870-1920; 212 items), owner of the Crescent City Stockyards.

The Manuscript Section has only a small group of papers relating to labor but includes Covington Hall's manuscript, "Labor Struggles in the Deep South" (n.d.). Also included are the papers of the New Orleans Street Railway Union (1927-1931; 7,077 items) and some of the New Orleans Typographers Union (1865-1873; 34 items).

The papers of Louisiana political leaders in the antebellum and modern periods include the personal, business, and political papers of U.S. Representative and Senator Randall Lee Gibson (1848-1893; 341 items); the congressional papers of Representative F. Edward Hébert (1915-1977; 350 cu. ft.); the gubernatorial and campaign papers of Sam Houston Jones (1939-1973; 54 cu. ft.); and the congressional papers of Representative David Connor Treen (1972-1977; 250 cu. ft.). The deLesseps Morrison collection includes family, military, mayoralty, gubernatorial, and campaign papers and Morrison's Organization of American States ambassadorial papers (1929-1965; 176 cu. ft.). The Morrison Mayoralty Papers from 1956 are at the New Orleans Public Library.

Of a related nature are the papers of David R. McGuire (1928-1971; 16 cu. ft.). These describe McGuire's role as head of the Public Relations Office, as chief administrative officer of the city of New Orleans, and as a leader in the Morrison and Sam Jones gubernatorial campaigns. A section of the Scott Wilson Papers (1937-1967; 73 cu. ft.) documents Wilson's role in the Morrison, Schiro, McKeithen, and Eisenhower campaigns in Louisiana. The Jefferson Democratic Association Papers (1950-1955; 7 cu. ft.) and the Democratic Conservative Parish Committee Records (1879-1889; 3

volumes) contain material on political organizations. The League of Women Voters Papers (1915-1972; 4,325 items); Ethel Hutson Papers (1908-1922; 3,714 items); and Martha G. Robinson Papers (1927-1971; 93 cu. ft.) all contain material on the growing political participation of women.

The William B. Wisdom Collection on Huey Long (775 items) contains books, pamphlets, broadsides, newspapers, and periodicals reflecting Long's career. The Cecil Morgan Papers (1923-1971; 4,800 items) stress his role in the impeachment of Long and in the establishment of the Louisiana Civil Service League. The papers of the league itself and those of Charles Dunbar (1939-1970; 40 cu. ft.) concern the creation and operation of the league and include a complete run of the Earl K. Long-endorsed *Louisiana Watchman* (1946-1948).

The papers of the Louisiana League for the Preservation of Constitutional Rights (1934-1948; 1,828 items) and those of its ideological successor, the Louisiana American Civil Liberties Union (1956-1978; 35 cu. ft.), record efforts to protect dissenters. The papers of the American Protective League (1918; 49 items), on the other hand, concern efforts to identify opposition to the United States's participation in World War I.

The Louisiana section of the Political Ephemera Collection contains seven cubic feet of advertising material for candidates for office in the state and twelve cubic feet of periodicals and flyers about groups and individuals who espoused extremist political views.

The Manuscripts Section includes a number of collections of papers from charitable and assistance organizations. Included are those of the Camp Nicholas Soldiers Home (1883-1941; 3,899 items, in the Louisiana Historical Association Collection); Charity Organization Society (1896-1924; 35 items); Christian Woman's Exchange (1881-1967; 1,304 items); Community Chest of New Orleans (1924-1957; 71 volumes); Council of Social Agencies (1923-1961; 29 cu. ft.); Family Service Society (1927-1975; 2,943 items); Fatherless Children of France (1917-1920; 1,819 items); Fink Asylum (1896-1924; 3 volumes); Friends of Widows and Orphans of the French Resistance (1946-1950; 131 items); the Gaudet Home (1935-1959; 67 items); German Protestant Home for the Old and Infirm (1910-1918; 1 volume); Jewish Children's Home (1940-1970; 11,424 items); La Société Française (1849-1937; 334 items); Orleans Parish Neighborhood Council (1937-1966; 26 cu. ft.); Poydras Home (1865-1960; 40,000 items); Poydras Home for Elderly Ladies (1960-1975; 26 cu. ft.); Protestant Children's Home (1861-1963; 520 items); Silver Thimble Fund (1925-1950; 591 items); Sophie L. Gumbel Home (1918-1966; 1 minutebook); Touro-Shakespeare Alms House (1901-1929; 3 minutebooks); Travelers' Aid of Louisiana (1918-1966; 16 cu. ft.); Waldo Burton Home (1824-1965; 68 items); and the Young Women's Christian Association (1911-1966; 84 cu. ft.).

Collections dealing with the practice of law in Louisiana include those of St. Clair Adams (1936-1946; 648 items), mainly his defense of Governor Richard W. Leche; Gustave Breaux Diary (1859; 1 volume); William K.

Dart (1916-1918; 170 items); Judge George Whitfield Jack (1895-1924; 95 items); Richard McConnell (1864-1934; 4,565 items); Clarence J. Morrow (1932-1941; 44 items); Charles O'Neill Speeches (1912-1949; 991 items); William S. Parkerson (1880-1902; 108 items); Judge Robert Reid (1888-1901; 244 items); Christian Roselius Lectures (ca. 1854; 2 volumes); and the papers of Gustavus and Charles E. Schmidt (1816-1908; 1,274 items).

Among collections of papers of physicians and medical organizations are those of Charles Cassedy Bass (1875-1975; 465 items); Stanhope Bayne-Jones (1914-1963; 778 items); Stanford Emerson Chaillé (1847-1911; 95 items); Marcus Feingold (1908-1937; 97 items); Joseph Jones (1869-1899; 2,600 items); dentist Charles Edmund Kells (1856-1928; 105 items); Rudolph Matas (1862-1960; 51 cu. ft.); Edmond Souchon (1895-1925; 317 items); the Isaac Delgado Memorial Fund (1912-1954; 1,181 items); the Howard Association Journals (1878; 2 volumes in the Grinder Papers); the Louisiana Dental Society (1942-1949; 3,073 items); the New Orleans Medical and Surgical Society Minutebooks (1873-1874; 1 volume); and the Orleans Infirmary Papers (1869; 18 items). In addition to these, twenty-five miscellaneous small collections mention yellow fever and cholera outbreaks in the state.

The largest collection of religious papers for the postbellum period are those of the Episcopal Diocese of Louisiana Archive, which contains over 10,000 items. The papers include records of Christ Church, Saint Paul's Trinity, Calvary, Saint James (Alexandria), Saint James (Baton Rouge), and a number of other Louisiana Episcopal churches. The archive holds the records of various bishops, the Diocesan Office, the triennial conventions, and the Women's Auxiliary. The archive also contains a number of pamphlets, newsletters, and programs. Separate from the archive are the papers of Saint Luke's Episcopal Church, a black church (1864-1971; 1,131 items) and microfilm of the records of Trinity Church. The McConnell Family Papers (1865-1911; 298 items) contain material on Saint Paul's and on Richard McConnell's tenure as chancellor of the diocese.

There are many other collections concerning religious matters, such as those of the German Lutheran Church (1838-1902; 10 volumes); Norman A. Holmes Recordbook (1929-1949; 1 volume) from the Central Congregational Church; A. Gordon Blackwell Sermons (1880-1895; 20 items); the Leesville Conference of the Methodist Episcopal Church Minutebook (1900-1903, 1 volume); Methodist minister S. H. Werlin Sermons (1882-1910; 46 items); Lafayette Presbyterian Church (1866-1932; 20 items, in the Louisiana Historical Association Collection); Presbyterian minister Robert Q. Mallard (1851-1889; in the Charles Colcock Jones Papers); and the papers of W. Reid Stryker (1923-1927; 195 items) while he served as deacon of the Saint Charles Presbyterian Church. The notes of Roger Baudier for his history of the Catholic church in Louisiana (n.d.; 1 volume) and the papers of Jesuit Alvin J. Pilié (1965-1968; 252 items) represent the Catholic denomination. The papers of Temple Sinai (1840-1973; 1,318 items); Touro

Synagogue (1830-1969; 73 items); and Rabbi Roy A. Rosenberg (1966-1970; 1,940 items) represent the Jewish community.

Recently the Special Collections Division of the Howard-Tilton Memorial Library established the Southeastern Architectural Archives to house better its growing collection of papers of architects and architectural firms from the region. These collections, which contain correspondence, specifications, photographs, and drawings, date chiefly from the late nineteenth and twentieth centuries. They constitute the most extensive historical record of buildings within the state. Among the papers are those of the firm of Benson and Riehl, William R. Burke, Hayward Burton, Arthur Feitel, the firm of Freret and Wolf, James Gallier, Sr., James Gallier, Jr., Moise Goldstein, Henry Howard, the firm of Koch and Wilson, William T. Nolan, Edward B. Silverstein, the firm of Stone Brothers, Thomas Sully, the firm of Toledano, Wogan and Bernard, and the firm of Weiss, Dreyfous and Seiferth. Closely related to the architectural collections are a number of photographic collections relating to Louisiana buildings.

Collections dealing with the development of arts in the state include the papers of individuals such as John James Audubon (1807-1827; 25 items); Werner Conrad Höehn (1929-1940; 89 items); Will Henry Stevens (1930-1945; 105 items); Ellsworth Woodward (1905-1925; 529 items); and William Woodward (1893-1901; 280 items). Papers of organizations include the New Orleans Fine Arts Club (1916-1975; 89 items) and the Southern States Art League (1921-1946; 40 cu. ft.).

Bridging the gap between art and journalism are the editorial cartoonists. The Manuscripts Section holds the works of John Chase (ca. 1929-1975; 12,600 items); Keith Temple (1923-1966; 74 volumes); and Trist Wood (1869-1953; 295 items).

For the performing arts, the sections contain material from the Federal Theatre Project (1935; 1 volume); the French Opera House (1889-1916; 169 items); the Group Theatre (1926-1938; 323 items); the New Orleans Friends of Music (1956-1978; 2,597 items); and Le Petit Théâtre (1922-1971; 1,429 items). From individuals, the Leon Ryder Maxwell Papers (1870-1957; 1,181 items) record the progress of music in New Orleans and Newcomb College, and the Henry Brunswick Loeb Papers (1911-1956; 176 items) help document the French Opera House and the New Orleans Symphony. Within the Kuntz Collection there is a large number of theatre programs and broadsides. The collection also contains libretti and programs from operas performed in New Orleans, mainly at the French Opera House.

Collections of Louisiana fiction and nonfiction writers include those of Hewett L. Ballowe (1918-1951; 341 items); Christopher Blake (1945-1980; 8 cu. ft.); Roark Bradford (1930-1948; 155 items); George Washington Cable (1871-1947; 22,290 items); James Broadman Cable (1893; 1 manuscript); Thomas Ewing Dabney (1911-1969; 1,174 items); Mollie Moore Davis (1891-1909; 106 items); Hermann B. Deutsch (1894-1968; 22 cu. ft.); Charles L. Dufour (1937-1979; 10 cu. ft.); Alexander Federoff (1955-1973; 6 cu.

ft.); Julius W. Friend (1915-1961; 685 items, including papers relating to *The Double Dealer*); Charles Etienne Arthur Gayarré (1848-1895; 150 items, including 31 items in the Kuntz Collection and 81 items in the John Minor Wisdom Collection); Lyle Saxon (1879-1946; 3,389 items); and Mary Ashley Townsend (1850-1911; 908 items). Papers produced by literary societies are also included. The major ones are L'Athénée Louisianaise (1876-1888, 1978-1980; 197 items); the Literary Club of New Orleans (1882-1887; 1 volume in the Charles Colcock Jones Papers); and the Alliance Franco-Louisianaise de l'Enseignement du Français (1890-1943; in the Lafargue Papers).

Reasonably, the Manuscripts Section of the Howard-Tilton Memorial Library would have a number of collections dealing with the development of education in the state, in addition to the holdings of the University Archives. These papers include those of administrators and faculty and education-related material. Foremost are the papers of William Preston Johnston (1850-1899; 6,500 items), covering his career as aide to Jefferson Davis, college teacher in Virginia, and president of Louisiana State University and Tulane University. The Richard McConnell Papers in the McConnell Family Collection, the Paul Tulane Papers, and the Randall Lee Gibson Papers all deal with the founding and early administration of Tulane University. The Pierce Butler Papers (1902-1943; 2,706 items) and the Brandt V. B. Dixon Papers (1887-1901; 121 items) contain material on the administration of Newcomb College. The John H. Stibbs Papers (1939-1975; 530 items) cover his career as dean of students at Tulane. There are numerous collections of faculty member papers. The diaries of Edwin Lewis Stephens (1873-1937; 46 volumes) record the development of a sister institution, the University of Southwestern Louisiana. Other collections deal with secondary education and bibliographical resources of the region. In addition, there are numerous collections of family papers that contain information on education at the tutorial, public, private, and sectarian levels in Louisiana, especially New Orleans.

Among collections dealing with scientific and technical matters is that of Pierre Gustave Toutant Beauregard (1822-1888; 242 items) who, although better known for his Civil War activities, had a longer career as an engineer. This interest in engineering, rather than his martial endeavors, is reflected in these papers. Other collections are those of chemist Robert Glenk (1897-1950; 2,744 items); botanist Joseph Finley Joor (1869-1892; 123 items); engineer John A. Klorer (1920-1943; 160 items); ornithologist Henry H. Kopman (1893-1952; 5 volumes); and naturalist and chemist George P. Meade (1932-1975; 5 volumes). Material about such pioneering engineers as Arthur Monroe Shaw (1892-1942; 44 diaries) and mechanical engineer James M. Todd (1908-1975; 450 items) should prove useful. Institutional records include the series *Tulane Studies in Zoology* (1950-1964; 3,299 items); the New Orleans Society of Plant Science (1932-1936; 252 items); and the New Orleans Academy of Science (1853-1943; 15 cu. ft.).

The papers of various organizations and societies include those of the Boston Club (1870-1966; 457 items); the New Orleans Lawn Tennis Association (1875-1972; 622 items); the Swiss-American Society (1865-1969; 65 items); the Quarante Club (1888-1977; 760 items); and the Lyceum-Tulane Association (1915-1958; 1,193 items).

The focal point of the printed sources on Louisiana history in the Howard-Tilton Memorial Library is the Louisiana Collection. The Louisiana Collection is a noncirculating holding of over 15,000 volumes, 600 cubic feet of vertical files, 300 cubic feet of pictorial material, and nearly 1,000 maps relating to the state. Given the size of the collection, it is difficult to describe it in anything but the most general terms. The guidelines for inclusion in the collection include any work principally about Louisiana or about an individual identified with the state. Some early nineteenth-century works are included within the Louisiana Collection because they are early Louisiana imprints, regardless of the author or subject matter.

The collection contains most standard state, regional, and local histories, historical serials, biographies, travel accounts, including nearly all of the eighteenth- and nineteenth-century accounts that focused upon the area, and governmental documents dating from 1805 on the state level and concerning Orleans Parish. The Louisiana Collection is not, however, a complete Louisiana documents repository. The collection contains numerous works of fiction and literary criticism. The medical section contains not only medical journals from the state dating from 1884 and tracts on the treatment of yellow fever but also a series of medical theses defended by Louisiana physicians at the University of Paris. The Louisiana Collection contains over 7,000 pieces of sheet music either published under a Louisiana imprint or written by a Louisiana composer. There is an extensive collection of opera, symphony, and theatre and costume designs, and ball programs dating from 1857.

The Vertical File contains clippings, broadsides, and pamphlets arranged by subject and covering a range of topics from "Abbeville" to "Zoning." The Vertical File also contains a biography section. The Pictorial File includes photographs, clipped pictures, sketches, and postcards and engravings relating to Louisiana topics. The Map Collection has original and duplicated maps covering the state, dating from 1713.

Access to material in the Louisiana Collection is facilitated by a special additional subject index, or citation file, which can inform the user about the location of information concerning a person, place, or event.

The Howard-Tilton Memorial Library also houses a number of Louisiana newspapers in both microform and hard copy. These newspapers include most of the main New Orleans papers, a number of important papers from other sections of the state, and a run of less prominent publications.

The William Ransom Hogan Archive of New Orleans Jazz concerns the evolution of music in New Orleans and a great deal more. The Jazz Archive contains over 15,000 jazz recordings, 13,000 pieces of sheet music, 5,000 photographs, 16,000 notes, clippings, posters and memorabilia, and, most importantly, nearly 1,500 reels of tape of interviews with more than 500 jazz musicians and other persons involved in the evolution of jazz in Louisiana. Many of these interviews contain significant information on the social history, lifestyle, and folk culture of New Orleans. For instance, one interview with the mother of a noted jazz clarinetist mentions life in Reconstruction New Orleans, a grandmother who still carried traditions from Senegal and the use of the French language among black Creoles.

Clearly, the Tulane University Special Collections and affiliated materials offer rich and varied opportunities for scholars. The Civil War era, military affairs, antebellum and postbellum agriculture and commerce, science and medicine, education, the arts, parish and municipal government, local, state, and regional politics, and religion, are topics to be mined for doctoral dissertations and monographs. Together with other major archives in the *Guide*, the collections provide the opportunity to reconstruct the state's history from many perspectives.

19
THE HISTORIC NEW ORLEANS COLLECTION: THE KEMPER AND LEILA WILLIAMS FOUNDATION

ROBERT D. BUSH

Street address:	533 Royal Street
	New Orleans, Louisiana 70130
Mailing address:	Same
Telephone:	(504) 523-7146
Days and hours:	Tuesday-Saturday, 10:00 A.M. to 4:30 A.M.

THE HISTORIC NEW ORLEANS Collection was created in 1966 by General and Mrs. L. Kemper Williams. Situated in the heart of the French Quarter, it was established from their private collection in order to preserve and exhibit items of cultural and historical importance. Housed in a historic architectural complex, each building significant in its own right, the collection includes a research center, public exhibition galleries, two museum residences, and a gift shop.

The main exhibition gallery at 533 Royal Street presents changing displays on local cultural and historical subjects at no charge. A modest fee is assessed for guided tours of the ten permanent exhibition galleries in the 1792 Merieult House and another for conducted tours of the 1889 Williams Residence. This latter beautiful nineteenth-century structure, adapted in the 1940s as one of the opulent "hidden houses" of the French Quarter, is maintained today as it was when the Williamses lived there. Tours of both the exhibition galleries in the Merieult House and the Williams Residence are available Tuesday through Saturday from 10:00 A.M. to 3:45 P.M..

The Historic New Orleans Collection Research Center consists of archives, a library, and the museum curatorial research area. Each offers collections on social, cultural, political, economic, and military developments in the Gulf South, Louisiana, and New Orleans.

Continuing to build upon the nucleus of items assembled by General and Mrs. L. Kemper Williams, the archives maintains and makes available for study unique textual sources on New Orleans and Louisiana history and culture. With complementary broadsides, newspapers, sheet music, and libretti, more than one hundred linear feet of manuscripts have recently been processed. Indexes on manuscript sources include a survey of collections and single items arranged under topical headings, and similar listings are available for printed materials. Most of the larger manuscript groups have also been calendared, and these item-by-item descriptions are on file for use in the archives reading room at 720 Toulouse Street. Approximately one-third of the manuscript holdings have been catalogued in detail, with all substantial subject references included in the card catalog. Microfilm and microfiche collections of New Orleans and Louisiana newspapers and periodicals provide useful primary sources. Additionally, a vertical file of theatre and concert programs of local interest is maintained here. The researcher may wish to consult a brief description by Robert D. Bush and Blake Touchstone, "A Survey of Manuscript Holdings in the Historic New Orleans Collection," *Louisiana History*, 16 (Winter 1975), 89-96. Copies of the *Guide to Research at the Historic New Orleans Collections*, 2nd ed. (New Orleans, 1980), 29 pages, are available upon request.

A substantial library includes rare books, pamphlets, periodicals, microfilm and microfiche collections, and city directories of New Orleans. The comprehensive architectural study known as the Vieux Carré Survey, containing 130 notebook-type folios, details property changes in the French Quarter. Additional sources of reference on architecural history (conveyance office books, notarial archives books, and over one hundred drawings) complement this collection; other holdings in the curatorial department provide much additional research information on this general subject, including photographs.

The curatorial department plays a major role in the research activities of the collection. Many facets of state and local history may be researched among the thousands of prints, maps, drawings, photographs, paintings, and objects contained here. Several thousand photographs, for example, provide an extensive resource on such topics of regional interest as city views, river life, local architecture, and famous personalities.

As a unit, the holdings of the Historic New Orleans Collection constitute one of the most comprehensive research facilities on regional history ever privately assembled. The collection has sought to make its holdings known to and used by researchers since its opening to the public in 1974. Simultaneously, the Kemper and Leila Williams Foundation has followed a discriminating policy of developing its collection in ways to strengthen and supplement the original materials.

The Historic New Orleans Collection is responsible for the administration, preservation, and availability of its collections to qualified patrons. As with any research institution, the possession of a valuable and fragile collection imposes an obligation for their care and protection; accordingly all materials are maintained in closed stacks. The reading rooms are equipped with tables, card catalogs, and additional location aids and are serviced by professional staff. Items used must be properly credited, and all costs incurred for reproduction and copying must be paid promptly.

Certain research procedures must be followed by all patrons, including, but not limited to, the following rules: each guest must register upon his arrival; browsing in the stacks is not permitted; no pens of any kind are permitted in the reading rooms, only pencils; no smoking or eating is allowed in the reading rooms; cameras are not permitted in the research areas; and there is a modest charge for all photoduplication or copying of materials. Printed registration forms and a schedule of photoduplication costs are available in all of the research areas.

The Historic New Orleans Collection's holdings offer a diverse selection in materials of regional importance. Military history, political events, social and economic development, architecture, literature, and the performing arts are subjects most commonly represented, with important subtopics under each of these headings.

The colonial discovery and exploration of Louisiana and the Mississippi Valley are well documented in all departments. Numerous published accounts are contained in the library, and all provide commentary by Europeans and later Americans on several topics. An extensive cartographic collection numbers more than 400 items and depicts political boundaries, river courses, landscapes, fauna and flora, and Indian encampments. A great deal of material—reports and maps in particular—discusses the expansion of America's frontier after the Louisiana Purchase of 1803. Thus, many published works, letters, journals, maps, and prints combine to provide excellent descriptions of Louisiana and the Mississippi Valley in the era of transition from European colony to statehood.

Manuscripts concerning the transfers of Louisiana from Spain to France and then from France to the United States are found in the Pierre Clément de Laussat Papers (606 items) and the Claude Perrin Victor Papers (36 items). The Laussat Papers are described in detail in Robert D. Bush, "Documents on the Louisiana Purchase: The Laussat Papers," *Louisiana History*, 18 (Winter 1977), 104-7, and Laussat's own account is available in Pierre Clément de Laussat, *Memoirs of My Life* (Baton Rouge, 1978), volume 2 in the Historic New Orleans Monograph Series.

A superb selection of maps and prints provides additional information beyond those contained in the manuscripts. The Laussat Papers contain correspondence between French, Spanish, and American officials and Laussat while he was acting in his official capacity as colonial prefect for Louisiana and then commissioner of the French government. Of special interest are the descriptions of Laussat's arrival in Louisiana, impressions of the colony's resources, and correspondence with numerous inhabitants. Also of note are the inventories, compiled in French and Spanish, furnishing conditions and values of government buildings, stores, disbursements for repairs and supplies, lists of munitions, fortifications, and church parishes. Other sources of information about the Louisiana Purchase are found among the published materials housed in the library. Books, pamphlets and bibliographical guides are available to assist researchers here.

The territorial period in Louisiana (1803-1812) is documented and illustrated in numerous holdings of the archives, curatorial department, and library. Such collections reveal the rapid growth and expansion of New Orleans during this era. For example, a collection of rare pamphlets and ephemera on political and legal subjects illustrates the changes that took place in Louisiana during the early years of American sovereignty. Additional accounts are among the diaries, travelogs, and journals of exploration (such as those of Lewis and Clark), with artifacts and visual materials on hand to provide useful illustrations.

Few events in American history have served to capture the popular imagination and to be represented in such diverse forms of expression as the Battle of New Orleans in 1815. General Andrew Jackson's defeat of the British forces below New Orleans established that Louisiana would remain permanently an American possession. This battle and the personalities involved in it have continued to be favorite subjects for generations.

The Historic New Orleans Collection provides a wealth of research materials on this subject. As with the Louisiana Purchase, books, pamphlets, prints, paintings, maps, and documents combine to form a unique collection of research items. Among the archival holdings are some from the British point of view that detail the perspectives of a campaign in Louisiana and plans for dealing with the populace. American movements in connection with the battle are represented in isolated letters, orders and commissions, orders for the assembly of the Tennessee militia, U.S. Army Morning Reports (1814-1815), and a large body of materials from the 10th Regiment, Louisiana Militia. Several prominent Louisiana families, such as

Jacques Phillipe Villeré, on whose plantation the Battle of New Orleans was fought, are represented here.

The Battle of New Orleans provided a rich theme for artists and printers. Among the many prints and other items located in the curatorial department is a superb collection of military drawings on fortifications drawn by Barthelemy Lafon from 1813 to 1814. The art of military engineering at this time is well represented in this collection.

The Historic New Orleans Collection houses a diverse assortment of material pertaining to the years between the Battle of New Orleans and the Civil War. Political, economic, religious, social, intellectual, and artistic subjects are interdependent in so many collections that only a cursory explanation is possible. One of the best methods to research the interdependence of subjects is to examine family collections, in which several members of a family discuss these subjects intimately and in detail. For example, see the Henri Saint-Geme Collection, described briefly by Robert D. Bush, in "Les Bulletins de Louisiane addressés au Baron de Saint-Geme," *Revue de Louisiane*, 4 (Winter 1975). Among the many printed items, the New Orleans *City Directories*, beginning with that of 1805, provide abundant information. Additional contemporary reviews, reports, documents, pamphlets, books, and other published sources are maintained in the library.

Most of the archival sources on Louisiana during the Civil War and Reconstruction focus on local men serving with the armies of Tennesee and of Northern Virginia, on their families in occupied New Orleans after April of 1862, and on political exiles. The curatorial department has a wide variety of sources on the Civil War—prints, proclamations, broadsides, and dramatic renderings of important military encounters in Louisiana. Published records sources and reference works located in the library assist researchers. Books, published maps and document series, periodical literature, vertical file entries, and bibliographical guides complete the reference materials in the library.

Important topics in Louisiana history and a sampling of the materials in the Historic New Orleans Collection's archives, curatorial department, and library have been discussed in the preceding pages. However, to discuss only these subjects would be to do a disservice to the many items and collections that do not fit neatly into orthodox historical categories. Virtually thousands of items, which cover topics falling generally into the broad category of social and cultural history, deserve mention.

Among the social and cultural collections, the Butler Family Papers is a fine example. In the correspondence of family members with friends and relative across almost two centuries, a record of one of the nation's outstanding families becomes a history of the United States itself. From Pennsylvania to Louisiana, one or more family members saw military service in the Revolutionary War, frontier Indian wars, Mexican War, and Civil War.

Similar information is found among other family papers housed in the archives, with supporting materials contained in the curatorial department (such as paintings of the subjects), and additional data in the library.

Cultural life in Louisiana and the city of New Orleans is the subject of other diverse collections. The role of music in the Creole City, for example, is demonstrated in several hundred pieces of sheet music and copies of libretti from operas, many of which were performed at the famous French Opera House in New Orleans. Numerous theatre, concert, and ballet programs provide additional information on the status of the performing arts during different eras in the history of the city. There are extensive holdings on the World's Industrial and Cotton Centennial Exposition (1884-1885), open-air markets of New Orleans, life along the Mississippi River and the levee in New Orleans during the halcyon era of the steamboats, and growth of the port of New Orleans as reflected in prints, paintings, drawings, maps, and photographs.

A systematic attempt by the Williams Foundation to collect representative works of Louisiana artists or of Louisiana subjects as portrayed by travelers makes the curatorial holdings of great research value. The most extensive collection representative of this effort is the Alfred R. Waud Collection, consisting of over 1,000 drawings and prints, as well as some correspondence, illustrating life along the Mississippi River during the second half of the nineteenth century.

In conclusion, the Historic New Orleans Collection offers researchers an opportunity to use one of the finest private collections in the nation open to the public. Manuscripts, documents, books, periodicals, prints, paintings, photographs, and extensive memorabilia on local subjects are available for study. From the rarest of single items to numerous records series, research files, and collections on architectural history, the Historic New Orleans Collection offers an enormous number of source materials.

20
THE AMISTAD RESEARCH CENTER

CLIFTON H. JOHNSON

Street Address:	Old U.S. Mint
	400 Eslpanade Avenue
	New Orleans, Louisiana 70116
Mailing address:	Same
Telephone:	(504) 522-0432
Days and hours:	Monday-Saturday, 8:30 A.M. to 5:00 P.M.

THE AMISTAD RESEARCH Center is an independent and privately supported archive that collects manuscripts and other source materials relating to the history of America's ethnic minorities, with particular emphasis on blacks, native Americans, and Americans of Hispanic and Asian descent or origin. The center's holdings include over 8 million manuscript pieces, 100,000 photographs, 200 tapes of speeches and interviews, 1,966 reels of microfilm, 295 pieces of microfiche, 15,000 reference books, and runs of 195 periodicals. The scope of the collections is national, and the manuscript collections include the personal papers of 160 individuals and families; the records of 32 national, regional, state, and local institutions and organizations; and 7 special collections documenting selected subject areas. The collections date from 1783 to 1980, but only a small number of items predate 1826. Approximately 80 percent of the center's collections relate to the history of black Americans, civil rights, and relations between blacks and whites.

The center receives its basic support from the American Missionary Association of the United Church Board for Homeland Ministries. It also receives support from Friends of Amistad, a membership organization with local chapters. Additional support comes from private gifts and foundation grants. The center maintains a cooperative relationship with Dillard University.

Fifty of the center's manuscript collections have materials relating to the history of Louisiana. The most significant of these are the following:

THE ARCHIVES OF THE AMERICAN MISSIONARY ASSOCIATION
(1839-1960; 227.4 lin. ft.)

The American Missionary Association, which grew out of the famous Amistad incident of 1839, was incorporated in 1846 in New York a nonsectarian, evangelical, abolitionist and missionary society supporting both home and foreign missionary activities. In 1861 the association began educational work among the contrabands (fugitive slaves) at Fortress Monroe in Virginia. Its missionaries and teachers followed Union troops into the South, and hundreds of schools were established for the freedmen during the Civil War and Reconstruction period. The AMA has continued to support black education to the present day. From its beginning, it progressively developed closer connections with Congregational churches and in 1914 became an official agent of Congregationalism.

The AMA began its work in Louisiana in 1864, establishing schools in New Orleans and neighboring towns, but withdrew in 1865, not to return until 1869. In 1870 the association was supporting forty schools in Louisiana, including Straight University in New Orleans, which would, in 1929, merge with the Methodist-supported New Orleans University to form Dillard University. About four linear feet of the AMA archives deal with activities in Louisiana. These records are an invaluable source for studying not only the association's educational work but also the beginnings of black Congregationalism in Louisiana. In addition, the reports of the teachers and missionaries and political conditions at the end of the Civil War and during Reconstruction.

PAPERS OF DANIEL ELLIS BYRD
(1947-1977; 4.4 lin. ft.)

Daniel Byrd was born in Arkansas in 1910. After graduation from Northwestern University he played professional basketball with the Harlem Globetrotters. He moved to New Orleans in 1937. He was an organizer and president for eight years of the Louisiana Conference of Branches of the NAACP. After serving for a decade as regional coordinator for the NAACP, he became, in 1950, field secretary of the NAACP Legal Defense and Education Fund, holding that position until 1977. Also, from 1941 to 1977, he served as a researcher for both the Legal Defense Fund and Louisiana's leading civil rights attorney, A. P. Tureaud, whose papers are also held by the center. The Byrd Papers include 1,700 pieces of correspondence, plus reports, research notes, petitions, and records of the Louisiana Education Association and the Louisiana Committee for Dismantling of a Dual System of Higher Education.

RECORDS OF THE CATHOLIC COUNCIL ON HUMAN RELATIONS, NEW ORLEANS
(1961-1964; 2 lin. ft.)

The New Orleans Catholic Council on Human Relations was organized by members of the laity in 1961. The records cover the entire period of its existence and include correspondence, minutes, accounts, biographical data, clippings, press releases, newsletters, speeches, scrapbooks, and the articles of incorporation, constitution, and bylaws. In addition to the council's efforts to promote racial justice, the records include information on desegregation of schools, both public and Catholic, throughout Louisiana and the nation. There are materials on the activities of the South Louisiana Citizens Council, the Citizens Council of Greater New Orleans, the NAACP, Save Our Schools, Inc., and Education Unlimited.

Three collections, records of the Congregational Church Building Society, the Congregational Church Extension Boards and the Congregational Home Missionary Society (80 lin. ft.), contain a total of about two linear feet of documents relating to black, white, and Indian Congregationalism in Louisiana, particularly churches in New Orleans, Lake Charles, Kinder, New Iberia, Jennings, Gueydan, Monroe, Thibodeaux, Roseland, Elton, Erath, Eros, Grand Bayou, Abbeville, and Drew. The manuscripts in these collections date from about 1885 to 1930. In addition to the reports and other correspondence between the home offices and the pastors and missionaries, these collections contain many valuable photographs. The Archives of the American Home Missionary Society (1816, 1826-1894, 1936; 243.2 lin. ft.) also contain a few documents on Congregationalism in nineteenth-century Louisiana.

PAPERS OF GILES ALFRED HUBERT
(1881-1977; 9.6 lin. ft.)

After a distinguished career in the United States and abroad, Giles Alfred Hubert (1907-1977) came to Dillard University in 1954 as professor of economics. In addition to teaching, he served as Dillard's director of admissions from 1963 to 1972. He retired in 1974. The collection spans Hubert's career. Those segments relating to Louisiana deal largely with Dillard University, the Urban League of New Orleans, Hubert's writings about

New Orleans, and collected materials grouped under Coordinating Council of Greater New Orleans and Black Enterprises of New Orleans. Hubert was an experienced and talented photographer, and the collection contains many exceptionally valuable photographs of people and places in New Orleans.

PAPERS OF RIVERS FREDERICK
(1893-1958; 0.8 lin. ft.)

Rivers Frederick (1874-1954) was born in Pointe Coupee Parish and received his early education in New Orleans, graduating from New Orleans University. After receiving the M. D. degree from the University of Illinois, he became, in 1901, associate professor of surgery at Flint Medical College and chief surgeon at Sarah Goodridge Hospital, both of which were affiliated with New Orleans University. With the organization of Flint-Goodridge Hospital as a unit of Dillard University in 1932, he was named chief of the surgical department, a position he held until 1950. He was a leader of the NAACP and the National Urban League and active in other civil rights organizations and civic activities in New Orleans. He joined the Louisiana Life Insurance Company's board in 1923 and soon became president and principal stockholder. Although the papers in this collection indicate the many achievements and contributions of Frederick, they do not document his day-to-day activities. The papers are composed mostly of congratulatory letters and telegrams, a collection of awards and citations, and clippings.

PAPERS OF JOSEPH A. HARDIN
(1904-1975; 1.2 lin. ft.)

Joseph A. Hardin (1875-1954) was born in Scooba, Mississippi, and lived in New Orleans from 1889 until his death. He graduated from Flint Medical College. While practicing and teaching medicine, he became a leading figure in New Orleans politics, influencing the city government to provide better facilities for blacks and at the same time organizing blacks to vote and exert political pressure. He served as a delegate to five Republican National Conventions from 1932 to 1948. He was named consul of the Republic of Liberia in 1940 and held that position until 1953. The Hardin Papers include correspondence, newspaper clippings, photographs, reports, certificates of honors and awards, programs, and collected items.

PAPERS OF ROBERT ELIJAH JONES
(1872-1965; 4 lin. ft.)

The first black bishop in the Methodist Episcopal church to be elected as a general superintendent of the entire church was Robert E. Jones (1872-

1960), elected in 1920 as resident bishop of New Orleans. From 1904 to 1920, he was editor of the New Orleans-published *Southwest Christian Advocate*. A close associate of Booker T. Washington, he was president of the first Negro Business League in Louisiana. Bishop Jones was a founding trustee of Dillard University and helped establish the reorganized Flint-Goodridge Hospital. He was also a trustee of Philander Smith College, Rust College, Bennett College, and Gammon Theological Seminary. He established Gulfside Assembly in Waveland, Mississippi. His papers contain correspondence, speeches, other writings, receipts, photographs, and collected items.

PAPERS OF ERNEST NATHAN MORIAL
(58.8 lin. ft.)

The mayor of New Orleans has given to the center papers that document his life and career up to his inauguration in 1978. Born in New Orleans in 1929, Ernest Morial was educated at Xavier and Louisiana State University, being the first black to graduate from the LSU School of Law. He was the first black in the twentieth century and the first black Democrat to be elected to the Louisiana legislature. After serving as a Juvenile Court judge in New Orleans, he was elected to the Louisiana Court of Appeals, from which he resigned in order to run for mayor of New Orleans. Morial has been a leader of the NAACP and, with A. P. Tureaud, prosecuted many significant civil rights cases in the 1960s. He was one of the organizers of the Lawyers Committee for Civil Rights Under Law. His papers document his early life and entire public career.

RECORDS OF THE NATIONAL ASSOCIATION FOR THE ADVANCEMENT OF COLORED PEOPLE, OFFICE OF THE FIELD DIRECTOR OF LOUISIANA
(1964-1976; 21 lin. ft.)

These records cover the entire period of the office's existence. The largest part of the collection (ca. 8 lin. ft.) is made up of correspondence, with the remaining part consisting of reports, press releases, minutes, newsletters, complaints, newspaper clippings, and photographs. The records cover an important period in the civil rights revolution, and they document efforts in voter registration, economic boycotts, housing, education, and other areas.

PAPERS OF JOHN P. NELSON
(1957-1977; 7.2 lin. ft.)

A native of Gulfport, Mississippi, Nelson grew up in New Orleans, where he is now a member of the law firm of Nelson, Nelson and Lombard and a professor of law at Loyola University. He has been the attorney for many landmark civil rights cases in Louisiana and Mississippi, including suits to desegregate Tulane University and the Louisiana State Athletic Association and a school desegregation case for Houma Indians of Terrebonne Parish. He founded and led organizations in New Orleans to effect school desegregation, and he was one of the founders of the National Catholic Conference for Interracial Justice. He has served as a director and on the legal council of the Southern Regional Council. His papers contain 1,227 pieces of correspondence, briefs, reports, minutes, memoranda, speeches, and magazine articles (about Nelson and his interests).

PAPERS OF ORLANDO CAPITOLA WARD TAYLOR
(1936-1979; ca. 3.5 lin. ft.)

O.C.W. Taylor (1891-1979) was a native of Huntsville, Texas, who came to New Orleans after his graduation from Wiley College. For forty-two years he was a teacher and principal in the Orleans Parish schools. He was one of the organizers and first editors of the *Louisiana Weekly*. For twenty years he served as the state agent and reporter for the Pittsburgh *Courier* and the Chicago *Defender* and as Southern representative for the Associated Negro Press. Beginning in 1943, he hosted a talk show on WNOE radio, and for two years he was the announcer and producer of a show for WWOM-TV. During World War II, he served as a dollar-a-year deputy administrator for war bond sales in Louisiana, and he is credited with sales totalling $12 million. He was a thirty-third degree Prince Hall Mason and an active member of the United Supreme Council, Thirty-third Degree Ancient and Accepted Scottish Rite of Freemasonry. Taylor was an organizer of the Bunch Club and served as its president and also as president of the Original Illinois Club. His papers contain correspondence, newspaper clippings of hundreds of articles written by him, scrapbooks, broadsides, and photographs.

PAPERS OF ALEXANDER PIERRE TUREAUD
(1783-1977; 31 lin. ft.)

A. P. Tureaud (1899-1972) of New Orleans was a nationally prominent civil rights attorney and Catholic layman. He initiated over thirty cases for the desegregation of Louisiana's public schools and also prosecuted suits to equalize salaries for public schoolteachers, to admit black students to Louisiana State University, to desegregate buses, parks, playgrounds, and other public facilities, and to compel the Louisiana State Board of Education to use textbooks portraying the black experience. In addition to being a crusading practicing attorney, Tureaud was employed at times in the U.S. Department of Justice and as deputy comptroller in the U.S. Customs Office in New Orleans. He served for twenty-five years as legal counsellor for the Louisiana Education Association. He taught in Xavier University's

School of Social Work and the YMCA School of Commerce. He was appointed judge (ad hoc) of the Traffic Court of New Orleans and to membership on the Louisiana Commission on Human Relations, Rights, and Responsibilities and to the Board of Commissioners of the Housing Authority of New Orleans. He was an organizer of the Louisiana State Conference of NAACP Branches, the Federation of Civic Leagues of New Orleans, and the Orleans Parish Progressive Voters League. He served as president of both the New Orleans Branch of the NAACP and the Louisiana Conference of Branches. A member of the Knights of Peter Claver, he was elected in 1932 as the order's first national advocate, a position he held for sixteen years. He later served as national secretary and national editor, and he received the order's highest honor, the Gold Medal of Saint Peter Claver. He was the first black member of the Board of Trustees of the Catholic University of America. In 1969, Tureaud was cofounder of the Louisiana Archives of Negro History, and he personally collected documents relating to Louisiana black history, many of which are included in his papers. The collection contains correspondence, briefs, family documents, minutes, resolutions, newspaper clippings, photographs, and other memorabilia.

CIVIL RIGHTS AND THE COURTS, DOCUMENTATION ON MICROFILM (162 reels)

This collection of microfilm contains the records of the Southern office of the NAACP Legal Defense and Education Fund, Inc., the Lawyers Committee for Civil Rights Under Law, and the Lawyers Committee for the Defense of the Constitution. These records, which encompass the South, include briefs, correspondence, and other documentation of over 500 Louisiana civil rights cases that reached state and federal courts.

RECORDS OF WESLEY (METHODIST) CHAPEL, NEW ORLEANS, LOUISIANA (1864-1912; 4 reels of microfilm)

The microfilm copy of these records was obtained from the Commission on Archives and History of the United Methodist church. Wesley Chapel was established in 1838 as an interracial church but became an all-black church during the schism of 1844 in the Methodist Episcopal church. The records contain a history entitled "Mother Wesley" (24 pages), covering the period from 1839 to 1931. Also included are minutes, records of memberships, marriages, baptisms, finances, church and civil trials, and reports.

Additional materials of significant quantity or quality on Louisiana history and Louisianians are found in the Beecher Memorial Church Papers (10 items); Frederick Leslie Brownlee Papers (1894-1966; 6.4 lin. ft.);

Records of the Catholic Committee of the South (1939-1955; 0.8 lin. ft.); Creole Affair Collection (1842-1854; 0.4 lin. ft.); Kenneth Bronstorph M. Crooks Papers (1905-1959; 0.8 lin. ft.); Countee Cullen Papers (1921-1969; 10.6 lin. ft.); Nellie De Spelder Diary (1895-1899); Microfilm Edition of the Paul Lawrence Dunbar Papers (1873-1936; 9 reels); William T. Handy Autobiography (1894- ; 70 typewritten pp.); Nicholas Hood Papers (1945-1960; 0.6 lin. ft.); Anna Marie Hansen Jamison papers (1917-1972; 0.4 lin. ft.); Rosa Freeman Keller Papers (1961-1979; 0.4 lin. ft.); Archives of the Race Relations Department of the United Church Board for Homeland Ministries (1942-1970; 87.6 lin. ft.); Race Relations Clippings Files (1895-present; 95 lin. ft.); Rockefeller Archives, Selected Records of the General Education Board (1902-1969; 12 reels of microfilm); Rosenwald Fund Archives (1917-1948; 117 reels of microfilm); and Robert Tallant Collection (ca. 1895-1952; 9 reels of microfilm).

The ten items in the Beecher Memorial Church Collection date from the beginning of this New Orleans church in 1893 to 1967. They include a short history of the church, programs showing the church's community involvement, and a poster showing photographs of its pastors. Frederick Brownlee was general secretary of the American Missionary Association, and his papers contain a few items relating to the history of Dillard University. The Records of the Catholic Committee of the South contain correspondence from priests and Catholic laymen of Louisiana. The Creole Affair Collection contains photocopies and microfilm from materials in the National Archives relating to the slave revolt on the *Creole* while the ship was en route from Virginia to New Orleans. The Kenneth Bronstorph M. Crooks Papers contain a few items relating to his tenure as professor of biology at Southern University. The Countee Cullen papers, an invaluable source for studying the life of Cullen and the Harlem Renassiance, contain a few items relating to Dillard University. The Nellie De Spelder Diary covers the period when Miss De Spelder was teaching in New Orleans in the Daniel Hand School of Straight College. Paul Laurence Dunbar married Alice Ruth Moore of New Orleans, and a large part of the microfilm edition of his papers—the originals are in the Ohio Historical Society—are the papers of his wife. However, only a few items date from her New Orleans years. The seventy-page autobiography of William T. Handy was written for his grandchildren. Handy served as longtime pastor of Ray Avenue and Williams Methodist Episcopal churches in New Orleans. Nicholas Hood, currently city councilman and pastor of Plymouth United Church of Christ in Detroit, was pastor of Central Congregational Church in New Orleans from 1949 to 1958. Several items in his papers document his work in New Orleans. Anna Marie Hansen Jamison taught at several of the American Missionary Association's schools for blacks, including Straight College and Dillard University in New Orleans from 1935 to 1937. A few of the items among her papers date from her New Orleans tenure. Rosa Freeman Keller has been deeply and widely involved in civic affairs and race relations in

New Orleans. She is currently a member of the board of trustees of Dillard University and was formerly chairman of the board of directors of Flint-Goodridge Hospital and of the National Urban League of New Orleans. Her papers include an autobiography written in 1979 for her children and records pertaining to the suit to desegregate Tulane University, which John P. Nelson litigated and she financed. The Archives of the Race Relations Department of the United Church Board for Homeland Ministries contain the records of a race relations institute held in New Orleans in 1945. The race relations clipping files contain several thousand clippings from national and local newspapers dealing with civil rights and race relations in Louisiana. The microfilm of Selected Records of the General Education Board, obtained from the Rockefeller Archives which holds the original records, contains information on Straight College, New Orleans University, and Dillard University. The microfilm of the Rosenwald Fund Archives, taken from originals at Fisk University and the University of Chicago, contains information on Louisiana's Rosenwald schools, Grambling State College, Southern University, Straight College, New Orleans University, and Dillard University. The records are particularly valuable for the establishment of Dillard University, for which the Rosenwald Fund assumed the initiative and leadership and to which it contributed more than $1 million. The microfilm copy of the Robert Tallant Collection was obtained from the New Orleans Public Library, which holds the originals.

All these collections are open for research use. A printed register or guide is available for each collection. The center provides photocopying services, and microfilm may be borrowed on interlibrary loan.

21
LOUISIANA DIVISION: NEW ORLEANS PUBLIC LIBRARY

COLLIN B. HAMER, JR.

Street address:	219 Loyola Avenue
	New Orleans, Louisiana 70140
Mailing address:	Same
Telephone:	(504) 586-4912
Days and hours:	Tuesday-Saturday, 10 A.M.to 6 P.M.

THE LOUISIANA DIVISION came into being through the consolidation of several city agencies and collections. From 1769 the New Orleans City Archives was maintained in the city hall (or its equivalent) with a custodian directly responsible to the Cabildo prior to 1803 and to the mayor after 1805. It eventually became a separate bureau of city government.

Plans for reorganization were often considered, and as early as 1903 it was recommended that the City Archives be transferred to the public library. This goal was realized in October 1946, during the administration of Mayor de Lesseps S. Morrison, when the City Archives was made a division of the New Orleans Public Library. The City Council passed an ordinance that defined the archives and prescribed the methods by which material was to be collected and ownership transferred to the library. Maintenance of the City Archives was considered so important as to merit inclusion in the 1954 Home Rule Charter as a specific library function.

Prior to 1961, parts of the City Archives Collection were housed in several locations, including the old City Hall and its Annex and the basements of two library buildings. A roving staff was required to operate this nebula of historical material. After the present central library was completed in 1948, the scattered material was gradually brought together so that by 1961, fifteen years after the library took custody, the City Archives were finally under one roof. At this time the department was greatly expanded with the transfer from other library departments of all books by or about Louisianians, the Louisiana state documents, Louisiana magazines, and the circulating books on Louisiana travel and history. The name of the combined collection was changed to the Louisiana Department and later to the Louisiana Division.

The *raison d'être* for the Louisiana Division is the collection and organization for research of every type of printed oral or visual record relative to the study of Louisiana and its citizens. Because the state documents, newspapers, and published books are listed in standard published finding aids, they will not be described, even though these areas are comprehensive within the division's collection. Two descriptive guides have been published: *Genealogical Material in the New Orleans Public Library* (1975), by the author; and *Researching the History of Your House* (1976), by Wayne Everard. Although the scope of the first guide is manifest in its title, the latter is a procedural handbook describing the many resources that relate to land records: tax assessment and paid tax rolls, plan books, building permits, maps, blueprints, city directories, and newspapers. All twentieth-century books, state and city documents, and microfilm are available for unrestricted use within the physical confines of the Louisiana Division; however, rare material, including books, manuscripts, and maps, can only be used after completing an "Application to Use Rare Material" form and presenting proper identification and credentials to the director of the Louisiana Division. Certain items in frail condition may be usable only in microform or other facsimile. Questions concerning copyright, literary rights, and photocopying will be addressed on a case-by-case basis.

In order to bridge the gap between collected resource material and easy access by the researcher, a number of indexes, amounting altogether to over one million cards and containing at least twice that number of references, have been created by the staff since the 1930s. Each of these contains exact citations to the source of the data in books, newspapers, or manuscripts.

The Louisiana News Index was begun by the Works Progress Administration in the City Archives Department and covers what was thought to be important from 1804 to 1939. Since the library's own comprehensive indexing project began in the 1940s to access all articles in New Orleans daily newspapers (except sports and society), the index grew until it contained 528,000 cards at the time of its unfortunate demise in 1966. At that time indexing of papers for the periods of the war of 1812, the Civil War, and the post-World War II era (through 1963) had been completed. Although contained in one alphabet with chronological subfiling, the difference between the selective approach of the WPA and the comprehensive method of the library is readily apparent to the researcher, who encounters an abundance of references on a topic during certain time spans and a reduced number in others.

The division maintains a separate Louisiana Biography Index containing 523,000 cards, to which are added about 20,000 per year through the efforts of a team of volunteer indexers and typists. While most of the cards refer to obituaries appearing in New Orleans daily newspapers, the index also contains references to biographies of Louisianians appearing in hundreds of monographs and collected biographies. Supplementing these indexes is the card index to the newspaper morgue file of the *Times Picayune* (1922-1944), which is available in an eight-reel set of microfilm, and the card index to station WVUE-TV, Channel 8 (New Orleans) news programming from 1969 to 1973.

Additional indexes have been compiled over the years for a number of periodicals that deal primarily with the New Orleans region: *Architectural Art and Its Allies*, *De Bow's Review*, *Double Dealer*, *Our Home Journal*, *Roosevelt Review*, *Figaro* (New Orleans), *New Orleans Magazine and Courier*. Subject indexes to reference works and source material have been created for Louisiana place names, forts, landmarks, plantations, and geographic points. The division staff also maintains a glossary of terms unique to Louisiana's vocabulary.

The division's substantial Carnival Collection is of particular interest to the social historian. This group of research materials includes over 10,000 items representing every type of activity relating to the annual Mardi Gras or carnival season from the 1850s to date. Included are original sketches for costumes and floats, ball invitations, programs, commemorative medals, medallions and memorabilia, scripts, slides, and photographs. Many of the late nineteenth-century items are excellent examples of lithography from Belgium and France. Also included are a large number of "Carnival editions" of newspapers from the 1890s through the 1920s, each containing color illustrations of the floats in a particular parade. Approximately 300 additional pieces are acquired annually as gifts from generous donors.

Social history is also well documented in the Louisiana and New Orleans Picture File, which contains approximately 30,000 photographs dating from the late 1880s to modern times. Buildings, scenes, and persons of every type and class are represented in the form of color slides, glass slides, and black and white enlargements, 10,000 of which are indexed. Also included are about 6,400 aerial photographs of the state and region and 2,400 reels of motion picture film acquired from WVUE-TV. The collection is arranged by photographer, when known, or by subject. Although the frozen images that record events of the past are of paramount importance to historians, certain groups, such as the Works Progress Administration Collection, 1936-1941, and the U.S. Army Corps of Engineers Collection, 1947-1964, have in recent times become more valuable to the allied fields of social history, government, architecture, and the environmental sciences.

Because it includes unique compilations of material from a wide variety of sources, the Scrapbook Collection presents to the researcher concise packages of data that would not otherwise be encountered except by accident. Some of the more important collections are Alcée Fortier High School (1931-1946; 23 volumes), Daneel School (1918-1942; 2 volumes), deLesseps Story Morrison (1945-1969; 23 volumes), French Market (1943-1945; 1 volume), Henry Dickson Bruns (1888-1904; 1 volume), Huey Pierce Long (1928-1940; 6 reels of microfilm), Yves R. Lemonier (1862-1910; Civil War, 6 volumes), Neville Levy, (1941-1963; 9 volumes), La Salle Elementary School (1902-1942; 12 volumes), Louisiana and New Orleans (6 volumes), Municipal Auditorium (1934-1968; 13 volumes), New Orleans Public Library (1906-1963; 10 volumes), New Orleans Tidewater Ship Channel (1943-1958; 6 volumes), Robert Sidney Maestri (1936-1958; 20 volumes), Robert Tallant (1938-1957; 11 volumes), Spanish American War, (1898-1899; 2 volumes), and Victor Hugo Schiro (1946-1968; 10 volumes).

The Louisiana Division's Microfilm Collection now contains over 22,000 reels of microfilm, 600 pieces of microfiche, and 10,000 microcards. Almost one-third of it is comprised of newspapers, our collection of New Orleans newspapers being probably the most complete in existence. All dailies and most weeklies have been microfilmed. We also have the Baton Rouge *Morning Advocate* from 1940 to date, along with many nineteenth-century papers from Alexandria, Natchitoches, Vidalia, and New Iberia, as well as Baton Rouge. Current subscriptions have been in effect since January 1973 for the Alexandria *Daily Town Talk* and the Shreveport *Journal*. The division maintains complete files of all black newspapers in the state. These include the *News Leaders* of Alexandria, Baton Rouge, Lafayette, Lake Charles, and Monroe and the *Louisiana Weekly* of New Orleans.

An assortment of graduate theses and dissertations on Louisiana subjects is another frequently used segment of the Microfilm Collection. This collection consists of almost 800 dissertations from various universities throughout the country and over 700 theses from universities in Louisiana and Texas. Topics range from subscription libraries in New Orleans to the food habits of the garfish. Research for many of these was undertaken in the Louisiana Division.

The division's map collection contains approximately 1,300 maps, plans, and drawings concentrating primarily on the New Orelans area. Many are original nineteenth-century pen and ink creations of the old City Surveyor's Department. Also included are photographic copies of rare maps and later published ones. In addition, all Jefferson Parish Subdivision surveys through 1964 are represented in four reels of microfilm. The twentieth-century New Orleans Sanborn Insurance maps in atlas form range from

1908 to date. With the exception of two volumes, we have uncorrected as well as corrected copies of most editions. They are extremely valuable for the amount of detail they offer concerning buildings and utilities, for example, type of building, construction material, and location of outbuildings and fire hydrants. *Robinson's Atlas* of 1883 is similar to the Sanborn map books. Even the locations of wells are indicated.

The James Harrison Dakin Collection numbers 376 original ink and wash drawings from the period 1832-1847 and represents a major historical insight into the trend toward Greek Revival architecture in the early nineteenth century. Among the types of buildings depicted are churches and government buildings, including jails (a prison in Havana), and the old state capitol at Baton Rouge. In a number of cases, such as the New Orleans Custom House, Dakin's plans were not accepted, and the completed structure was totally different in concept.

Spanning the period 1710 to the present, private manuscripts collections in the Louisiana Division display an array of formats ranging from a palm leaf book in one of the languages of the Indian Subcontinent to the working papers of the Curtis and Davis New Orleans Neighborhood Study in the 1970s.

New Orleans business leaders and concerns are well represented. The John McDonogh Papers (1803-1804; 12 items) and the business papers of the McDonogh and W. C. Payne concern (1801-1803; 223 items) trace the early career of one of New Orleans's most prominent and best-remembered businessmen. Included among cultural collections are the George W. Booth Theatre Collection (1880-1896; 2 volumes) and the La Variete Association (1822-1904; 3 volumes). Civic organizations represented substantially include the Equal Rights Association Club (1914-1919; 1 volume), the Local Council of Women (1889-1901; 2 volumes) and the Women's Anti-Lottery League (1891-1892; ca. 200 items). The Robert Tallant Collection (1937-1957; ca. 470 items) documents the career of one of New Orleans's prominent literary figures, while the Lyceum and Library Society Collection (1854-1881; 5 volumes) describes cultural developments in the nineteenth century.

The development of social agencies, including the Girdo Asylum (1841-1874; 326 items) and the Volunteer Relief Committee (1862; 3 volumes) are described in large bodies of documents. Important political figures represented in the holdings include Governor William Charles Cole Claiborne (1804-1814; 122 items), while the Martha G. Westfeldt Papers (1934-1937; 43 items) contain documents relating to Huey Long. A recent acquisition, the Walter C. Carey Collection (ca. 1920-1979) contains voluminous material relating to the development of flood control works on the lower Mississippi River.

The New Orleans City Archives Collection is a comprehensive and unique record of the Crescent City and its history. Containing 8,905 manuscripts and 7,442 printed volumes along with 3,700 reels of microfilm and over 850,000 pieces of correspondence, this collection covers the entire history of the New Orleans municipal government from 1769 to the present. Classified by governmental department or function, the records are in continuous use by researchers interested in city planning, urban studies, architecture, and government. An archives card catalog lists the materials by their archives classification and is cross-referenced by subject. The City Archives Collection can be roughly divided into time periods based largely on the various charter changes that affected local government. In addition, the division includes records of former cities that were eventually absorbed into the city of New Orleans. Holdings for city departments, advisory boards, committees, and other offices are voluminous. There is sufficient material to support an institutional history of almost every city agency. In order to illustrate the varied and comprehensive nature of the city's records, some examples of the holdings for particular agencies are offered below. The records of the Mayor's Office, 1805-present, include over 200 volumes and 22 reels of microfilm along with over 300 linear feet of unbound correspondence. Most of the latter files are twentieth-century records and include the letters of Martin Behrman (1904-1925; 1.5 lin. ft.), Arthur Joseph O'Keefe (1926-1930; 1.5 lin. ft.), Andrew James McShane (1920-1925; 1.5 lin. ft.), Robert Sidney Maestri (1936-1946; 3 lin. ft. and 31 reels of microfilm), deLesseps Story Morrison (1946-1961; 117 lin. ft.), Victor Hugo Schiro (1957-1970), and Moon Laudrieu (1970-1978; 16.5 lin. ft.). Also included are over 200 reels of motion picture film chronicling mayors' activities along with numerous tapes of annual reports and other mayoral speeches from 1950 to date.

Among the many interesting documents filed with the Mayor's Office over the years are four volumes of registers containing the names of free persons of color allowed to remain in the state. Beginning with 1840 and continuing as late as 1864, these records are alphabetized to the first letter and give the name, sex, age, occupation, place of birth, date of arrival, and date of recordation for each individual.

City Council minutes have been preserved since 1769. The earliest records are in manuscript form beginning with the records and deliberations of the Cabildo during the Spanish period through 1803. For the years 1909-1970, we have the complete record of the proceedings for each meeting. These include not only the official published version of the minutes but also reports to the council, petitions from citizens, and the full text of all proposed motions and resolutions. For the years 1951-1954 and 1961-1969 there are also sound recordings of the council meetings. In this form the researcher has access to the most complete—and the most intriguing—record of the council's debates. Official papers of a number of city councilmen are available for use in the City Archives: Bernard McCloskey (1946-1950; 11 cu. ft.), Victor Hugo Schiro (1950-1954; 14 cu. ft.), James E.

Fitzmorris (1954-1966; 46 cu. ft.), John J. Petre (1961-1967; 16 cu. ft.), Joseph V. DiRose (1962-1978; 40 cu. ft.), Daniel Kelley (1962-1966; 4 cu. ft.), John D. Lambert, Jr. (1970-1971; 1 cu. ft.), Frank Friedler (1974-1980; 4 cu. ft.), and Abraham Lincoln Davis (1975-1978; 9 cu. ft.).

A large and varied group of records deals with the city's finances. Annual reports of the city comptroller dating back to 1853 contain printed records of the receipts and expenditures of the city government. These volumes have been used to research various public projects such as the paving of Esplanade Avenue. The microfilmed real estate assessment rolls date back to 1857 and show the assessed value of each piece of property in the city. They are useful in determining the periods when the various sections of the city were subdivided and settled.

Most of the Health Department records date only from the turn of the century. These include annual reports and minutes of the Board of Health along with statistical reports on morbidity and mortality. Originally created by the Recorder of Births, Marriages and Deaths and later passed on to the Health Department are microfilmed death certificates from 1805 to 1916 and marriage certificates from 1870 to 1915. A set of some 175 marriage record books created by the first through seventh justices of the peace from 1845 to 1870 are slowly being indexed by volunteers. Closely related to the death certificates are the records of the various city cemeteries extending back to 1835.

From the Coroner's Office are Autopsy Reports (1844-1967), Records of Property Found on Deceased Persons (1906-1930), and Records of Insane Persons (1881-1930). The latter group includes descriptions of the psychological behavior of individuals judged to be insane.

Records of the city surveyor, city engineer, and other offices dealing with real estate provide glimpses into the growth and development of the Crescent City. Among these are plan books from as early as 1852 showing property ownership and existing structures throughout the city. Correspondence from these departments contains references to the construction of public buildings and to the opening and paving of city streets, bridges, and canals.

Registers of the Wharfinger and Collector list the flatboats, steamships, and other craft using the harbor facilities as early as 1806.

The Fire Department records are primarily for the central business area and date back to the 1890s. Log books of the various fire companies detail the day-to-day routine of the firemen, and the fire report books record the alarms received and actions taken to combat the fires. These records extend into the 1960s.

Among the materials from the Police Department are arrest records, 1826-1968, and detailed reports of homicides from 1898 to 1947, as well as the verbatim testimony of witnesses to these crimes for the years 1930-1945. Correspondence of the department contains numerous references to establishments of the day.

The growth of the city and changing architectural patterns are documented in extensive collections. Included with the bound maps and atlases are several splendid surveyor's atlases dating from the 1870s, including two concerned with Carrollton, and seven-volume set of plans of the first municipal district from the 1860s created by the city auctioneer. These record property lines and owners and in some cases show the plan view of all buildings in the area.

Since 1972 the division has been receiving from the Safety and Permits Department at City Hall a collection of 1,200 sets of blueprints dating from 1892 through 1972. Most nonresidential buildings in the city are represented because a requirement for a building permit calls for the deposit of one set of plans. This collection takes on extra value when one considers how many buildings have been torn down over the years or remodeled to the point of being unrecognizable. The arrangement is chronological, with the early ones gradually being converted to microfilm. A card index has been devised that accesses the blueprints by fronting street, architect, and name of building or functional use.

In 1974 the Orleans Parish Civil District Court placed its pre-1900 records on deposit with the library. Dating from 1805, they include 1,800 manuscript volumes, 1,200 reels of microfilm, approximately 100 cubic feet of exhibits, and over 275,000 original suit records, ranging in size from single sheets to foot-high bundles of documents. Most of the pre-1880 materials, representing the nineteen predecesser courts to the present body, have been at least partially arranged. The 61,000 Civil District Court suit records (1880-1900), however, are so disarranged as to require several more years before they are fully accessible. This vitally important body of information includes wills, successions, naturalizations, and damage suits. In addition, the documents provide insight into personalities, social customs, economic climate, and many of the major events of the era.

Research into the rich and diverse history of the Queen City of the South and the metropolitan center of Louisiana has only begun to scratch the surface. Few cities offer such extensive and accesible source material for the study of local and regional culture. Together with the other archival, library, and museum sources described in this guide, the Louisiana Division's materials insure that New Orleans historical research will be limited only by the researcher's imagination.

22
THE EARL K. LONG LIBRARY ARCHIVES AND MANUSCRIPTS DEPARTMENT

D. CLIVE HARDY

Street address:	Earl K. Long Library, 1st floor University of New Orleans, Lakefront, New Orleans, Louisiana 70122
Mailing address:	Same
Telephone:	(504) 286-6543
Days and hours:	Monday-Friday, 8:00 A.M. to 4:30 P.M.; Saturday, 9:00 A.M. to 1:00 P.M.; closed all university holidays due to limited staff. Out-of-town researchers are advised to make appointments if possible.

THE ARCHIVES AND Manuscripts Department of the Earl K. Long Library of the University of New Orleans is a relatively new repository, having only recently marked its thirteenth year of operation. In this short span, however, it has fulfilled a need that should prove increasingly important to scholars in several disciplines. An appreciation of the collection's strength can be gained from a summary of the department's inception and growth to date, which will also illustrate the evolution of the rationale behind the department's goals.

In the spring of 1968 the Earl K. Long Library acquired and accessioned its Italian Clubs Collection (ca. 1893-1963; 5 lin. ft.). Consisting of records and memorabilia from eleven different Italian fraternal organizations that had existed in New Orleans since the late nineteenth century, the collection was significant in several ways. Other manuscript collections had been given previously to the library but, because of an institutional orientation that favored books and other secondary sources, had remained in odd storage areas, forgotten until years later when rediscovered. Unlike these earlier gifts, the Italian Clubs Collection was accessioned, and that formality marked the birth of the Archives and Manuscripts Department within the library.

If the accessioning of the Italian Clubs Collection established the Archives and Manuscripts Department as an entity, its subject matter suggested that the department's collecting endeavors be directed to local ethnic materials. This stress was appropriate in several ways to the university's own urban cast. Such groups are primarily an urban phenomenon, and the school's student body is a representative cross section of the city's ethnic populations. An additional advantage in collecting such material was its more ready availability, a result of having been largely overlooked up to that time by most depositories in the New Orleans area. Thus, the department has acquired by gift or deposit a fair number of collections that could be considered ethnic. An excellent example would be the Marcus Bruce Christian Collection (ca. 1910-1976; ca. 200 lin. ft.), mainly personal papers, book and article manuscripts, and other records of the black poet, historian, and printer. The collection also contains Christian's extensive library and a large body of original documents concerning the black experience in Louisiana's history. It would be hard to exaggerate the importance of this collection as a primary source for understanding that experience.

Collections that reflect Louisiana's black heritage as it merged with the state's French cultural base are the Société des Jeunes Amis Collection (ca. 1885-1920; 332 items incl. 8 bound volumes), the Société des Francs-Amis (1907-1926; 4 items, including 3 bound volumes), and the Peter Joseph Collection (ca. 1874-1978; 0.67 lin. ft.), which includes records of the Société Prospérité and the Arts et Metier BMAA. Organized initially to provide medical and funeral benefits for members, these organizations evolved into community institutions with significant social ramifications. Although certainly fragmentary, the records of these fraternal groups provide an insight into a talented, close-knit social group, the Creoles of Color, that has today all but disappeared. Finally, no review of the department's holdings on the Creoles of Color would be complete without citing the René Grandjean Collection (1835, 1858-1938, 1954, 1977; 32 lin. ft.). At the heart of this collection are thirty-four manuscript volumes that record in meticulous French the details of séances held by a New Orleans spiritualist group between 1857 and 1890. These volumes would seem to be an ideal source for a psychohistorical examination of a complex group about which very little is known.

Documentation of the black experience in more recent years may be gained by studying the papers of two current black leaders, Louisiana State Representative Louis Charbonnet, III (ca. 1972-1975; 20 lin. ft.), and New Orleans City Councilman Sidney J. Barthelemy (1974-1977; 7 lin. ft.). The department's largest and perhaps most important holding of documents reflecting on the city's black history during the post-World War II era is the National Association for the Advancement of Colored People, New Orleans Branch Collection (1928, 1942-1971; 75 lin. ft.). With an as yet unprocessed augmentation for the years 1971-1972 of 37 linear feet it will no doubt prove a rich source for scholars interested in the many local aspects of the changes that have occurred since the *Brown* v. *Topeka* decision.

In addition to the already cited Italian Clubs Collection, material on the city's Italian population can be found in the Antonio Lanata Sr. Collection (1873-1900; 60 items) and the Octavia Benintende DiLeo Collection (1915-1952; 0.67 lin. ft.). Much interesting material on the New Orleans German community is to be found in the very large Lutheran Church-Missouri Synod, Southern District Collection (ca. 1882-1972; 58 lin. ft.). On the other hand, scholars interested in the Crescent City's large Irish population will find material in the Saint Joseph's Roman Catholic Church Collection (1864-1935, 1951; 2 lin. ft.). Material on the city's relatively small but elite French-speaking white community may be examined in the Athénée Louisianais Collection (1913-1970; 1,201 items) and the Bezou-France Amérique Collection (1951, 1952, 1954-1968; 1,155 items). These collections reflect the attitudes and actions of a well-educated and largely cosmopolitan French group. The Saucier phonodiscs in the Louisiana Folklore Society Collection (ca. 1948; 50 items), on the other hand, reveal the rustic lore and culture of Louisiana's Acadian population. Consisting of folk songs and stories recorded in Vermillion Parish, they disclose a charming and once thriving culture that is changing rapidly.

Labor union material constitutes another area of special interest with significant holdings. Among the most important of these are the Stoddard Labor Collection (ca. 1899-1903, 1944, 1957; 10 items, including 1 bound volume), which was compiled and donated by A. P. Stoddard, a former president of the Greater New Orleans AFL-CIO, and the Operative Plasterers' and Cement Masons' International Association of the United States and Canada, Local 93 (1917-1968; 27 lin. ft., including 55 bound volumes), which will be augmented as the union retires current records. This union, incidentally, has been racially integrated since its inception in 1901, an uncommon phenomenon for the time and place. Other labor union collections include those of the New Orleans Printing Pressmen's Union, Local 26 (ca. 1920-1973; 1.5 lin. ft., including 1 bound volume), and the New Orleans Typographical Union, Local 17 (1852-1946, 1952, 1954, 1959; 64

items, including 20 bound volumes), the oldest union in the city and one of the oldest in the South. The typographical records include bank deposit books; constitution, bylaws, and minutes; convention proceedings; union contracts; ledger books; and publications.

Two of the department's largest holdings of labor materials are the Greater New Orleans AFL-CIO Collection (1953, 1957-1975, 1977; 29 lin. ft. and an unprocessed addendum of 17 boxes) and the records of the New Orleans Classroom Teachers' Federation (1921-1975; 36 lin. ft.) in the Sarah Towles Reed Collection. Much smaller but significant labor union holdings are the records of the Bricklayers', Masons', and Marble Masons' International Union No. 1 of Louisiana (1908-1960; 6 bound vols. and related miscellany) and the New Orleans Federation of Classroom Teachers, Local 527 (1937-1945; 1 bound volume) in the William H. Davis, Sr. Collection. Local 527, incidentally, was a black union, and New Orleans Classroom Teachers' Federation was a white union. The two locals are today merged as the United Teachers of New Orleans, Local 527, and that union has deposited fifteen feet of records, which have not yet been accessioned. Finally, the Firemen's Charitable Association of the Seventh District Collection (1876-1892; 1 bound volume) should probably be listed with the department's holdings of labor records. Not a union by strict definition, it was one of those organizations out of which the union movement grew.

Among the department's oldest urban-oriented materials are three tax assessment field books in the Orleans Parish Board of Assessors Collection (1857, 1859; 3 bound volumes). Holdings for a much later period include the Community Services Council of New Orleans Collection (ca. 1921-1972; 20 lin. ft.), records generated by the forerunner of today's United fund; the Community Services Council of Jefferson Collection (ca. 1960-1973; 5 lin. ft.), records for a sister agency of the aforementioned devoted to the amelioration of social problems in adjoining Jefferson Parish; and the Goals Foundation Council Collection (1968-1975; 250 lin. ft.), records produced by that organization together with its studies, conclusions, and recommendations concerning the general welfare of metropolitan New Orleans. Additional urban-related collections are the Audubon Park Commission Collection (1886-1960; 58 lin. ft.), consisting of minutes, account books, correspondence, scrapbooks, photographs, plans, and miscellany of the agency that administers the city's second oldest public park, and the Vieux Carré *Courier* Collection (1960-1978; 60 lin. ft.), which documents the founding and eventual failure of a small but influential New Orleans newspaper that is now defunct.

The neighborhood and architectural preservation movement has had a considerable influence on the city's development in recent decades and is, therefore, a subject of interest to the department. The Andrew R. Sullivan Collection (1971-1977; 4.5 lin. ft.) is an example of such material. Consisting of files compiled by several members of the Governor's Advisory

Committee for the Comprehensive River Area Study and the Governor's Citizen Advisory Committee for the Metropolitan New Orleans Transportation Planning Program, the collection is an in-depth source on the transportation system of New Orleans and its many problems. Other significant holdings in this category are the papers of Mark P. Lowrey (1965-1970; 473 items), Suzanne L. Ormond (1951-1974; 2.5 lin. ft.), and David L. Campbell (1968-1976; 0.67 lin. ft.). These papers, while primarily concerned with such issues as a proposed riverfront expressway through the city's Vieux Carré and the location of a second Mississippi River bridge within the city, also treat such issues as transportation planning and neighborhood zoning. Additional material bearing on similar topics can be found in the Curtis and Davis Planning Department "New Orleans Housing and Neighborhood Preservation Study" Collection (1973, 1974; 5 lin. ft.) and the Louisiana Department of Public Works Collection (1937-1961; 21 lin. ft.), this last consisting of planning files prepared by that agency for various Louisiana cities, including New Orleans. Finally, the Chamber of Commerce of the New Orleans Area Collection (1913-1970; 250 lin. ft.) consists of records germane to all major aspects of the city's history during the twentieth century.

Emphasis on collecting urban, ethnic, and labor records of the New Orleans area has not precluded efforts to acquire other types of material. A few examples of the department's diverse range of holdings are the Newman Louisiana Aviation Collection (ca. 1916, 1928-1932, 1945; 1,628 items), consisting of correspondence, photographs, newspaper clippings, aircraft catalogs, and business records primarily of the Wedell-Williams Air Service and other early (1928-1932) commercial aviation activities in the state; and the Herman B. Deutsch Collection (ca. 1920, 1930-1940, 1945; 2 lin. ft.), compiled by the late newspaperman and centering mainly on Louisiana politics with significant material on Senator Huey P. Long. Additional material on Huey P. Long can also be found in the collection of Gladys McGuffey Rogers (ca. 1930, 1934-1935, 1941; 151 items), who was employed as a secretary to Governors O. K. Allen and James Noe and on occasion worked for Senator Long.

The Weiblen Memorial Collection (ca. 1914-1972; 15 lin. ft.) provides the history of a marble and granite business that was one of the city's few manufacturing activities during part of that period. The Orleans Gallery Collection (1956-1972; 11 lin. ft.) contains virtually all existing records of a now defunct art gallery that was the city's first and possibly most important post-World War II gallery to exhibit serious contemporary art. The Abram Kaplan Collection (1890-1935; 8.5 lin. ft.) includes business records and personal papers of a Polish immigrant who became a Louisiana merchant, land developer, and rice industry entrepreneur and for whom Kaplan, Louisiana, is named. Included in the collection is a very detailed fifty-volume diary, which Kaplan kept from 1908 through 1934. The Monnot/Lanier Family Collection (1821-1958; 5 lin. ft.) contains business and personal records and papers of a family and its sugar plantation in Assumption Parish. The U.S. Army, Corps of Engineers, New Orleans Office Collection (1965-1970) consists of 150,000 photographic prints of aerial views of Louisiana's coastal marshes, the Mississippi and Red rivers, and their tributaries and contiguous land areas. The Delta Steamship Lines Collection (1919-1930, 1935-1952; 55 volumes) details all freight carried by the company to and from New Orleans and ports in Europe, West Africa, and Latin America.

Finally, the diversity of the department's holdings is well illustrated by the following three collections of legal records, which individually and collectively reflect the broadest range of subjects: the Dart and Dart Collection (1848-1975; 6.5 lin. ft.); the Herman L. Midlo Collection (1916-1964, 1978; 6 lin. ft.); and the Supreme Court of Louisiana Collection, which consists of legal files compiled by the state's oldest law firm on behalf of such important clients as Louisiana author Grace King, land and lumber entrepreneur Joseph Rathborne, and the Interstate Natural Gas Company. The Herman L. Midlo Collection, on the other hand, is composed of records Mr. Midlo compiled while defending individuals and groups of modest circumstance involved in immigration and naturalization proceedings, union organizing, and litigation over civil liberty questions. The Supreme Court of Louisiana Collection, consisting of the court's legal archives, is, of course, a major holding by any criterion, and the broad range of its subjects will no doubt attract scholars from many disciplines.

Because of the limited staff facilities, only a very modest amount of copying can be permitted at this time. For additional information and to obtain copies, please inquire of attendant. No incoming correspondence found in the collection of a contemporary person (any person whose career extended past 1915) can be photoduplicated without the written consent of the writer of these letters or his heirs.

23

SOURCES IN NORTHWEST LOUISIANA

PATRICIA L. MEADOR

ARCHIVES DEPARTMENT, LOUISIANA STATE UNIVERSITY—SHREVEPORT

Street address:	8515 Youree Drive
	Shreveport, Louisiana 71115
Mailing address:	Same
Telephone:	(318) 797-5226
Days and hours:	Monday-Friday, except university holidays, 8:00 A.M. to 4:30 P.M.

THE HISTORY OF Northwest Louisiana, which is seriously lacking in reliable publications, offers numerous untapped sources for research. Most topics are completely untouched by research, and, except for Perry Snyder's unpublished Ph.D. dissertation, "A History of Shreveport, Louisiana, 1839-1877" (Florida State University, 1977), there are no comprehensive and reliable studies of the history of Shreveport/Bossier City or of Northwest Louisiana. A few dissertations and articles provide documented historical research into a limited number of topics related to the area of Northwest Louisiana, but the few general works on Shreveport and Caddo Parish history are sketchy, somewhat unreliable, and seldom footnoted.

Until the establishment of the LSU-Shreveport Archives in 1975, there had been no sustained effort to collect and make available the primary sources necessary for historical research and writing in this area of the state. The establishment of the North Louisiana Historical Association (NLHA) in 1954 did show evidence of an awareness of North Louisiana history, and Centenary College of Shreveport encouraged this movement by providing a depository for the records of the association and for donations of material on area history. The association's records and historical materials were housed at Centenary, and Mrs. Lucille Tindoll, a founding member of the NLHA and a school librarian, volunteered her time to catalog many of these records.

The LSU-Shreveport Archives Department was established in 1975 for the purpose of collecting, preserving, and making available the historical manuscripts and records of Northwest Louisiana. The major collections in the LSU-Shreveport Archives document seven major aspects of the region: the Red River, government and politics, agriculture and plantation life, business and industrial activity, the oil and gas industry, architecture, and social and cultural activity. At the present time the archives has more than 200 collections with approximately 950 linear feet of material in addition to more than 500 maps, 3,000 photographs, 300 reels of microfilm, and 220 oral history tapes and transcripts. The shelf capacity is approximately 3,500 linear feet.

The acquisition of source materials on the Red River has been one of four top priorities. Important records for research are available on the Red River Raft, its clearing and impact on the region, and the politics of funding for Red River improvement and for studies of shipping on the Red River and the physiographic and cartographic changes in the Red River.

Among the earliest acquired documents on area history was the *Red River Raft Book*, a series of 107 rare photographic views of the Red River Raft and its final clearing in 1872-1873 by the U.S. Corps of Engineers. This volume of photographs is one of only two extant. The other volume is in the Library of Congress in Washington, D.C. The photographs portray the conditions of the raft, the methods used in clearing, and other Red River scenes.

In his position as superintendent of western water improvement, Captain Henry Miller Shreve surveyed, analyzed, and supervised improvement on the Ohio, the Mississippi and Red rivers. Approximately 240 of his letters written to the secretary of war were selected and brought together as the Henry Miller Shreve Letters (1827-1841; 1 reel of microfilm). These letters provide considerable information on the early attempts at clearing the raft and contain descriptions of the Red River, Shreve's requests for funds for improvement projects, and his comments on the navigation and economic situation of that period.

The records of the Red River Valley Association (1927-1980; 60 lin. ft.) are on deposit at the LSU-Shreveport Archives. The association was organized in July 1927, as the Red River Valley Improvement Association, for the purpose of developing land and water resources of the basin of the Red River, which along with its tributaries drains portions of Oklahoma, Texas, Arkansas, and Louisiana. The records, including correspondence, minutes, reports, hearings, legislation, and membership lists, consist of material on projects of land and water improvement undertaken by the association and material of an administrative nature, including membership and annual conventions of the association. There are also scrapbooks of newsclippings, 1938-1968, as well as maps, photographs, and biographical material of area congressmen and other annual meeting participants. Numerous publications on water resources, waterways, the environment, and flood and pollution control supplement the records.

These sources are untapped and provide an excellent basis for investigation of the economics and politics of the Red River as well as a number of other more narrowly defined topics. A very significant contribution could be made through the compilation and editing of nineteenth- and twentieth-century maps of the Red River to determine and define the constantly changing course of the Red River over a given period of time. The Map Collection at present is modest, but maps are of high priority in the collection development and are continually being added.

The history of the Red River and of steamboating are tied closely together in the collection of Dewey A. Somdal (1780-1972; 33 lin. ft. and 31 maps). As an avid collector of historical materials, Somdal brought together numerous letters, news clippings, freight receipts, and judicial briefs and depositions related to steamboats and steamboat captains as well as correspondence, receipts, agreements, and notes on the Red River. The collection is highlighted with more than 300 photographs of numerous steamboats and river scenes. The Somdal Collection also contains correspondence, inventories of successions, slave bills of sale, and land papers (1798-1866) on Louisiana plantation life, a portion of the J. Fair Hardin papers, and photocopies of the correspondence with President Harry S. Truman regarding the architectural plans for the Truman Library in Independence, Missouri, 1950-1965.

For the study of shipping on the Red River, the William Joseph Hutchinson Plantation Records (1820-1969; 24 lin. ft.) provide a large number of shipping lists and freight receipts. Similar records may be found in the F.M.&S.B. Hicks Cargo Records (1889-1903; 1 volume of 66 pages), the Captain M. S. Scovell Reminiscences (1865-1908; 16 leaves, typescript), the J. Frank Glen Riverboat Logs (1879-1891; 5 items), and the Albert Harris Leonard Memoirs (1835-1861; 66 pages, photocopy). The archives has microfilmed the records of the Caddo Levee Board Minute Books (1892-1975; 2 reels) and the Caddo-Bossier Port Commission Records (1963-1979; 5 inches), and these are also available for research concerning the Red River.

Sources are available but largely unresearched for the study of agriculture and the plantation life and economy of the Northwest Louisiana. Topics that need research include the impact of the Civil War on the economy, post-Civil War agricultural and economic trends, tenant and sharecropping systems, changing production and marketing conditions, and the impact of technological developments on cotton production and marketing.

The largest and most complete collection is the William J. Hutchinson Family and Plantation Records (1740, 1820-1965; 28 lin. ft. and 194 volumes). The records of the plantation, which was established in 1852 and known as Caspiana, are almost complete from the Civil War to the 1890s. Post-Civil War agricultural and economic trends may be investigated through the ledgers, account books, bills, receipts, shipping lists, and correspondence. Family correspondence, diaries, and notes dating from the 1820s reveal social, cultural, and educational aspects of the period.

The Marshall-Furman Papers (1824-1903; 8 reels of microfilm; originals in Centenary College Archives include 12 lin. ft. and folio) extensively document the business, economic, social, and political developments of the antebellum period, the Civil War, and the post-Civil War period. Henry Marshall, who settled in DeSoto Parish in the 1830s, built Land's End Plantation and became a wealthy slaveholder. He was a member of the Louisiana Senate, the state secession convention, the Provisional Congress, and the First Regular Congress of the Confederate States of America. The papers, however, are under restriction and may not be used without special permission.

More business and financial information is found in the William V. Robson Plantation Records (1873-1941; 6 lin. ft. and 36 volumes) and the Allandale Plantation Ledgers (1866-1900; 1 reel of microfilm includes 4 volumes).

For a study of area business and agriculture, the Frierson Company Records (1878-1974; 42 lin. ft.) provide an unbroken run of ledgers from the company's beginning in 1878 in DeSoto Parish until its closing in 1974. The Frierson Family, in addition to operating the area store, purchased cotton and operated a cotton gin. The records include some correspondence in the 1930s, the Frierson Company Corporation Record Book (1932-1970), and the tax records and other financial records (1953-1974).

The papers of Samuel J. Webb (1880-1940; 2 lin. ft.) offer a good source for research. Webb, merchant and farmer from Minden, Louisiana, invented and patented the cotton compress in the mid-1890s, and his papers include his patent and correspondence regarding the sale of the compress throughout the South. Other family correspondence relates to the single tax movement of the late nineteenth century.

Records of the Louisiana State Fair Association (1906-1975; 2 reels of microfilm; originals at the State Fair Office) have been microfilmed and are available for supplementary studies of business and agriculture. Materials include the charter, minutes, financial statements, and reports from the date of its origin in 1906. The records reflect local and national economic and agricultural trends, the organizational problems and development of the fair, and the association's relationship with the city, state, and federal governments. The George Freeman Papers (1849-1932; 8 lin. ft.) supply other materials regarding the building and development of the State Fair.

The LSU-Shreveport Archives has made a concerted effort since its establishment to acquire the basic records of the area's governmental bodies. The department has completed microfilming the proceedings and minutes of the Shreveport City Council (1839-1979; 23 reels; originals at the City Council Office; index available, 1839-1955), the Bossier City Council Minutes and Records (1907-1976; 6 reels; originals at Bossier City Council), the Bossier Parish Police Jury Minutes (1881-1973; 24 reels; originals at the Bossier Parish Police Jury Office), the Caddo Parish Police Jury Minute Books (1840-1973; 10 reels; originals at the Police Jury Office), the Caddo-Bossier Port Commission Records (1963-1979; 5 inches), and the Caddo Parish Levee Board Minute Books (1892-1975; 2 reels; originals at Levee Board Office). Plans are being made to microfilm additional records of this nature. These provide excellent and unbroken accounts of the official acts of local and area government. Varied research topics may be supplemented in these records.

Documentation of the political and legal history of Northwest Louisiana in the nineteenth century is scattered and relatively scarce. The Marshall-Furman Family Papers include some materials of Henry Marshall as a member of the Louisiana Senate in the antebellum period and as a member of the state secession convention, the Provisional Congress, and the First Regular Congress of the Confederate States of America. A diary kept by Henry G. Hall (1870-1873; 1 reel of microfilm), a Shreveport attorney in the 1850s and a Caddo Parish judge in the 1870s, gives short daily accounts of the years 1870-1873. National political developments of the 1820s are discussed in the brief correspondence between Dr. Alfred Flournoy, Sr., and James K. Polk in the Alfred Flournoy Sr. Family Papers (1824-1944; 1.5 lin. ft.).

A prime subject for biographical research is Newton Crain Blanchard, an early Shreveport lawyer, chair of the Caddo Parish Democratic Committee, Constitutional Convention delegate in 1879, state representative 1889-1894, senator, associate justice of the Louisiana Supreme Court, and governor of Louisiana, 1904-1908. Unfortunately there is no collection of Blanchard papers yet available, but the Archives does have the Newton Crain Blanchard Scrapbooks (1892-1906; 2 reels of microfilm, originals in Shreve Memorial Library, 4 volumes), which do offer some insight into Blanchard's life.

Recent political history is much better documented. The right-wing conservative movement dating from the 1940s is well documented in the papers of William M. Rainach (1930-1977; 48 lin. ft.). Rainach, who served two terms in the Louisiana House of Representatives (1940-1948) and three terms in the State Senate (1948-1960), was instrumental in the formation of the White Citizens' Councils. In 1955 he organized and was elected first president of the Louisiana Association of Citizens' Councils, and in the

1959 Democratic primary he made an unsuccessful bid for governor. His papers amply document his support of segregation and other conservative causes as well as his legislative and business career. The papers include his correspondence from 1938 to 1978, his speeches, numerous news clippings, and a large quantity of right-wing literature.

The papers of other Democrats include those of former Representative Algie Brown (1948-1972; 4 lin. ft.), former State Senator Jackson B. Davis (1956-1980; 14 lin. ft.), and former State Senator Don Williamson (1971-1980; 3 inches) and the scrapbooks of J. Howell Flournoy, Caddo Parish Sheriff (1939-1966; 16 scrapbooks).

Urban politics of Shreveport may be examined in the scrapbooks and papers of Shreveport mayors, Clyde E. Fant (1945-1946, 1954-1970; 12 scrapbooks), James Gardner (1954-1958; 7 scrapbooks), and L. Calhoun Allen (1962-1978; 14 lin. ft. and 20 scrapbooks).

Sources for the study of legal history are found in the papers of several judges and lawyers. The papers of Judge Benjamin C. Dawkins, Sr. (1924-1953; 39 lin. ft.) of the Federal Court for the Western District of Louisiana provide not only a study of a unique father-son judicial succession but also the records of some very significant and influential decisions particularly affecting the Caddo Parish educational and social structure. Additionally the Hollingsworth B. Barret Papers (1892-1959; 52 lin. ft.) represent his work as a Shreveport lawyer and his membership on the State Supreme Court Committee on Ethics and Grievances.

Business and industrial activity in Northwest Louisiana is another of many topics virtually void of serious study. There are fewer sources for the nineteenth century than for the twentieth, but merchant records are available in the Frierson Company Records (1878-1974; 42 lin. ft.) and the Sibley Country Store Ledger (1855-1856; 1 volume). And there are numerous bills and receipts in the William J. Hutchinson Plantation Records as well as in a number of other collections.

Business and industrial activity of the twentieth century has somewhat better documentation. Potential research exists for the study of the oil and gas industry, the development of aviation, and the growth of the lumber industry in the area. Some of the basic trends and prominent leaders in the business community of Shreveport may be discovered in the records of the Shreveport Chamber of Commerce (1910-1977; 7 reels of microfilm, originals at the Chamber of Commerce office). The Goodloe Stuck Industrial Collection (1893-1976; 2.5 lin. ft.) contains catalogs, pamphlets, reports, and advertising materials on industrial and manufacturing companies. These often reflect the development and growth of the companies and their significance to the economic progress of Shreveport.

The oil and gas industry, which has played a most significant role in this area's development, needs new and careful examination. At present the LSU-Shreveport Archives has the Arkansas-Louisiana Gas Company Records (1906-1975; 6.5 lin. ft.) and the Rendall Martin Papers and

Cadastral Map Collection (1838-1974; 10 lin. ft., 140 maps, 35 volumes). The Arkla Gas Records include reports, charts, surveys, historical surveys, and summaries and fragmentary correspondence files of a number of early gas and pipeline companies that eventually merged to form the Arkansas-Louisiana Gas Company. The Martin Papers include a large number of cadstral maps, land and geological surveys, and accounting records relating to Arkla Gas Company, plus a small series of materials relating to the Louisiana State Federation of Labor, 1916-1942.

Aviation development in the Shreveport-Bossier City area may be examined in the Colonel D. W. Spurlock Correspondence (1918-1935; 8.5 inches). This correspondence, which has never been used in research, documents Spurlock's instrumental role in the establishment of local airfields for a transcontinental airway, an air mail route through Shreveport in the 1920s, and Barksdale Air Force Base in 1935. The department has recently microfilmed the newspaper that has served Barksdale since 1941. Another recent acquisition relating to aviation history is the Edwin Hefley Papers (1907-1975; 4 lin. ft., ca. 120 photographs). These are the papers of a well-known commercial and executive pilot, and they include photographs, correspondence, pilot logs, and news clippings. To supplement these records, an oral history interview was conducted with Hefley and is available in the archives.

Although the lumber industry is of major importance to this area, holdings are quite small. Records of this industry may be found in some quantity at Stepehen F. Austin University in Nacogdoches, Texas, and at LSU-Baton Rouge. However, two collections available at LSU-Shreveport are the S. H. Bolinger Lumber Company Records (1906-1978; 4 lin. ft.) and the George Freeman Papers (1703-1938; 8 lin. ft.). Freeman was affiliated with the Victoria Lumber Company in Shreveport for a number of years, and his collection contains a small but interesting series of correspondence related to problems of the Bayano River Lumber Company in Panama.

Music and theatre offer research possibilities. The Nathaniel S. Allen Papers (1860-1910; ca. 5 lin. ft. and 25 drawings) when completely accessioned will include the first known musical compositions native to the Shreveport area. Allen, considered by some a Renaissance man, could be an excellent subject for a biographical work. The Jan Garber Papers (1916-1972; 5 lin. ft.) provide clippings and numerous photographs representing the Big Band Era beginning in the 1930s and extending well into the 1970s.

The creation, development, and activities of the Shreveport Symphony Association are documented in its records (1948-1978; 2 reels of microfilm; originals in Symphony House). Oral history interviews supplement this collection and add much to our knowledge of music in the area.

The archives is in the process of accessioning the John Wray and Margaret Young Papers (1939-1979; 3 lin. ft.), which record the growth and development of the Shreveport Little Theatre, the oldest continuously operating community theatre in the United States. The papers document over thirty years of the theatre and include many of the best-known writings on community theatre in the United States.

Another unexploited collection is the Paul L. Carriger Papers (1928-1975; 1,140 leaves). These letters, photographs, and news clippings represent the first attempt to establish an experimental television station in this part of the country as well as the excitement of some of the earliest radio stations in the area.

Education as a topic for study has received little attention, but resources are available on such topics as private education in the nineteenth century, education of freedmen, the problems of beginning public education, and the integration issue since 1954. Mid-nineteenth century education may be investigated in the George Pendleton Letters (1848-1904; 1 reel of microfilm) the Emerson Bentley Diary (1861-1889; 4 inches and 1 reel of microfilm), the fragmented records of the Freedmen's Bureau in Shreveport after the Civil War and the correspondence of several collections of family papers in the department.

The Pendleton Letters discuss some of the obstacles and difficulties of a teacher in the 1850s, and the Bentley Diary was kept by a young teacher from Ohio employed by the Freedmen's Bureau to teach freedmen's children in the post-Civil War period near Donaldsonville, Louisiana. The Wiley B. Grayson Papers (1818-1880, 1924-1939; 4 lin. ft.) offer much detail on education and family life in Catahoula and Franklin parishes and in Grimes County, Texas.

Education of the late nineteenth and early twentieth centuries may be examined in the Caddo Parish School Board Records (1877-1908; 1 reel of microfilm), and after the turn of the century one of many private schools is partially documented in the Ella Dingle Hicks Collection (1876-1969; 2.5 lin. ft.).

Many of the important developments in education from the 1950s through the 1970s may be examined in the Caddo Parish School Board Scrapbooks (1934-1964; 23 scrapbooks), the E. L. McGuire Papers (1926-1970; 5 lin. ft.), the Charles Beard Papers (1969-1973; 2.5 lin. ft.), and the judicial decisions of Judge Ben C. Dawkins, Jr. (1953-1979; 4 lin. ft.). The William M. Rainach Papers also include the records of a private school established during the desegrgation controversy.

The impact of certain religious groups has been considerable on this area's history, but records for churches or religious groups tend to remain in the individual church or instituion. Access to such records for scholarly intent, however, is generally easy to obtain.

A considerable amount of information regarding church affairs, religious movements, and related matters is often found in nineteenth-century correspondence and diaries. The archives has a series of correspondence of J. Franklin Ford (1847-1865; 30 leaves, typescripts, photocopy), which details many activities of a mid-nineteenth-century preacher. Records of the Keatchie

Presbyterian Church (1858-1888; 52 leaves, photocopy) and other small congregations may be found in some of the collections of plantation records, and the Rabbi Abraham Brill Papers (1900-1940; 3 lin. ft.) provide a good source for the study of one of the Jewish congregations in Shreveport between 1920 and 1940.

Study of architectural development in Northwest Louisiana is facilitated by several good sources. One of the most important collections of architectural records is the Samuel G. Wiener, Sr. Records (1921-1976; 5 lin. ft., 60 blueprints and tracings, ca. 400 photographs). These records include drawings and blueprints, photographs, articles, and correspondence, and they document the work of the Jones, Roessle, Olschner and Wiener firm (1922-1935) and Wiener's independent work (1922-1976). The development of Wiener's style from that of Art Deco, as represented in the Municipal Auditorium of the 1920s, to the International Style of the Shreveport Incinerator in the 1930s and the Municipal Airport in the 1950s is well documented and a very fertile but untapped source for study.

The Van Os-Flaxman Architectural Records (1935-1970; 2 lin. ft. and ca. 50 drawings) provide further documentation of the International Style covering roughly the same period as the Wiener Collection. When completely accessioned the Nathaniel S. Allen Papers will document the life and work of an architect who not only designed more than 300 residential and commercial buildings in Shreveport between 1870 and 1910 but also was a musician, composer, and popular band leader.

To supplement the architectural development of Shreveport, the archives has many of the Sanborn Insurance Maps (1885, 1909-1916, 1935-1949; 8 volumes) as well as the records of the Historic Preservation Society of Shreveport (1970- ; 1 file cabinet). The comments and observations about architectural development in the state were recorded by fourteen prominent Louisiana architects in a project sponsored by the Louisiana Architects Association and entitled the Louisiana Heritage Collection (1972; 19 tapes). These tapes are available in the LSU-Shreveport Archives, but they are not transcribed.

Medical and hospital records are quite slim. Sources for medical developments in the nineteenth century include the War Department Records of the General Hospital, Shreveport, Louisiana (1864-1865; 1 reel of microfilm) and include orders, letters and a Register of Patients (1864-1865). Household books of cures and remedies are found in plantation records such as those of the William J. Hutchinson Family. Many collections of family papers and correspondence contain much information regarding family health problems and illnesses as well as regional epidemics.

Medical developments of the twentieth century may be examined in the Willis P. Butler Papers (1916-1973; 56 lin. ft.). These records consist of several files of the Caddo Parish Coroner's Office from 1916 to 1963 and include autopsy, pathology and police reports, mental case files, and drug case files, correspondence, news clippings, and some photographs. The only files that have been researched to any extent are those of the controversial Drug Clinic opened by Dr. Butler in Shreveport in 1919 and closed under controversy by the Louisiana State Medical Society in 1924. These records provide a wealth of material for various statistical studies in criminology, social behavior, mental health, and medical pathology. To supplement research in these records, an oral history interview and transcript with Dr. Butler is available.

The cultural character of the Shreveport-Bossier City area is well represented in the Holiday-in-Dixie Records (1949-1979; 60 lin. ft.). The charter, minutes, financial records, correspondence, and photographs fully document the establishment and development of this spring event. The archives is also the repository for the records of the Red River Revel (1972-1976; 12 lin. ft.). The revel was established in conjunction with the American Bicentennial Celebration in 1976 and has become a widely recognized fall event. The LSU-Shreveport Archives also has records of other groups as well as service organizations.

Numerous ethnic groups have added different dimensions to the growth and development of the Shreveport-Bossier City area. The archives has a full run of the Italian newspaper the *Italia Moderna*, later the *News Record* (1929-1973; 17 volumes; 6 reels of microfilm). The newspaper, which was printed in both Italian and English, was edited by Frank Fulco, the first Italian American to be elected from the area to the Louisiana State House of Representatives. Records are continually sought that document ethnic groups within the community.

The LSU-Shreveport Archives has some records concerning war and military affairs. Although records of the Civil War period are not plentiful, several small collections record wartime events. The Alfred Flournoy, Jr. Correspondence (1861-1864; 93 leaves) is comprised of letters between Flournoy, who was in and around Richmond, Virginia, in 1861 and 1862, and his wife, who resided in Greenwood, Louisina. His letters are rich in detail of Confederate camp life, and hers are filled with home life activities in Greenwood.

The department has a microfilm copy of the Louisiana State Government Records (1850-1888; 24 reels; originals in the National Archives). The records primarily concern the period from 1861 to 1865. The War Department evidently recovered them in Shreveport in June of 1865. See *A Guide to the Records of the Louisiana State Government in the War Department Collection of Confederate Records . . . National Archives*, comp. Thomas J. Harrison (Washington, D.C., 1957). Already mentioned on microfilm are some of the records of the General Hospital in Shreveport, Louisiana (1864-1865).

Information regarding veterans' organizations is located in the records of the Spanish-American War Veterans (1898-1980; 12 lin. ft.). The records include bylaws, minutes, correspondence, general orders, resolutions, rosters, reports, some artifacts, and photographs. The Walter B. Martin Scrapbooks (1939-1945; 9.5 lin. ft., or 38 volumes) contain daily news accounts from the Dallas *Morning News*, the *Reporter Telegram*, and *Time* magazine on World War II. These clippings were accumulated very methodically and provide good material for a journalistic view of World War II.

The archives has a number of collections of family papers that contain research material for studies of immigration patterns, home life, religious, social, and cultural values, education, and regional economic crises, as well as genealogy. The Booher-Martin Family Papers (1824-1946; 250 items) contain correspondence largely between 1824 and 1865 relating family health and economic problems and conditions in central Arkansas. The family papers of Wiley B. Grayson (1818-1880, 1924-1939; 4 lin. ft.) consist of some excellent correspondence relating to family life, education, and general social and business conditions in and around Grayson, Franklin Parish, Louisiana. The Mary Elizabeth Rives Diary (1865-1869, 1888-1900; 1 reel of microfilm, 360 leaves) is another untapped resource for social and cultural activities in the post-Civil War period. Other personal papers include the George Freeman Papers and the John F. Tomkies Papers (1825-1935; 152 leaves; photocopy).

Subjects for family or biographical studies may be found in the papers of the Flournoy family. The Alfred Flournoy, Sr. Papers (1824-1944; 1.5 lin. ft.) and the J. Howell Flournoy Scrapbooks (1939-1966; 16 scrapbooks) offer two good subjects for biographical studies. Alfred Flournoy, Sr., was a pioneer settler in Greenwood in the 1830s, and J. Howell Flournoy, Caddo Parish sheriff from 1940 to 1966, was several times commended by J. Edgar Hoover for his work. The American Forum of Shreveport named him "Outstanding Conservative of the Year 1965." The archives also has the Alfred Flournoy, Jr. Correspondence and the Wayne Spiller Papers (1813-1925; 2 lin. ft.), containing the correspondence, clippings, and genealogical data for the book *Branches from the Flournoy Family Tree* (Seagraves, Tex.: Pioneer Book Publishers, n.d.).

Other genealogical collections include the Bickham Christian Collection (1672-1970; 2 lin. ft.) and the Martin Wallace Collection (1765-1946; 2 lin. ft.).

There are opportunities for investigation of the civil rights struggle in Northwest Louisiana. The collection of published opinions of Judge Ben C. Dawkins, Jr. (1953-1979; 4 lin. ft.) partially documents the U.S. district judge's decisions in several important civil rights cases and his decision in 1978 striking down the city of Shreveport's commission form of government.

The Caddo Parish School Board Scrapbooks (1943-1970), the E. L. McGuire Caddo Parish School Board Papers, and the Charles Beard Papers provide a substantial amount of information on the desegregation of schools in Caddo Parish.

The political papers of William M. Rainach, former State Senator Jackson B. Davis, and former State Representative Algie Brown address aspects of the civil rights issue from a conservative viewpoint.

The integration movement of the 1950s is well represented in the Monsignor Joseph Gremillion Papers (1951-1958; 3 reels of microfilm; originals are in and controlled by the Notre Dame Archives; includes 7 boxes).

Maps, photographs, and oral history interviews supplement many of the collections, and they offer opportunities for scholarly work. For further information on the LSU-Shreveport oral history holdings, see Hubert Humphreys, "Oral History in Louisiana: An Overview," *Louisiana History*, 21, no. 1 (Winter 1980).

The Map Collection includes more than 500 maps representing many of the cities and parishes of Northwest Louisiana. The Arkansas Louisiana Gas Company Records (1905-1976) and the Rendall Martin Papers and Cadastral Map Collection (1838-1977) contain more than 150 maps relating to oil and gas properties of the region. The archives also have maps from insurance and architectural firms and real estate companies as well as many topographic and township plate maps.

The Photograph Collection contains approximately 1,100 catalogued photographs and some 3,500 additional unprocessed photographs. Plans are underway for a full-scale photographic laboratory, and holdings are expected to increase considerably.

Detailed inventories for most collections and a Cumulative Name Index (CNI) are available to researchers, and a Guide to the Collections was published in the summer of 1982. The archives welcomes inquiries, and research assistance can be provided on a limited basis for those unable to visit the campus. Facilities for limited photocopying are available.

CLINE ROOM, CENTENARY COLLEGE

Street address:	Magale Library
	Centenary College
	Shreveport, Louisiana 71104
Mailing address:	Same
Telephone:	(318) 869-5202
Days and hours:	Monday, by appointment; Tuesday, and Friday, 8:00 A.M. to 4:30 P.M.; Wednesday, 8:00 A.M. to noon; Thursday, by appointment; closed on weekends except by appointment.

The Cline Room of Centenary College, also located in Shreveport, Louisiana, has several groups of records potentially useful for studies on Northwest Louisiana. Since the founding of the North Louisiana Historical

Association, the Centenary Archives has housed the association's records as well as additional materials collected from a variety of sources reflecting aspects of Shreveport's history. These materials were catalogued by item and cross-referenced in a card catalog, which, although incomplete, is helpful. The materials were not maintained as collections or record groups, so general headings from the catalog are noted here.

In addition to the records, newsletters, president's reports, bulletins, articles, and clippings on the association, there are articles and clippings on Huey P. Long, the Louisiana Purchase, the Civil War, the Red River, the Shreveport Symphony, the Civic Opera Association, the Caddo Indians, and Louisiana State Fair. A few copies of letters from Henry M. Shreve regarding the Red River Raft, bills of lading from a Red River Packet Book, a Hopewell Plantation Book, and some area maps are available. Several photographs depict the Red River Raft removal and Shreveport around the turn of the century.

Several collections of personal and family papers, a major collection of political and legal materials, and institutional records of the college comprise the main sources for research. Nineteenth-century family life, education, and local political activity are recorded in the Watson Family Papers (1840-1903; 2.5 inches), the Robert T. Gibbs Papers (1846-1873; 2.5 inches and folio); the Hale-Hawkins-Allen-Hitchcock Family Papers (1849-1873; 2.5 inches), and the Roland Jones Papers (1850-1920; 5 inches).

The Watson Family Papers contain correspondence on the children's education, the transfer of slaves, and the 1860 election, as well as Matthew Watson's documents relating to his duties as Caddo Parish sheriff and tax collector, 1846-1855. The correspondence between Robert Gibbs and his wife relates his experiences as a Civil War surgeon. The family correspondence, receipts, and financial records from 1860 to 1913 in the Hale-Hawkins-Allen-Hitchcock Papers provide a record of experiences of the Hale family, who were settlers in Caddo Parish before 1845.

A major source for the study of segregation and state's rights is the collection of Robert G. Chandler (1935-1970; 20 boxes). Chandler (1899-1972) was a Shreveport lawyer very active in the Citizens' Council of Shreveport and on the States' Rights Democrats Committee in 1948 and 1956. His papers include correspondence, financial records, legal documents, and organizational files. Of particular importance are those papers relating to the States' Rights Democrats of Louisiana and the Association of Citizen's Councils of Louisiana. The segregation materials deal with efforts to organize the Citizen's Council and other legal challenges to segregation. Other correspondence relates to the states' rights movements of 1948, his membership on the States' Rights Democrats committee, and his candidacy as an elector for president on the States' Rights ticket in 1956. Some of his principal correspondents include W. Scott Wilkinson, William M. Rainach (papers in the LSU-Shreveport Archives), and Leander Perez.

The bulk of the records in the Cline Room pertain to the history and operation of the college itself. The Centenary College Records (1825-1906, 1908- ; ca. 30 lin. ft.) contain the charter, amendments, minutes, correspondence and incomplete runs of Business Office records, faculty records, presidential papers, and student records, largely from 1908 to the present.

The Centenary Women's Club Papers (1928-1970; 5 inches and scrapbook), Albert Lutz Papers (1874-1941; 2.5 inches and folio), William G. Phelps Scrapbooks (1927-1940; 4 scrapbooks), and Robert E. Smith Papers (1933-1961; 2 lin. ft.) provide news clippings, photographs, programs, and memorabilia reflecting the activities and development of the college.

The Centenary Archives is the repository for the records of the United Methodist church, Louisiana Conference (1847-date). These records are relatively unexploited and available for research. The records of the League of Women Voters and the Southwest Renaissance Society are also on deposit here.

In addition the Cline Room has the papers of Dodd College (1930-1941; 5 inches), a private junior college for women in Shreveport founded in 1927 by M. E. Dodd, pastor of the First Baptist Church of Shreveport. After the college closed in 1943, the buildings were purchased for Centenary, and the permanent student records of Dodd College are now in the custody of the Centenary College registrar. Records in this collection include account books, press releases, student and faculty lists, 1928-1940, and other papers, photographs, and publications.

Collection use is by appointment, and photocopying facilities are available. For information concerning these collections, contact Carolyn Garrison, Archivist, Cline Room, Magale Library, Centenary College, Shreveport, Louisiana.

ARCHIVES, LOUISIANA TECH UNIVERSITY

Street address:	Ruston, Louisiana 71272
Mailing address:	Same
Telephone:	(318) 257-2577
Days and hours:	Monday-Friday, 8:00 A.M. to 4:00 P.M.; other times by appointment only.

Several significant collections of Northwest Louisiana materials are found at Louisiana Tech University Library in Ruston. The Henry Hardtner Room in the library houses three groups of materials significant for the study of the Louisiana forestry industry. The unprocessed papers of Henry E. Hardtner consisting of one file drawer of papers and a scrapbook of clippings, and the records of the Louisiana Forestry Commission (1913-1940; 4 file drawers) provide excellent basic sources for the study of forestry in

Louisiana. The records of the Louisiana Chapter of the Society of American Forestors (1963-1974; 3 file drawers) are also located there.

The Archives of Louisiana Tech house a number of other important collections for the study of regional history. The major topics with research potential are forestry, nineteenth-century family life, and agriculture. Source material relating to the nineteenth-century legal profession, education, the Civil War, the history of North Louisiana parishes, and genealogy would profitably supplement regional studies.

The Sidney Seth Tatum Family Papers (1868-1970; ca. 105 items) record the life and work of a large landholder and farmer in Claiborne and Lincoln parishes during the late nineteenth and early twentieth centuries. Tatum, a merchant and private school teacher in Hico, Louisiana, was active in the Farmers' Union Movement in Lincoln Parish and helped establish the Dubach State Bank. The business and financial papers (1885-1913) record agricultural development, including the improvement of a planter and agricultural distributor in 1892. Documents and publications of the Farmers' Union and the proceedings and publications of the Farmer's Union National Farmers' Alliance (1886-1906) provide an excellent source for study. School records and personal correspondence give other details of education, family, and social life.

Antebellum agricultural activities (1844-1850) and the Grange movement in Catahoula Parish may be examined in the Ernest Adalbert Treuman Breithaupt Family Papers (1844-1899; ca. 75 items; photocopy). The records include correspondence and a journal of a Catahoula Parish planter's agricultural activities (1844-1850), records of the Grange movement in the parish (1868-1877), and some Civil War correspondence.

The social, cultural, and political activities of a Yankee in Red River Parish during the Reconstruction are reflected in the family correspondence and legal records of Marshall Harvey Twitchell (1851-1938; ca. 600 items; originals and some photocopies). The papers discuss the outrages committed by the White League of Red River Parish and its harrassment of Twitchell. The business, legal, and financial records relate activities on Twitchell's Starlight Plantation, such as publication of the Sparta *Times* (November 26, 1870-May 27, 1871, issues included). There is also an autobiography of Twitchell in the collection.

Plantation correspondence of the Pickett family and a ledger of Gold Point Plantation (1902-1903) is included in the Roland Jones Family Papers (1840-1969; 850 items; photocopy).

Three generations of the Hoss family are reflected in the deeds, business records, and correspondence of the family papers (1847-1971; 302 items; photocopy). The business records of Nathaniel Hoss (1849-1874), an early Caddo Parish settler, planter, and commission merchant, and his son, James M. Hoss, Sr., founder and benefactor of Hosston, Louisiana, would provide good material for a study of business in this early period.

The Samuel Worth Jones Diary and Family Papers (1806-1931; 10 ledger books and ca. 125 items; photocopy) provide a good, consistent run of ledgers (1870-1925). Kept by a prosperous farmer in Webster Parish, these business accounts, family legal records, and personal papers and correspondence document the family and business activities from the 1850s through the 1920s. Of particular note is a small group of papers relating to Floyd Jones, sheriff of Red River Parish and member of the Ku Klux Klan.

Family papers of John Murrell, pioneer settler of Claiborne Parish, Louisiana, are found in the Bessie Murrell Gray Family Papers (1848-1965; 85 items; photocopy) and include legal, business, and genealogical records as well as personal correspondence.

Some potential for research into the legal profession and the politics of Northwest Louisiana is found in the Tech Archives. The legal papers, correspondence, and plantation ledgers of Roland Jones (1840-1969; 850 items; photocopy) provide information on his activities as a lawyer, pioneer resident, U.S. congressman, and Caddo Parish district judge. The correspondence of Montfort Stokes Jones, post-Civil War Coushatta lawyer, and of Annie Jones Randell (1871-1947) further document the legal profession. The papers also include information on home life in the antebellum period, the yellow fever in Shreveport, education, and the Civil War.

The James A. Ramsey Correspondence (1862-1887; 3 volumes; carbon copies) is comprised of the letter books of an attorney and prominent citizen of Farmerville, Union Parish, Louisiana, and includes his personal and business correspondence. The bulk of each of the letter books consists of civil and legal matters such as successions, notes, property sales, and lawsuits. Other correspondence relates to the Concord Baptist Association, Keatchie College, and Ramsey's difficulties with J. E. Tremble, editor of the Farmerville *Gazette*. Potential research material may be found in his political correspondence as chairman of the Democratic Executive Committee in Union Parish, letters concerning proposed whiskey elections, and letters regarding the overthrow of the McEnery "ring" in Union Parish.

The Judge J. G. Taliaferro Personal Papers (1814-1902; 38 items) include correspondence from 1845 to 1876 and provide some interesting detail on family relations and living conditions of the period.

Studies in education may be supplemented through use of the Roland Jones Family Papers, the Sidney Seth Tatum Family Papers, and the catalogs of the Mount Lebanon University and Mount Lebanon Female College (1855-1866), in the Charles S. Cox Collection (1855-1866; 7 items; photocopy).

Supplementary information on Civil War experiences in North Louisiana and other parts of the South may be found in the correspondence of John B. Wise (1861-1864; 5 items; photocopy) and the family papers of Ernest Adalbert Treuman Breithaupt (1844-1899).

The Tech Archives has several collections that provide documentary materials for study of the individual parishes in Northwest Louisiana. The Earl R. Hester Papers (1850-1965; ca. 700 items) relate mainly to the history of Arcadia and Bienville Parish, Louisiana, but also have materials on Bossier, Claiborne, Union, and Sabine parishes. Records include the Bienville Parish Incorporating Act, legal records, maps, church histories, correspondence, articles, and miscellaneous notes on various landmarks and events, including the Arcadia Male and Female College, E. A. Seminary, and the Electric Light Plant in Arcadia.

A number of historical notes and articles on Bienville Parish were brought together in the Lavinia Egan Papers (1926-1940; 56 items; photocopy). Egan collected many notes on the history of Bienville, Red River, and other parishes and wrote a number of short articles, including information on the economy, social conditions, and regional folkways, in preparation for writing a history of Northwest Louisiana.

Materials on Claiborne Parish are found in the Bessie Murell Gray Family Papers and the Sidney Seth Tatum Family Papers. Sources for nineteenth-century Caddo Parish include the Hoss Family Papers and the Roland Jones Family Papers.

The Samuel Worth Jones Diary and Family Papers and the Marshall Harvey Twitchell papers contain important source materials for the study of Red River Parish.

The history of Winn Parish is well documented in the Harley B. Bozeman Papers (1858-1971; 1,080 items; originals and photocopies). Bozeman was a longtime resident of Winn Parish, a state politician, and friend of Huey P. Long and his famly. In later years he became known as the historian and genealogist of Winn Parish. Included are the numerous writings of Bozeman, transcripts of taped interviews with Bozeman, a biography of Bozeman, and some of his correspondence. Included also are some materials relating to Huey P. Long and a 1959 interview with Governor Earl K. Long.

Although the Tech Archives does not house any major documents regarding the Long family of Winn Parish, they have two small collections of interest. The Earl K. Long Newspaper Clippings (1938-1963; 1,500 pages; photocopy) include articles covering the career of Earl K. Long between June 1938 and his death in 1960. And the William C. Boone Correspondence (1928-1930; 9 items) consists of letters written from Baton Rouge by the Claiborne Parish state senator and attorney to his wife during the first two years that Huey P. Long was governor of Louisiana. The correspondence deals with political matters, including the impeachment proceedings against Long.

Genealogical records include the Willie Lee Pace Dillon Memoirs and Genealogical Notes (1818-1957; 200 pages; photocopy), the Burt Family

Genealogy (1665-1965; 5 volumes; photocopy), the Christian Bubenzer-Cheatham Bible Records (1829-1888; 1 volume), and a work compiled by Rosa Colvin Barksdale, *The Colvins of North Louisiana, 1730-1958*.

The records of the Salem Baptist Church, Bossier Parish, Louisiana (1844-1972; 7 volumes; photocopy) and a historical sketch of the Bistineau Baptist Church by Ernell Montgomery Thrash (n.d.; 6 pages photocopy) provide documentation for some of the religious activity of the area.

Collections of writers and writings include the Garnie W. McGinty papers and Publications (1895-1969; 10 items; originals, typed copies, and page proofs), consisting of the works of a retired Louisiana Tech University history professor, 1928-1965. Page proofs, reprints of articles, and other addresses and publications by Dr. McGinty are included. The Lavinia Egan Papers consist of materials collected or written for a history of Northwest Louisiana, 1926-1940.

For information concerning the holdings and use of the Louisiana Tech University Archives, contact Mrs. Nowlan Nichols, Librarian/Archivist.

24

LOUISIANA'S SMALLER ARCHIVES

GLEN JEANSONNE

ARCHIVES AND SPECIAL COLLECTIONS
NORTHEAST LOUISIANA UNIVERSITY

Street address:	Sandel Library
	700 University Avenue
	Monroe, Louisiana 71309
Mailing address:	Same
Telephone:	(318) 342-3111
Days and hours:	Monday-Friday, 8:00 A.M. to 5:00 P.M.

THE NORTHEAST LOUISIANA University Archives and Special Collections, established in 1977, began acquiring collections the following year. The archives document the development of northeastern Louisiana, the area served by the Monroe university. Persons wishing to undertake research should write Scott D. Swanson, Director of Archives and Special

---

I wish to thank the following individuals for their contributions to this chapter: Scott D. Swanson, Northeast Louisiana University; Dudley S. Johnson, Southeastern Louisiana University; Mark W. Flynn, Loyola University; Philip D. Uzee, Nicholls State University; Landrum Salley, Louisiana College; Kathy Gardner, McNeese State University; and John Milton Price, Northwestern State University.

Collections. Limited xeroxing requests are processed by the staff. Most collections have been reproduced in microfilm and are available through the micrographics unit of the library. Individual pages may be reproduced, but reproduction of the entire microform is prohibited.

Because of its recent establishment, holdings on Louisiana's colonial period are limited. Nonetheless, several collections make available sources that otherwise would necessitate considerable travel. One such document is Paulmier D'Annemours, *Memoire on the District of Ouachita . . . 1803*, a transcribed translation written to describe French Louisiana to President Jefferson. The Ouachita District Seville Papers and the papers of Intendant Juan Ventura de Morales include fourteen reels of microfilmed documents found in the Spanish archives at Seville. An original copy of the U.S. Supreme Court case *United States* v. *Philadelphia and New Orleans, 1851* deals with disputed territory given to the Baron de Bastrop, 1796-1797.

The archives are rich in nineteenth-century social and economic documents, particularly for the antebellum years. Plantation data is available in the Robert Forbes McGuire Diary (1818-1852), the Civil War diary of Ellen Power (1862-1863), the day book compiled by Bossier Parish planter Leonidas Spyker (1846-1860), and the James Monette Diary decribing community and plantation life in Morehouse Parish (1848-1864) in the George Patton Collection. The large James Sterling Milling microfiche collection is valuable for life in Bossier and Caddo parishes from antebellum times through the mid-twentieth century. The seven-reel microfilm collection of the John Cooper Rolfe family provides much information about the communities of Mer Rouge and Oak Ridge during approximately the same span, complemented by the John Rolfe Windsor and Gertrude Rolfe White Papers.

Four collections deal with religious organization in the nineteenth and twentieth centuries. Most important are the Morehouse Parish Methodist Church Records, over 1,000 pages pertaining to eight churches of the Methodist Episcopal Church, South. The detailed diary of Henry O. White, circuit rider for the Methodist church from 1861 until his death in 1912, provides an account of church activities from northeast parishes to Opelousas. The microfilmed journal of the Bartholomew Methodist Episcopal Church relates births, deaths, marriages, and membership for the oldest Methodist church in Louisiana. The twenty-seven-volume papers of Reverend Dr. Ernest D. Holloway for 1939-1971 include his dissertation, reviews, sermons, prayers, devotionals, speeches, and television meditations. The diary of Father Louis Gergaud, rector of Saint Matthew's at Monroe, 1856-1871, sketches the development of an important Catholic church.

The Northeast Louisiana University Archives also includes partial files of newspapers published in the northeastern parishes, some dating back to the late nineteenth century. Most of these are available in the Louisiana State

University microfilm collection, but holdings include some originals not found elsewhere.

The single most valuable and extensive twentieth-century acquisition is the papers of former Fifth District Congressman Otto E. Passman (served 1947-1976), the inventory of which runs to 142 pages.

Besides the Passman Collection, several others concern twentieth-century Louisiana politics. The papers of Luther Hall, governor, 1913-1917, include 209 items, chiefly newspaper articles, telegrams, and political speeches for the 1912 campaign. For a somewhat later period, 1921-1924, the Morehouse Parish Ku Klux Klan microfiche promises to illuminate activities of the Klan in North Louisiana, particularly the infamous Mer Rouge murders. This group is closed to researchers until June 6, 1989. More recent political developments are represented in the extensive Paul H. Goodman Collection about Louisiana's Constitutional Convention of 1973. Goodman, a delegate, donated 150 items, reproduced on eight reels of microfilm. The collection is subdividied by subject, committee, and delegate, and access is facilitated by a key-word index.

The Northeast Louisiana University Archives suggests topics dealing with settlement patterns in Louisiana parishes, parish histories, Confederate regimental histories, Governor Luther Hall, Congressman Passman, and biographies of other politicians, church and community leaders, and military commanders.

ARCHIVES AND SPECIAL COLLECTIONS, SOUTHEASTERN LOUISIANA UNIVERSITY

Street address:	Southeastern Louisiana University Library Western Avenue Hammond, Louisiana 70402
Mailing address:	University Station Hammond, Louisiana 70402
Telephone:	(504) 549-2194
Days and hours:	Hours flexible and varied. During fall and spring semesters hours are usually 8:00 A.M. to 12:00 P.M., Monday-Friday. Visitors should check at the main library.

The Southeastern Louisiana University Archives and Special Collections began collecting in 1972. Its holdings are limited chronologically to the nineteenth and twentieth centuries and geographically to the Hammond area. There is a small microfilm collection of local newspapers and some church records. The microfilm copy of the journals of Dr. George Colmer, a resident of Springfield, Louisiana, from the 1840s until his death in the 1870s constitutes the only other nineteenth-century holding. The original journals are in the Howard-Tilton Memorial Library at Tulane University.

The largest single collection is the James H. Morrison Papers (1943-1967; 200 lin. ft.), encompassing the period Morrison served as congressman for the Sixth District of Louisiana. Arranged by subject, these include correspondence from constituents dealing with pensions, jobs, legislation, and other matters. Very little correspondence is about his three campaigns for governor of Louisiana. There is a large collection of photographs, which is unarranged at the present time.

There is little other political material, but some collections will be of interest to economists and local historians. The Maurice Plauche Collection (ca. 1940-1960s; 20 lin. ft.) consists of the receipts and correspondence of a Saint Tammany Parish businessman and police juror (county legislator). These include details of cattle and rice farming and the retail oil business.

Local historians may find useful the Velmarae Dunn Collection (1930-1970; 2 lin. ft.). Miss Dunn was a schoolteacher and prominent local historian who researched some of the early settlers of Hammond, including Peter Hammond, for whom the city was named. In addition, there is a collection of family genealogies of some of the early settlers of the Florida parishes and several local histories (1880-present; 8 lin. ft.).

The Clifford Webb Map Collection (one hundred items) consists of maps of parishes (except Tangipahoa Parish) and subdivisions of Southeast Louisiana. The collection is not yet catalogued or ready for use.

NEW ORLEANS SPECIAL COLLECTIONS AND ARCHIVES, LOYOLA UNIVERSITY

Street address:	6363 Saint Charles Avenue
	New Orleans, Louisiana 70118
Mailing address:	Same
Telephone:	(504) 865-3346
Days and hours:	Monday-Friday, 8:00 A.M. to 4:45 P.M.

The Loyola University Special Collections and Archives is housed in the university library. The purpose of the archives is to collect and provide access to records relating to the history of Louisiana and the Society of Jesus. The secondary purpose is to support historical studies pertinent to the curriculum of Loyola University. Material in English, Spanish, and French for the area encompassed by the Louisiana Purchase is available. There are no chronological limitations to the collection, but emphasis is on the colonial period and the territory of Louisiana. The Archives and Special Collections includes papers, documents, books, serials, microforms, and ephemera.

By far the most extensive holding is the Spanish Documents Collection (1762-1810; 234 reels). The Loyola University Special Collections and Archives is the depository of the only microfilm copy of Spanish colonial documents from Sección de Gobierno—Audiencia de Santo Domingo. This collection, known as the Santo Domingo Papers, consists of 35 mm. positive microfilm copies of official correspondence from Spanish officials in colonial Louisiana to respective officials in Spain.

Father Charles Edwards O'Neill, S. J., has written a history and overview of the Spanish document undertaking in "Catalogues and Microfilm: The Louisiana Project of Loyola University (New Orleans) in the Archivo General de Indias," *Homenaje a Don José María de la Peña Camara* (Madrid, 1969). Father O'Neill's *Catálogo de documentos del Archivo General de Indias* (New Orleans, 1968) serves as a description of the content of the Santo Domingo Papers.

The Spanish Documents Collection also includes the Papeles Procedentes de Cuba (Papers Brought from Cuba), a continuing microfilming project which when completed will consitute along with the Santo Domingo Papers more than half a million items. Descriptive materials for the Papeles de Cuba include *Anexo de la publicación en microfilm*: *Indice general,* which relates *legajo* and folio to microfilm reel, and *Papeles de Cuba, Secciones para microfilm.* The latter is the Loyola schedule for microfilming the Papeles de Cuba as housed in the Archivo General de Indias in Seville. Thus far the archives has only completed filming for *legajos* 488-560, a small part of the entire project.

Under agreement with the Spanish government, no paper or microfilm copies may be made of the collection at Loyola. Any individual may order directly from the Archivo General de Indias, Seville. Such orders must include the *legajo* and folio number. The only practical way to learn this without going abroad is to consult the Loyola Collection.

The Spanish Documents Collection also includes mircofilmed Cabildo Records from Spanish Louisiana (1769-1803; 4 reels). An index to the English Transcription of the Records and Deliberations of the Cabildo is available and calendared.

The French Documents Collection (1713-1762; 71 reels) includes microfilmed records relating to the governance of Louisiana under France. Included is section C13 a, b, c, of the Bibliothèque National in Paris, consisting of documents produced for the French royal government of Louisiana. An index entitled *France: Archives de Colonies de la Louisiane Subseries* relates microfilm reel to series number. The Loyola French Documents Collection partly duplicates the microfilm collection of French Colonial Documents at the University of Southwestern Louisiana.

The Special Collections and Archives also houses nineteenth- and twentieth-century collections. The Lafcadio Hearn Correspondence (1884-1896; 38 items) consists of letters from the New Orleans journalist, novelist, and chronicler of the lore of New Orleans and Old Louisiana to Page Baker, his former employer as editor of the *Times-Democrat*, after Hearn had moved to Japan.

The University Archives (1912-present; 200 lin. ft.) consists of administrative records documenting the growth of Loyola University and its day-to-day operations and is constantly expanding.

The H. L. Mencken Correspondence (1927-1955; 69 items) consists of correspondence between Mencken and Lou Wylie, a New Orleans poet and reporter for the *Times-Picayune*.

The Louis J. Twomey, S.J. Papers (1947-1969; 85 lin. ft.) documents Twomey's activities as a Catholic social worker in Louisiana and contains information on labor struggles in the Pelican State. The bulk of the material deals with Twomey's founding of the Institute for Human Relations and its work. This collection lacks any inventory or register at this time, but one is due to be prepared.

Cultural historians and students of creative writing will find useful the *New Orleans Review* Collection (1968-present; expanding). This collection represents all manuscripts, business records, and correspondence pertaining to the publishing of this literary and cultural publication from its inception to the present. The collection includes the original manuscripts of many stories and essays published in the review and elsewhere, among them the late John Kennedy Toole's highly acclaimed novel *A Confederacy of Dunces* (Baton Rouge, 1980).

The Moon Landrieu Collection (1960-1978; 80 lin. ft.) consists of correspondence, reports, speeches, and records relating to the government of New Orleans. Landrieu served as city councilman (1966-1969), mayor (1970-1978), and secretary of housing and urban development in the Carter administration. The collection is unprocessed, but a preliminary inventory is available.

The Loyola University Special Collections and Archives promise much to researchers interested in the social, political, and cultural development of colonial and territorial Louisiana, nineteenth- and twentieth-century literature, labor, and politics, and the history of Loyola University itself and the Society of Jesus in Louisiana. Duplicating services are available at five cents per page, subject to restrictions placed on individual collections.

ALLEN J. ELLENDER ARCHIVES, NICHOLLS STATE UNIVERSITY

Street address:	Ellender Memorial Library
	Nicholls State University
	Thibodaux, Louisiana 70301
Mailing address:	Same
Telephone:	(504) 446-8111, extension 406
Days and hours:	Monday-Friday, 8:00 A.M. to 4:00 P.M.; weekends by appointment.

The Ellender Memorial Library, named for the late U.S. Senator Allen J. Ellender, a native of Terrebone Parish, opened in September 1980. A three-story building of modular construction, it contains 122,000 assignable square feet of floor space. It is the third largest academic library in Louisiana, with a capacity of over 300,000 volumes for the main collection and a seating capacity of 1,500. The Ellender Archives division, located on the first floor, has its own reading room with a seating capacity for twenty patrons. The large stack area is equipped with motorized compact shelving. The division is a repository for historical manuscript and photographic materials for the parishes of south central Louisiana.

The Ellender Archives includes a substantial body of materials related to plantation and business enterprises in south central Louisiana. The holdings include the records of two sugar plantations and a plantation store. The Martin-Pugh Collection (1831-1925; 32 lin ft.) consists of correspondence, business records, and genealogical materials of the Robert C. Martin, Sr., family of Albemarle Sugar Plantation, Assumption Parish, Louisiana. The J. Wilson Lepine Collection (1896-1926; 130 lin. ft.) consists of correspondence, business records, plantation diaries, and sugar mill records of the Laurel Valley Sugar Plantation, Lafourche Parish, Louisiana. The Laurel Grove Plantation Store Collection (1856-1870, 1884, 1900-1953; 20 lin. ft.) is comprised of the business records of a typical sugar plantation store located in Lafourche Parish, Louisiana. Also included are the business records of a small-town store, the Henry Riviere Store Collection (1900-1921; 16 lin. ft.), located in Thibodaux, Louisiana.

The Jeanne Delas Gremillion Collection (1875-1935; 30 lin. ft.) consists of manuscript and sheet music collected by the Emmanuel Chol family of Thibodaux, Louisiana. It includes original compositions and arrangements of religious music by Emmanuel Chol, a music teacher who was the organist and choir director of Saint Joseph's Catholic Church. The collection also includes compositions and arrangements by his daughter, Clothilde Chol.

By far the largest and most important collection is the Allen J. Ellender Papers (1937-1972; ca. 900 lin. ft.). These consist of the correspondence and data files covering the span of Ellender's service in the U.S. Senate, from January 1937 until his death in July 1972. While they are being processed, the papers are kept in the boxes in which they were shipped from Washington. However, each box has been inventoried, and the files have been assembled according to categories approximating the order in which they were kept in the senator's office. These include campaign correspondence, speeches, patronage, foreign travels, and outgoing mail sent daily from the senator's office.

The most recent addition to the archives is the Heritage '76 Collection of the Lafourche Parish Bicentennial Commission (1974-1976; 20 lin. ft.). The collection is comprised of scrapbooks, photograph albums, slides, tapes, and films relating to the history, crafts, architectural, and cultural developments of Lafourche Parish, Louisiana.

MT. LEBANON-KEATCHIE ROOM, LOUISIANA COLLEGE

Street address:	1140 College Boulevard
	Pineville, Louisiana 71360
Mailing address:	Richard W. Norton Memorial Library
	College Station
	Pineville, Louisiana 71360
Telephone:	(318) 487-7201
Days and hours:	Monday-Thursday, 7:45 A.M. to 10:00 P.M.; Friday, 7:45 A.M. to 5:00 P.M.; Saturday, 10:00 A.M. to 5:30 P.M.; closed Sunday.

Louisiana College is a coeducational college in the geographical center of the state, founded in 1906. It is the only college financially supported by Louisiana Baptists today.

Louisiana College does not have a separate archives department, but archives, historical materials, and rare books are housed in the Mt. Lebanon-Keatchie Room. Norton Library does collect materials related to the history of Louisiana College and its predecessor institutions, Mt. Lebanon and Keatchie; the history of Louisiana Baptist churches and the Louisiana Baptist Convention; and the history of central Louisiana. Louisiana College is not the sole depository for Louisiana Baptist materials. Other collections are at the New Orleans Baptist Theological Seminary, in the Mae Lee Library in the Louisiana Baptist Convention building in Alexandria, at Louisiana State University in Baton Rouge, and at Northwestern State University in Natchitoches. The papers of Dr. Claybrook Cottingham, president of Louisiana College from 1910 until 1941, are housed at LSU.

The collection on Louisiana Baptists (1880-present; 10 lin. ft.) includes photographs, catalogs, diplomas, concert programs, and commemorative programs and booklets related to special events in Baptist churches in Louisiana through the years. There are also materials from Mt. Lebanon University (est. 1853, a men's college throughout most of its history) and Keatchie College (est. 1857, a college for women), both founded in the nineteenth century but closed soon after the turn of the century. Until about the time of their closing, they had no official connection with the Louisiana Baptist Convention, but they received support from Baptists and Baptist churches and were regarded as Baptist institutions. The room in the library that houses these materials is named for these predecessor institutions. A smaller room, the Acadia Room, houses annuals, photographs, and archival materials from Acadia Baptist Academy, established in 1917 and closed in 1973.

The B. B. McKinney Collection (1906-1952; 5 lin. ft.) relates to an alumnus of Louisiana College who spent most of his adult life in Texas and Tennessee and became probably the best-known music leader among Southern Baptists. These materials include photographs, letters, photostatic copies of original music scores by this prolific composer, and taped interviews with his widow and relatives. A larger collection of materials related to McKinney is located at Oklahoma Baptist University, Shawnee, Oklahoma.

The Robert Hunter MacGimsey Collection (1930-1979; 12 lin. ft.) includes scrapbooks, tapes, phonodiscs, and original scores of Robert Hunter MacGimsey, composer and performer. MacGimsey spent his musical career in New York City and retired to Phoenix, Arizona, but was born and reared in Pineville. Born on September 7, 1898, to one of Pineville's leading white families, he early developed an interest in black music, and many of his compositions are in the style of the Negro spiritual. The son of a lawyer father and an organist mother, he was educated in both the law and music. After practicing law for a time at Lake Providence, Louisiana, he was "discovered" by the famous recording artist, Gene Austin, who persuaded MacGimsey to accompany him to New York. There he gained celebrity status as a whistler, earning a hundred dollars a minute in the depth of the Depression as a network whistler. A prolific composer, he perhaps has received his widest acclaim as the creator of "Shadrack" and "Sweet Little Jesus Boy." When he died in Phoenix in 1979, his body was returned to his native state to be buried in Shreveport. Just prior to his death, he sent his musical holdings home to Pineville to be housed in Norton Library.

Norton Memorial Library provides self-operated copy machines.

MCNEESE STATE UNIVERSITY ARCHIVES

Street address:	Lether E. Frazar Library
	Ryan Street
	McNeese State University
	Lake Charles, Louisiana 70609
Mailing address:	Same
Telephone:	(318) 477-2520, extension 270
Days and hours:	Monday-Thursday, 8:00 A.M. to 10:00 P.M.; Friday, 8:00 A.M. to 4:00 P.M.; Saturday, 8:00 A.M. to noon; Sunday, noon to 10:00 P.M.

McNeese State University has a rudimentary archival center specializing in materials dealing with southwestern Louisiana. The small collection is housed along with rare books in Frazar Library. Scholars interested in specific collections should contact Archivist Kathy Gardner.

NORTHWESTERN STATE UNIVERSITY ARCHIVES

Street address:	Eugene P. Watson Library
	College Avenue
	Northwestern State University
	Natchitoches, Louisiana 71457
Mailing address:	Same
Telephone:	(318) 357-4586
Days and hours:	Monday-Friday, 8:00 A.M. to 5:00 P.M.

The archives date from 1956, when Eugene P. Watson created the North Louisiana History Collection. The archives have been greatly expanded in recent decades. It is an important depository for Louisiana history and education containing materials on the following eras: Louisiana colonial history and the Mississippi valley, 1699-1812; the Spanish borderlands to 1812; Louisiana folklore; the educational history of the state; science; Indians of Louisiana; commerce and business; and numerous other topics dealing with every period in the state's history. The archive operates in conjunction with the Southern Studies Institute and has, in recent years, undertaken programs to increase its holdings greatly. For additional information, contact John Milton Price, Director of the Southern Studies Institute, Northwestern State University.

Appendix I
CHRONOLOGY OF LOUISIANA HISTORY

1513	Ponce de Leon, first Spaniard to explore mainland of North America.
1527	Panfilo de Narvaez explores Gulf Coast.
1537	Cabeza de Vaca, survivor of Narvaez expedition, arrives in Mexico.
1539-1543	Hernando de Soto explores Southeast; first Spaniard to sight Mississippi River.
1534	Jacques Cartier explores Northwestern Coast of North America; two subsequent voyages (1535-1536; 1541-1542).
1608	Samuel de Champlain founds Quebec. First permanent French colony in North America.
1673-1674	Father Jacques Marquette and Louis Jolliet explore Mississippi River to mouth of Arkansas River. Prove Mississippi empties into Gulf of Mexico.
1682	René Robert Cavalier, Sieur de la Salle explores Mississippi River. Reaches mouth (April 9), claims for France, and names "Louisiana" for Louis XIV.
1699	Pierre Le Moyne, Sieur de Iberville finds mouth of Mississippi from south (March 2). Founds Fort Maurepas at Biloxi, first

	French settlement on Gulf Coast. Later founds Fort de la Boulaye in present-day Plaquemines Parish, La. Le Sieur de Sauvole becomes governor.
1701	Jean Baptiste Le Moyne, Sieur de Bienville, Iberville's younger brother, becomes governor.
1702	Iberville founds Mobile.
1706	Death of Iberville.
1712	Louisiana becomes propriety colony of Antoine Crozat. Superior Council established by royal decree.
1713	Antoine de la Mothe Cadillac replaces Bienville as governor. Louis Juchereau de Saint Denis founds Natchitoches, first permanent town in present state of Louisiana.
1717	Jean Michiele, Seigneur de Lepinay appointed governor. Crozat renounces charter. Company of the West (Mississippi Company), headed by John Law, becomes proprietor of Louisiana.
1718	Bienville becomes governor again. Founds city of New Orleans.
1719	First cargo of African slaves reaches Louisiana.
1720	Collapse of Mississippi Bubble. Law flees France.
1724	Code Noir (Black Code) defines status of blacks in Louisiana. Bienville recalled. Pierre Dugue, Sieur de Boisbriant appointed governor ad interim.
1726	Etienne Périer becomes governor.
1727	"Casket Girls" arrive to provide wives for settlers. Ursuline nuns arrive in Louisiana.
1729	Settlers at Fort Rosalie (Natchez) massacred by Natchez Indians.
1731	Colony returned to the French Crown.
1736-1740	Chickasaw War.
1737	Jean Louis established Charity Hospital of New Orleans.
1743	Pierre François de Rigaud, marquis de Vaudreuil becomes governor.
1753	Louis Billouart, chevalier de Kerlérec becomes governor.
1755	Acadians forcibly expelled from Nova Scotia by British troops.
1754-1763	French and Indian (Seven Years') War. French defeated by British, lose colonies. France cedes Louisiana east of Mississippi to England.

Chronology of Louisiana History

1762	Secret Treaty of Fountainbleu cedes Isle of Orleans and Louisiana west of Mississippi to Spain.
1763	Treaty of Paris ends French and Indian War. Spain cedes Florida to England in exchange for Cuba. Jean Jacques D'Abbadie becomes director-general of Louisiana.
1764	Acadians begin arriving in Louisiana.
1765	After death of D'Abbadie Captain Charles Philippe Aubry, senior military officer, heads government. First large group of Acadians reaches Louisiana.
1766	Don Antonio de Ulloa arrives to take possession of Louisiana for Spain.
1768	Rebellion by French colonists against Spanish rule.
1769	General Don Alexandro O'Reilly replaces Ulloa, crushes revolt, executes leaders. Abolishes Superior Council. Establishes Cabildo in its place as legislative and judicial body. Don Luis de Unzaga installed as governor.
1775	American Revolution begins.
1776	Don Bernardo de Gálvez becomes military commander of Louisiana.
1777	Gálvez becomes governor.
1779	Spain declares war on England as ally of French and American colonies. Gálvez captures Baton Rouge, Manchac, Natchez.
1780	Gálvez captures Mobile.
1781	Gálvez captures Pensacola.
1783	Treaty of Versailles ends war of American Revolution. Spain receives East and West Florida from England.
1785	Don Esteban Rodriguez Miró becomes governor. Sixteen hundred Acadians migrate from France to Louisiana.
1788	Great Fire of New Orleans.
1791	Francois Louis Hector, Baron de Carondelet becomes governor.
1792	Second Great Fire of New Orleans.
1795	Etienne de Boré perfects process for granulating sugar. Pinckney's Treaty sets boundary of United States at thirty-first parallel and gives United States "Right of Deposit" at New Orleans.
1797	Manuel Gayoso de Lemos becomes governor.

Appendix I

1799	Francisco Bouligny becomes governor. Marquis de Casa Calvo becomes acting governor.
1800	Secret Treaty of San Ildefonso returns Louisiana to France.
1801	Don Juan Manuel de Salcedo becomes governor until French assume control.
1803	Louisiana Purchase (April). France takes posession from Spain (November). United States takes possession from France (December). William C. C. Claiborne appointed territorial governor.
1804	Louisiana Purchase divided at thirty-third parallel into Territory of Louisina (above) and Territory of Orleans (below).
1810	Revolt by West Florida settlers against Spain. Annexed by United States.
1812	Louisiana becomes a state (April 30). Constitution adopted. Claiborne elected governor.
1814	Captain Henry Miller Shreve travels down Mississippi in *Enterprise*. Treaty of Ghent ends War of 1812 (December 24).
1815	Unaware of the war's end, Andrew Jackson defeats British at Battle of New Orleans (January 8).
1816	Jacques Philippe Villeré elected governor.
1820	Thomas Bolling Robertson elected governor.
1823	First theater opened in New Orleans.
1824	Robertson resigns as governor to become federal district judge. Henry Schuyler Thibodeaux finishes Robertson's term. Henry S. Johnson elected governor.
1825	Civil Law Code produced by Edward Livingston adopted.
1828	Pierre Derbigny elected governor.
1829	Derbigny dies. Armand Beauvais becomes governor. Jacques Dupré claims governorship.
1830	André B. Roman elected governor. First Whig governor. State capital moved from New Orleans to Donaldsonville. Capital returned to New Orleans.
1835	Edward Douglas White elected governor.
1837	Panic of 1837.
1839	André B. Roman becomes governor. Last Whig governor.

1840	Red River above Alexandria opened to navigation by Captain Henry Miller Shreve.
1842	Alexandre Mouton becomes first Democrat elected governor.
1845	New constitution adopted.
1846	Isaac Johnson elected governor.
1848	Zachary Taylor (a Louisianian) elected president.
1850	Joseph Marshall Walker elected governor.
1852	New constitution adopted.
1853	Paul O. Hébert elected governor.
1856	Robert C. Wickliffe becomes governor.
1860	Thomas Overton Moore becomes governor. Abraham Lincoln elected President.
1861	Louisiana secedes from union (January 26). Secession convention ratifies Confederate Constitution (March 21).
1862	New Orleans taken by federal troops.
1863	Port Hudson taken.
1864	Red River Campaign. Henry Watkins Allen becomes governor of Confederate Louisiana. Michael Hahn becomes governor of Union Louisiana. New Constitution adopted.
1865	Assassination of President Abraham Lincoln. Hahn resigns as governor to become U.S. Senator. J. Madison Wells succeeds Hahn as governor; elected in special election.
1866	Race riot in New Orleans. Wells removed as governor by General Philip Sheridan, military commander in Louisiana.
1867	Benjamin Franklin Flanders appointed governor by General Sheridan.
1868	Joshua Baker appointed governor. New constitution adopted. Henry Clay Warmoth elected governor.
1868	Louisiana readmitted to Union. Louisiana Lottery chartered.
1871	Lieutenant Governor Oscar J. Dunn dies. Pinckney Benton Stewart Pinchback elected president protempore of State Senate, making him ex-officio lieutenant governor.

Appendix I

1872	Impeachment charges voted against Warmoth; suspended as governor. Pinchback becomes acting governor; only black governor in Louisiana's history. Elections held for governor and legislature. Rival governors inaugurated: William Pitt Kellogg (R), and John McEnery (D). President Grant recognizes Kellogg as governor.
1873	Depression of 1873.
1874	White League battles Metropolitan Police in New Orleans. Federal troops restore order.
1876	Both Francis T. Nicholls (D) and Stephan B. Packard (R) claim election as governor.
1877	Compromise of 1877. Rutherford B. Hayes becomes president. Nicholls recognized as governor. Federal troops withdrawn. End of Reconstruction in Louisiana.
1879	New constitution adopted. Louisiana Lottery Company given monopoly.
1880	Louis Alfred Wiltz becomes governor.
1881	Wiltz dies; Samuel Douglas McEnery becomes governor.
1884	McEnery re-elected. World Industrial and Cotton Exposition held in New Orleans.
1886	Louisiana Farmers' Union founded.
1887	Louisiana Farmers' Union merges with Texas Farmers' Alliance to form Farmers' Alliance.
1888	Francis T. Nicholls elected governor.
1891	Eleven Italians lynched in New Orleans for allegedly murdering Police Chief David Hennessy.
1892	Populist party nominates Robert L. Tannenhill for governor. Only true Populist to run for governor of Louisiana. Murphy J. Foster elected governor. Louisiana Lottery outlawed.
1896	Foster re-elected governor. Choctaw Club of Louisiana founded in New Orleans.
1898	New constitution adopted. Disfranchises most blacks.
1900	William Wright Heard elected governor.
1904	Newton Crain Blanchard elected governor.
1908	Direct primary adopted. Blacks excluded from voting in Democratic primary. Jared Young Sanders elected governor.

Chronology of Louisiana History

1911	Democratic Good Government League formed under leadership of John M. Parker.
1912	Luther E. Hall elected governor.
1916	Ruffin G. Pleasant elected governor.
1920	John M. Parker elected governor.
1921	New constitution adopted.
1922	Ku Klux Klan lynches two men at Mer Rouge.
1924	Henry L. Fuqua elected governor.
1926	Death of Fuqua. Oramel Hinkley Simpson becomes governor.
1927	Great Mississippi River Flood.
1928	Huey Pierce Long elected governor.
1929	State House of Representatives votes to impeach Long. Senate clears Long of one charge, adjourns without voting on the others.
1930	Long elected U.S. Senator.
1931	Long resigns governorship to take seat in Senate. Alvin Olin King finishes Long's term.
1932	Oscar K. Allen elected governor.
1934	Long founds Share-Our-Wealth Society.
1935	Long assassinated.
1936	Governor Allen dies in office. James A. Noe finishes term. Richard Webster Leche elected governor.
1939	Louisiana Scandals break. Governor Leche resigns. Earl Kemp Long completes term.
1940	Leche and Louisiana State University President James Monroe Smith sentenced to prison for role in Scandals. Sam Houston Jones elected governor. Civil Service Commission, State Crime Commission created.
1943	Jones puts down challenge to his authority in Plaquemines Parish by sending State Guard; incident dubbed "The Little War."
1944	James Houston ("Jimmie") Davis elected governor.
1948	Earl Kemp Long elected governor. Governor Long calls, then cancels constitutional convention.
1952	Judge Robert Floyd Kennon elected governor.
1956	Earl Kemp Long elected governor.

1958	Louisiana State University football team wins national championship.
1959	Governor Long suffers nervous breakdown.
1960	Jimmie Davis elected governor. New Orleans public school desegregation begins.
1964	John J. McKeithen elected governor. Code of Ethics for State Officials adopted.
1966	Constitutional amendment adopted permitting governor to serve two consecutive terms. Bond issue authorizes construction of New Orleans "Superdome."
1967	New Orleans Saints football team established.
1968	Governor McKeithen re-elected.
1970	All state colleges except Grambling designated universities.
1972	Edwin W. Edwards elected governor.
1974	New constitution adopted.
1976	Governor Edwards re-elected. Open Primary Law adopted.
1980	Dave Treen elected governor. First Republican governor since Reconstruction.

Appendix II

SELECTED LIST OF ORGANIZATIONS WITH SPECIAL INTERESTS IN LOUISIANA HISTORY

Alexandria Historical and Genealogical Library
505 Washington Street
Alexandria, La. 71301

American Association for State and Local History
1315 8th Avenue South
Nashville, Tenn. 37203

Anglo-American Art Museum
Louisiana State University
Baton Rouge, La. 70803

Art Center for Southwestern Louisiana
P.O. Drawer 4-4290, USL
Lafayette, La. 70504

Ascension Heritage Association
Mrs. R. N. Sims, President
P.O. Box 7
Donaldsonville, La. 70346

Association for the Preservation of Historic Natchitoches
Mrs. Lucille T. Carnahan
Cloutierville, La. 71416

Baton Rouge Area Convention and Visitors Bureau
P.O Box 3202
Baton Rouge, La. 70821

Baton Rouge Historical and Genealogical Society
10236 S. Riveroaks Avenue
Baton Rouge, La. 70815

Bayou Folk Museum
Mrs. Mildred McCoy
Cloutierville, La. 71416

Brimstone Historical Society
Dr. Joe Bruce, President
P.O. Box 242
Sulphur, La. 70663

Calcasieu Historical Preservation
Society
Box 5621, Drew Station
Lake Charles, La. 70606

Camp Moore Confederate Museum
Mrs. Irene Morris, Curator
Tangipahoa, La. 70465

Civil War Roundtable of Baton Rouge
Mr. John P. King
735 Cora Drive
Baton Rouge, La. 70806

Colonial Dames of America
Mrs. Gordon Riley
3009 Nelson
Alexandria, La. 71301

DeSoto Parish Historical Society
Bridges Plaza
Mansfield, La. 71052

Caroline Dormon Nature Preserve, Inc.
P.O. Box 226
Natchitoches, La. 71457

East Carroll Historical Society
P.O. Box 93
Lake Providence, La. 71254

East Feliciana Historical Preservation
Society, Inc.
c/o Mrs. William Bennet
Bennet-Brame House
Clinton, La. 70722

East Feliciana Pilgrimage and Garden
Club
c/o Mrs. Bob R. Jones
Blairstown Plantation
Route 1, Box 334
Clinton, La. 70722

Evangeline Genealogical and Historical
Society
P.O. Box 664
Ville Platte, La. 70586

Firefighters Historical Association
Mr. J. B. Gwin
3108 45th Street
Metairie, La. 70001

Foundation for Historical Louisiana, Inc.
900 North Boulevard
Baton Rouge, La. 70802

Genealogy Research Society of New
Orleans
Mrs. Alice Daly Forsyth
Genesis (New Orleans) Editor
P.O. Box 51791
New Orleans, La. 70150

Historical Association of Central
Louisiana
P.O. Box 843
Alexandria, La. 71301

Historical Preservation of Shreveport,
Inc.
P.O. Box 857
Shreveport, La. 71162

The Historic New Orleans Collection
533 Royal Street
New Orleans, La. 70130

Iberia Parish Cultural Resources
Association
Mrs. Eleanor L. Holleman,
Corresponding Secretary
Route 1, Box 46
New Iberia, La. 70560

Jefferson Parish Historical Commission
3330 N. Causeway Boulevard
Metairie, La. 70002

Jennings Genealogicial Society
Mrs. William Tuthill, Secretary-Treasurer
1610 State Street
Jennings, La. 70546

Kent Plantation House, Inc.
Mrs. James C. Harris, President
P.O. Box 2003
Alexandria, La. 71301

La Commission des Avoyelles
P.O. Box 28
Hamburg, La. 71339

Lafayette Historic Preservation Society
Mr. Bill James, President
P.O. Box 2282
Lafayette, La. 70501

Lafourche Heritage Society, Inc.
P.O. Box 913
Thibodaux, La. 70301

Selected List of Organizations

LaSalle Art and Historical Association
Mrs. Fred Windham, Corresponding Secretary
Rt. 1, Box 181
Trout, La. 71371

Le Comite des Archives
Mr. Damon Veache
P.O. Box 44370
Baton Rouge, La. 70804

Edward Livingston Historical Association, Inc.
P.O. Box 44492, Capitol Station
Baton Rouge, La. 70804

Louisiana Children of the Confederacy
Beau Bowman, President
9366 Jessica Drive
Shreveport, La. 71106

Louisiana Genealogical and Historical Society
P.O. Box 3454
Baton Rouge, La. 70821

Louisiana Historical Association
Box 40831
The University of Southwestern Louisiana
Lafayette, La. 70504

Louisiana Historical and Confederate Museum
929 Camp Street
New Orleans, La. 70130

The Louisiana Historical Society
509 Cotton Exchange Building
231 Carondelet Street
New Orleans, La. 70130

Louisiana Landmarks Society
St. Mary Chapter
Mrs. H. H. Dinkins
517 Main Street
Franklin, La. 70538

Louisiana Preservation Alliance
P.O. Box 1587
Baton Rouge, La. 70801

Louisiana State Museum
Dr. Robert R. McDonald, Director
P.O. Box 2458
New Orleans, La. 70116

Mansfield Battle Park
Wilber H. Lewis
P.O. Box 447
Mansfield, La. 71052

Morehouse Historical Society
309 Cox
Bastrop, La. 71220

Mount Lebanon Historical Society
Rt. 2, Mount Lebanon Road
Gibsland, La. 71028

Natural History Museum and Planetarium
Mrs. Beverly Latimer, Director
637 Girard Park Drive.
Lafayette, La. 70503

North Louisiana Historical Association
Dr. Philip Cook, President
Department of History
Louisiana Tech University
Ruston, La. 71270

Preservation Press of New Orleans
The Preservation Resource Center of New Orleans, Inc.
823 Perdido St., Suite 200
New Orleans, La. 70112

River Road Historical Society
P.O. Box 5
Destrehan, La. 70047

Sons of Confederate Veterans, Louisiana Division
c/o J. Patrick Terrell, Commander
3921 Audrey Drive
Baton Rouge, La. 70809

Southeast Louisiana Historical Association
Dr. Joy Jackson
Department of History
Southeastern Louisiana University
Hammond, La. 70401

Southwest Louisiana Genealogical Society
Mrs. J. G. Miltner, President
P.O. Box 5652
Lake Charles, La 70606

Southwest Louisiana Historical Association
Lake Charles *American Press*
Lake Charles, La. 70601

St. Helena Historical Association
P.O. Box 4
Greensburg, La. 70441

St. Tammany Historical Society
Dr. C. Howard Nichols
Southeastern Louisiana University
Hammond, La. 70401

Terrebonne Historical and Cultural Society
P.O. Box 2095
Houma, La. 70360

United Daughters of the Confederacy
Kate Beard Chapter No. 397
P.O. Box 113
Mansfield, La. 71052

Welsh Genealogical and Historical Society
Mrs. Mary Sue Lyon, President
201 Pine
Welsh, La. 70591

West Baton Rouge Historical Association
Box 502
Port Allen, La. 70767

West Feliciana Historical Society
P.O. Box 338
St. Francisville, La. 70775

INDEX

Abbadie, Jean-Jacques-Blaise d', 12
Abbot, John Stevens, 5
Abernethy, Thomas P., 20, 29
Acadia Baptist Academy, 254
Acadian Bicentennial Celebration, 172
Acadian Creole and Folklore Project, 168, 172
Acadians, 13-14; archival material, 172, 225
Ackel Family Papers, 186
Acosta Rodriguez, Antonio, 23, 24
Adam, John Moreau, 62
Adams, St. Clair, Papers, 193
Adams, William H., 33
Adams Family Papers, 36
Adeline Sugar Refining Company Papers, 191
Ader, Emil Bertrand, 63
Affleck, Thomas, Papers, 157
Agriculture, 11; antebellum, 28, 37; archival materials, 170, 177, 186-87, 232, 237, 243
Aiken, Earl Howard, 52-53
Aime, Valcour, Diaries, 177
Aiton, Arthur S., 12
Alcée Fortier High School Scrapbooks, 218
Alexander, Charles C., 81
Allain, Mathé, 9, 10, 13, 72, 97
Allandale Plantation Ledgers, 232
Allen, Henry W., 150
Allen, Henry Watkins, Monument Association Papers, 190
Allen, L. Calhoun, Papers and Scrapbooks, 232
Allen, Nathaniel S., Papers, 235, 237
Allen, O. K., 227
Allen, Richard B., 81, 105, 106, 112
Alliance Franco-Louisianaise de l'Enseignement du Francais Papers, 196
Allison, Stephen H., Papers, 191
Almonester y Pontalba, Barnoness Michaela de, 97
Alter, Charles, Papers, 187
Alvord, Clarence W., 7, 20
Amato, Pasquale, 164
American Association of University Women, 100, 161, 170
American Colonization Society, 177
American Forum of Shreveport, 239
American Home Missionary Society, 98
American Institute of Architects, 93
American Missionary Association, 206, 212; Archives, 206, 207
American Protective League Papers, 193
American Revolution, 22
Amistad Research Center, 205-13
Ampère, J. J., 30
Ancelet, Barry, 168
Anderson, John Q., 42
Andreassen, John C., 38, 154
Andreu Ocariz, Juan José, 21, 24
Andrieu, Jules, Letterbook, 191

Index

Antebellum period, 27-40; archival materials, 177, 186-89, 203, 243, 248; blacks in, 73-76; New Orleans during, 85-87
Arcadia Electric Light Plant, 245
Arcadia Male and Female College, 245
Architecture, 93, 174; archival materials, 195, 200, 219, 222, 226-27, 237
Archive de Colonies, 169
Archive de la Marine, 169
Archive de Ministère de la France d'Outre-Mer, 169
Archives Coloniales, 186
Archives de la Guerre, 169
Archives du Ministère des Affaires Etrangères, 169
Archives Nationales de France, 155
Archives of Spanish Governors of West Florida, 176
Archivo de la Contaduria del Consejo de Indias de Madrid, 180
Archivo del Ministerio de Asuntos Exteriores (AMAE), 133
Archivo del Servicio Histórico Militar, 132
Archivo General de Indias (AGI), 129, 133-36, 142, 155, 156, 169, 180, 186, 251
Archivo General de la Nacion, 136
Archivo General de Simancas (AGS), 129-30, 136, 155, 169, 180
Archivo General Militar, 132-133
Archivo Historico Nacional (AHN), 21, 129-31, 135, 136, 169
Arena, C. Richard, 21
Arkansas-Louisiana Gas Company Records, 234-35, 241
Armas Medina, Fernando de, 22
Armas Vicente, José A., 24
Armstrong, Lillian, 99
Armstrong, Louis, 175
Arthur, Stanley Clisby, 135
Arts et Metier BMAA, 224
Aseff, Emmett, 35
Associated Negro Press, 210
Association of Citizens' Councils of Louisiana, 233, 241
Association of the Army of Northern Virginia Papers, 190
Aswell, James G., Papers, 162
Aswell, James, Jr., Papers, 164
Athenée Louisianaise, 196; Collection, 225
Attakapas Day Book, 169
Attorney General records, 152

Aubry, Charles Philippe, 14
Aucoin, Sidney J., 34
Audiencia de Santo Domingo, 134
Audubon, John James, 175; Papers, 195
Audubon Park Commission Collection, 226
Austerman, Wayne R., 79
Austin, Gene, 255
Autopsy Reports, 221
Avoyelles Indians, 142
Avoyelles Parish records, 150, 151, 181

Bagwell, Harrison G., Papers, 162
Baillardel, A., 10
Baker, Page, 251
Baker, Riley E., 55, 80
Baker, Vaughn, 30
Baldwin, John T., 66
Ballinger, Captain John, Papers, 189
Ballowe, Hewett L., Papers, 195
Bancroft Library (Berkeley), 127, 135-36
Banking. *See* Economic history
Bank of New Orleans records, 156
Bank of the United States-Natchez Office records, 156
Banks, General Nathaniel, P., 41, 42, 88,
Bannon, John Francis, 19, 20
Baptist church records, 254-55
Barbé-Marbois, François, 3, 15
Barker, Danny, 81, 90
Barksdale, Rose Colvin, 246
Barksdale Air Force Base, 235
Barnidge, James L., 69
Barnwell, Colonel John, 145
Barret, Hollingsworth B., Papers, 234
Barrow, Bennet H., 74
Barrow, David, 191
Barrow, Robert H., Photography Collection, 158
Barrow, Robert Ruffin, Papers, 186
Barrow Family Archives, 185, 191
Barthelemy, Sidney J., Papers, 225
Bartholomew Methodist Episcopal Church Journal, 248
Bartley, Numan V., 82
Baruc, B., 178
Bass, Charles Cassedy, Papers, 194
Bass, Jack, 66
Bassett, John S., 32
Basso, Hamilton, 60, 63
Bastrop, Baron de, 248

Baton Rouge Business and Professional Women's Club records, 100, 161
Battle of New Orleans, 32-33; archival materials, 177, 189, 202-3
Baudier, Roger, 39, 194
Bautista Muñoz, Juan, 133
Bayano River Lumber Company, 235
Baynes-Jones, Stanhope, Papers, 194
Bayou Teche Railroad and Light Company Minutebook, 192
Beale, Howard K., 48
Beals, Carlton, 60
Beard, Charles, Papers, 236
Beauregard, Pierre Gustave Toutant, 42-43, 178, 189; Papers, 178, 196
Bechel, Thomas, 81
Bechet, Sidney, 175
Becnel, Thomas, 53, 107
Bedsole, Vergil L., 136, 154
Beebe Papers, 177
Beecher Memorial Church Papers, 211, 212
Beer, William, 13, 184
Beerman, Eric, 21-23, 132
Behan, Mrs. William J., 190
Behrman, Martin, 54-55, 90-91, 174; Letters, 220
Beiderbecke, Bix, 175
Bellin, Jacques Nicolas, 145, 147
Belting, Natalie Marie, 7
Bemis, Samuel Flagg, 20
Benjamin, Judah P., 34, 163, 178; Papers, 187
Bennett College, 209
Benson and Riehl Papers, 195
Bentley, Emerson, Diary, 236
Bentley, George R., 47
Bergeron, Arthur W., Jr., 149-52
Berlin, Ira, 75, 76
Bermudez Plata, Cristobal, 134
Bernard, A. C., 172
Bernard, Francisco, 175
Bernard, John Frédéric, 184
Bernstein, Barton J., 80
Berry, Mary F., 77
Bestoff, Frank M., Collection, 187
Bethell, Tom, 81
Bexar Archives, 136
Bezour-France Amérique Collection, 225
Bibb, Henry, 73
Biblioteca Nacional, 131-32
Bibliothèque Nationale, 169, 251

Biddle, Nicholas, 36
Bienville, Jean-Baptiste Le Moyne, sieur de, 7, 143, 144
Bienville Parish Incorporating Act, 245
Bilbo, Theodore G., 162
Bistineau Baptist Church, 246
Bjork, David, 19
Black Enterprises of New Orleans, 208
Black history, 24, 71-83; archival materials, 158-59, 205-13, 224-25; Civil War, 43; free blacks, 10; Gilded Age, 52-53; New Orleans, 87-92; Progressive Era, 55-56; Reconstruction, 47-49. *See also* Slavery
Blackwell, A. Gordon, Sermons, 194
Blake, Christopher, Papers, 195
Blanchard, Newton Crain, Scrapbooks, 233
Blassingame, John W., 43, 47, 52, 74, 76, 77, 79, 83, 88
Blumenthal, Walter Hart, 8, 97
Board of Appraisers records, 152
Board of Audit and Exchange records, 152
Board of Commissioners for the Port of New Orleans minutes, 152
Board of Health records, 152
Board of Pension Commissioners minutes, 152
Boeta, José Rudolfo, 22
Bogan, Harvey, 109
Bogue, Allan G., 120
Bolden, Buddy, 81
Bolinger, S. H., Lumber Company Records, 235
Bolton, Herbert Eugene, 6, 19, 20, 127
Bonaventure Plantation Ledger, 177
Bonds of Free Persons of Color in the First Municipality, 188
Booher-Martin Family Papers, 239
Boone, William C., Correspondence, 245
Booth, George W., Theatre Collection, 219
Borja Medina, Francisco de, 22
Bossier City Council Minutes and Records, 233
Bossier Parish Police Jury Minutes, 233
Boston Club Papers, 197
Boudreux, C. Dreaux, Papers, 158
Bouligny, Francisco, 131, 186
Bourbons, 51, 62, 89
Bowers, Claude G., 46, 47

272 Index

Bowles (adventurer), 131
Boyd, David French, Papers, 165
Boyd, Thomas Duckett, Papers, 165
Bozeman, Harley B., Papers, 245
Brackenridge, Henry M., 29
Bradford, Roark, Papers, 195
Bragg, Jefferson Davis, 42
Brassaux, Carl A., 3-15, 72
Breaux, Gustave, Diary, 193
Breese, Sydney, 7
Breithaupt, Ernest Adalbert Treuman, Family Papers, 243, 244
Brent, George W., 190
Brent, John L., Papers, 190
Brent Collection, 178
Briant family, 178
Bricklayers', Masons', and Marble Masons' International Union No. 1 of Louisiana, 226
Brigham, Jerry, 68
Briley, Richard, III, 64
Brill, Abraham, Papers, 237
Bringier Papers, 185
Brinkley, Alan, 63
British, archival material on, 169
Brizzard Collection, 187
Brooks, Charles P., 32
Brooks, Overton, Papers, 162
Brooks, Philip C., 20
Brou Plantation Papers, 186
Broutin, Ignace, 148
Brown, Algie, Papers, 234, 240
Brown, Wilbur S., 32
Brownlee, Frederick Leslie, Papers, 211, 212
Bruns, Henry Dickson, Scrapbook, 218
Bubenzer-Cheatham, Christian, Bible Records, 246
Buchanan, James, Papers, 36
Buerkle, Jack V., 81, 90
Bullard, Henry A., 35
Bumstead, Gladys, 40
Bunch Club, 210
Burke, Glendy, 187
Burke, Walter J., Papers, 169
Burke, William R., Papers, 195
Burns, Frances P., 79
Burr, Aaron, 29, 176
Burrus, Ernest J., 137
Burson, Caroline M., 22
Burt Family Genealogy, 245-46
Burton, Hayward, Papers, 195

Burton, Waldo, Home Papers, 193
Burton, Walthall, Papers, 186
Bush, Robert D., 199-204
Butler, General Benjamin F., 41, 88, 188
Butler, E. G. W., Papers, 32
Butler, Pierce, 34; Papers, 196
Butler, Willis B., Papers, 237-38
Butler Family Papers, 203
Byrd, Daniel Ellis, Papers, 206-7

Cabildo Records, 251
Cable, George Washington, 30, 46; Papers, 164, 195
Cable, James Broadman, Papers, 195
Cadastral Map Collection, 235, 241
Caddo-Bossier Port Commission Records, 233
Caldo Indians, 241
Caddo Levee Board Minute Books, 231, 233
Caddo Parish Coroner's Office, 237
Caddo Parish Police Jury Minute Books, 233
Caddo Parish School Board Records and Scrapbooks, 236, 239
Cadillac, Lamothe, 8
Caffrey, Donelson, 169; Papers, 162
Caffrey, Jerrerson, Papers, 170
Caldwell, Norman W., 10, 11
Caldwell, Stephen A., 38
Calhoun, Robert Dabney, 35
Cameron, John, 119
Campbell, Clara Lopez, 52
Campbell, David L., Papers, 227
Campbell, Edna F., 11
Campbell, Marie, Papers, 171
Campbell, Randolph, 117-18
Camp Nicholas Soldiers Home Papers, 193
Canal Bank records, 191
Canby, E. R. S., 178
Canonge, L. Placide, 159
Capers, Gerald W., 47, 88
Carey, Cora E., Papers, 161
Carey, Walter C. Collection, 219
Carleton, Mark T., 55, 68, 69, 81
Carmel Archives, 99
Carnival, 90; Collection, 217
Carondelet (Spanish governor), 128, 155, 176
Carpetbaggers, 45

Carriere, Marius M., 33-34, 116
Carrigan, Jo Ann, 22, 39, 87
Carriger, Paul L., Papers, 236
Carroll, General William, 189
Carroll, Hoy and Company Papers, 187
Carrollton records, 188
Carter, Betty W., 39
Carter, Clarence E., 28
Carter, Doris Dorcas, 81-82
Carter, Hodding, 39, 67, 79
Carter, Samuel, 32
Cartier, Jacques, 142
Cartography, 139-48, 179, 218-19, 231, 240, 250
Cartwright, Samuel A., Papers, 164
Caruso, John Anthony, 5
Carver, Ada Jack, Papers, 99
Casa Calvo (Spanish governor), 128, 155
Casey, Joseph, 178
Caskey, Willie M., 46
Cassidy, Vincent H., 13, 42
Castillo, Antonio, 21
Castle, Joseph D., 139-48
Catholic church records, 170
Catholic Committee of the South Records, 212
Catholic Council of Human Relations Papers, 207
Catholic University of America, 211
Caughey, John W., 19, 22, 127
Caulfield, Ruby B., 39
Cenas Family Papers, 179
Census Bureau, U.S., 31
Census of New Orleans (1805), 188
Centenary College, 99, 230; Cline Room, 240-42; Records, 242; Women's Club Papers, 242
Central Congregational Church, 194, 212
Chaffraix, D. A., Papers, 177
Chaillé, Stanford Emerson, Papers, 194
Chaise, Alexandrine de la, 155
Chalaron, Joseph A., Papers, 190
Chalmers, David M., 81
Chamberlain, Grace, Papers, 179
Chamber of Commerce of the New Orleans Area Collection, 227
Chambers, Henry Edward, 4, 5
Champomier and Giraud Papers, 177
Chandler, David L., 89
Chandler, Robert G., Collection, 241
Charbonnet, Louis, III, Papers, 225
Charest-DeGournay-Duborg Papers, 185

Charity Hospital Papers, 176
Charity Organization Society Papers, 193
Charles, Robert, 53, 81
Charles III, King, 19
Charters, Samuel B., 81
Chase, John, Papers, 195
Chennault, William C., 86
Chevrillon, André, 5
Chiaves, Hieronymo, 140, 142
Chicago, University of, 213
Chinese immigrants, 160
Choctaw Club, 89, 91
Chol, Clothilde, 253
Chol, Emmanuel, 253
Christ Church records, 188, 194
Christian, Bickham, Collection, 239
Christian, John T., 39
Christian, Marcus, 76
Christian, Marcus Bruce, Collection, 224
Christian Women's Exchange Records, 100, 193
Christovich, Mary Lou, 93
Chubbuck, James, 116
Cior, Charles, 164
Citizens Bank and Trust Company Papers, 187, 191
Citizens Council of Greater New Orleans, 207
Citizens Council of Shreveport, 241
Civic Opera Association, 241
Civil Courts, U.S., 36
Civilian Conservation Corps, 65
Civil rights movement, 82; archival materials, 206-13, 239-40
Civil War, 41-44, 149; archival materials, 150, 158-60, 163, 169, 177, 178, 189-90, 203-4, 206, 238, 241, 244; blacks during, 77; New Orleans during, 88
Civil Works Administration, 65
Claiborne, J. F. H., Papers, 32
Claiborne, William Charles Cole, 161, 177; Papers, 219
Clapp, Theodore, 31
Clark, Daniel, Papers, 29
Clark, George Rogers, 202
Clark, John G., 11, 23, 30, 72, 85-86, 131
Clay, Floyd Martin, 68
Clay, Henry, 36
Clayton, Ronnie W., 65, 82
Clegg, Richard, Jr., 175
Clemens, Samuel, Papers, 164
Code Noir of 1724, 180

Index

Coffey, Thomas P., 29
Coker, William S., 18, 21, 23, 24, 137
Cole, Fred, 105
Coles, Harry L., 74
Coles, Harry L., Jr. 37
Coles, Robert C., 92
Colección Muñoz, 132
Colles, James: Letterbooks, 177; Papers, 32
Collins Family Papers, 187
Colmer, George, Journals, 249
Colomb Plantation Papers, 186
Colonial period, 6-8, 10; blacks in, 72-73; archival materials, ¹68-69, 181, 185-86. *See also* French Louisiana; Spanish Louisiana
Commerce. *See* Economic history
Commercial Bank of Natchez records, 156
Commercial-Germania Trust and Savings records, 191
Commercial National Bank records, 191
Commercial Trust and Savings records, 191
Community Chest of New Orleans Papers, 193
Community Services Council of Jeffersen Collection, 226
Community Services Council of New Orleans Collection, 226
Compagnie d'Assurance de la Nouvelle Orléans Dividend Ledger, 187
Company of the Indies, 12, 186
Company of the West, 180
Compromise of 1877, 79
Conaway, James, 67, 82
Concord Baptist Association, 244
Confederacy. *See* Civil War
Confederate Cavalry Veterans Association, 190-91
Congregational church records, 207
Connelly, Marc, Papers, 170
Connor, William P., 78
Conrad, Glenn R., 9, 11, 14, 30, 68, 69, 168
Conrotte, Manuel, 20
Conservation, Louisiana Department of, records, 171
Consolidated Association of Planters of Louisiana records, 156
Constitutional Convention of 1973, 162
Coody, Archibald S., Papers, 162
Cooley, L. V., 158
Cooley Family Papers, 192

Coordinating Council of Greater New Orleans, 208
Corbitt, Duvon C., 136
CORE, 82
Corine Plantation, 179
Cornish, Dudley T., 77
Coroner's Office records, 221
Cortés Alonso, Victor, 24
Cortés Alonso, Vincenta, 21
Costa Solano, Fernando, 21
Cottingham, Claybrook, Papers, 254
Coulon, George, 175, 179
Coulter, E. Merton, 42, 47, 48
Council of Social Agencies Papers, 193
Court Proceedings of Spanish Cabildo of Louisiana, 181
Coutts, Brian E., 135, 166 n
Cowdrey, Albert Edward, 63-64
Cox, Charles S., Collection, 244
Cox, Isaac Joslin, 5, 20, 29
Cox, Lawanda, 48
Cox, Nathaniel, Papers, 176
Coxe, John E., 89
Craig, Charles R., 34
Crain, Robert L., 82
Crane, Verner W., 13
Craven, Avery O., 73, 95-96
Cravens, John N., 73
Crawford, Charles A., Papers, 192
Creek Indians, 25
Creole Affair Collection, 212
Creoles: archival material on, 172, 224; of color, 75, 224; in New Orleans, 86
Crescent City Democratic Association, 91
Crescent City Stockyards, 192
Crittenden, John J., 36
Crooks, Kenneth Bronstorph, M., Papers, 212
Crosset Lumber Company records, 157
Crouse, Nellis M., 7
Crozat, Antoine, 180
Cruzat, Heloise Hulse, 10, 97
Cullen, Countee, Papers, 212
Cultural history: antebellum, 39-40; archival material, 163, 164, 195-96, 203-4, 219, 238, 252; of Reconstruction, 47, 49
Cummins, Light Townsend, 17-25
Cunningham, George E., 80
Curley, Henry Hosford, Papers, 187
Currell, James, Papers, 178
Curry, Thomas, 35

Curtis and Davis New Orleans Neighborhood Study, 92, 219, 227
Customs Office, U.S., 210

Dabney, Thomas Ewing, 48; Papers, 195
Daigle, Jean, 14
Dakin, James Harrison, Collection, 219
Daley, T. A., 76
Dallas Calmes Affair, 170
Dalrymple, Margaret Fisher, 24, 153-66
Damaré, James, Recordbook, 187
Daneel School Scrapbooks, 218
D'Annemours, Paulmier, 248
D'Antoni, Blaise C., 118
Darby, William, 29
Dargo, George, 28-29
Dart, Henry P., 10, 14, 35-36, 72
Dart, William K., Papers, 194
Dart and Dart Collection, 228
Daugherty, Dennis, 67
David, Paul A., 117
Davis, Abraham Lincoln, Papers, 221
Davis, Edwin Adams, 4, 37, 74, 149-50, 153-54
Davis, Forrest, 59-60
Davis, Jackson B., Papers, 234, 240
Davis, Jefferson, 178, 196; Papers, 179
Davis, Jimmie, 67
Davis, Mollie Moore, Papers, 195
Davis, William H., Sr., Collection, 226
Dawkins, Benjamin C., Jr., Papers, 236, 239
Dawkins, Benjamin C., Sr., Papers, 234
Debaillon Family Papers, 169
Debien, Gabriel, 9
Debouchel, Victor, 4
De Bow, J. D. B., 39; Papers, 32
Declouet Family Papers, 169
Deep South Writers' Conference Papers, 170
Deiler, J. Hanno, 9
Delanglez, Jean, 5, 8, 11, 13
Delgado, Isaac, Memorial Fund Papers, 194
Delta Airlines, 158
Delta Steamship Lines Collection, 228
Democratic Conservative Parish Committee Records, 192-93
Denechaud, Justin F., Collection, 179
Department of Agriculture and Immigration records, 152
Department of Commerce and Industry records, 152

Department of Education records, 152
Department of Highways records, 152
Depôt des Cartes et Plans de la Marine, 169
Desdunes, R. L., 76
Desegregation, 82, 91-92; during Reconstruction, 48. *See also* Civil rights movement
Desmond, John, 40
De Spelder, Nellie, Diary, 212
Dethloff, Henry C., 52, 61-62, 80, 168
Deutsch, Hermann, 64; Collection, 227; Papers, 195
DeVries, Walter, 66
Dew, Charles B., 43
Dibble, Ernest F., 25
Diket, Albert L., 34
DiLeo, Octavia Benintende, Collection, 225
Dillard project, 65
Dillard University, 206-9, 212, 213
Dillon, Willie Lee Pace, Memoirs and Genealogical Notes, 245
Dimitry, Charles Patton, Papers, 179
Din, Gilbert, 21-25, 72, 127-37
Diocese of Louisiana and the Floridas Records, 181
Dirección General de Archivos y Bibliotecas, 129
DiRose, Joseph V. Papers, 221
Dispatches from U.S. Consuls in New Orleans, 181
Dispatches of the Spanish Governors of Louisiana, 156, 176
Dispersed of Judah Papers, 189
Dixon, Brandt V. B., Papers, 196
Dodd College Papers, 99, 242
Dollar, Charles, 122-23
Domínguez Bordona, Jesús, 132
Donelson, Andrew Jackson, 36
Donnelly, Joseph P., 5
Dorman, James H., 73
Doucet, D. J. "Cat," 68
Douglas, Judith Haynes, Papers, 100, 161
Douglas, Walter B., 19
Douthit, Leo Glenn, 63
Dubach State Bank, 243
Dudley (cartographer), 179
Dudley and Nelson, 177
Duffy, John, 39, 73, 87
Dufossard Landry Accountbook, 187
Dufour, Charles L., 42

Dufour, Cyprien, 31
Duke University, 32
Dumez, Eugene, 159
Dunbar, Charles, Papers, 193, 195
Dunbar, Paul Laurence, Papers, 212
Dunbar-Nelson, Alice, 73
Duncan, Greer B., Papers, 188
Dunlop, John, Papers, 187
Dunn, Velmarae, Collection, 250
Dunn, William Edward, 6
Dupont, Albert L., 34-35
Dupré, Edith Garland, Papers, 99, 170
Dupré, Garland, 170
Durham, Marshall, Photograph Album, 165
Durieux, Caroline, 166
Durnford, Andrew, 75, 177; Papers, 186
du Ru, Paul, 143

Eakin, Sue, 73, 106
E. A. Seminary, 245
East Baton Rouge Parish records, 151
Eaton, Clement, 76
Eaton, John Henry, 32
Eccles, William J., 4
Economic history, 23; antebellum, 28, 30, 36-38; archival materials, 156-58, 171, 176-77, 187, 191-92, 232, 234-35, 248; oral, 106-7; quantification and, 116; Reconstruction, 44; urban, 85
Edmundson, Munro, S., 82
Education: antebellum, 30, 39-40; archival materials, 196, 206, 207, 210, 212-13, 236, 244; of blacks, 76, 79, 82; and women, 98-99
Education Unlimited, 207
Edwards, Edwin W., 69
Egan, Lavinia, Papers, 245, 246
Eisenhower, Dwight D., 192
Ellender, Allen J., 70, 253; Papers, 253
Ellis, J. Tuffly, 90
Emery, Emma Wilson, Papers, 161
Englesman, John Cornelius, 77
Episcopal Diocese of Louisiana Archive, 188, 194
ERA Club, 100, 179; Papers, 219
Erwin, Joseph and Lavinia, 74
Essex, Mark, 82
Ethnic Heritage Oral History Project, 110
Ethnic minorities. See *specific groups*
Evans, Harry Howard, 38
Everard, Wayne, 35, 52, 89, 216

Everett, Donald E., 10, 73, 75, 77, 87
Evia, José de, 132
Ewing, Don, 108
Ewing, Jasper E., and Sons, 166
Ewing, Quincy, 56
Exploration, 4-6
Exxon Corporation, 106

F. M. & S. B. Hicks Cargo Records, 231
Fabre-Surveyer, E., 10
Family History Project Papers, 156
Family Service Society Papers, 193
Fant, Clyde E., Scrapbooks, 234
Farmers' Union Movement, 243
Farm Security Administration, 65
Farragut, Commodore David, 41
Farrand, Edward, 178
Fatherless Children of France Papers, 193
Favrot, Claude Joseph, 185
Favrot, Philogène, Papers, 189
Favrot, Pierre Joseph, 185
Favrot Family Papers, 185
Favrot Library, 184
Fay, Edwin W., 39
Federal Emergency Relief Administration, 65
Federal Theatre Project, 195
Federal Writers' Project, 65
Federation of Civic Leagues of New Orleans, 211
Federoff, Alexander, Papers, 195
Feingold, Marcus, Papers, 194
Feitel, Arthur, Papers, 195
Fer, Nicholas de, 144
Ferchand, Jean Baptiste, Papers, 186
Ferguson, Kate Lee, Papers, 161
Ferguson, Ted, 35
Fernandez Duro, Cesareo, 6
Ferry, Alexis, Papers, 186
Ficklen, John R., 3, 15, 46
Fiehrer, Thomas, 72
Field, Betty Marie, 63, 64
Fields, Harvey G., 60
Filhiol, Juan, Papers, 155
Fineran, John Kingston, 59
Fink, Steven D., 116
Fink Asylum Papers, 193
Fire Department records, 221
Firemen's Charitable Association of the Seventh District Collection, 226
First Presbyterian Church Recordbook, 189
Fischer, Roger A., 48, 76, 78

Fisk University, 213
Fitzmorris, James E., Papers, 220-21
Fitzpatrick, John, 24
Flanders, Benjamin F., Papers, 162
Flathers, John, Papers, 177
Fleitas, John B., Diary, 179
Fleming, Walter L., Collection, 165
Fletcher, Stahl, 12
Flint, Timothy, 30
Flint-Goodrich Hospital, 208, 209, 213
Flint Medical College, 208
Florida, University of, Stetson Collection, 155
Floud, Roderick, 122, 123
Flournoy, Alfred, Jr., Correspondence, 238, 239
Flournoy, Alfred, Sr., Family Papers, 233, 239
Flournoy, J. Howell, Scrapbooks, 234, 239
Folmer, Henry, 6, 11
Foner, Laura, 10
Fontainebleau, Treaty of, 12
Fontenot, Mary Alice, 68, 69
Foote, Henry S., 31
Ford, J. Franklin, Papers, 236
Fordyce Lumber Company records, 157
Forest History Society, 157
Forrest, Nathan Bedford, 178
Forstall, Edmond J., 37, 38
Forstall, Eugene, Papers, 186
Fortier, Alcée, 15, 18
Fortier, James A., 60
Fossier, A. E., 39
Foucault, Denis-Nicolas, 14, 15
Fournet, John B., 69; Papers 162
Foy, Prosper, Papers, 186
Franck and Danneel Papers, 192
Franquelin, Jean Baptiste Louis, 143
Frederick, Rivers, Papers, 208
Freedmen's Bureau, 47, 77-78, 236
Freeland Collection, 171
Freeman, Arthur, 34
Freeman, George, Papers, 233, 235, 239
Freeman, Margery, 110
Freemantle, Lieutenant Colonel Arthur, J. L., 42
Free Night School for Working Men and Boys, 99
Fregault, Guy, 7
Frehrer, Thomas M., 23
French and Indian War, 145
French Louisiana, 3-15; archival materials, 169, 180, 185-86, 201-2, 251; women in, 96-97
French Market Scrapbook, 218
French Opera House, 195, 204
French Superior Council of Louisiana, 176
Freret and Wolf Papers, 195
Freret Collection, 177
Friedler, Frank, Papers, 221
Friedman, Robert S., 82
Friend, Julius W., Papers, 196
Friends of Amistad, 206
Friends of the Cabildo, 179
Friends of Widows and Orphans of the French Resistance Papers, 193
Frierson Company Records, 232, 234
Froitzheim Pictorial Collection, 171
Fruge, J. Cleveland, Papers, 163
Fulco, Frank, 238
Funding Board minutes, 152
Fuqua, Henry L., Papers, 162
Fur trade, 7

Gallatin, Albert, Papers, 29
Gallier, James Sr., Papers, 195
Gálvez, Bernardo de, 22, 128, 130, 133, 155, 176
Gálvez, José de, 133
Gambino, Richard, 89
Gammon Theological Seminary, 209
Garber, Jan, Papers, 235
García Melero, Luis Angel, 22
García Navarro, Luis, 21
Gardner, Frank, 178
Gardner, James, Scrapbooks, 234
Gardner, Joel, 104
Gardner, Kathy, 255
Garrison, Carolyn, 242
Gates of Mercy Papers, 189
Gatewood, Willard, 53, 56
Gaudet Home Papers, 193
Gay, Edward, Jr., Papers, 162
Gay, Edward J., 100; and Family Papers, 156
Gayarré, Charles E. A., 3, 15, 18, 30, 33, 39, 127, 180; Papers, 164, 196
Gayoso de Lemos, Manuel, 155, 185
General Education Board, Selected Records, 212, 213
Gênet (adventurer), 131
Genovese, Eugene D., 74
Gentry, Judith, 119
George III, King of England, 147

Geraghty, James F., 13
Gergaud, Louis, Diary, 248
German American National Bank records, 191
Germania National Bank records, 191
Germania Savings Bank and Trust records, 191
German immigrants, 9; archival materials, 160, 225
German Lutheran Church records, 194
German Protestant Home for the Old and Infirm Papers, 193
Gerteis, Louis G., 77
Gerwick, Fred, Collection, 171
Gibbs, Robert T., Papers, 241
Gibson, Randall Lee, Papers, 192, 196
Gilded Age, 51-53; New Orleans in, 89
Gilkinson, Helen, Papers, 161
Gillette, Michael L., 63
Gilmore, H. W., 92
Giraud, Marcel, 4, 7, 8, 96
Giraud, P. A., Papers, 177
Girdo Asylum Papers, 219
Givens-Hopkins Papers, 169
Gleig, George Robert, 32
Glen, J. Frank, Riverboat Logs, 231
Glenk, Robert, Papers, 196
Goals Foundation Council Collection, 226
Goldin, Claudie, 86-87
Goldstein, Moise, Papers, 195
Gómez del Campillo, Miguel, 21, 131
Gonichon (surveyor), 148
Gonzales, John Edmond, 48
Gonzalez Palencia, Angel, 131
Goodloe Stuck Industrial Collection, 234
Goodman, Paul H., Collection, 249
Goodspeed, Winston Arthur, 4
Gordon, Jean, 56-57
Gosnell, H. Allen, 42
Gottschalk, Louis Moreau, 164
Gould, C. P., 11
Graham, Hugh Davis, 61, 82
Grambling State College, 213
Grandjean, René, Collection, 224-25
Grange movement, 243
Granger, G., 178
Gravier, Gabriel, 5, 97
Gravier, Henri, 8
Gray, Bessie Murrell, Family Papers, 244, 245
Gray, Lewis C., 36
Grayson, Wiley B., Papers, 236, 239
Great Depression, 64-65

Greater New Orleans AFL-CIO, 225; Collection, 226
Green, George D., 38
Green, Joe L., 62
Greer, James G., 33
Grégault, Guy, 12
Gregory, Hiram "Pete," 109-10
Gremillion, Jeanne Delas, Collection, 253
Gremillion, Monsignor Joseph, Papers, 240
Grenier, Charles E., 69, 116
Grenier, Emile P., 38
Griffin, Lucile Mouton, Papers, 170
Griffith, Connie G., 110, 135
Griffith, Willis P., Papers, 186
Grima Family Papers, 185, 186
Groner, Samuel B., 35
Grosseilliers, Médard Chovart, sieur des, 142
Grosz, Agnes Smith, 78
Group Theatre, 195
Grummond, Jane de, 32
Gruss, Louis, 34
Guibert, Marie-Claude, 9
Guillemart, Gilberto, 128
Gulfside Assembly, 209
Gumbel, Sophie L., Home Papers, 193
Gutman, Herbert G., 43, 74

Haas, Edward F., 64, 67-68, 71-83, 91, 107, 173-81
Hackett, Derek L. A., 33, 118-19
Hair, William I., 51-57, 79-81, 88
Haldimand, Frederick, Papers, 155
Hale-Hawkins-Allen-Hitchcock Family Papers, 241
Hall, Basil, 30
Hall, Covington, 192
Hall, Henry G., Diary, 233
Hall, Luther, Papers, 249
Hallowell, James S., 178-79
Hamer, Collin Bradfield, Jr., 104, 118, 215-22
Hamer, Philip M., 137
Hamilton, Peter J., 8
Hamilton, Raphael N., 5
Hamiter, Joseph B., Papers, 163
Hamlin, Walter B., Papers, 163, 179
Hammack, Rudolph Carrol, 64-65
Hammond, Bray, 38
Hammond, Hilda Phelps, 66
Handy, William T., Autobiography, 212
Hansen, Eduard, 160
Hardee, W. J., 178
Hardin, J. Fair, 31; Papers, 231

Hardin, Joseph A., Papers, 208
Hardtner, Henry E., Papers, 242
Hardy, D. Clive, 223-28
Hardy, James D., Jr., 8, 15
Harlan, Louis H., 48, 88
Harlem Renaissance, 212
Harrington, Fred H., 42
Harris, Thomas H., 39
Harris, Thomas O., 60
Harrison, John H., Papers, 188
Harrison, William Henry, 36
Hart, E. J., Records, 191
Haskins, James, 75, 78
Hatcher, William B., 29, 34
Hatfield, Joseph T., 29
Havard, William C., 66, 115, 116
Haynes, Robert V., 22
Hayot, Emile, 73
Head, William H., and Family Papers, 163
Health Department records, 221
Hearn, Lafcadio: Collection, 184; Correspondence, 251
Hearsey, Clem G., 12
Heberle, Rudolph, 117
Hébert, A. Otis, Jr., 137
Hébert, F. Edward, 68; Papers, 192
Hébert, Paul Octave, 35
Hébert Papers, 170
Heck, Harold, 38
Hefley, Edwin, Papers, 235
Heinrich, Pierre, 8
Hellman, Lillian, 99
Hendrix, James Paisley, Jr., 74
Henley, William Ernest, 60
Hennepin, Louis, 143
Hennessey, Melinda Meek, 79
Hennessy, David C., 89
Hentoff, Nat, 90
Heritage '76 Collection, 253
Hernon, Peter, 82
Hesseltine, William H., 46
Hester, Earl R., Papers, 245
Heywood Papers, 171
Hicks, Ella Dingle, Collection, 236
Hicky, Philip, Papers, 155
Hidy, Ralph W., 38
Higginbotham, Jay, 7, 8
Hill, Roscoe R., 134, 136
Hinckley, Orramel, Papers, 158
Hinding, Andrea, 100-101
Historical Architectural Buildings Survey, 179

Historic New Orleans Collection, 98, 100, 148, 198-204
Historic Preservation Society of Shreveport Records, 237
Hodge, Frederick Webb, 13
Hodgson, Daisy L., Papers, 190
Hoëhn, Werner Conrad, Papers, 195
Hoese, Dickson H., 6
Hoey, John, Papers, 186
Hoffman, Paul, 24
Hogan, William Ransom, 105, 106, 112, 154; Archive of New Orleans Jazz, 197-98
Holiday, Billie, 99
Holiday-in-Dixie Records, 238
Holloway, Ernest D., Papers, 248
Holly, Donald, 65
Holmes, Jack D. L., 11, 18, 21-25, 72, 129, 132, 137, 155
Holmes, Norman A., Recordbook, 194
Holzman, Robert S., 42
Homann, Johann, 141
Home Institute, 99
Hood, John T., 35
Hood, Nicholas, Papers, 212
Hoover, Herbert, 56
Hoover, J. Edgar, 239
Horowitz, Murray H., 77
Hoss, James M., Sr., 243
Hoss, Nathaniel, 243
Hoss Family Papers, 243, 245
Hotel Dieu Hospital Library, 99
Houck, Louis, 19, 136
Houghton Library, Harvard University, 29
Houma Indians, 210
Houssaye, Sidonie de la, Papers, 159, 161
Hout, V., 4
Howard, Charles L., Papers, 188
Howard, Henry, Papers, 195
Howard, Milo B., 25
Howard, Perry H., 33, 54, 69, 115, 116
Howard Association Journals, 194
Huber, Leonard V., 40, 97
Hubert, Giles Alfred, Papers, 207-8
Hubert-Robert, Régine, 4
Hudson, Charles M., 25
Hudson, Julien, 175
Hughes, Howard Sr., 108
Humphreys, Hubert D., 65, 103-13, 240
Hunt, Charles Havens, 34
Hunt and Smith Company, 177
Hutchinson, William J., Family and Plantation Records, 231, 232, 234, 237
Hutson, Ethel, Papers, 193

280   Index

Hyams, H. M., Letterbook, 177
Hyde, H. Montgomery, 8
Hyde and Goodrich, 175
Hyman, Harold M., 48

Iberville, Pierre Lemoyne d', 7, 8, 143, 144
Immigrants, 8-11; female, 86-97; urban, 86. See also *specific ethnic groups*
Independent Petroleum Association of America, 158
Indians, 11-13, 24-25; archival materials, 160; oral history, 109-10
Inger, Morton, 82
Ingraham, Joseph H., 30
Ingram, Lawrence Franklin, 67, 68
Insane Persons, Records of, 221
Institute for Human Relations, 252
Interstate Natural Gas Company, 228
Interstate Oil Pipeline Company, 105
Inter-University Consortium for Political Research (ICPR), 120-21
Irish immigrants, archival materials, 160, 225
Italian Clubs Collection, 224, 225
Italian immigrants, 89, 160; archival materials, 225, 238

Jack, George Whitfield, Papers, 194
Jacks, J. V., 5
Jackson, Andrew, 33, 36, 177, 202; Papers, 32
Jackson, Joy J., 52, 89, 106
Jackson, Riddle and Company Papers, 187
Jackson Brewing Company records, 191
Jackson Lumber Company records, 157-58
Jacobs, Miller, 13
Jahncke, Ernest Lee, Sr., Papers, 162
James, James A., 20
Jamison, Anna Marie Hansen, Papers, 99, 212
Jastremski, Leon, Papers, 162
Jayhawkers, 44
Jazz, 81, 90, 175-76; archival materials, 197-98; oral history, 105-6; and women, 99
Jeansonne, Glen, 59-70, 82, 107, 247-56
Jefferson, Thomas, 147, 248; Papers, 29
Jefferson Democratic Association Papers, 192
Jefferson Parish Subdivision surveys, 218
Jeffreys, Thomas, 146, 147
Jenkins, John Carmichael, Papers, 157

Jennings, Louisiana Women's Auxiliary to the Grand Army of the Republic, 100
Jennings-Heywood Oil Syndicate Records, 158
Jennings Nursery Collection, 170
Jensen, Richard, 122-23
Jewish Children's Home Papers, 193
Jewish life, 159-60
John, Elizabeth, A., 13
Johns-Manville Timberlands records, 158
Johnson, Clifton H., 83, 205-13
Johnson, Isaac, 34, 177
Johnson, Lyndon, B., 105
Johnson, Marie White, 79
Johnston, Albert Sidney, 189
Johnston, Joseph E., 178
Johnston, Josiah Stoddard, Papers, 32, 34, 36
Johnston, William Preston, Papers, 196
Joliet, Louis, 5, 142
Jones, Carl, 108
Jones, Charles Colcock, Papers, 194, 196
Jones, Floyd, 244
Jones, Howard J., 78
Jones, Joseph, Papers, 164, 194
Jones, Joseph Merrick, Collection, 192
Jones, Montfort Stokes, 244
Jones, Robert Elijah, Papers, 208-9
Jones, Robert R., 52, 80
Jones, Roessle, Olschner and Wiener (architects), 237
Jones, Roland, Family Papers, 241, 243-45
Jones, Sam Houston, 67, 166; Papers, 70, 192
Jones, Samuel Worth, Diary and Family Papers, 244, 245
Joor, Joseph Finley, Papers, 196
Joseph, Peter, Collection, 224
Judicial records, 179-80
Justice Department, U.S., 210

Kane, Harnett T., 60; Papers, 164
Kaplan, Abram, Collection, 227
Keatchie College, 244, 254
Keatchie Presbyterian Church records, 236-37
Keep, Edward H., Papers, 191
Keller, Rosa Freeman, Papers, 99, 212-13
Kelley, Daniel, Papers, 221
Kellogg, L. P., 4
Kellogg, William Pitt, 48; Papers, 162
Kellogg Lumber Company records, 158
Kells, Charles Edmund, Papers, 194

Kemp, John R., 55, 91, 173-81
Kemper, James Parkerson, Papers, 179
Kendall, John S., 74, 76, 89
Kendall, Lane Carter, 73
Kenner, Duncan, Papers, 178
Kennon, Robert F., Papers, 162
Kenyon, Karlie K., 68
Key, V. O., Jr., 61, 66
Keyes, Frances Parkinson, Papers, 161
Kilman, Grady W., 10
King, Grace, 3, 7, 10, 15, 228; Papers, 32, 99, 161, 164
Kinnaird, Lawrence, 19, 127. 135
Kirby, Jack Temple, 55, 57
Kitchen, Thomas, 146
Kleinpeter Family Papers, 160
Kleppner, Paul, 119, 120
Klingamen, David C., 120
Klorer, John A., Papers, 196
Kmen, Henry A., 76, 87
Knights of Peter Claver, 211
Know-Nothing movement, 116, 169
Koch and Wilson Papers, 195
Kondert, Reinhart, 9
Kopman, Henry H., Papers, 196
Kotlikoff, Laurence J., 74, 116, 117
Kousser, J. Morgan, 55, 56, 80, 89
Krupa, Gene, 175
Ku Klux Klan, 79, 81, 162, 170, 244, 249
Kunkel, Paul A., 80
Kuntz, Rosemond E. and Emile, Memorial Collection, 184, 186, 188, 189, 195, 196
Kurtz, Michael L., 66, 68, 107

Laborde, Adras, 66-67
Labor history, 192, 225-26
Labranche, Jean, Papers, 170
Lafargue Papers, 196
Lafarque, André, 6
Lafayette, Andrew, and Steele Chapels records, 189
Lafayette Insurance Company records, 191
Lafayette Presbyterian Church, 194
Lafayette Realty Company records, 191-92
Lafayette records, 188
Lafitte, Jean, 32
Lafon, Barthelemy, 203
Lafourche Parish Bicentennial Commission, 253
Lambert, John D., Jr., Papers, 221
Lambert, Pierre Antoine and Pierre Alexander, Papers, 188
Lanata, Antonio, Sr., Collection, 225

Landrieu, Moon: Collection, 252; Letters, 220
Landry, Stuart Omar, 47, 48
Landry, Thomas, 35
Lang, Herbert H., 18
Larsen, Lawrence H., 86
La Salle, and René-Robert Cavelier de, 5-7
La Salle, Robert Cavalier, sieur de, 143, 144
La Salle Elementary School Scrapbooks, 218
Latour, A. Lacarrière, 32
Laumet, Antoine, 8
Laurel Grove Plantation Store Collection, 253
Laurent, Lubin F., 9
Laussat, Pierre Clement de, 186; Papers, 201, 202
Laut, Agnes C., 8
Lauvrière, Emile, 14
Laval Université, 172
Lavie, Gabriel, 187
Law, John, 8, 9, 145
Law, William, 145
Lawson, McGhee Library, 136
Lawyers Committee for Civil Rights Under Law, 209; Records, 211
Lawyers Committee for the Defense of the Constitution records, 211
Lazaro, Ladislas, Papers, 162
Leacock, William T., Papers, 188
Leadbetter, Huddie (Leadbelly), 104
League of Women Voters: Papers, 193; records, 242
Leathers, Thomas P., Papers, 158, 192
LeBlanc, Coozan Dudley, 68
LeBlanc, Sam A., Papers, 163
LeBreton, Dagmar, 39
LeBreton, Marietta, 29
Leche, Richard W., 60, 193; Papers, 162
Le Conte, René, 9
Lee, Robert E., 178
Leesville Conference of the Methodist Episcopal Church Minutebook, 194
Legal history: antebellum, 35-36; archival material, 162-63, 179-80, 193-94, 228, 244
Legan, Marshall Scott, 38
Legendre, David Louis, 64
Lehman Stern Company, 191
Le Jeune, Emilie, 76
Lelong Papers, 177
Lemann Family Papers, 191
Lemieux, Donald J., 12, 14

Index

Lemonier, Yves R., Scrapbooks, 218
Leon, Alonso de, 141
Leonard, Albert Harris, Memoirs, 231
Leonard, Irving A., 6
Leper Home Records, 165
Lepine, J. Wilson, Collection, 253
Leprohon, Pierre, 5
Leslie, J. Paul, Jr., 62, 66
Le Sueur, Pierre Charles, 143
Levasseur, Emile, 8
Levy, Neville, Scrapbooks, 218
Lewis, George, 81
Lewis, Meriwether, 202
Lewis, Pierce J., 92
Lewis family, 178
Liberty Place, Battle of (1874), 47-48, 79
Library of Congress, 29, 32, 35, 36, 43, 136, 172, 230
Liebling, A. J., 65-66
Lieutard, Albert, Collection, 187
Liljegren, Ernest R., 72, 131
Lincoln, Abraham, 41, 46
Lind, Jenny, 164
Linden, Fabian, 37
Lion, Jules, 175
Lionpacher, Louis, 160
L'Isle, Guillaume de, 140, 141, 143-45
Lislet, Louis Moreau, 35
Literary Club of New Orleans Papers, 196
Literature. *See* Cultural history
Livingston, Edward, 34
Local Council of Women of New Orleans, 100; Papers, 219
Loeb, Henry Brunswick, Papers, 195
Logsdon, Joseph, 73
Lomax, Alan, 81, 90
Lomax, John Allan, 104
Long, Earl K., 61, 65-66, 245; archival materials, 193; Newspaper Clippings, 245; Papers, 162
Long, Huey P., 5, 53, 54, 57, 59-67, 105, 108-11, 116, 165, 170, 219, 227, 241, 245; archival materials, 193; Papers, 162; Scrapbooks, 218
Long, Russell, 61, 66
Longstreet, Stephen, 81
Lonn, Ella, 46
Loos, John, 105, 106, 112
López, Thomás, 145
Louis XIV, King of France, 6, 141
Louisiana, University of, 184
Louisiana American Civil Liberties Union Papers, 193

Louisiana and New Orleans Picture File, 217-18
Louisiana and New Orleans Scrapbook, 218
Louisiana Architects Association, 149
Louisiana Archives of Negro History, 211
Louisiana Archives Survey, 149
Louisiana Bank, 187
Louisiana Baptist Convention, Mae Lee Library, 254
Louisiana Biography Index, 217
Louisiana Camellia Society Papers, 170
Louisiana Civil Records, 177
Louisiana Civil Service League, 193
Louisiana College, Mt. Lebanon-Keatchie Room, 254-55
Louisiana Commission on Human Relations, Rights and Responsibilities, 211
Louisiana Committee for Dismantling of a Dual System of Higher Education, 207
Louisiana Committee for the Humanities, 112
Louisiana Dental Society Papers, 194
Louisiana Department of Public Works Collection, 227
Louisiana Education Association, 207
Louisiana Engineering Society Papers, 179
Louisiana Folklore Society Collection, 225
Louisiana Forestry Commission records, 242-43
Louisiana Heritage Collection, 237
Louisiana Historical Association, 112; Collection, 189-90
Louisiana Historical Records Survey (HRS), 149, 154, 155
Louisiana Iris Society Papers, 170
Louisiana League for the Preservation of Constitutional Rights Papers, 193
Louisiana Life Insurance Company, 208
Louisiana Lottery Company, 52
Louisiana Militia Book, 177
Louisiana Music Teachers Association Papers, 164
Louisiana National Bank records, 191
Louisiana News Index, 216-17
Louisiana (steamship) records, 187
Louisiana Relief Committee records, 152
Louisiana State Advisory Commission on Civil Rights, 91
Louisiana State Archives, 112, 149-52
Louisiana State Athletic Association, 210
Louisiana State Bank records, 156

Louisiana State Board of Agriculture and Immigration Papers, 179
Louisiana State Board of Education, 210
Louisiana State Fair, 241; Records, 232
Louisiana State Federation of Labor, 235
Louisiana State Government Records, 238
Louisiana State Legislature, 35
Louisiana State Library, 98
Louisiana State Museum, 93, 97, 148; Archives, 112, 173-81; Louisiana Historical Center, 148, 176-81
Louisiana State Nurses' Association, 161
Louisiana State University, 43, 44, 46-47, 69, 210; Agricultural Extension Service Papers, 157, 159; Department of Archives and Manuscripts, 98-100, 104, 105, 153-66
Louisiana State University—Baton Rouge, 135, 235, 254
Louisiana State University—Shreveport, 69-70, 108-9, 111; Archives Department, 229-41
Louisiana Sugar Planters' Association Records, 157
Louisiana Sugar and Rice Exchange Records, 157
Louisiana Tech University Archives, 242-46
Louisiane Concessions, 176
Louisiane Correspondence Générale, 176
Louisiane Etat Civil, 176
Louisiane Générale, 176
Louisiane Passage, 176
Louisiane Recensements, 176
Lovrich, Frank M., 31
Low, Nicolas, Papers, 185
Lower, Richard, 117-18
Lowery, Woodbury, 18
Lowrey, Mark P., Papers, 227
Lowrey, Walter M., 38, 48
Loyola University of New Orleans, 135, 155; Special Collections and Archives, 250-52; University Archives, 252
Lutheran Church Missouri Synod, Southern District Collection, 225
Lutheran church records, 170, 225
Lutz, Albert, Papers, 242
Lyceum and Library Society Collection, 219
Lyceum-Tulane Association Papers, 197
Lyell, Charles, 30
Lyon, E. Wilson, 12, 20
Lyons, Charlton H., 69; Papers, 158, 162
Lyons, Grant, 36
Lytle, Andrew, 165

McCaleb, E. Howard, Papers, 162
McCaughan, Richard B., 66
McCloskey, Bernard, Papers, 220
McClung Collection, 136
McClure, Captain John W., Papers, 163
McConnell, Elizabeth Logan, 100
McConnell, Richard, Papers, 194, 196
McConnell, Roland C., 73, 75, 77
McConnell Family Papers, 100, 194, 196
McCoy, Donald R., 61
McCrary, Peyton, 77
McCulley, Paul Ted, 56
McCurdy, Raymond, R., 39
McDermott, John Francis, 7, 18, 137
McDonogh, John, 73; Papers, 177, 186-87, 219
McDonogh and W. C. Payne Papers, 219
McEnery, Samuel D., 51
McFeely, William, 78
MacGimsey, Robert Hunter, Collection, 255
McGinty, Garnie W., 52; Papers and Publications, 246
McGloin, Frank, Papers, 192
McGowan, James Thomas, 10, 72
McGowan, Thomas M., 24
McGuire, David R., Papers, 93, 192
McGuire, E. L., Papers, 236, 239
McGuire, Robert Forbes, Diary, 248
McKeithen (politician), 192
McKinney, B. B., Collection, 254-55
McMillan, John, 68
McNeese State University Archives, 255
McSeveney, Samuel T., 119-20
McShane, Andrew James, Letters, 220
McTigue, Geraldine, 80, 116, 117
McWhiney, H. Grady, 48
McWilliams, Richebourg Gaillard, 7
Madison, James, Papers, 29
Maestri, Robert Sidney, 91; Letters, 220; Scrapbooks, 218
Magnam, D.M.A., 4
Mallard (cabinetmaker), 175
Mallard, Robert Q., 194
Many, Anna Estelle, Papers, 98-99
Margavio, Anthony V., 92
Marigny, Bernard, 33
Marine Bank and Trust records, 191
Marine Paint and Varnish Company records, 191
Marino Perez, Luis, 133
Markham, Thomas R., Papers, 189
Marquette, Jacques, 5, 142
Marquis, Donald M., 81, 90

284   Index

Martin, François-Xavier, 3, 15, 18, 33
Marshall-Furman Papers, 232, 233
Martin, Claude, 9
Martin, Francois Xavier, 3, 15, 18, 33
Martin, Jerry B., 87
Martin, Rendall, Papers, 234, 235, 241
Martin, Robert C., Sr., 253
Martin, Thomas, 61, 65
Martin, Walter B., Scrapbooks, 239
Martin, Williams, 81
Martin-Pugh Collection, 253
Massachusetts Historical Society, 36
Massé, G.C.E., 8
Matas, Rudolph, Papers, 194
Maury, Dabny H., 178
Mavis Grove Plantation Journal, 177
Maxwell, George Hebard, Papers, 179
Maxwell, Leon Ryder, Papers, 195
May, Thomas J., 48, 77-78
Mayer, Norman, Papers, 191
Meade, George P., Papers, 196
Meade, Robert D., 34
Meador, Patricia L., 229-46
Medicine, 87, 164-65; archival materials, 188, 194, 237-38
Meeker, Edward, 117
Meier, August, 82
Memphis State University, John Brister Library, 136
Mencken, H. L.: Correspondence, 252; Papers, 164
Meneray, Wilbur, 183-98
Merchants' Bank of New Orleans records, 156
Merrick Collection, 100
Merrick Family Papers, 100
Merrill, William Stetson, 137
Mer Rouge murders, 249
Messner, William F., 77
Methodist Episcopal church, 208-9, 211
Meyer Brothers Store Records, 157
Meyer and Hymel Daybook, 187
Micele, Jerry, 14
Middletown, Ernest J., 82
Midlo, Herman L., Collection, 228
Miers, Earl S., 42
Military Reconstruction Acts, 44
Miller, E. T., 6
Miller, M. Stone, Jr., 154
Miller, Minos D., Jr., Papers, 163
Miller, W. James, 23
Miller, Zane L., 80
Milling, James Sterling, Collection, 248

Mills, Gary, 10
Mills, John, Papers, 169
Ministerio de Educación Nacional, 129
Miró, Esteban, 22, 128, 155, 176
Mississippi Department of Archives and History, 136
Mississippi Valley Association, 187
Mississippi Valley Collection, 136
Missouri Historical Society, 136
Mitchell, Gary C., 39
Mitchell, Virgil L., 65
Mitchell, William S., Papers, 178
Mobley, James W., 39-40
Moll, Herman, 144
Molyneaux, J. Lambert, 92
Monette, James, Diary, 248
Monnot/Lanier Family Collection, 227-28
Montero de Pedro, José, 21
Moody, V. Alton, 71, 73
Moore, Alice Ruth, 212
Moore, John Preston, 14, 15, 21, 22, 34
Moore, Thomas Overton, 150; Papers, 162
Moorman, George, Scrapbooks, 190-91
Morales Padrón, Francisco, 21, 24
Moran, Robert E., 65
Morazan, Ronald R., 72
Morehouse Parish Methodist Church Records, 248
Morgan, Cecil, 35, 109; Papers, 193
Morgan, David, Papers, 189
Morgan, David B., 177
Morgan, Otis P., 67
Morial, Ernest Nathan, Papers, 209
Morrison, deLesseps S., 66-68, 82, 90, 91, 93, 107, 215; Letters, 220; Papers, 192; Scrapbooks, 218
Morrison, James H., Papers, 250
Morrison, Jimmy, 70
Morrow, Clarence J., Papers, 194
Morse, Isaac Edward, Papers, 187
Morse, Jedediah, 29
Morton, Inger, 91
Morton, Jelly Roll, 81
Moss, George, Papers, 178
Mossmeier Papers, 180
Mount Carmel Generalate, 98
Mount Lebanon Female College, 244
Mount Lebanon University, 244, 254
Moussier, J. B., 38
Mouton, Alexander, Papers, 169, 170
Mower, Joseph A., Post of the Grand Army of the Republic Papers, 191
Mugleston, William F., 63

Mugnier, George François, 165, 175
Muller, Mary Lee, 82, 92
Municipal Auditorium Scrapbooks, 218
Murray, Charles A., 30
Murrell, John, 244
Murphy, E.R.M., 7
Murphy, J. M., 75
Museo Naval (Madrid), 132
Music. *See* Cultural history; Jazz

Nasatir, Abraham, 19, 20, 25, 127, 131, 135
Nash, Gerald D., 116
Natchez Indians, 11-12
Natchitoches, Parish records, 151, 155
National American Woman's Suffrage Association, 179
National Archives, 31, 36, 38, 43, 150, 151, 212; Machine-Readable Archives Division, 121
National Association for the Advancement of Colored People, 206-9, 211; New Orleans Branch Collection, 225; Office of the Field Director of Louisiana Records, 209
National Catholic Conference for Interracial Justice, 210
National Endowment for the Humanities, 103-4, 118, 119, 181; for Francophone Studies, 171
National Historical Publications and Records Commission, 171
National Irrigation Association, 179
National Organization for Women (NOW), 161
Nau, Joseph, 86
Negro Business League, 209
Negro Writers' Project, 104
Neilli, Humbert S., 89
Nelson, John P., 213; Papers, 209-10
Neu, Irene D., 38
Nevins, Allen, 103
Newcomb College, 184, 195, 196
New Deal, 64-65
Newman Louisiana Aviation Collection, 227
New Mexico State Archives, 136
New Orleans, Battle of. *See* Battle of New Orleans
New Orleans Academy of Science Papers, 196
New Orleans and Carrollton Railroad records, 192
New Orleans Art Museum, 104

New Orleans Baptist Theological Seminary, 254
New Orleans Board of Underwriters Records, 191
New Orleans Botanical Garden Papers, 170
New Orleans Canal and Banking Trust Company records, 191
New Orleans Canal Bank and Trust Company Papers, 187
New Orleans Charity Hospital Record Books, 164-65
New Orleans City Archives Collection, 215-16, 219-22
New Orleans City Council records, 104, 176, 220-21
New Orleans *City Directories,* 203
New Orleans Classroom Teachers' Federation: Local 527, 226; Records, 226
New Orleans Commission Merchant Ledger, 187
New Orleans Committee of Subsistence Papers, 189
New Orleans Cotton Broker Correspondence, 187
New Orleans Cotton Exchange records, 191
New Orleans Fine Arts Club Papers, 195
New Orleans Friends of Music, 195
New Orleans Housing Authority, 211
New Orleans Lawn Tennis Association Papers, 197
New Orleans Medical and Surgical Society Minutebooks, 194
New Orleans Municipal Records, 155, 186, 188
New Orleans Printing Pressmen's Union, Local 26 Collection, 225
New Orleans Public Library, 93, 100, 104, 213; Louisiana Division, 215-22
New Orleans Railway and Light Company Papers, 192
New Orleans Review Collection, 252
New Orleans Riot (1866), 46
New Orleans Society of Plant Science Papers, 196
New Orleans Street Railway Union Papers, 192
New Orleans Symphony, 195
New Orleans Tidewater Ship Channel Scrapbooks, 218
New Orleans Traffic Court, 211
New Orleans Typographers Union Papers, 192
New Orleans Typographical Union, Local

286 Index

17 Collection, 225-26
New Orleans University, 93, 206, 208, 213; Earl K. Long Library Archives and Manuscripts Department, 223-28
New Orleans Wharfinger's General Cargo and Vessel Book, 192
New Orleans Wholesale Merchant Ledger, 187
New Orleans Wine Merchant's Daybook, 187
Newton, Earle W., 25
Newton, Lewis W., 30-31
New York Historical Society, 29
New York Public Library, 29, 32
Nicholls, Francis T., 51, 52
Nicholls State University, 70, 111; Allen J. Ellender Archives, 252-53
Nichols, Clarence Howard, 52
Nichols, Nowlan, 246
Nicolet, Jean, 142
Niehaus, Earl F., 40, 86
Noble, Stuart, 30
Noe, James, 227
Nolan, William T., Papers, 195
Nolte, Vincent, 31
Norman, E. B. and N. Philip, Collection, 158
North Carolina, University of, Chapel Hill, 29, 32, 43, 44
Northeast Louisiana University Archives and Special Collections, 247-49
North Louisiana Historical Association (NLHA), 230, 240-41
Northrup, Solomon, 73
Northwestern State University, 99, 100, 104, 111, 254; Archives, 256; Folklife Center, 110
Notarial Records of Notaries of Spanish Louisiana, 181
Notre Dame Archives, 240
Nuebling, Max, Letter Book, 160
Nussbaum, Raymond O., 52, 85-93
Nute, Grace Lee, 7

Ocerín, Enrique de, 133
O'Connor, Rachel Weeks, 95-96, 98
O'Donnell, James H., III, 22
Odum, Edwin Dale, 38
O'Fallon (adventurer), 131
Official Journal of the Convention of the State of Louisiana, 178
Ogden, Henry D., Papers, 189
Ogg, Frederick Austin, 5

Ohio Historical Society, 212
O'Keefe, Arthur Joseph, Letters, 220
Oklahoma Baptist University, 255
Oliver, King, 81, 175
Oliver, André, Papers, 159
Olmstead, Frederick Law, 30
Olsen, Otto H., 80
O'Neill, Charles A., Speeches, 194
O'Neill, Charles Edwards, 8, 13, 18, 21, 76, 251
Opelousas District Papers, 155
Openweyer Cypress Lumber Company records, 191
Operative Plasterers' and Cement Masons' International Association of the United States and Canada, Local 93 Collection, 225
Opotowsky, Stan, 61, 65
Oral history, 103-13, 166, 172
Orcuitt, William Dana, 5
O'Reilly, Alejandro, 14, 15, 22, 176, 184
Original Illinois Club, 210
Orleans, College of, 184
Orleans Gallery Collection, 227
Orleans Guard Artillery, 190
Orleans Infirmary Papers, 194
Orleans Parish Board of Assessors Collection, 226
Orleans Parish Civil District Court records, 222
Orleans Parish Neighborhood Council Papers, 193
Orleans Parish Progressive Voters League, 211
Ormond, Suzanne L., Papers, 227
Ortel (Ortelius), Abraham, 140, 142
Osage Indians, 25
Osler, Edmund Boyd, 5
Osterhaus, P. G., 178
Oszucik, Philippe, 40
Otis Lumber Company records, 191
Ott, C. Ellis, Papers, 163
Ouachita District Seville Papers, 248
Oubre, Claude F., 78
Oudard, Georges, 4, 8
Overdyke, W. Darrell, 34
Overton, John Holmes, Papers, 64, 162

Page, John, Papers, 188
Painter, Nell Irvin, 53
Palacio de Oriente, 132
Palfrey Family Papers, 29

Palmer, J. Norris, Papers, 163-64
Panton, Leslie, and Company, 24
Panzeri, Louis, 40
Papeles de Cuba (PC), 133, 155, 186, 251
Paris, Treaty of, 12
Park, Kathryn, 65
Parker, John, 53-57, 66; Papers, 170
Parker, Joseph B., 68, 69, 91
Parkerson, William S., Papers, 194
Parkman, Francis, 4, 5, 13
Parks, Joseph Howard, 42
Passman, Otto E., Papers, 249
Patronato Nacional de Archivos Históricos, 130
Patti, Adelina, 164
Patton, George, Collection, 248
Paz, Julian, 132, 135
Pearson, Sophie Colley, Papers, 158
Peckham, Howard H., 4, 13
Peña y Cámera, José Maria de la, 134, 135
Peñalosa, Diego, 6
Peñalver, Luis, 128
Pendleton, George, Letters, 236
Penney, Edward L., 82
Pennsylvania Historical Society, 29, 32, 36
Peoples, Morgan D., 53, 66, 79
Perez, Leander, 67, 82, 107, 241
Perkins, A. E., 78
Perrin, William H., 31
Perrin du Lac, F. M., 29
Peters Family Letters, 29
Petit Théâtre, Le, 195
Petre, John J., Papers, 221
Petroleum Archives, 171
Phares, Ross, 11
Pharr Family Papers, 156
Phelps, William G., Scrapbooks. 242
Philander Smith College, 209
Philbrick, Francis S., 29
Phillips, U. B., 35
Pickett family, 243
Pierce, Billie, 99
Pierce, Neal R., 66
Pierce, Franklin, 36
Piernas, Colonel Pedro, 128
Pierson, David, 189-90
Pierson Family Letters, 189-90
Pilié, Alvin J., Papers, 194
Pintado, Vicente, Survey Papers, 156
Pittman, Philip, 12
Planter's Bank of Natchez records, 156
Plauche, Maurice, Collection, 250
Plaza, Angel de la, 130

Pleasant, John R., Jr., 63
Plessy v. *Ferguson,* 80
Poe, David A., 64
Poitevent-Favre Lumber Company records, 191
Polad, Michael, 81
Police Department records, 221
Political history, 59-70; antebellum, 33-36; archival materials, 161-62, 169-70, 187-88, 192-93, 233-34, 249; Gilded Age, 51-52; Great Depression, 64-65; Long era, 59-64; New Orleans, 89-91; Progressive Era, 53-56; quantitative study, 115-16; women's, 100
Polk, James K., 36, 233
Polmer Brothers Papers, 191
Ponce de Leon, Juan, 142
Pontalba-Almonester-Miró Papers, 180
Pontchartrain, Jerome Phelypeaux, Comte de, 7
Pontchartrain Railroad Company Minute Book, 187
Pontiac's Uprising, 13
Populism, 52, 62
Porter, Alexander, 34
Porter, Betty, 76
Porteus, Laura L., 72
Post, Lauren C., 11
Power, Ellen, Diary, 248
Power, Tyrone, 30
Poydras, Julien, Letterbook, 180; Recordbook, 185
Poydras Home for Elderly Ladies, 193
Poydras Home Papers, 188, 193
Pradel, Jean-Charles, Papers, 154-55
Price, John Milton, 73, 154, 256
Priestly, William, Narrative of the Expedition of General Carroll, 189
Prioult, A., 10
Pritchard Rice Milling Company Papers, 171
Proctor, Samuel, 18, 25
Progressivism, 52-57, 62, 66
Property Found on Deceased Persons, Records of, 221
Protestant Children's Home Papers, 193
Provident Bank and Trust records, 191
Prudhomme, Lestan, Papers, 186
Public Affairs Research Council, 69
Purvis, John T., 190

Quantification, 115-23
Quarante Club Papers, 197
Queyrouse, Leona, Papers, 99, 161

Race Relations Clippings Files, 212, 213
Radical Republicans, 44-46
Radisson, Pierre d'Esprit, sieur de, 142
Railroad Commission records, 152
Rainach, William M., 70, 108, 241; Papers, 233, 236, 240
Ramke, Diedrich, 34
Ramsey, James A., Correspondence, 244
Randell, Annie Jones, 244
Rankin, David C., 73, 78, 79, 83, 87, 88, 116, 117
Ransdell, Joseph E., 100; Papers, 162
Rathbone, Joseph, 228
Raynall, Abbé Guillaume T. F., 3
Rea, Jesse K. Bell, Papers, 158
Rea, Robert, 12, 21, 23, 25
Rebellion of 1768, 14-15
Reconstruction, 41-42, 44-49, 149; archival materials, 158-59, 163, 206, 243; blacks during, 77-79; end of, 51-52; New Orleans during, 88-89; women during, 98
Red River Raft Book, 230
Red River Revel Records, 238
Red River Valley Association records, 239-31
Reed, Germaine A., 80
Reed, Merl E., 37, 38, 86
Reed, Sarah Towles, Collection, 226
Rees, David, Papers, 186, 189
Reeves, Miriam G., 68-69
Reid, Robert, Papers, 194
Reilly, Robin, 32
Reinders, Robert C., 74-76, 86, 87
Religions of the Sacred Heart, 98
Religious history, 13; antebellum, 39; archival materials, 163-64, 170, 188-89, 194, 211, 236-37, 248, 254
Renwick, Edward Francis, 64, 116
Replier, Agnes, 5
Reynaud, John, Papers, 158
Reynolds, Donald E., 78-79
Reynolds, George M., 55, 89
Rice Archives, 171, 172
Rice Millers' Association Archive, 171
Richland Parish Library, 112
Richter, William L., 74
Rickels, Milton, 39
Riddell, William, 72
Riddell, W. P., Diary, 177
Ridell, John Leonard, Papers, 188
Riedel, Johnnes, 81
Riehl, Vincent, 68
Riley, Martin L., 30

Ripley, C. Peter, 43, 76, 77, 83
Rives, Mary Elizabeth, Diary, 239
Rives, William C., 36
Riviere, Henry, Store Collection, 253
Roberts and Company Papers, 187
Robertson, James Alexander, 19, 136
Robertson, Thomas Bolling, 161
Robin, C. C., 29
Robinson, Martha G., Papers, 193
Robson, William V., Plantation Records, 232
Roca, Pedro, 132
Rockefeller Archives, 212, 213
Rodríguez, Mario, 22
Rodríguez Casado, Vicente, 21
Rodríguez Villa, Antonio, 132
Roeder, Robert Earl, 30, 37
Rogers, Gladys McGuffey, Collection, 227
Rogers, M. A., Papers, 191
Rohrer, John H., 82
Roland, Charles P., 43, 76
Rolfe, John Cooper, Collection, 248
Roman, Bernard, 146
Roman Family Papers, 186
Romero, Sidney J., 69
Roosevelt, Franklin D., 62-65, 170
Rose, Al, 81, 90
Roselius, Christian, Lectures, 194
Rosenberg, Roy A., Papers, 195
Rosenwald Fund Archives, 212, 213
Ross (cartographer), 146
Roudanez, Louis and Joseph, 45
Rouquette, Adrien-Emmanuel, 39; Papers, 159
Roussève, Charles Barthelemy, 71, 76
Rowland, Dunbar, 7, 28
Royal Academy of History (Madrid), 132
Rudwick, Elliott, 82
Ruigomez y Hernandez, Maria Pilar, 22
Rule, John C., 7
Rupert, Anton J., 74, 116, 117
Rush, N. Orwin, 22
Rust College, 209
Ruteledge, Joseph L., 4

Safety and Permits Department Collection, 222
Sage, Bernard Janin, Papers, 178
St. Charles Hotel Papers, 192
Saint Charles Parish Library, 112
Saint Charles Parish records, 151, 180
Saint Charles Presbyterian Church, 194
Saint-Denis, Louis Juchereau de, 143, 145

Saint-Geme, Henri, Collection, 203
Saint James Church (Alexandria) records, 194
Saint James Church (Baton Rouge) records, 194
Saint James Parish records, 151
Saint John Parish election records, 187
Saint Joseph's Roman Catholic Church Collection, 225
Saint Landry Parish records, 150, 151, 180-81
Saint Luke's Episcopal Church records, 188, 194
St. Martin, Louis, Papers, 187
Saint Paul's Trinity Church records, 194
Saint-Père, Rameau de, 4
Saint Vincent Sisters of the Daughters of the Cross Convent, 98
Salcedo (Spanish governor), 155
Salem Baptist Church records, 246
Sanborn Insurance Maps, 218-19, 237
Sanchez-Fabres Mirat, Elena, 24
Sanders, Jared Y., Papers, 162
Sanders, Joe W., Papers, 162-63
Sanson, Jerry P., 67
Sanson d'Abbeville, Nicolas, 140-41
Santo Domingo Papers, 251
Sarah Goodrich Hospital, 208
Saucier phonodiscs, 225
Saulls, Louis de, 187
Saussure, Daniel de, Papers, 192
Sauvolle, Ensign, 7
Save Our Schools, Inc., 207
Saxon, Lyle, 65, 90; Papers, 164, 196
Sayer, Robert, 145
Schafer, William J., 81
Schiro, Victor Hugo, 192; Letters, 220; Papers, 220; Scrapbooks, 218
Schlesinger, Arthur M., Jr., 61
Schlesinger, Dorothy, 110
Schmidt, Gustavus and Charles E., Papers, 194
Schmitz, Mark, 37
Schoonover, Thomas, 115-23
Schott, Matthew J., 56, 66, 69, 120
Schroeder, Martha Mays, 64
Schweringer, Loren, 74
Scott family, 179
Scovell, Captain M. S., Reminiscences, 231
Screwmen's Benevolent Association Records, 159
Scruggs, William O., 56
Scully, Arthur, 40

Sears, Louis M., 34
Sección de Gobierno-Audiencia de Santo Domingo, 251
Secession Convention, 41, 43
Sefton, James E., 47
Segregation, 79-80; antebellum, 76; archival materials, 241; in New Orleans, 88; during Reconstruction, 79
Seignouret (cabinetmaker), 175
Seip, Terry L., 74, 75, 116
Semple, Henry C., 13
Senex, John, 145
Serrano y Sanz, Manuel, 20
Servies, James A., 18
Seven Years' War, 12
Shanahuch, Charles, 119
Shapiro, Nat, 90
Share Our Wealth Society, 63, 64, 107
Shaw, Arthur Monroe, Papers, 196
Shepherd, William R., 12, 129
Shepley, General George G., Letterbook, 189
Sherman, John, 178
Sherman, William T., Papers, 165
Shorter, Edward, 121-23
Shreve, Henry Miller, 241; Letters, 230
Shreveport Chamber of Commerce records, 234
Shreveport City Council records, 233
Shreveport Little Theatre, 109, 235-36
Shreveport Symphony, 109, 241; Association records, 235
Shugg, Roger W., 34, 35, 48, 53, 54, 90, 119
Sibley Country Store Ledger, 234
Sicilian immigrants, 89
Sigel, Elise, 160
Sigel, General Franz, 160
Silverstein, Edward B., Papers, 195
Silver Thimble Fund Papers, 193
Simkins, Francis Butler, 46-48
Simpson, Amos E., 9, 42
Simpson, Vaughan Baker, 9, 95-101, 168
Sindler, Alan P., 53, 54, 60-61, 65, 116
Sigletary, Otis A., 47, 79
Sitterson, J. Carlyle, 37, 76
Skipper, Otis C., 39
Slavery, 10, 24, 72-76; archival materials, 286; quantitative studies, 117-18; urban, 86-87; and women, 98
Slidell, John, 34, 163; Papers, 177, 187
Smith, Al, 56
Smith, Bessie, 99

Smith, G. W., 178
Smith, Gerald L. K., 64, 107
Smith, Hubbard and Company Papers, 187
Smith, John, Collection, 176
Smith, General Kirby, 41, 42
Smith, Robert E., Papers, 242
Smith, Webster, 59
Smithfield Plantation Records, 156
Smithsonian Institution, 171
Snyder, Perry, 229
Snyder, Robert E., 62, 63
Social history: antebellum, 39-40; archival materials, 203, 217-18, 248; Reconstruction, 47, 49
Social Science Data Archive (SSDA), 121
Société des Francs-Amis Collections, 224
Société des Jeunes Amis Collections, 224
Société Française, La, Papers, 193
Société Prospérité, 224
Society of American Forestors, 243
Socola, Edward M., 39
Solomon, Clara, 160
Somdal, Dewey A., Collection, 231
Somers, Dale A., 52, 80, 88, 90
Soniat, Meloney C., 73
Soto, Fernando de, 141, 142, 145
Souchon, Edmond, 81, 90; Papers, 194
Soulé, Pierre, 34; Papers, 187
Southeastern Louisiana University, 70; Archives and Special Collections, 249-50
Southern Baptist Convention, 164
Southern Forest Products Association records, 157
Southern Regional Council, 210
Southern States Art League Papers, 195
Southern University, 212, 213
South Louisiana Citizens Council, 207
South Methodist Episcopal Church, Louisiana Conference of, Minutes, 170
Southwell, Owen, Papers, 170
Southwestern Louisiana, University of, 111, 135, 196; Archives and Manuscripts Collection, 167-72; Women in Louisiana Collection, 99-100
Southwest Library Association, 112
Southwest Renaissance Society Papers, 242
Spain, Daphne, 92
Spanish-American War: Scrapbooks, 218; Veterans records, 238-39
Spanish Louisiana, 12, 14-15, 17-25; archival materials, 127-37, 169, 176, 180-81, 185-86, 201-2, 250-51; women in, 97-98

Spanish Office of Cultural Relations, 129
Spanish West Florida Records, 155-56
Sparks, W. H., 31
Speeg, George, Papers, 160
Spiers, Patricia Loraine, 100
Spiller, Wayne, Papers, 239
Sprague, Marshall, 5
Springfield Lumber Company Corporation records, 158
Spurlock, Colonel. D. W., Correspondence, 235
Spyker, Leonidas, Day Book, 248
Stagg, Louis, Papers, 169
Stahl, Annie Lee West, 75
Stallworth, Elsie Booth, 63
Stampp, Kenneth M., 74
Standard Fruit and Steamship Company records, 187
Starobin, Robert S., 74
Starr, J. Barton, 21, 22
State Advisory minutes, 152
State Agricultural Credit Corporation Papers, 157
State Auditor records, 152
State Board of Equalization minutes, 152
State Board of Health minutes, 152
State Land Office records, 152
States' Rights Democrats Committee, 241
State Treasurer records, 152
Steinbeck, John, 92
Stephen F. Austin University, 235
Stephens, Edwin Lewis, Diaries, 196
Stephenson, Wendell Holmes, 34, 42, 47
Sterkx, H. E., 75
Stern, Edgar B., Papers, 191
Stern, Laurence, 66
Stevens, Will Henry, Papers, 195
Stibbs, John H., Papers, 196
Stielow, Frederick J., 167-72
Stoddard, Amos, 29
Stoddard Labor Collection, 225
Stone Brothers Papers, 195
Story, Benjamin, Diary, 189
Straight College, 212, 213
Straight University, 206
Stryker, W. Reid, Papers, 194
Stuck, Goodloe, 112-13
Sturdivant, Sheila T., 8
Suarez, Raleigh A., 37, 39
Sugar Archives, 171
Sullivan, Andrew R., Collection, 226-27
Sully, Thomas, Papers, 195
Supreme Court of Louisiana Collection, 228

Surrey, Nancy Miller, 11
Survey of Federal Archives, 155
Surveyor's Department maps, 218
Swanson, Betsy, 31
Swanson, Scott D., 247
Swanton, John R., 13
Swierenga, Robert P., 119, 120
Swiss-American Society Papers, 197

Taliaferro, James Govan, Papers, 163, 244
Tallant, Robert, 90; Collection, 212, 219; Scrapbooks, 218
Tanner, Helen Hornbeck, 25
Tansey, Richard, 116
Tasistro, Louis F., 30
Tate, Albert, Jr., Papers, 163
Tatum, Sidney Seth, Family Papers, 243-45
Tavern Bonds, 188
Taylor, Ethel, 44
Taylor, F. Jay, 42
Taylor, Joel Gray, 41-49, 69, 72-74, 76, 78
Taylor, Orlando Capitola Ward, Papers, 210
Taylor, Lieutenant General Richard, 42, 178; Papers, 189
Taylor, William R., 5
Tebbs, Robert, 175
Tebo, Julie C., Papers, 165
Teche Lines records, 192
Temple, Keith, Papers, 195
Temple Sinai Papers, 194
Tennessee Historical Society, 32
TePaske, John J., 24, 25
Territorial period, 28-30; archival materials, 176, 202
Teunesson, John, 175
Texada, David K., 15, 22
Texas, University of, 99
Tharp, James Burton, 4
Thernstrom, Stephen, 120
Thevenot (author), 143
Thomas, D. H., 11
Thomas, William H., 190
Thompson, Richard, 81
Thomson, Buchanan Parker, 22
Thorpe, Thomas Bangs, 39
Thrash, Ernell Montgomery, 246
Times Picayune card index, 217
Tindall, George B., 80
Tindoll, Lucille, 230
Tinker, Edward L., 39
Tirion, Isaak, 141
Todd, James M., Papers, 196
Toledano, Wogan and Bernard Papers, 195

Tomkies, John F., Papers, 239
Tonti, Henri de, 143
Toole, John Kennedy, 252
Tornero Tenajero, Pablo, 23-24
Torres Ramirez, Bibiano, 21, 22
Touchstone, Blake, 76, 200
Tourgee, Albion Winegar, 80
Touro-Shakespeare Alms House Papers, 19
Touro Synagogue Papers, 194-95
Toutant family, 178
Townsend, Mary Ashley, Papers, 196
Trans-Mississippi Army, 41
Trans-Mississippi Department, 178, 190
Transportation: antebellum, 38; archival materials, 158, 187, 192; and urban history, 86
Travelers' Aid of Louisiana Papers, 193
Treen, David Connor, 51; Papers, 192
Tregle, Joseph G., Jr., 27-40, 86, 119
Trelease, Allen W., 79
Tremble, J. E., 244
Trenholm, G. A., 178
Trevigne, Paul, 45
Trinity Church records, 194
Trist, Nicholas P., Papers, 29, 32, 36
Trudeau, Carlos, 148
Trufant, Samuel A., Papers, 192
Truman, Harry S., 231
Tulane, Paul, Papers, 187, 196
Tulane University, 93, 99-101, 110, 210, 213; Howard-Tilton Library, 70, 135, 148, 183-98, 250; Jazz Archive, 99, 105-6, 197-98; Louisiana Collection, 197; Rare Books section, 184; University Archives, 184
Tunnell, T. B., Jr., 49, 77, 78
Tureaud, Alexander Pierre, 209; Papers, 185, 207, 210-11
Turner, Arlin, 80
Twitchell, Marshall Harvey, Papers, 243, 245
Twomey, Louis J., Papers, 252
Tyler, Bruce, 23

Ulloa, Antonio de, 14, 15, 128, 176
Uncle Sam Plantation Records, 156
United Church Board of Homeland Ministries, 206; Race Relations Department Archives, 212, 213
United Confederate Veterans' Association records, 163
United Confederate Veterans Papers, 190
United Daughters of the Confederacy Papers, 190

United Methodist Church: Commission on Archives and History, 211; Louisiana Conference records, 242
United Sons of Confederate Veterans Papers, 190
United States Trust and Savings records, 191
United States v. *Philadelphia and New Orleans*, 248
United Teachers of New Orleans, Local 527, 226
Unzaga (Spanish governor), 128, 176
Urban history, 85-93
Urban League of New Orleans, 207, 213
Urquhart Collection, 185
Ursuline Convent Archives, 97, 98
U.S. Army Corps of Engineers, 230; Collection, 218; New Orleans Office Collection, 228
Usner, Daniel H., Jr., 72
Uzee, Philip D., 35, 52, 78

Van Buren, Martin, 36
Van Deusen, John, 79
Van Os-Flaxman Architectural Records, 237
Variete Association, La, Papers, 219
Vaudechamp, Jean Joseph, 175
Vaudreuil, Pierre Rigaud de, 12
Vaughn, Courtney, 62
Veddes, Richard E., 120
Ventura de Morales, Juan, 128; Papers, 248
Vergne, Hugues de la, Papers, 189
Vergne, Jules de la, 187
Verret, J. Emile, 170
Verret Canal and Land Company Records, 192
Victor, Claude Perrin, Papers, 201-2
Victoria Lumber Company, 235
Vidal, José, Papers, 155
Vietnam War veterans, 166
Vieux Carré *Courier* Collection, 226
Vieux Carré Survey, 200
Vigilence Committee, 177
Vignaud, Henry, Papers, 159
Villere, Jacques, 189
Villeré, Jacques Phillipe, 203
Villere Plantation, 179
Villiers du Terrage, Marc de, 6, 7, 10-12, 15
Vincent, Charles, 43, 47, 78, 79
Vogel, Claude L., 13
Volunteer Relief Committee Papers, 219
Voorhies, Albert, 36, 170
Voorhies, Felix, Papers, 159
Voorhies, Jacqueline K., 14

Wade, Richard C., 74, 76, 86, 87
Wagner, Jacob, 29
Waldo Burton Home, 188
Walke, Juan Pedro, 141-42
Walker, Joe E., 116
Walker, Samuel, Papers, 186
Walker, William A., 175
Wall, Bennett, H., 106
Wall, Helen, 12
Wallace, Joseph, 7
Wallace, Martin, Collection, 239
Walton, James B., Papers, 190
War Department Records of Shreveport General Hospital, 237
War of 1812, 189. *See also* Battle of New Orleans
War of the League of Augsburg, 6
Ware, Eleanor Percy, Papers, 161
Ware, Marion, 97
Warmoth, Henry Clay, 44, 45
Warner, Charles Dudley, Papers, 164
Washington, Booker T., 209
Washington Artillery, 190
Water Resources Congress, 187
Watson, Arthur, 109
Watson, Dalton, Papers, 169
Watson, Eugene P., 256
Watson, Thomas D., 25
Watson Family Papers, 241
Watt, John, 187
Waud, Alfred R., Collection, 204
Webb, Allie Bayne Windham, 52, 79
Webb, Clifford, Map Collection, 250
Webb, Lewis Henry, Diaries, 177
Webb, Samuel J., Papers, 232
Webster, Daniel, Papers, 36
Weddle, Robert S., 6
Wedell-Williams Air Service, 227
Weeks, David, 95
Weiblen Memorial Collection, 227
Weill, Gus, 67
Weisberger, Bernard, 49
Weiss, Carl Austin, 64
Weiss, Dreyfous and Seiferth Papers, 195
Wells, James Madison, 48, 178; Papers, 178-79
Wells, Tom H., 74
Werlin, S. H., Sermons, 194
Wesley Chapel Records, 211-12
Westfeldt, Martha G., Papers, 219
Weydemeyer, Luise, Family Correspondence, 160
Wharfinger and Collector Registers, 221
Wharton, Edward Clifton, Papers, 164

Wharton, Vernon Lane, 47, 80
Wheeler, Joseph, 178
Whisenhunt, Donald W., 63
Whisler, Ernest J., Papers, 170
Whitaker, Arthur P., 14, 20, 136
Whitaker, John S., 31
White, Alice Pemble, 74
White, Edward Douglas, 34, 177
White, Gertrude Rolfe, Papers, 248
White, Henry O., Diary, 248
White, Howard Ashley, 47, 77
White, John T., 52
White, Mansel, Papers, 32
White Citizens' Council, 162, 233
White League, 169; of Red River Parish, 243
Whitley, Merna W., 166 n
Whitten, David O., 37, 73-75, 116, 117
Whittington, G. P., 31
Wickliffe, Robert Charles, 35, 177
Wickoff family, 185
Wiener, Samuel G., Sr., Records, 237
Wilcox, Henry, Papers, 177
Wilerson, Helen C., Papers, 98
Wiley, Bell Irvin, 43, 76, 77
Wilkinson (adventurer), 131
Wilkinson, James, Papers, 29, 176
Wilkinson, W. Scott, 241
William III, King of England, 143
Williams, Archibald P., Papers, 186
Williams, David Reichard, Papers, 170
Williams, Espy, Papers, 170
Williams, Kemper and Leila, Foundation, 199-204
Williams, Kenneth P., 42
Williams, Mary Lou, 99
Williams, Robert W., Jr., 90-91
Williams, T. Harry, 42, 46, 54, 61-62, 78, 104-6, 108-10, 112, 162
Williamson, Don, Papers, 234
Willis, Edwin E., 68, 170
Wilson, Scott, Papers, 93, 192
Wilson, Woodrow, 170
Windsor, John Rolfe, Papers, 248
Wingo, Barbara C., 116
Winsor, Justin, 4
Winston, James E., 75
Winters, John D., 42, 43
Winzerling, Oscar W., 14
Wisdom, John Minor, Collection, 186, 188, 189, 193, 196
Wisdom, William B., Collection, 184
Wise, John B., Correspondence, 244
Witcher, Robert C., 39

Woessner, Charles Herman, 74-75
Woessner, Herman C., 87
Women, 95-101; archival materials, 160-61, 170-71, 179, 193; black, 82; immigrant, 9; in Progressive Era, 56-67
Women in Louisiana Collection, 9, 168, 171, 172
Women's Anti-Lottery League, 100; Papers, 219
Wood, Trist, Papers, 195
Woodman, Harold D., 116
Woods, Frances Jerome, 75, 82
Woods, Patricia D., 12
Woodward, C. Vann, 48, 63, 80, 88, 89
Woodward, Ellsworth, Papers, 195
Woodward, Ralph Lee, Jr., 22
Woodward, William, Papers, 195
Woody, Robert S., 46-47
Woolman, Collett Everman, Papers, 158
Wooster, Ralph A., 36
Works Progress Administration (WPA), 154, 176, 180, 216-17; Collection, 217; Ex-Slave Narrative Project, 98; Papers, 98; Writers' Project, 104, 112
World's Industrial and Cotton Centennial Exposition, 204
World's Panama-Pacific Exposition Commission Papers, 179
World War II, 239
Wray, John, Papers, 235
Wright, Donald T., Papers, 192
Wright, Gavin, 119
Wright, J. Leitch, Jr., 18, 21-23
Wright, Sophie Bell, 99
WVUE-TV news programming card index, 217
Wylie, Lou, 252
Wynes, Charles E., 56, 80

Xavier University, 210-11

Yela Utrilla, Juan J. F., 20
YMCA School of Commerce, 211
Yoes, Henry, III, 9
Young, Margaret, Papers, 235
Young, Perry, 90
Young, Tommy R., II, 73
Young Women's Christian Association Papers, 193

Zatta, Antonio, 141
Zimmer Papers, 171
Zink, Stephen, 55-56
Zinman, David H., 64

ABOUT THE CONTRIBUTORS

ARTHUR WILLIAM BERGERON, JR., previously served as Archivist with the Louisiana State Archives and Records Service. He received both M.A. and Ph.D. degrees in American history from Louisiana State University. He has taught courses in Louisiana history and has authored numerous articles and book reviews in several scholarly journals. He has also had experience as an editorial assistant for *Louisiana History*.

CARL A. BRASSEAUX received his B.A. in political science from the University of Southwestern Louisiana in 1974 and his M.A. in history from the same institution. He joined the Center for Louisiana Studies as Assistant Director, and, in 1980, became Director of the center's large colonial records collection. His publications include four books and thirty-five scholarly articles dealing primarily with the French experience in the Mississippi Valley.

ROBERT D. BUSH was Assistant Director and Head of Research at the Historic New Orleans Collection from 1974 to 1982. In addition to his more than one dozen articles in professional journals, he has edited three volumes in the Historic New Orleans Collection Monograph Series, of which he is the General Editor. Dr. Bush holds a Ph.D. degree from the University of Kansas and is interested in the era of the Louisiana Purchase. He is currently director of the Wyoming State Archives, Museums, and Historical Department in Cheyenne.

JOSEPH D. CASTLE is a native of West Virginia. He lived for several years in Spain. He has a B.A. and an M.A. in history from West Virginia University. He is a specialist in colonial Louisiana history. He serves as Associate Curator of Colonial Manuscripts of the Louisiana Historical Center, Louisiana State Museum, in New Orleans.

About the Contributors

LIGHT TOWNSEND CUMMINS recieved a Ph.D. in history from Tulane University. He lived for several years as a Fulbright Scholar in Spain, where he conducted extensive research on Spanish Louisiana. He is the author of various studies dealing with the southeastern Spanish borderlands, especially during the era of the American Revolution. He is currently Chairman of the History Department at Austin College in Sherman, Texas.

MARGARET FISHER DALRYMPLE is currently an editor at the Louisiana Sate University Press, having formerly served as an archivist at the Department of Archives and Manuscripts, Louisiana State University. She is the editor of *Merchant of Manchac: The Letterbooks of John Fitzpatrick* and coauthor, with Max Saville, of *The Origins of American Diplomacy*.

GILBERT DIN is a native of California and an historian of Latin America. He is Professor of History at Fort Lewis College. He studied at the University of California at Berkeley and received a Doctorate in history from the University of Madrid, Spain. He is the author of numerous books and articles dealing with Spanish Louisiana, including *Louisiana in 1776* and *The Imperial Osages*.

EDWARD F. HAAS is the Chief Curator of the Louisiana Historical Center, Louisiana State Museum. He studied at Tulane University and received a Ph.D. from the University of Maryland. He is the author of *DeLesseps S. Morrison and the Image of Reform: New Orleans Politics, 1946-1961*, associate editor of *Readings in Louisiana History* and *Louisiana's Black Heritage*, and a contributor to *The City in Southern History* and *The Encyclopedia of Southern History*.

WILLIAM IVY HAIR is a native of Louisiana. He is currently the Fuller E. Callaway Professor of Southern History at Georgia College, having previously taught at Florida State University. He is the author of numerous studies on Louisiana history, including *Bourbonism and Agrarian Protest: Louisiana Politics, 1877-1900* and *Carnival of Fury: Robert Charles and the New Orleans Race Riot of 1900*.

COLLIN B. HAMER, JR. attended Tulane University, received a B.A. from LSU-New Orleans and an M.S. in library science from LSU. He has been a member of the staff of the New Orleans Public Library since 1963 and Head of the Louisiana Division since 1968. He has authored several journal articles on historical matters and contributed a chapter on the New Orleans Public Library for the *Encyclopedia of Library and Information Science*.

D. CLIVE HARDY is Archivist and Associate Librarian of the Earl K. Long Library, University of New Orleans. He holds advanced degrees from Tulane University and the Archival Institute of the University of Texas. He is the author of *The World's Industrial and Cotton Centennial Exposition*.

HUBERT HUMPHREYS is Assistant Professor of History and Coordinator of Archives and Oral History at Louisiana State University in Shreveport. He has advanced degrees from Louisiana State University and the University of Texas, has done additional work at Stanford, Tulane, the Georgia State Archives, and the seminar/colloquia of the Oral History Association. He is past President of both the

Louisiana Historical Association and the North Louisiana Historical Association and is active in several other professional groups. He has published numerous articles on Louisiana history.

GLEN JEANSONNE is Associate Professor of History at the University of Wisconsin-Milwaukee. He has also taught at the University of Southwestern Louisiana and Williams College and has been associate editor of *Louisiana History*. He is author of *Leander Perez: Boss of the Delta* and *Race, Religion and Politics: The Louisiana Gubernatorial Elections of 1959-60*.

CLIFTON H. JOHNSON is Executive Director of the Amistad Research Center. He holds a Ph.D. in history from the University of North Carolina. He has taught at Fisk University and East Carolina University. He is the author of various studies dealing with Afro-American history.

JOHN KEMP is a journalist with the New Orleans *Times-Picayune/States-Item*, having formerly served as Director of the Louisiana Historical Center. He is a native of New Orleans, having received an M.A. in history from the University of Southern Mississippi. He is the author of *Martin Behrman of New Orleans: Memoirs of a City Boss, Louisiana Images, 1880-1920*, and *New Orleans*.

PATRICIA L. MEADOR is Archivist and Assistant LIbrarian of Louisiana State University at Shreveport. She has an M.A. in History from the University of Oklahoma and a Master's of Library Science from Louisiana State University. She has taught at Emporia College and is active in numerous professional archival associations.

WILBUR MENERAY is Head of Rare Books and Manuscripts, Special Collections Division, Howard-Tilton Memorial Library, Tulane University. He holds a Ph.D. in history from the University of North Carolina, having served in the Southern Collection of the University of North Carolina and in the Colegio Medical de Guatemala. In addition to his archival activities, he is a specialist in eighteenth-century Latin American history.

RAYMOND O. NUSSBAUM is a native of New Orleans. He received a Ph.D. in history from Tulane University. He has conducted extensive research on New Orleans urban history, especially during the Progressive Era. He currently serves as an archivist at the Earl K. Long Library of the University of New Orleans.

THOMAS DAVIS SCHOONOVER received a Ph.D. in history from the University of Minnesota. He is the author of *Dollars over Dominion: The Triumph of Liberalism in Mexican-United States Relations, 1861-1867* and over twenty-five articles. He currently resides in Lafayette, Louisiana.

VAUGHAN BAKER SIMPSON is Director of the Women in Louisiana Collection at the Center for Louisiana Studies and Adjunct Assistant Professor of History at the University of Southwestern Louisiana. She holds a Ph.D. in modern European history and has published several books and articles on European and Louisiana history.

About the Contributors

FREDERICK J. STIELOW is the coauthor of *Grand Isle on the Gulf* and a number of articles on southern Louisiana. He received a Ph.D. in history and American studies from Indiana University and an M.S. from the University of Rhode Island. He has taught at Indiana University, Grinnell College, and Simpson College in Iowa and has served as University Archivist and Curator of Archives and Special Collections for the University of Southwestern Louisiana.

JOE GRAY TAYLOR received a B.S. from Memphis State and an M.A. and Ph.D. from Louisiana State University. He has taught at Memphis State, Francis T. Nicholls State University, the Air University, Southeastern Louisiana University, and McNeese State University. He has been head of the Department of History at McNeese since 1968. He is the author or editor of eleven books, including *Negro Slavery in Louisiana, Lousiiana, A Student's Guide to Localized History, Louisiana Reconstructed, 1863-1877,* and *Louisiana: A Bicentennial History*. He is a past president of the Louisiana Historical Association.

JOSEPH G. TREGLE, JR., currently resides in New Orleans. He recently retired from his teaching career at the University of New Orleans. He is the author of various studies dealing with the history of Louisiana, including studies of the early nineteenth-century tariff and Louisiana during the Jacksonian era.

About the Editors

LIGHT TOWNSEND CUMMINS is Assistant Professor of History at Austin College, Sherman, Texas. Articles reflecting his interest in the Spanish borderlands of the revolutionary United States have appeared in *Southern Studies*, *El Escribano*, *Louisiana Review*, and *Revistade Historia*.

GLEN JEANSONNE, a prolific scholar in Louisiana and recent American history, is Associate Professor of History at the University of Wisconsin, Milwaukee. He is author of *Race, Religion and Politics: The Louisiana Gubernatorial Elections of 1959-1960*, and *Leander Perez: Boss of the Delta* as well as numerous articles.